The Shock of Medievalism

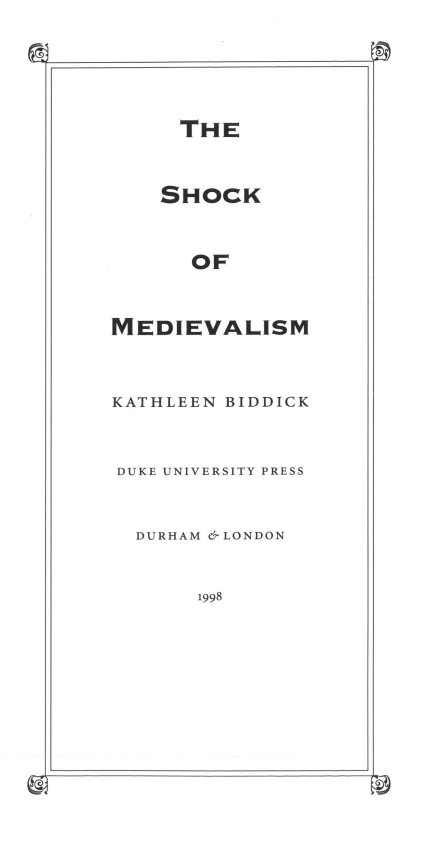

The Shock of Medievalism

KATHLEEN BIDDICK

DUKE UNIVERSITY PRESS

DURHAM & LONDON

1998

Printed in the United States of America

on acid-free paper ∞

Typeset in Adobe Minion with Copperplate display

by Keystone Typesetting, Inc.

Library of Congress Cataloging-in-Publication Data

appear on the last printed page of this book.

This volume is made possible in part by support from the Institute for Scholarship in the Liberal Arts, College of Arts and Letters, University of Notre Dame.

For Nettie and John

Contents

ACKNOWLEDGMENTS

Imagine Magritte (b. 1898) as a child leafing through Jules Verne's *Histoires des Grands Voyages et des Grand Voyageurs* (1878). He comes upon the illustration of the assassination of Pizarro taken from an engraving published by Theodore de Bry in his *America* (1594). When Magritte returned to this print in 1927 he disarmed the figures, linked them like acrobats, and rendered their faces invisible, a motif that appears here for the first (but not the last) time in his work. His visual interrogation of the historical gaps between Verne, de Bry, and Pizarro helped me to embark on this project. A web of colleagues, classrooms, and funding institutions gave me courage to continue.

First, my loyal "referees," Judith Bennett, Michael Camille, Barbara Hanawalt, Joan Wallach Scott, remained steadfastly curious about what would come next. Kerry Walk, coach extraordinaire, would not let me stop too soon. The lively transitivity of colleagues at the Center for Cultural Studies and the Pre- and Early Modern Studies Program at U.C.–Santa Cruz helped me to reimagine my work in medieval studies. I would like to offer special thanks to the intellectual hospitality of Karen Bassi, Harry Berger, Jim Clifford, Carla Frecerro, Donna Haraway, Susan Harding, Margo Hendricks, Virginia Jansen, Sharon Kinoshita, Linda Lomperis, Lisa Rofel, and Catherine Soussloff. The members of three reading groups in Boston, South Bend, and Santa Cruz lavished on drafts their provocation and learning. In Boston I thank Lily Kay and Sandra Joshel and the members of the Narrative Intelligence seminar at the Media Lab at M.I.T. In South Bend I thank my rigorous interlocutors, Doris Bergen, Mary Rose D'Angelo, Julia Douthwaite, Barbara Green, Jill Godmilow, Glenn Hendler, Graham Hammill, and Katherine O'Brien O'Keeffe. I especially thank Lisa Rofel, Graham Hammill, and Michal Kobialka in Minneapolis not only as interlocutors but for the resources they shared at crucial moments.

My colleagues in the Medieval Institute, especially John Van Engen and Dan Sheerin, along with the program's intrepid graduate students, encouraged me to think about the future of Medieval Studies. The exuberance of Notre Dame undergraduates, who have made my teaching life such a pleasure, would not let me be daunted for long.

Fellowships gave me gift of time that can never be repaid, only acknowledged. I am grateful for a Lilly Fellowship to study at M.I.T. and a Rockefeller Fellowship at the Center for Cultural Studies at U.C.–Santa Cruz. Jennifer Warlick, Associate Dean of the Institute for Scholarship in the Liberal Arts at the University of Notre Dame, indulged my taste for Magritte by supporting subvention for publication. The Vice-President of Graduate Studies, Jim Merz, found money to support some of the clerical tasks involved in producing the manuscript. Ken Wissoker, his colleagues at Duke University Press, and two readers encouraged the manuscript to grow into a book.

Much of the research for this book was conducted in the New York Public Library. The openness of Wayne Furman in the Office of Special Collections epitomizes the extravagance of that wonderful collection. Likewise the staff of the Interlibrary Loan at Notre Dame were indefatigable in their service.

My friend Bob has given more to this book than he knows. I dedicate this book to my parents. My mother and father dreamed of educating their children and worked day and night to realize that dream. My father's work of dying and the work of publication were closely bound in joy and grief. His death underscored the question I leave to myself and to the reader: how can the study of history be open to the risks of futurity?

I am grateful for permission to reprint the following: "Humanist History and the Haunting of Virtual Worlds: Problems in Memory and Rememoration," *Genders* vol. 18 (1993): 167–184; "Stranded Histories: Feminist Allegories of Artificial Life," *Research in Philosophy and Technology* 13 (1993): 167–189; "Genders, Bodies, Borders: Technologies of the Visible," *Speculum* 68 (1993): 389–418, reprinted in Nancy Partner, ed.; *Studying Medieval Women* (Cambridge, Mass.: Medieval Academy of America, 1993): 87–116.

Introduction

The Shock of Medievalism

Though the difference or "otherness" or "alterity" of the Middle Ages is thus urged upon us, the interpretive deal is one in which hermeneutic otherness, difference, or disagreement, is in fact purged.

—Louise O. Frandenburg, " 'Voice Memorial' "[1]

These collected essays explore the contemporary consequences of the methods used to institute medieval studies as an academic discipline in the nineteenth century. In an outpouring of studies brilliantly critical of the "fathers" of medieval studies, medievalists have recently assured us that this nineteenth-century heritage can now be put safely behind medieval studies.[2] *The Shock of Medievalism* cautions against this disciplinary security, arguing that the consequences of the fathers' work still elude full acknowledgment. This book traces the ways in which medieval studies is still intimately bound to the fathers, showing that our disavowal of them actually reflects an inability to historicize the discipline. It returns to those political and cultural problems that were and still are excluded by the discipline, using those excluded objects as a way to think about what medieval studies might become.

The methods used to establish medieval studies as an academic discipline in the nineteenth century are well known and can be summarized as follows. In order to separate and elevate themselves from popular studies of medieval culture, the new academic medievalists of the nineteenth century designated their practices, influenced by positivism, as scientific and eschewed what they regarded as less-positivist, "nonscientific" practices, labeling them *medievalism.* They isolated medieval artifacts from complex historical sediments and studied them as if they were fossils. Scholars such as Gaston Paris in literature, Viollet-le-Duc in art history, and Bishop Stubbs in history each used versions of these isolating methodologies.[3] Gaston Paris's insistence on documentary readings of medieval poetry in his new philology severed the study of medieval literature from poetics. Viollet-le-Duc produced a scientific medieval art history by splitting off images from their material milieu. Stubbs refused to teach any constitutional history beyond the seventeenth century on the grounds that it was too presentist. Through these different kinds of exclusions, justified as avoiding sentimental medievalisms, these scholars were able to imagine a coherent inside to the discipline of medieval studies. Medievalism, a fabricated effect of this newly forming medieval studies, thus became visible as its despised "other," its exteriority.

Histories of the fabricated rupture between an authoritative, "scientific" medieval studies and nonscientific medievalism have so multiplied over the past decade that medievalists have felt secure enough to announce a *new medievalism.* By this they mean a medieval studies that no longer negatively produces medievalisms, as did the "old" medieval studies. *The Shock of Medievalism* questions this confidence (attractive as it is for its exuberance) and traces how medievalism (old and new) intimately inhabits medieval studies as, I shall show, an abiding historical trauma.

One sign of trouble in recent histories of medieval studies is their tendency to be paradoxically yoked to the scientific victors of the nineteenth century. Brilliant studies of the scientific "fathers" of medieval studies abound. Critically mindful that these victors effaced history by fabricating objects for their own nationalist and imperialist ends, these studies have nevertheless failed to address others excluded by such methods. The new medievalism thus both repeats the exclusionary process under study and retraces a rigid topography of interiority and exteriority. There is, however, one difference—they expel the now suspect "fathers" to the exterior of the discipline. Recent critical studies are also ambivalently aware that, under the tutelage of these nineteenth-century predecessors, positivist medieval studies institutionalized the techniques that many medievalists regard as the mainstay of academic medieval studies today and, indeed, created these skills as a defining point of difference between medievalists and a "homogenous field of disciplinary uniformity"[4] in the American academy. The maintenance of these techniques (diplomatics, paleography, text edition) poses a conundrum: How can contemporary medievalists conserve these techniques in view of their heritage?

The common solution is to distance medieval studies, not from the techniques, but from the "fathers." For example, the editors of *Medievalism and the Modernist Temper* conclude their introduction by referring to Abbé Mignè, famous for editing the series *Patrologia latina* (1844–55) and *Patrologia graeca* (1857–60): "We are not he, nor do we and the volume's contributors share the philosophy of the founders of the discipline, as much as we admire and respect their legacy."[5] The new medievalism thus achieves its own disciplinary purity by reinforcing the interior and exterior boundaries of the discipline.

Yet there is something to be learned by shifting attention from the fathers to those excluded on the exterior of medieval studies in the nineteenth century.[6] Take, for example, the case of Jules Michelet. Regarded as a typical "Romantic" historian and not a scientific victor, his work was exiled as medievalism (a corpus for the new scientific medievalists to bury *extra muros*), and he barely figures in recent histories of medievalism. Jacques Rancière (himself not a medievalist) has recuperated the profound challenge of Michelet to the exclusionary processes of medieval studies. Michelet questioned the foundational aspect of exteriority on which the institutionalization of medieval studies relied in the nineteenth century: "Romantic writing, which makes the new history possible, is from the outset situated beyond the classical alternatives of mimetic naïveté and interpretive science. These always supposed an exteriority: that of the model one imitates or of the meaning hidden beneath the fable. Michelet, however, installs himself in the continuity of the narration that excludes the two figures of exteriority: imitation, and interpretation."[7]

The Shock of Medievalism reopens this problem of exteriority in medieval studies. If the work of Michelet could once end up as an abject corpse on the exterior, who or what else will be pushed to the exterior as medieval studies attempts to rethink its connection to the past? How can a critical medieval studies imagine an exterior produced by productive openness to futurity rather than negative processes of expulsion? Recent debates in medieval studies do not hide that something must be sacrificed to retain a purified notion of the interior of the discipline. "Theory" is to be moved to the outside since it is imagined as threatening history, whose function in the new medievalism is to guarantee the "hard-edged alterity we need to discover in our [medieval] period."[8] Yet, even though the advertised agenda of recent critical studies (to "historicize the field of critical theory")[9] invokes history, paradoxically historians are mostly absent as contributors to critical literature on the state of medieval studies. The contributors to the recent critical volumes come largely (although not exclusively) from literary fields. History is their silent partner. The repetitious invocation, then, of images of the "hard-edged alterity" of the Middle Ages is suspect. These images mark a desire rigidly to separate past and present, history and theory, medieval studies and medievalism. They foreclose exploration of how critical theories might historicize medieval studies, theories that are crucial to what Joan Scott has called "historicizing interpretation."[10]

This book turns such a topography inside out; it historicizes through theorizing.[11] The essays in it return to the moment of fabricating an inside and an outside to the establishment of medieval studies in the nineteenth century, and, through them, I try to rethink our complex relations to different pasts. In so doing I do not intend to reinstall some retro version of nonscientific medieval studies that the scientific medievalists sought to overcome, nor do I think there ever was a perfect unity out of which interiority and exteriority was falsely carved. Instead, I am retracing the epistemological violence at stake in producing a hard-edged exteriority for medieval studies. Only through understanding that disciplinary wound can we rework medieval studies today and move it away from the repetitious name-calling and policing of "theory" that hovers over a discipline already melancholy over past amputations. I thus intend this collection to be a work of history as imagined by Walter Benjamin: "Historical materialism wishes to retain that image of the past which unexpectedly appears . . . at a moment of danger. The danger affects both the content of the tradition and its receivers."[12]

The Sounds of Silence

These stranded objects would be composed of symptoms. . . . Symptoms as Freud has taught, are traces of another, unconscious reality that haunts one's conscious reality like a revenant being. In the present context, they would be traces of knowledge denied, of deeds left undone, of eyes averted from pain, of shades drawn, of moments when it might have been possible to ask a question or to resist, but one didn't ask and one didn't resist.

—Eric L. Santner, *Stranded Objects*[13]

An example of what I mean by the *shock of medievalism* is the story about the danger surrounding the appointment of William Stubbs as Regius Professor of Modern History at Oxford in 1866. His career exemplifies the formation of professional subjects in the mid-nineteenth-century English academy.[14] Lodged within the histories of professionalization in medieval studies may be found fragments from an "oppressed past" (the very fragments that caused Walter Benjamin so much concern in his "Theses on the Philosophy of History"). My intention in retelling this story is, not to claim that "we are not Stubbs," but to show instead how that claim would continue a complicity with a shocking history of silencing and keeping separate the joined academic histories of medieval studies in Europe and North America.

William Stubbs served as Regius Professor at Oxford from 1866 to 1884. His tenure overlapped a crucial period in the production of a professional cadre of British historians. This transformation is conventionally schematized along the line of the following institutional, civic, and curricular events: (1) the inauguration of open examinations for the Indian Civil Service and the specification of modern history as an examination field in 1855; (2) the opening of the public search rooms at the Public Record Office in 1866; (3) the appointment of William Stubbs on 2 August 1866;

(4) the establishment by 1872 of modern history as an independent honors degree at Oxford; (5) the appearance of an English edition of Ranke's *History of England* in 1875; and (6) the founding of the *English Historical Review* in 1886 and its decision not to remunerate authors, thus placing the journal outside the lucrative literary marketplace.

What is the legacy of William Stubbs? Is it his scholarly work, especially *The Constitutional History of England* (1873–78), which marked medieval history for the next century, or his exemplary formation as a professional historian, which dictated an institutional model of withdrawal from the political contest of public culture ("I desire to use my office as a teacher of facts and of the right habit of using them")?[15] His Oxford appointment helped remap the moral mission of history to accommodate the school-based professional education and certification introduced into the British university in the mid-nineteenth century. The archivally based "scientific" history embraced by scholars such as Stubbs did not undermine the deeply religious and moral "mission" of history; it produced prestige in new ways. In my view, the scholarly career of Stubbs suggests that we should not think of the professionalization of the university and the discipline of history as *secularization* but instead explore scientific history as a new site of moralization.

Stubbsian institutionalization favored an economy of "silence pays" among historians. This claim about silencing becomes persuasive when we remember that Stubbs's predecessor, Goldwin Smith, resigned his Regius professorship in 1866 in the aftermath of the furor over his political response to the Jamaica uprising in 1865.[16] To put both Smith's resignation and Stubbs's appointment in perspective, remember that the British colony of Jamaica had been the site of a slave revolt in 1831–32, that Britain abolished slavery as a legal institution in 1833, and that it emancipated the slaves in its colonies in 1838. Jamaica then became a "laboratory" wherein both British conservatives and British liberals could observe the development of a postplantation economy. In particular, these factions were curious to follow the unfolding of peasant proprietorship in the wake of emancipation. The success or failure of the emancipated economy touched, not only on British colonial interests from Ireland to

India, but also on the "European" question of Russia. British pundits began to watch Jamaica even more anxiously in the wake of the India Mutiny of 1857, the Maori war in New Zealand, and the clashes leading to the American Civil War.

Their worst fears were confirmed when telegrams arrived in London reporting the Jamaica uprising. On 11 October 1865, black settlers had gathered at the courthouse to protest the arbitrary behavior of the local magistracy. The militia fired into the crowd, killing seven of the protesters and wounding several others. The protesters then set on the courthouse and burned it. Disorder spread to a number of estates, where hated white overseers were killed. Governor Edward John Eyre declared martial law and proceeded to execute 439 blacks, flog about 600 others, and burn over 1,000 dwellings belonging to the protesters. Most dramatically, without due process Eyre executed George William Gordon, a prominent mulatto political figure and preacher in the Native Baptist Church.

The news shocked the British public, and the government moved quickly to recall Eyre and set up a royal commission of inquiry. The Victorian intelligentsia polarized around this incident. The Eyre Defence and Aid Committee included such notable conservatives as Thomas Carlyle, John Ruskin, Alfred, Lord Tennyson, and Charles Dickens. The liberal Jamaica Committee, which wanted to see Eyre officially tried for his actions, numbered among its members John Stuart Mill, Thomas Huxley, Herbert Spencer, Thomas Hughes, Frederic Harrison, John Bright, and Goldwin Smith. Carlyle persuasively portrayed Eyre to the public as a chivalric hero protecting England from anarchy and Englishwomen from sexual violation by black men. He succeeded in arousing middle-class opinion in Eyre's favor. Goldwin Smith came under fierce attack for speaking against Eyre. He resigned his professorship at Oxford in July 1866, accepting another, which he took up in 1868, at the newly founded Cornell University.[17]

The government moved quickly to fill the empty Regius chair.[18] The fourth earl of Carnarvon, the secretary of state for the colonies, wrote his undergraduate mentor, the Reverend Henry Longueville Mansel, Waynefleet Professor of Metaphysical Philosophy and fellow of St. John's (later appointed Regius

Professor of Ecclesiastical History in December 1866), asking for advice about the appointment.[19] Mansel recommended Stubbs on the basis of his conservative politics and strong Anglican religious convictions. Carnarvon then drew up a shortlist in which religious and political affiliations figured prominently in the ranking of candidates. Stubbs topped the list, and Lord Derby officially offered the professorship to Stubbs in August 1866.

As Catherine Hall has shown in her important analysis of gender, race, and the prestige at stake in the Eyre case,[20] liberals and conservatives shared common ground on the importance of Englishness and masculinity but defined the path to these desired goals differently. I thus do not intend here to mark some stark contrast between Smith and Stubbs. My immediate concern is instead with establishing what kind of academic behavior gets rewarded and how academic prestige is produced and consumed. Goldwin Smith, whom Disraeli called "an itinerant spouter of stale sedition . . . a wild man of the cloister, who goes about the country maligning men and things,"[21] was active on education reform commissions and contributed regularly to the press (the *Morning Chronicle,* the *Daily News,* and the *Saturday Review*). In strong contrast, once Stubbs moved to Oxford, he never again published in the literary press (he had once contributed to the *Gentleman's Magazine*).[22] He also refused to teach modern history beyond the early seventeenth century. As Reba Sofer has noted, his "insistence that contemporary history, because it was controversial, had to be avoided was among his most permanent legacies to the History School."[23]

Paradoxically, Stubbs, a passionate advocate of "scientific" history, believed the past to be dead. He regarded the study of ancient history as akin to the "study of death," as he stated in his inaugural lecture in 1867. Christianity protected the historian from the study of death: "It is Christianity that gives to the modern world its living unity and at the same time cuts it off from the death of the past."[24] Thus, positivism and the Christian mission of history were closely bound.

Stubbs preserved his silence as Regius Professor and was rewarded for it, although he could be found voicing his political views in personal correspondence.[25] He did not publicly align himself with controversial political debates, or write in literary journals, or draw attention to himself other than as a textual editor and as a scholar of medieval constitutional history.[26] His silence paid. He was amply rewarded, especially by his nomination to the bishoprics of Chester (1884–89) and Oxford (1889–1901).

But, in my view, Stubbs did engage in one deeply political project. As I show in "Gothic Ornament and Sartorial Peasants," he buttressed the imperial project of Gothic Architectural Revival with its churches and government buildings that stretched from Bombay to Oxford. We can tell from the list of his printed sermons that he frequently presided over the dedication of restored churches during his tenure as Regius Professor. As bishop of Chester, he oversaw a major and very successful church-building campaign.[27] The questions of renovation and preservation raised by the Gothic Architectural Revival put Stubbs in the center of a Victorian debate over memory, pleasure, and history. This debate lingers today in medieval studies. What Robert Brentano has called Stubbs's "renunciation of art"[28] is also, along with his withdrawal of history from public culture, one of his permanent and most problematic legacies to medieval studies. At the center of an incipient medieval studies we thus hear the monastic-like silence of Bishop Stubbs. This silence continues to leave unspoken the conditions of his appointment in the midst of a traumatic debate over British colonial race relations conjoined with the colonial transformation of the British university. The silence still lingers.

Trauma and the Possibility of History[29]

> Mourning always follows a trauma. . . . [T]he work of mourning is not one kind of work among others. It is work itself, work in general, the trait by means of which one ought perhaps to reconsider the very concept of production—in what links it to trauma, to mourning, to the idealizing iterability of exappropriation, thus to the spectral spiritualization that is at work in any tekhne.
>
> —Jacques Derrida, *Specters of Marx*[30]

The shock of medievalism imparted in the Stubbs story cannot be undone by expelling Stubbs to the exterior for the sake of a "new medievalism" or by dismissing the story as an unfortunate inevitability of nineteenth-century politics unthinkable now in postcolonial times. Another kind of history needs to be thought, one that imagines temporality as something other than hard-edged alterity and one that avers that unrecognized losses become traumatic. Louise Frandenburg has already brilliantly delineated the damage that results from constructing intellectual community in medieval studies without such histories. It produces "an overreliance on a common sense that implies a sense of community that may no longer be so common."[31]

Conventional historical chronologies (past, present, future) are not the guideposts to such a history. Trauma is a temporal process that is located, not in one moment alone, but in the relation between two moments. Since its content is not grasped when it occurs, a traumatic loss has no present and therefore resists conventional contextualization based on either diachrony or synchrony. Trauma also resists representation since its traces recur fragmentarily in flashbacks, nightmares, and other repetitive phenomena. Past and present symptomatically fuse in such repetition, and, in so doing, the possibility of futurity—change—is foreclosed. Such fusing is typical of melancholy. To unfuse past, present, and future, to return to the narrative relation of temporality, requires the work of mourning. Mourning does not find the lost object; it acknowledges its loss, thus suffering the lost object to be lost while maintaining a narrative connection to it.

Mourning and melancholy work in different registers (which can overlap). Melancholy is mimetic; it refuses loss and mimics the lost object. It has been called a kind of "theft" that reappropriates the lost object. Mourning, by contrast, is performative in that it is only in action (to be distinguished from traumatic repetition) that the suffering of the loss of the lost object can be constituted. Mourning and melancholy thus have to do with the gestural and narrative status of objects. The study of objects implies their identity and our relations to them. A history of trauma opens itself up, then, not only to psychoanalysis, but also to the diverse and lively critical projects in feminist, queer, and postcolonial studies that have undertaken the historicization of identity and the analysis of the political work in identification.[32]

Studies of trauma fill self-help shelves in bookstores. This trivialization is thinkable because traumatic processes have (as Michael Roth has noted of memory) become "privatized" and "ghettoized" as a defense against both thinking of how trauma refigures any linear notion of an integral biographical self and the political, intergenerational implications of trauma. Trauma is also mistakenly reduced in some psychoanalytic readings to castration, a notion of exteriority as invariant, transhistorical.[33] This has the effect of reducing psychoanalysis to a melancholic mimesis rather than opening it up to the important work of thinking its own relation to particular historical trauma and mourning. Some readers may also object to my contention that medievalism inhabits medieval studies as an abiding trauma, believing that it transposes inappropriately, indeed reductively, painful debates on the status of history after the catastrophe of the Holocaust. It may also transpose, through its use of psychoanalytic literature, the trauma that haunts the institutionalization of early psychoanalysis.[34] The concern would be that the history of trauma I am proposing could reduce history to trauma and thus lose both history and trauma in a further reduction to some notion of experience. Yet, although this history of trauma precipitated by the professionalization of medieval studies might be risky, it is nevertheless urgently necessary.

These gathered essays think of such risk otherwise. They wager that historians do not yet know enough about particular histories as works of mourning to know in advance how they can actually enable rather than diminish the historical work of mourning for the Holocaust. Rather than anachronism (or despair and solipsism, as some medievalists have experienced it), this work of mourning in medieval studies, a discipline that emerged within well-articulated racisms, imperialisms, and nationalisms, can actually help disable what Eric Santner has eloquently described as the "elegiac loop," that is, the displacement, disavowal, and dispersal of particular, historical tasks of mourning.[35] Put another way, elegiac loops foreclose the formidable historical challenge of constructing solidarity in mourning and an openness to futurity. Elegiac loops fix us in identity politics, a politics that Wendy Brown has eloquently characterized as "states of injury."[36] For medieval studies, its melancholic fixation on an identity politics imagined as hard-edged alterity neither saves history (with the desire that it redeem us), nor ends it, but stifles it.

Works of Mourning

Even though chronology places regularity above permanence, it cannot prevent heterogeneous, conspicuous fragments from remaining within it.

—Walter Benjamin, "On Some Motifs in Baudelaire"[37]

Diverse as these essays are, problems of trauma, melancholy, and mourning in medieval studies thread through them all. The three essays of part 1, "Sounds of Silence," trace how medieval studies fabricated powerful melancholic objects in the nineteenth century, notably the "Gothic peasant" and the "mother tongue," melancholically resuscitating these objects at moments of disciplinary crisis in the twentieth century, especially during decolonization following World War II and the corporatization of the university during the 1980s.

"Gothic Ornament and Sartorial Peasants" explicates a crucial crisis in medieval studies and medievalism that I designate the *melancholy for work,* a melancholy that displaces works of mourning. During the Gothic Revival in the nineteenth century, the hands of industrialized and colonial laborers severed from production by power machinery came to be spoken of in terms of a discourse of Gothic peasants and Gothic handicraft. I call the ways in which Victorian intellectuals and artists (such as John Ruskin and William Morris) responded to the shock of industrialization as a melancholy for work. Rather than join in a particular work of mourning—join the outcry of workers in their strikes—Victorian intellectuals practiced another "economics of the mind" (as Freud designated it), a melancholy for work; that is, they concentrated, not on the disturbing lost objects, all those disembodied industrial workers whose disembodiment threatened their own imagined integrity, but on a *sense of loss* that they articulated as the "hand" of an imagined Gothic handicraft.[38] Put in other terms, the melancholy for work protected from an awareness of the loss that would bound disembodied workers most intimately and most painfully to such elites, in a solidarity of mourning. The melancholy for work ensured that "the corpse must remain dead, in its place the corpse; one must at all times be assured of this. It must not return, nor be allowed to return and with it the dream of the lost object."[39]

The obsession with Gothic ornament and the debates over handicraft and taste that proliferated in nineteenth-century Britain enacted the repetition of loss rather than recognizing the contemporaneous disembodiments at stake in the industrial fabrication of labor. In the course of the debate over the material proliferation of Gothic ornament, the Gothic peasant emerged as a figure that functions as the metaphor for elite male sorrow over the radical disembodiment attending industrialization. The Gothic hand of handicraft as incorporated in the ornament of the nineteenth-century Gothic Revival produced the melancholy for work in medieval studies as a specific affective process: "The 'grievous' suffering of the melancholic artist is a gendered one, an eroticized nostalgia that recuperates loss in the name of an imaginary unity and that also gives to the melancholic man (homo melancholicus) a privileged position within literary, philosophical, and artistic canons."[40]

The discursive tracings of this melancholy for work as it manifests itself in the formation of English studies and in post–World War II peasant studies raise an important question about medievalism: Can this melancholy for work be translated into works of mourning? Part 2, "Works of Mourning," takes up the challenge of imagining passageways from melancholy to mourning. What kind of reading practices can work through the melancholy for work and perform works of mourning in medieval studies? The two essays in part 2 do not define an act of reading but rather attempt to find passageways through texts where previously there were none. The first seeks to rethink ways of reading what is arguably one of the most symptomatic texts produced in late medieval Europe, the *Malleus maleficarum* (Hammer of witches). It complicates my argument about the melancholy of medievalism initiated in part 1. The traumatic relations between medievalism and industrialization cascade over historic melancholies. Of special concern in part 2 is the deeply tenacious melancholy of Christians for Jews. Just as industrialization traumatically refigured the bodies of workers, medieval Christendom phantasmatically refigured Jewish bodies. Perhaps one of the most profound moments of Christian disembodiment of Jews came in the fifteenth century, the time of the writing of the *Malleus maleficarum*, the evidentiary focus of "The Devil's Anal Eye." In the fifteenth century, Christian intellectuals experimented with a new *historical* epistemology that entailed driving a "great parenthesis" between the "present" and the primitive church. That wedge permanently severed old Israel from the Jews among whom Christians lived.[41] My reading of the *Malleus maleficarum* leads to a meditation on the changing fabrications of Christocentrism and its relations to the formation of the European discipline of ethnography in the fifteenth century. The companion piece, "Genders, Bodies, Borders," traces the engendering of this melancholic ethnography in contemporary medieval studies.[42] My reading practice seeks to refigure a Christian melancholy for Jews into a historical work of mourning, striving after a notion of history that is not "naturally" referential but instead permits history to arise "where immediate understanding may not."[43]

Part 3, "Virtual Loops," turns to contemporary virtual worlds and their science fiction. Inspired by the work of medieval travel books, which fabricated the New World before it was ever apprehended by explorers, I read this science fiction as travel books. My interest in studying them was prompted by reading Marx's *Capital* as a travel guide to commodity fetishism. It intrigued me that Marx used the medieval to mark the trauma of the industrial transformation of embodiment. He prefaced the first edition, which he finished just as Bishop Stubbs was poised to give his inaugural address at Oxford, with a citation from canto 5 of Dante's *Purgatorio.* In this canto, Dante and Virgil walk among the souls who have met a sudden and violent death. Fatal wounds and pools of blood abound in the tales that these souls recount. The canto also teaches a minilesson in optical diffraction and differentiation. The souls are astonished to see the "broken light" around Dante's opaque body, through whose living form the light cannot pass, as it can through the ghostly Virgil.

It intrigues me that Marx prefaced *Capital* with a citation from a canto that is all about trauma, wounding, optics. As I show in part 3, trauma also haunts the travel literature of virtual worlds. If the industrial fabrication of labor in the nineteenth century constituted a profound trauma, how does this trauma repeat itself even as on the shop floor robotics displaces not only workers' hands but their bodies? The severed hand of the industrialized body now transforms itself into a robotic server. Consider, for example, the new robotic arm developed to aid in human genome research. One of the most arduous and time-consuming aspects of that laboratory work is the transfer of DNA into different sequencing protocols. Until quite recently, many skilled laboratory technicians could be found performing those sequencing steps manually. Scientists have now perfected a robotic arm that performs the work of all those technicians itself, requiring as its workstation only a single table. The spectrality of capitalism, which Marx knew well and which Derrida has evocatively elucidated,[44] comes full circle in virtual technologies. This virtual loop is an elegiac one, meaning that it disavows and disperses once again historical works of mourning. The essays in part 3 on cyberspace and artificial life show how the layers of melancholy excavated in this gathering of essays shroud the terminals for digital technologies. It is in these technologies, perhaps more than ever, that medievalism returns, asking medieval scholars to engage now in works of mourning.

Unclaimed Experience

> Insofar as grief remains unspeakable, the rage over loss can redouble by virtue of remaining unavowed.
>
> —Judith Butler, *Bodies That Matter*[45]

The more I studied medieval "*peasants*" in the 1980s, the more the historical similarities between this and other Victorian categories, especially *woman, race,* and *homosexuality,* troubled me. The violent epistemological work of these latter categories has not gone unquestioned, yet economic history seemed unwilling to historicize its basic terms. To find ways of doing just that, I turned to theoretical critiques of categories being developed in feminist, postcolonial, and queer studies. My problem gradually defined itself conceptually as a history of the discursive production of and attachment to categories as objects. The study of virtual technologies allowed me to experiment in the early stages of this project since the burgeoning literature on virtual worlds questioned such basic categories as *human, body, nature.* This literature offered me rich analogical material to characterize the intersections of transformative technologies and contested epistemologies. My opportunity for fieldwork among scientists producing virtual technologies at MIT in 1991 gave me insight into ways of working back to the cultural politics of the nineteenth century, when political economy forged its own epistemological categories (*peasant, labor, commodity, capital, production,* etc.) and new academic fields, including medieval studies, emerged.

My journey, a kind of "back to the future," has allowed medieval studies to have a fuller impact on my work. The shock of medievalism helped dislodge my research from its elegiac loop. That shock helped me move into intellectual and political communities beyond medievalists and also helped me rethink my own community in medieval studies. This shock brought me to the question that threads through these essays: How does trauma incurred in the academic institutionalization of medieval studies (then and now) affect the ways in which medievalists connect the past to the present and to the future?

The essays collected here offer no sure answers. Each chapter attempts to refigure politically the borders of the discipline. *The Shock of Medievalism* proposes a different kind of exterior for what medieval studies may become—not a discipline based on expulsion and abjection and bound in rigid alterity, but one permeable to the risk of futurity.

Sounds of Silence

GOTHIC ORNAMENT AND SARTORIAL PEASANTS

Gothic Ornament Then and Now

What does it mean to practice a discipline whose designs on the life and death, the pleasure and suffering of the body, however often effaced or repressed, are nonetheless a central part of cultural work?

—Louise O. Frandenburg and Carla Frecerro,
"The Pleasures of History"[1]

Embedded in the "oppressed past" of Gothic Revival ornament is a traumatic allegory of critical theory in medieval studies today. The ornaments fabricated during the Revival substantially materialized the built space of the "professionalizing" British university of the nineteenth century and still bear witness to the work of disciplinary architecture in extant monuments to be found from Oxford to Bombay.[2] Particularly telling is the proliferation of popular "guides" to Gothic architecture and the very popular pattern books of ornament (with page upon page illustrating fragments of moldings, tracings, and other Gothic detail) that brought the Revival to those Victorians who consumed a literature of "taste." In their dream-like condensations of the unstable sites of the artisanal hand, the steam engine, the factory worker, the Indian villager, the connoisseur, the Regius Professor, the Anglican churchgoer in the metropolis and the colony, these guides and pattern books participated in a "Gothic" economy of excess. How do these "grammars of ornament" (as these pattern books titled themselves), which once inflected Victorian "taste" wars, continue to inflect contemporary debate over theory in medieval studies?

The Case of the Missing Hand

Such as the hand is, I looked for its fellow. At first I thought it had been broken off, but on clearing away the dust, I saw the wretched effigy had only one hand, and was a mere block on the inner side.

—John Ruskin, *Stones of Venice*[3]

John Ruskin was writing this famous anecdote about the sculptured hands of the Vendramin tomb in Venice for *The Stones of Venice* just as Londoners streamed to the Crystal Palace in 1851. Not only did the Great Exhibition display the "manufacture" of industrial countries (the *Illustrated London News* dubbed the Medieval Court designed by Pugin "the most unique and best harmonised display of art and skill" [20 September 1851, 362]); it also exhibited colonial "handicraft." The India Exhibit caused nothing less than a scandal. The Victorian intelligentsia split over the question of "taste" in Indian handicraft in a way that oddly anticipated the case of Governor Eyre (discussed in the introduction).[4] Their contempt for the vulgarity of European manufacture was unanimous; all agreed that its workmanship showed a "disordered state." The nub of the debate lay with interpretations of the beauty of Indian handicraft. To supporters, it represented "a people faithful to their art and religion." To denigrators, such as Ruskin, it failed to represent a "natural fact"; for him, the "art whose end is pleasure is pre-eminently gift of a cruel and savage nation."[5]

In all corners of the debate, whether it be from the anti-manufacture advocates or the denigrators of Indian handicraft, the question of the "hand" comes to the foreground (and, as Ruskin so acutely observed, the hands of the Vendramin tombs). Owen Jones, who included a guide to the India Exhibit in his sumptuous, color-illustrated *The Grammar of Ornament* (1856), described one of the most popular pieces of the India display, an embroidered saddlecloth, as "beyond the power of a European hand to copy it with the same complete balance of form and color."[6] George Birdwood, who published a guide to the Indian

Court at the Paris Exhibition of 1878, introduced his reader to a village full of Indian "hands" by conjuring up a tour of handicraft production in an Indian village. For Birdwood, the aesthetic failure of British manufacture lay, not with British taste ("no people have by nature a truer feeling for art than Englishmen and Englishwomen of all classes"),[7] but with a crisis of the hand. It is as if the battle over English and Indian ornament became distributed over a body part. The Indian hand could produce plenitude and beauty; the British hand, cut off by the epistemology of industrial labor, failed and touched all with dead imitation and vulgarity. Gothic ornament worked as a kind of skin marking the border between hand and machine, labor and slavery, nation and colony, presence and loss, history and memory.[8]

The debate over ornament forged links between ornament, a body part (the hand), the social grouping of the village, and the moral injunction that Indians should not "hybridize" (i.e., they should wear only clothing and ornaments of "native manufacture and strictly native design"),[9] and much could be said about an imperial ideology developing around ornament. At this juncture, however, the hand is a convenient way into understanding why ornament had become a center of debate by the 1851 exhibition and how the hand is used in that debate to figure historical change in the very conceptualization of tactility and visibility, change that is crucial to understanding what ornament meant in the Gothic Revival and what critical theory means to medieval studies today.

Sleight of Hand

I address the problem of the hand in the Gothic Revival by comparing the frontispiece of two books on Gothic architecture published within six years of each other: *Attempts to Discriminate the Styles of English Architecture from the Conquest to the Reformation* (1819), by Thomas Rickman, the textbook for Gothic architecture for the next half century, and the earlier, large-format, and lavishly illustrated *Essay on the Origin, History and Principles of*

Gothic Architecture (1813), by Sir James Hall. Although close in time of publication, these two books come from different epistemological worlds. Hall is able to join hand and vision through a notion of a pregiven world of nature; in Rickman, the hand has been cut off from vision, and the act of seeing has become an optical discipline of discerning difference without any system of referentiality incarnated in tactile space. The epistemological differences between the two texts radically influence the readings of the architectural fragments they illustrate.

The frontispiece (fig. 1) to Hall's volume depicts a Gothic cathedral constructed from wicker and thatch that Hall erected on his estate as a scientific experiment. Hall relates that, during a trip to Europe in 1785, his Vasarian attitude toward the Gothic as a monstrous and barbaric architecture changed as he made his way north through France. He came to appreciate the intimate link of Gothic ornament with "utility" and noticed that the tracery, capitals, and vaulting of Gothic masonry resembled the craft of wickerwork that he saw in production and use among local peasants. He then subjected his ethnographic thesis—that Gothic building developed out of this wicker tradition—to an "experimental test," the "construction of a wicker fabric now standing in my garden, a view of which is given in the frontispiece."[10] He reported the results to the Royal Society of Edinburgh in 1792 and published his lavishly illustrated volume two decades later.

It is worth thinking about the content and arrangement of the book's engravings in relation to Hall's frontispiece. The engravings mix wickerwork architectural details (windows, tracery, roof vaults, spires, etc.) with examples of generic masonry details and sometimes with "historical" details drawn from specific cathedrals, mostly English. Both historical and generic details of Gothic structure and ornament are used as models to refer back to the organic wickerwork. Hall thus insists on an *organic origin* for ornament. He also mediates his aristocratic relations to Gothic ornament through the medium of a peasant ethnography (paradoxically in an English economy that had deterritorialized its peasantry and was in the process of relocating part of its labor force into factories).

Six years after Hall's *Essay* appeared, Thomas Rickman, a

Figure 1. Wicker gothic. From the frontispiece to Sir James Hall, *Essays on the Origins, History, and Principles of Gothic Architecture* (London, 1813). Courtesy the Art and Architecture Collection, New York Public Library, Astor, Lenox and Tilden Foundations.

Quaker accountant living in Liverpool and a member of the Liverpool Philosophical Society, published an essay on Gothic architecture at a size and at a "price that shall not present an obstacle to extensive circulation." Rickman's book constituted an optical tool to train the eye to make "such clear discriminatory marks on the buildings now existing."[11] His frontispiece (fig. 2), a "composition" showing the style markers of a "Decorated" (one of his subdivisions of English Gothic) interior, illustrates a virtual space that bears no relation to any tangible "historical" per-

Figure 2. A virtual Gothic interior. From the frontispiece to Thomas Rickman, *An Attempt to Discriminate the Styles of English Architecture* (London, 1819). Courtesy the Art and Architecture Collection, Miriam and Ira D. Wallach Division of Arts, Prints and Photographs, New York Public Library, Astor, Lenox and Tilden Foundations.

ceptual space that would join vision and touch. The engraving, drawn by Rickman himself, refers only to the internal criteria of his definitions of style. These criteria he has built from "scientific" observations of details of architectural fragments.

Figure 3 reproduces another plate from Rickman's work. Here, organized within one frame are seventeen architectural fragments, ranging from bits of moldings to mullions, that Rickman used to illustrate the traits of various styles. Three of the architectural fragments in this plate render pieces from actual Gothic buildings; the rest are virtual designs. Like the frontispiece, these fragments, too, refer only to his system of stylistic classification. This system has no origin in "nature" or ethnography, as did Hall's, nor does it have any anchor in what readers today might regard as "history" since Rickman is interested only in the details of the fragments. For Rickman, there is no "whole" building of which the fragments are a "part." His engravings for the 1819 edition are also exceptional for including no human beings whose presence would suggest some kind of inside to the space he is depicting, who might serve as a relay between a notion of part and whole, inside and outside. In other words, Rickman has dissolved the inside/outside distinction of ornament and building that Hall tried to preserve through his ethnographic fantasy of wicker origins for Gothic ornament. With Rickman's system there is now only ornament, which works like a skin. If there is any referent, it is the disciplined eye of the observer, which is trained through viewing ornament.

How might we think about the ways in which Rickman's "Gothic" breaks with Hall's "Gothic"? Jonathan Crary, who studies the new techniques of the observer emerging in scientific discourse on perception in the early nineteenth century (these being instantiated in the newly invented, popular optical devices such as the kaleidoscope, the diorama, and the stereoscope), can help us understand the difference between Rickman's eye and Hall's hands. Crary argues for a radical relocation of vision in this period. A model of vision that had constructed itself through the medium of the camera obscura, in which the observer is "inside" the viewing apparatus that frames and projects for the observer the "outside" of a pregiven world, relocates itself to the eye of the observer. Vision itself is redefined as "a capacity

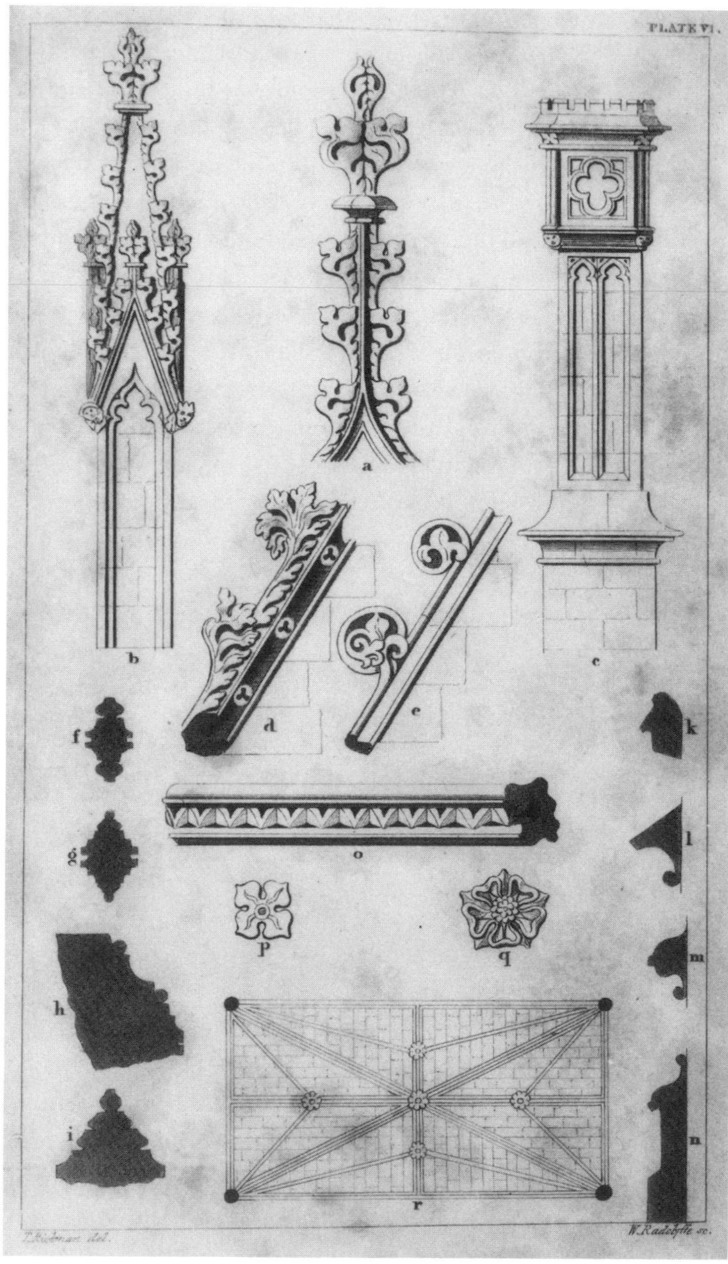

Figure 3. Gothic ornament. From pl. 6 of Thomas Rickman, *An Attempt to Discriminate the Styles of English Architecture* (London, 1819). Courtesy the Art and Architecture Collection, Miriam and Ira D. Wallach Division of Arts, Prints and Photographs, New York Public Library, Astor, Lenox and Tilden Foundations.

for being affected by sensations that have no necessary link to a referent, thus imperiling any coherent system of meaning." These new models of vision cut the sense of touch off from the sense of vision and "industrially remapped the body."[12] Thus, according to Crary, new techniques of the observer produce subjectivities working as cameras *before* the invention of the camera.

The epistemological contrasts between Hall's and Rickman's concepts of ornament exemplify Crary's argument. Another project of Rickman's can further elucidate this transforming empire of the senses and the changing categories *interior, exterior,* and *surface* in the early nineteenth century. During the 1830s, Rickman contributed to a publication that gathered together views of Norfolk architectural antiquities drawn by John Sell Cotman from 1812 to the 1830s. Cotman had a local antiquarian, Dawson Turner (the father-in-law of Sir Francis Palgrave, deputy keeper of the Public Record Office), provide commentary for the first set of views. When Rickman joined the project, he added his own commentary, set off by the publisher in brackets to distinguish it from Turner's.

It is instructive to compare the two commentaries. Turner belonged to the epistemological world of James Hall. He describes the buildings through their family or institutional histories, through a genealogy of antiquarian texts that reference or illustrate them. Thus, the architectural view is entangled in a description of both family history and textual genealogy. Turner also frequently comments on the overall condition of the architectural monument at the time of his writing. Cotman's engravings also come from Hall's epistemological world. They are picaresque and almost always include some ethnographic depiction of "locals" and their everyday life amid the monuments. Vegetation and shadowing are devices used to insert the architectural etching in some real time. In sharp contrast, Rickman's commentary works like a studio camera, deterritorializing the antiquarian grid of family and textual genealogy. It focuses strictly on architectural detail and is limited to instructing the disciplined and discriminating observer how to differentiate between the various architectural styles.

Take as a case in point Rickman's commentary on panels from a tomb in Hunstanton Church, Norfolk:

> The variations between the parts of this monument, which at once shows to the practiced eye the difference between decorated and perpendicular work, is a matter of nicety, and at first not easy of acquisition, but when it is in constant exercise and sharpened by frequent discrimination, not only between the styles, but the earlier ones also, it is a sort of faculty most useful to the antiquary, and which he should take every opportunity to exercise and keep in constant employment. In this monument the variety of forms merely but not quite alike is very visible.[13]

Here we see illustrated his emphasis on the disciplining techniques that the observer must follow in order to reconstitute himself or herself as the kind of studio camera that Rickman has become. Rhetorically, its "cut-up" quality also reminds us of the optical effects of the fragments represented by Rickman in his engravings. With the development of this "camera eye" before the actual invention of the camera, there is no place for touching!

Rickman's Gothic ornaments become the site of discipline; they are "useful" for training the eye. Not only do they break with any notion of an "organic origin" for ornament, but they further break links between peasant handiwork and ornament, as imagined in Hall's thesis on wickerwork. In the back of his 1819 edition, Rickman produced a gazetteer of English Gothic architecture organized by county. Here, his succinct descriptions of churches once again isolate them as ornamental fragments (the fragment is the structure). The impact of his guide was enormous. It chased other books out of the market and continued to be revised and reissued at more or less regular intervals until the 1880s.

I do not think that it is incidental that ornament is so important to Rickman. The study of ornament constitutes the new observer desired by an array of scientific and technical discourses under production in the early 1800s. As the eye became a surface that could be investigated (measured, graphed) like any other physical phenomenon, Rickman searched for a way to reinvent "humanness" in this new epistemology, which disincarnated historical relations of touch and visibility. He mapped Gothic ornament as English and Christian. But, since the ornament is the structure, then Englishness and Christianness are ornament. The ornament then must be a white skin, but its gender and sexuality have to do with the eye of the observer, not with the hand. Rickman's work, by implication, poses the question, What are the sex and gender of this eye produced by scientific discourse in the early nineteenth century and disciplined through such techniques as the discrimination of style in Gothic ornament?

Gothic ornaments seem to break off at the question of gender and sexuality, just as the hand broke off from vision in the new techniques of the observer. It is in such a gap, I believe, that the "history of sexuality" in the nineteenth century can be read against its grain. A study of the Victorian "attachment" to ornament can help us understand "how the production of sexualities came to look like repression."[14] Rickman wanted to create a traffic in Gothic ornament and, in order to do so, translated what was historical into what was optical. It is the *instability* of this translation, *the historical and the optical*, that would haunt Gothic ornament.

The project of Rickman and his colleagues deterritorialized architecture and reterritorialized it as ornament. This act cleared the space for an intensive and ubiquitously material internal colonization of England, its Gothicization. To understand how the "English" came to imagine and sustain a vision of the nation as "progressive," it is important to understand the crucialness of internal colonization through its own Gothicization during the Gothic Revival (between 1820 and 1870, over nine thousand churches underwent "Gothic" restoration in England, and the Gothic style proliferated, being applied to domestic structures, universities, hospitals, prisons, banks, railway stations, and the Houses of Parliament). Gothic ornaments also reproduced themselves in colonial channels.

It is interesting to note here as well that Rickman first circulated his essay one year after the appearance of Mary Shelley's *Frankenstein* (1816), a creature noted for its sutured skin. In the same year, Scott published *Ivanhoe,* in which the veil of the Jewish Rebecca, her "second skin," is so crucial. These experiments in skin—the skin of the ornament, the skin of the monster, the second skin of the Jewish woman—may actually inform each other.[15]

Bombay Gothic

Bombay, an Architectural Sodom.
—*Murray's Handbook for India and Ceylon*[16]

The Gothic Architectural Revival is typically regarded as the outcome of the Anglican Counter-Reformation.[17] This conventional textbook story overlooks the technological and colonial fragments embedded in the chronology, namely, the dissemination of popular optical devices in the early nineteenth century, such affordable "scientific" guides to Gothic style as Rickman's *Styles of English Architecture,* the state-supported competition to rebuild the Houses of Parliament in 1834, and the subsequent efforts to develop a Gothic architecture suitable for "tropical colonies." This alternative history of the Gothic Revival recasts in imperial ways the work of the Oxford and Cambridge Architectural Societies, which, in the 1840s, most certainly did enunciate Anglican Counter-Reformation ideologies for architecture.

Popular optical devices (the kaleidoscope, the diorama) must, I think, be regarded as the optical prosthetic of the Gothic Revival.[18] In 1815, David Brewster read a prizewinning paper to the Royal Society of Edinburgh outlining the principles of the kaleidoscope. The Liverpool Philosophical Society, of which Rickman was a member, would have taken note of this new invention. A "sensation," this optical device was sold by the hundred thousands in London and Paris, and "large cargoes were sent abroad, particularly to the East Indies." The kaleidoscope had, according to Brewster, special potential for application to architectural ornament. Through its focus on a section of architectural ornament, it could produce for the architect "an immense variety of the most beautiful designs . . . and as perfect as if they had been carved out of the stone by the most skillful workmen."[19] The eye replaces the hand! The architect could permanently record whatever design he so chose from this array by means of a camera lucida, or later a camera, or a kaleidoscope camera.

The many pleasures of ornament (amusement, industrial application, colonial export) crisscrossed like the refractions of the kaleidoscope. Having been trained by Rickman to exercise discrimination about Gothic style, the reader's eye was also being conditioned to see ornament through the optical device of the kaleidoscope. Five years after Rickman's *Styles of English Architecture* appeared, Daguerre's diorama came to London; subsequently, Liverpool, Manchester, Dublin, and Edinburgh built their own diorama buildings.[20] At Liverpool, Rickman could have seen, among other things, a diorama of Trinity Chapel, Canterbury, in 1825, of Holyrood Chapel in 1826, and of Roslin Chapel in 1828. With their bias toward depicting Gothic architectural sites, early dioramas thus further aroused popular interest in the Gothic and its ornament.[21]

The dissemination of kaleidoscopes, dioramas, and affordable "scientific" guides to Gothic ornament meant that by the 1830s (well before Ruskin's major commentary on architecture, *The Seven Lamps of Architecture* [1848]) the Gothic Architectural Revival was under way as a popular phenomenon. Someone like Rickman, who as a Quaker was denied access to education at Oxford and Cambridge and who certainly did not have the wealth to pay the high fees that archives charged in that day, could become, along with a network of amateur middle-class observers, a recorder of scientific detail in local Gothic architecture. Rickman went on to design and build several Gothic mansions, residences, and churches after the publication of his book. By 1827, at age fifteen, the young Pugin was designing the "Gothic" furniture for Windsor Castle.[22]

This heterogeneous and multistranded media interest in Gothic architecture and ornament became focused in the national debate that followed on the burning of the Houses of Parliament in 1834. The government sponsored a competition for the design of new buildings, mandating that entries be submitted in the Gothic style. The newly launched *Architectural Magazine* (1834) helped foment debate by questioning the exclusion of the classical style from the competition.[23] Charles Barry, with Pugin, won the contest, and the public called for an exhibition of the submissions. Thus, the Gothic Architectural Revival and the quest for ornament went national before it went ecclesiological. Charles Eastlake, the first historian of the Revival, wrote perceptively in 1872: "Who knows how far the taste for the Middle Ages might have been developed at all but for the timely patronage of the State?"[24]

At this juncture, the traditional story of the Gothic Revival would usually turn to the founding in 1839 of both the Cambridge Camden Society (later known as the Ecclesiological Society) and the Oxford Society for Promoting the Study of Gothic Architecture, a high point of the Anglican Counter-Reformation, which led to the publication of the *Ecclesiologist* by the Camden Society and to debates between Cambridge and Oxford over the Gothic Architectural Revival.[25] Let us instead leap forward to 1849 and *A History of Architecture* by Edward A. Freeman, an Oxford historian whose work on the Norman Conquest would help consolidate the new scientific history with a nationalistic Englishness. Freeman used his *History* to link Gothic architecture with the progress of civilization.

Freeman's choice for an epigraph was from Prescott's *Conquest of Peru:* "The surest test of the civilization for a people, at least as sure as any, afforded by mechanical art is to be found in their architecture." The purpose of its work, "the general idea which I have all along kept in my mind during the composition of the present work," is to initiate the "Historical Study of the Art of Architecture." The problem for Freeman is that architecture had become a "very popular study"—"in fact I am by no means clear that its popularity has not been injurious to it." Freeman is careful to distance his work from such populism. He makes no mention of Ruskin, even though Ruskin had links to the Oxford Archaeological Society and published his *Seven Lamps of Architecture* in the same year as Freeman published his *History.* Freeman also chose, in the end, not to illustrate his book with engravings of any of the churches or ornaments under discussion. Such a loss is not great, he claims, in that his history is not to be a "treatise on detail" or a record of "existing specimens." To distance himself further from the popular, he condemns Rickman: "They have provided a complete but lifeless body, and look with suspicion on any attempt to infuse a vital principle into the inert ones."[26] Archaeologists and ecclesiologists (his colleagues at Cambridge) also come under attack for failing to promote the study of architecture as an "art."

Freeman produced, not a history of architecture, but a nationalist geography mapped onto architecture. He excluded the possibility of Greek architecture as a national architecture, not an uncommon move in the wake of the Houses of Parliament competition, on the grounds that a national architecture must be Teutonic and Christian: "National feeling, if we have any left, any real love for the true glories of Teutonic England, would repudiate it [classical architecture] even for secular buildings, united national and religious feeling pronounce it unfit for the Christian temple."[27] Furthermore, Gothic architecture was for Freeman suitable only for Northern Europe. The Italian Gothic represented the "forsaking" of the principles of the Northern Gothic and internal proof that the Gothic style should not be exported to the British colonies, a move encouraged by the Cambridge Camden Society.

How can we unpack Freeman's architectural politics? By locating his architecture within an economy in which he Gothicizes "others" in order to purify his own interests. First, there are the heterogeneous observers of architecture that are in need of purification. The popular taint of ornament and those nonuniversity men interested in ornament must be rendered as some monstrous, dead thing. Second, there are the visual pleasures of ornament that must be chastened. Freeman refuses to illustrate architecture and ornament in his *History* in order to flatten out ornament, that is, to erase its Gothic effects of excess, pleasure, and opticality. His *History* is also important for reintroducing a language of interiority to the discussion of Gothic architecture. He claims that "architecture then is the soul, building the body."[28] In an uncanny way, Freeman produces for architecture the nineteenth-century discourse on body and soul that Foucault marked and challenged: "The soul is the effect and instrument of a political anatomy; the soul is the prison of the body."[29] In her reflections on Foucault, Judith Butler has shown how this discourse of the soul had the effect of producing the body, the surface, as the sign of lack, the soul, "a figure of interior psychic space inscribed on the body as a social signification that perpetually renounces itself as such."[30]

With Freeman, the Gothic paranoia of the Revival begins to take shape. Judith Halberstam has described the mobile nature of this male paranoia (Cambridge and Oxford and their learned societies being intensely homosocial) as follows: "Gothic is a narrative strategy that refuses purity and indeed, reveals the suspect ideological stakes of quests for purity. Paranoia, within this description of Gothic structures, is the fear that simultaneously blurs boundaries and calls for their resurrection."[31] What Rickman blurred, Freeman wanted to clarify as nonpopulist (read *manly*), Teutonic, Christian, and English. To resurrect borders, he must flatten out the excessive ornamental surface produced by Rickman and bury it inside the soul of architecture, which for Freeman is the pure spirit of Teutonic nationalism. He sutures history to architecture and buries ornament alive. That is why he *dare not* represent ornament visually in his book; it might look back, re-monstrate him.

Freeman's architecture anticipates a late Victorian plot like *Dr. Jekyl and Mr. Hyde* in which the monster, like the ornament, is buried within. A clue to the race and gender of that buried ornament comes from Freeman's colleagues in the Cambridge Camden Society writing in the *Ecclesiologist*.[32] The links of the Cambridge Gothic Revival with colonialism are announced in the first issue, which describes a request from the bishop of New Zealand that the society "furnish working models of the actual size of Norman capitals, sections of mouldings, ornamented piers, door, and window arches: and these, it is hoped, may be easy for the natives to imitate in the stone of their own country."[33] The *Ecclesiologist* began to include regular reports on the progress of Gothic church architecture in the colonies, ranging from Newfoundland to Calcutta. The secretary of the society, Benjamin Webb, urged that the "principles" of the Gothic be adapted to the colonies.[34] To facilitate that project, the society issued two pattern books, entitled *Instrumenta Ecclesiastica*, giving detailed drawings for copying Gothic ornament ranging from coffin lids to door handles. In keeping with their "virtual" notion of the Gothic, the designs "are taken from ancient examples, some are adaptations, and some are original designs, generally framed in accordance with the suggestions of the society."[35] The second of the two volumes included blueprints for church designs, such as the one illustrated in figure 4 of a wooden

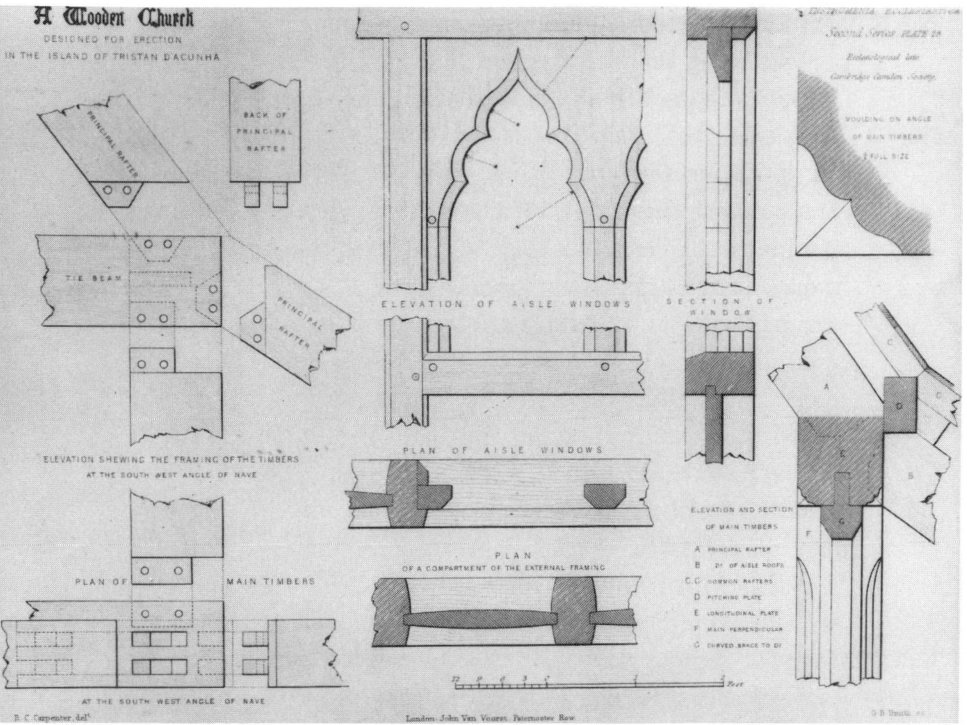

Figure 4. Modular Gothic for the colonies. From *Instrumenta ecclesiastica,* ed. Ecclesiological Society (Cambridge, 1856). Courtesy the Art and Architecture Collection, Miriam and Ira D. Wallach Division of Arts, Prints and Photographs, New York Public Library, Astor, Lenox and Tilden Foundations.

church for the colony Tristan da Cunha. The pattern books were to be distributed to bishops in the colonies.[36]

The extent of auto-Gothicization was stunning, as the 1876 parliamentary study of new church building and restoration undertaken in Britain from 1840 to 1875 made visible. The survey broke down the moneys spent on restoration and new church building by county. Overall, £9,704,033 had been expended. As a benchmark, consider that the parliamentary outlay for the Public Record Office for 1879–80 amounted to only £24,377.[37] The average annual expenditure for the Gothic Revival during this period was, then, around eleven times greater than government support for the Public Record Office. The success and ubiquity of Gothic autocolonization, its public spacing, produced a crisis of temporality, a historical crisis.

Gothic ornament had proliferated (from London to Bombay) to such an extent that a crisis arose over the notion of an "original" in Revival discourse.[38] The "soul" of architecture failed to imprison ornament as Freeman had imagined in 1849. Autocolonization by the Gothic in England had its intimate counterpart in the colonization of the colonies with Gothic ornament. Then ornament, a skin, stretching across metropolis and colony, became too hybrid (not white, not quite); it seemed utterly confused (indeed, sodometrical, as the epithet of the Bombay Gothic as an "architectural Sodom" indicates), even monstrous, as Charles Eastlake intimated: "It is lamentable to reflect how many monstrous designs have been perpetuated under the general name of Gothic."[39]

William Morris intervened in the mounting crisis over copy and original in 1874 when he prohibited the sale of Morris and Company stained glass and upholstery to any ecclesiastical Revival projects, on the grounds that consumers could no longer distinguish between the work of Morris and Company and the work of "history." Many restorers actually preferred to rip out original fabric in order to install Morris designs.[40] In other words, Morris intuited that there was no sense of original or copy at work in Gothic restoration. Today, we might say that these Revival ornaments had become queer or were always already queer.

Recent work in queer theory can help us understand Morris's intervention, his misgivings about how his ornaments "passed" all too well as the "real thing," and the political implications of their withdrawal.[41] Judith Butler has offered us important insights into the relation between copy and original that troubles gender and compulsory heterosexuality today. Rather than imagining the parodic effects of a gay identity as a copy or simulation of some original ("natural" heterosexuality), such parodic effects instead expose heterosexuality as "an incessant and panicked imitation of its own natural idealization."[42] The play of Morris's ornament in the Gothic Revival materializes the problem that Butler is discussing, and, since, as we have seen, ornaments functioned as skin, they bear on corporeal embodiment. When he realized that his ornaments exposed the panicked imitation at work in the nationalistic and colonial idealization of Gothic ornament, Morris himself panicked. His ornaments were interrupting the desired linear, familial continuity implied in the "national" inheritance of the English Gothic in Victorian Britain. In a lecture given in New York in 1882, Oscar Wilde described William Morris as "the greatest handicraftsman we have had in England since the fourteenth century."[43] Morris was to realize that such an "inheritance was never given, it is always a task."[44] He and his ornaments were coming to stand *before* the fourteenth-century peasant, rendering authentic Gothic fabrics belated in the restoration.

Morris could have embraced this "inversion" as political consciousness of what Sedgwick calls "foundational and/or incipient national difference already internal to national definition."[45] Instead, he insisted on restoring linearity, "order." He sealed off the historical fabric of Gothic churches in England through his business decision and his concomitant work with the Society for the Protection of Ancient Buildings (SPAB).

Along with leading intellectuals and artists (e.g., John Ruskin and Thomas Carlyle), Morris founded the SPAB in 1877 to police the binary of copy and original in the Revival. The SPAB attempted to stop what its members regarded as a kind of parasitism in which the industrially produced ornament fed off the historical Gothic by killing the host. They declared that no one should dare "touch" a Gothic "monument" except to protect it from age and weather. Gothic churches, they announced, were to be regarded as national relics—to sustain such relics new technologies of restoration needed to be invented. The SPAB used the public media, especially newspapers, to stop what the group regarded as destructive restoration projects and to educate the public about the appropriate sacral behavior toward national ecclesiastical relics. Through the SPAB and his embargo on the use of his company's ornaments in "national monuments," Morris effectively produced as so many architectural relics Gothic "originals." He thus inverted the dangerous situation whereby the reproduction ornaments exposed the absence of such a historical original. Linear inheritance was restored through the SPAB's construction of the category *the original.* The firmly drawn line between ordered and disordered ornament staved off any further proliferation of monstrosity. Morris produced, in short, the "hard edge of alterity" for Gothic ornament. His ornaments could no longer be "confused" with the authentic Gothic fabric because having the ornament and being the ornament could now never cross back on each other. Having the ornament was encrypted in history; being the ornament was encrypted in the consumer—or so a universalizing discourse about national monuments attempted to fix ornamental desire.

But, in so fixing the Gothic ornament, Morris and Company created new problems: "Just as one monster dies, another is always produced."[46] How could the company's ornaments, now secured from any panicky taint of queerness by their linear inheritance from an inviolable historical Gothic original, be distinguished from contemporary kitsch, circulating in English markets? Here, the case of the Indian ornament returns, ambivalently idealized as handicraft and excoriated as kitsch among the Victorian intelligentsia. As Sedgwick has observed, kitsch operates under the epistemology, "It takes one to know one."[47] If you have to ask the question, Is it kitsch? then the ornament becomes kitsch.

In "Rescuing" his ornament from one epistemological crisis, that is, the absence of the unified, national Gothic original that he had to construct through the SPAB, Morris plunged into a new epistemological problem: how to distinguish his ornaments from all the kitsch out there that he and Victorian connoisseurs repudiated? If the SPAB imagined that, having encrypted the ornament (sealed it over), it had buried the copy in the skin of the original, it was mistaken. Instead, it had merely exacerbated the tension between manufactured and handcrafted Gothic ornament, showing the instability of notions of *original* and *copy*.

Haunted Ornaments: Dreaming Sartorial Peasants

Through the notion of trauma . . . we can understand that a rethinking of reference is aimed not at eliminating history but at resituating it in our understanding, that is, at precisely permitting *history* to arise where *immediate understanding* may not.

—Cathy Caruth, *Unclaimed Experience*[48]

Enter the Gothic peasant! Morris (following Ruskin) publicized a universalizing, public rhetoric of medieval peasants and their handicrafts that produced medieval peasants as the belated examples of Morris and Company ornament. His invention of the "Gothic" peasant helped resolve an unbearable instability between original and copy. In a lecture on pattern designing that he delivered to the Working Man's College in 1881, Morris invoked the "Gothic" peasant in his (*sic*) imperial/colonial hybridity: "I am most sure that all the heaped up knowledge of modern science, all the energy of modern commerce, all the depth and spirituality of modern thought, cannot reproduce so much as the handiwork of an ignorant, superstitious Berkshire peasant of the fourteenth century, nay of a wandering Kurdish shepherd, of a skin-and-bone Indian ryot."[49] Morris conjured the Gothic peasant most fully in the novella *The Dream of John Ball* (*DJB*)—an "architectural dream" of the uprising of 1381—which he serialized in his socialist publication the *Commonweal*.[50] But in this novella Morris misrecognized the work of mourning as melancholy for work. That misrecognition persists even today among such strong new historicist readings of the uprising as Steven Justice's[51] and is thus doubly worthy of attention.

To read *The Dream of John Ball*, it is first necessary to consider Morris's design and entrepreneurial activities in the late 1870s and 1880s as a daydream. Writing, designing, capitalizing, and dreaming in Morris are closely bound. First, it should be noted that Morris significantly increased his entrepreneurial autonomy in 1875 when he bought out the shares of members of the Pre-Raphaelites with whom he had been in business since 1861. The early 1880s were a period of expansion for Morris. In 1881, he began negotiations to move the production lines of Morris and Company to Merton Abbey. He augmented advertising by publishing impressive brochures for the company in 1882 and extended the display space of his Oxford Street shop. Also in the same year he decided to add another showroom in Manchester, where he participated in the Manchester Fine Art and Industrial Exhibition. Morris delivered his first lecture in Manchester, "Art, Wealth, and Riches," after joining the Democratic Federation, a socialist organization, on 6 March 1883. The American market also lured Morris. In 1883, Morris and Company bought space in the Boston Foreign Fair and had printed an elaborate catalog for it. Morris enjoyed his greatest period of artistic productivity after announcing the embargo on ornaments to national monuments. Between 1875 and 1885, he produced seventy-six new designs for wallpaper and printed and woven fabrics, approximately 66 percent of his total design output between 1861 and his death. In short, Morris dreamed his dream of medieval peasants at the height of his creativity and entrepreneurialism.[52]

Let us turn to his dream. Once the SPAB encrypted historical Gothic fabric, put it beyond touch, there is no way back to that Gothic hand that fashioned the ornament. The hand is quite literally cut off from the present. This exclusion of the past rematerializes as an anxiety dream in the opening of *DJB.* Can Morris be in two places at once? "I had begun my sojourn in the Land of Nod by a very confused attempt to conclude that it was all right for me to have an engagement to lecture at Manchester and Mitcham Fair Green at half-past eleven at night on one and the same Sunday."[53] If Manchester and Mitcham Fair cannot work simultaneously for Morris, 1381 Kent and 1885 London can—in his dream. Medieval peasants, or, more precisely, their churches, houses, clothing, domestic goods, weapons, and landscape, haunt his dream. These dream peasants are not specters of a "lost" past, a "lost" handicraft. Instead, they are specters from some design supersession (a supersession is not a history that will be but a history that always was); belatedly, they materialize the designs advertised in Morris and Company catalogs. If the SPAB blockaded access to the nostalgic "ornamental" referent that was always already lost in any case, Morris recovered that referent as a catalog history that will have been in his dreams.[54] We can read *DJB* as a kind of "Gothic" catalog, a hieroglyph, whose translation is roughly this: "I know that I have encrypted Gothic ornament and cannot return to it; I know I have staged the loss of the nostalgic referent; nevertheless, I have the clothes, the architecture, the drinking cups. This is the history that will have been."

In *DJB,* Morris dreams history as the incorporated space of ornament. Compare this entry from Morris's Boston catalog (1883) to a description from *DJB:*

One use of these heavy cloths in England, is the hanging of the walls of churches or large halls. The Peacock and the Bird Pattern are very good for this use. Mr. Morris's own room is hung with the Bird pattern, from the skirting to within two feet of the ceiling.[55]

Also the walls, instead of being paneled, were hung with a coarse loosely-woven stuff of green worsted with birds and trees woven into it. (p. 101)

Morris's uncanny poetics of the catalog recurs again in an important encounter when Morris joins John Ball in the parish church, where lay the bodies of peasants and knights slain in the day's melee. In an echo of Hamlet (where Marcellus, speaking of the ghost, says to Horatio, "Thou art a scholar; speak to it, Horatio" [1.1.42], John Ball speaks to Morris as he pulls the linen cloth that covers the face of one of the dead peasants: "What sayest, thou scholar?" (p. 115). And Morris (speaking as if through the wound of trauma) says, "Nay, I feel no sorrow for this; for the man is not here: this is an empty house. . . . [B]ut here is no life nor semblance of life, and I am not moved by it; nay, I am more moved by the man's clothes and war-gear—there is more life in them than in him" (p. 116).

My reading of *DJB* might insinuate that Morris produces a history that will have been, in which he can participate as a parasite. He consumes his own ornament, a kind of autocannibalism that eerily resonates with the autocolonization set in motion by the Gothic Revival. Morris's anguished poetics of ornament, nevertheless, asks for a more nuanced reading. Morris himself points the way to such a reading when he experiences an unexplicable traumatic lapse in the middle of his dream. It occurs at the turning point of the "battle at township's end" (an encounter between the villagers and the forces of Sir John Newton of Rochester Castle), when "all mingled together" (p. 85). The villagers are getting the better, indeed, murdering "bailiffs and tipstaves, and lawyers and their men, who could not run and hoped for no mercy." At this point Morris, "blacks out":

I looked as on a picture and wondered, and my mind was at a strain to remember something forgotten, which yet had left its mark on it. I heard the noise of the horse-hoofs of the fleeing men-at-arms (the archers and arbalestiers had scattered before the last minutes of the play), I heard the confused sound of laughter and rejoicing down in the meadow, and close by me the evening wind lifting the lighter twigs of the trees, and far away the many noises of the quiet country, till light and sound both began to fade from me and I saw and heard nothing. (p. 86)

Why this lapse at such a crucial moment by an observer who (like Ruskin) seems never to miss detail? Morris blacks out presumably at the revolutionary high point, the death of the ruling class. This is a traumatic moment staged by Morris in which he points to the traumatic latency of his own socialist politics. Morris will "miss" the workers at the moment they begin to rise up. He will not be there: "I saw and heard nothing."

E. P. Thompson tells the story on which I base this claim. He traces how the editorial policy of *Commonweal* and Morris himself were out of touch with the emerging working-class movement in England.[56] Morris viewed the Leeds labor strike and the London dock strike of 1889 as something apart from the socialist movement, which he imagined as strictly devoted to education for revolutionary supersession. The ambivalence of this position is expressed in the Socialist League's executive memorandum published in the 12 October 1889 edition of *Commonweal*, a statement that Thompson stigmatizes as "the most pitiful in all its years of existence." "In answer to numerous enquiries, the Executive Council . . . desires to express its opinion that members of the League do not in any way compromise their principles by taking part in strikes, but asks them not to let the revolutionary propaganda suffer thereby."[57]

Thus, trauma haunts Morris's dream. He desires to fix medieval peasants and their handicrafts as the belated afterimage of the Morris and Company catalog and, in so doing, linearize and immunize his own historical identification with Will Green and John Ball. Morris wishes to translate such an intense identification safely as, "I do not love Will Green; I am Will Green." But, at the moment of murderous class struggle in which peasant kills lord, Morris faints at the trauma of class. Medievalism faints, too, at this traumatic moment. Morris, who missed the emerging politics of British workers by melancholy for work and not working to mourn, addresses medievalists today, a hundred years after.

This Is the Hand of the Lord

But who were "they"? The question has haunted the whole book; in a more general form, it has haunted the writing of rural history for a century.

—Steven Justice, *Writing and Rebellion*[58]

A century has passed since the appearance of Morris's *Dream of John Ball*, yet hands can still be found haunting historicist studies of medieval "rural" politics and "peasants." In one of the most notable examples of new historicist work (winner of the Modern Language Association's 1995 Best New Book Award), Steven Justice's *Writing and Rebellion,* the first hand to appear is the author's own: "My hands had held my Ph.D. before they ever held a manuscript." Hands are "matter out of which texts are made." They are thus a ground and a site of labor. When the author finally holds in his hands medieval manuscripts (Henry Knighton's *Chronicle* and Thomas Walsingham's *Historian anglicana*), he at last has the opportunity "really" to work: he transcribes.[59] Through an identification with paleography, today's medievalist, who dare not (according to Fredric Jameson) assimilate without glamorizing his or her "intellectual tasks" to alienated labor, can mourn for the alienated physical labor of the medieval scribal craft, the scribe's writing hand. The intellectual can have access to alienated labor through paleography and at the same time melancholically introject the hand of scribal handicraft. Melancholy and paleography are thus closely bound in Justice's call to engage in paleography to make available "new material" to transform the medieval literary canon. Rather than look critically at the disciplinary conditions of possibility productive of such canons, Justice simply reverses canonical practices (from editions to paleography) and thus reinstalls the very exclusionary canonical practices he would change.[60]

The detection of textual mistakes provides the fissures and gaps through which Justice is able "to see through and past," as if with X-ray vision, into history. That same methodology allows us to look at the case of the mistaken hands in *Writing and Rebellion* in an effort, not only to reverse Justice's melancholy for work, but also, as Judith Butler encourages, to mime it and render it hyperbolic, thus disabling it as a counterdiscourse that would, in fact, reinstall the canonical practices he protests.[61] How can medieval rural history, paleography, and canon formation be rethought as a work of mourning and not a melancholy for work?

Hands are crucial to the very performance of Justice's argument. In spite of disavowing his involvement with "a method (certainly not a theory) for interpreting historiographic narratives," Justice does map a goodly amount of theoretical and historiographical debate in his lapidary footnotes.[62] His use of the speech act theory of J. L. Austin is crucial to his conceptualization of insurgent writing. He uses Austin's notion of the performative utterance—formulaic words that accomplish action, like the "I do" of the wedding ceremony—to distinguish traditions of commentary (such as Langland's *Piers the Plowman*) from the documentary modalities that, he argues, peasants used in rebel writings during the uprising of 1381. In a long footnote on performative speech acts, Justice acknowledges (parenthetically) Derrida's challenging critique of Austin's notion of *mistake* but brushes it aside since he is interested in "what certain kinds of performance are conventionally taken by the performers to be."[63] Derrida questions the notion (implicit in Austin) of a writing space or an utterance present to itself and its content (thus self-identical) and notes that that assumption requires the exclusion of the very notion of a mistake on which both Austin and Justice (following Austin) want to draw. This means that Justice must repudiate Derrida's crucial observation that, without citational legacy, that is, prior quotation, there would be no recognizable performative utterance. In excluding (as Austin also does) what makes speech acts open to the nonserious, the nonordinary, and the parasitic, Justice imports into his book (the return of the repressed) an "I" (first-person singular, active), a rural, agrarian, peasant "I," as ahistorical presumption rather than the very basis of historical questioning.[64]

The implications of Justice's refusal of various poststructuralist debates (implicitly a refusal of feminist and queer critiques of copy and original) about speech acts can be exemplified in his reading of "the case of the mistaken hands." Different chronicle versions of the execution of the archbishop of Canterbury during the uprising conflict over the agency of the hand. These disagreements reveal Justice's refusal in his own work to imagine the "impure" [perverse?] relation of citation to performance and question the ideology of his own performative "I do" that produces such a mistake as an effect.

The execution of Simon Sudbury, archbishop of Canterbury and royal chancellor, on 14 June 1381 marks one of the most dramatic moments of the uprising. Different chronicle versions of the event disagree over a crucial detail of the execution. The continuator of the *Eulogium historiarium,* a Franciscan friar from either London or Canterbury, wrote that, as the rebels beheaded Sudbury, "they cried with each stroke, 'This is the hand of the Lord'" ("Ad quemlibet ictum dicentes: 'Haec est manus domini'"). Other chroniclers, including Walsingham and the L copy of the *Eulogium,* attribute this utterance to Sudbury. When Justice first presents to his readers this rebel "speech act," he relegates to a footnote the problem of evidentiary confusion about who spoke these words. In a later discussion, Justice glosses Walsingham's version as a kind of voice-over, thus arguing that these are rebel words: "It is there to deny, take away, obscure, and otherwise render inaudible anything the rebels might have said—by speech, script, purposeful action—and jumble all their words and actions into undifferentiated sound."[65] In what follows, I offer a different political reading of the confusion of who said what, whose hand smote Sudbury. The very confusion of the chronicles points to the conflicted terms of political crisis in the late fourteenth century, which can be stated succinctly as, What, indeed, are the embodied relations of citation to performance? or, What are the embodied relations of copy and original?

The Mouth of Richard, the Ear of the Wife of Bath

Writing cannot forget the misfortune from which its necessity springs; nor can it count on tacit, rich, and fostering "evidences" that can provide for an "agrarian" speaker his intimacy with a mother tongue.

—Michel de Certeau, *The Writing of History*[66]

The mouth of Richard II and the ear of the Wife of Bath offer ways into thinking about the discursive political crisis at stake in *Writing and Rebellion.* As we have seen, citation, the possibility for every performative utterance to be "quoted," is the condition of possibility for the recognition of performative utterance. Performative utterance is thus always reiteration, and, "to the extent that it acquires an act-like status in the present, it conceals or dissimulates the conventions of which it is a repetition."[67] Bearing this in mind, it is possible to read the different versions of performative utterance during Sudbury's execution as a rebel utterance ("Our hand is God's hand," as Justice reads it) or as Sudbury's utterance ("Done!" affirming, like Austin, the absolute singular uniqueness of a speech act and in so doing excluding the very problem of citation of which Sudbury's body is the subject). The two versions differ politically in their displacements between performance and citation.

The two different hands of God conjured at Sudbury's death anticipate in an uncanny way the kernel of political debate in contemporary speech act theory, the political debate that Justice brushes aside. By didactically resolving the confusion rather than exploring it, Justice misses how the conflicting versions are performative of the political crisis of performative utterance in late fourteenth-century England.[68] These conflicting chronicle versions show how suspect and unstable the relation of citation to performative utterance had become, how "unguaranteed," how "unwarranted." It is therefore crucial not to settle on one version but to use the historical confusion for what it might suggest about a historical politics of citation becoming unrecognizable, thus destabilizing recognizable performative utterance. In other words, the uprising precisely focused political crisis on the problem of performative utterance as a labor. And that labor must be understood as a work of mourning, not as a melancholy for work.

This crisis, the confusion between performance and citation, can be traced to the king's mouth, to his writing hand (his bureaucracy), and to the legislation regarding the use of English in different juridical and colonial venues. Consideration of these sites disrupts the binaries that organize *Writing and Rebellion* (town and country, commentary and documentary, Latinity and vernacularity, rebels and ideologues, performative utterance and citation) and refigures what Justice considers to be the "social outside" of the canon, those "great regions of rural experience and practice,"[69] to include the colonial vernaculars of Ireland, Scotland, and Wales.

The deposition of Richard II in 1399 exemplifies the political crisis over performative utterance and citation.[70] As Jesse Gellrich has noted, the deposing parliament accused Richard II of arrogating law to his own body, into his mouth and his breast:

> Item, idem Rex nolens justas Leges et Consuetudines Regni sui servare seu protegere, set secundum sue arbitrium voluntatis facere quicquid desideriis ejus occurrerit, quandoque et frequentius quando sibi expositi et declarati fuerant Leges Regni sui per Justic' et alios de Consilio suo, et secundum Leges illas petentibus justiciam, exhiberet; Dixit expresse, vultu austero et protervo, quod Leges sue erant in ore suo, et aliquotiens in pectore suo: Et quod ipse solus posset mutare et condere Leges Regni sui. Et opinione illa seductus, quam-pluribis de ligeis Justiciam fieri non permisit, set per minas et terrores quamplures a prosecutione communis Justicie cessare coegit.[71]

Richard is doing what Sudbury did when, according to some chronicle versions, he exclaimed at his execution, "This is the hand of God." The king and his archbishop arrogate performativity, not to the invocation of citation (a "chain of binding conventions," as Judith Butler has described it),[72] but to one body, God's or the king's. Richard conflated performative utterance and citation onto his body, thus producing the fantasy of a pure body, which is the fantasy of a pure speech act that is not part of a reiteration, that is, a body without temporality. Caught up in such conflation, performance fails, not because of some "infelicity" (a mistake, as Austin and Justice would construe it), but because of a phantasmatic political refusal to yield the body to the engendering and sexualization that is historically part of the process of citation. This refusal also refuses writing and therefore undermines whatever power might accrue to literary work. The king's mouth becomes the realm's writing pad.

The rebels worked to render performative utterance recognizable again (their intervention, however, works uncannily like William Morris's). They undertook to set the relations of citation back in motion again by writing on the chancellor's body with God's hand. In the versions that describe their act ("Our hand is God's hand"), the rebels enacted the hand of God as a citational hand, a writing hand, with the blade on Sudbury's neck. Through decapitation, the spacing of citationality reemerges. The rebels eschew the pure body of performativity through the decapitation of Sudbury and attempt to return to a production of Richard as the "felicitous" executor of speech acts.

But this reading of the two versions of the scene of execution has not yet answered the question, Why should the chancellor's body and not Richard's serve as the writing pad needed to reestablish the recognizability of performative utterance? A clue to the necessity comes again from the account of the parliamentary deposition (written not in French, as was often the case, but Latin) of Richard. The rolls inform us that, after having read out loud his agreement to renounce the crown to a group of temporal and spiritual lords in the Tower of London, and after having signed it, Richard took off his signet ring and put it on the finger of the duke of Lancaster ("I do"?), as a sign of his intention that the duke be declared his successor. At the ensuing session of Parliament, when the Commons acceded to the deposition, Henry, duke of Lancaster rose in Parliament, declared (recorded in English on the roll) the throne vacant, and waged his challenge for the throne. Lords and Commons were then asked what they made of this challenge, and they agreed without delay that the duke should rule over them. At that moment, Henry shows the Parliament Richard's signet ring.[73] What is the significance of this verbal consent to Henry's accession from Parliament, followed by his showing of the signet ring?

Jesse Gellrich has noted the importance of Richard's personal signet ring in the political conflict of what he calls *orality* and *literacy*, which I have refigured in this discussion of *Writing and Rebellion* as the relation between the performative utterance and citationality.[74] Increasingly, Richard had used his ring to make his wishes known directly to the chancellor through letters signet. The ring thus worked as a kind of loudspeaker grafted onto the chancellor's ear. The signet ring was the technological device whereby Richard was able to conflate performative utterance and citationality. To disable this technology and set performative utterance and citationality back into some kind of recognizable temporal sequence, the rebels needed to dislodge Richard's loudspeaker from the chancellor's ear. They accomplished this surgical task through beheading. The beheading thus enacted a double labor of writing on Sudbury, effacing the possibility of pure utterance and also spacing Sudbury's body from the conflation of performance and citationality practiced by Richard. Henry's showing of the signet ring to Parliament repeats and displaces the rebels' display of Sudbury's head on London Bridge. The signet ring, disseminated in Henry's ostentation across his body and the body of Richard, once and for all pulls the plug on Richard's loudspeaker, forecloses the possibility of Richard's plugging the signet ring into someone else's ear, setting in motion once again the collapse of citationality into performance. The duke and the rebels are thus on the side of a performativity that is not "pure," but neither the duke nor the rebels were politically willing to spin out the implications of citationality, to look too closely at what the "nonserious," the "nonordinary," and the parasitic might mean to the politics of speech acts (questions now engaged in the contemporary struggle over speech acts).

The unlikely character of the Wife of Bath did, however, address the deeper implications of the political crisis of the later fourteenth century. Given her florid status as one of the most symptomatic subjects of a mostly breathtakingly misogynistic Chaucerian criticism, my curiosity about her was aroused, as I read Justice's book, by his turning a deaf ear to questions of gender and sexuality in the ideology of the rebels, confected in "the lives of the villages themselves."[75] Justice's deaf ear reminded me of a different deaf ear, that of the Wife of Bath. This association offered the opportunity of returning the question of gender (so assiduously suppressed by Justice) to *Writing and Rebellion.*

In *Writing and Rebellion,* Justice distinguishes between commentary and documentary writing: "The written word in documentary record functions differently from the written word in Langland and the tradition of commentary."[76] The insurgents and Justice (influenced by Austin's speech act theory) read commentary as documentary and are thus able to critique commentary and rewrite it as performative enactment. The Wife of Bath's tale engenders a different relation between reading and writing commentary and documentary. The tale shows how coerced members of a textual community could reclassify genre in their reading practices. It thus traces how coercion materialized genders and sexualities in profoundly political ways.[77]

How is the engendering of commentary, documentary, and speech acts staged in the text of the Wife of Bath's tale? In the first two lines of the Wife of Bath's introduction in the general prologue of the *Canterbury Tales,* the reader learns first that the wife comes from "beside Bath" (line 445); she is on the border of town and countryside, an in-betweenness that complicates at the outset Justice's own ideology of the "ideology of locality" ("stonde manlyche togedyr") (130), which marks an ideological chasm between town and country.[78] Next the reader learns that the wife is "somdel deef, and that was scather" (line 446). The first body part of the Wife of Bath to be introduced to readers is not one of her sexual endowments celebrated later in the text but instead her deaf ear. The Wife tells the story of how she came to be deaf in the prologue to her own tale. The story begins with the Wife's best friend, Alisoun ("she knew myn herte, and eek my privitee" [line 531]; "so often tymes to my gossyb went for evere yet I lobed to be gay" [lines 544–45]). The Wife's traffic in men always passes through Alisoun, and the only one in the Wife's tale to know her "privitee" (when the Wife talks about her genitals in relation to men, she calls them her "bele chose" [line 510]) is her girlfriend.[79] Alisoun's boarder, the clerk Jankyn, becomes the Wife's fifth husband. It is a blow from him that renders the Wife of Bath deaf, and she tells this traumatic story twice. First, she describes how after their marriage Jankyn spurned her desire ("He nolde suffre nothyng of my list" [line 633]) and then links that spurning to the blow: "By God! he smote me ones on the lyst' for that I rent out of his book a leef" (line 634). She retells the story in more detail after she acquaints the reader with Jankyn's provocative reading habits, how he preaches and recites to his wife exemplary stories from antifeminist tracts. One night, as he regales her with such recitations, she exasperatedly tears three pages from the book as he reads and punches him on the cheek. Jankyn falls backward into the fire and then springs up and hits the Wife of Bath in the ear, thus deafening her. In the exchange that ensues, the Wife outmaneuvers the clerk. She recovers the "governance" of her house and land and has the clerk burn his book.

This story can be read as we have read Richard's mouth, his signet ring, and Sudbury's head. Antifeminist tracts, conventionally thought of as commentary, were for the Wife always already documentary, which she tries to reread and reconfigure as commentary, in order to disable their performative work of sexual politics in her household. They are performative because they call into question the "felicity" of the speech acts of her five marriages. The tracts from which Jankyn reads claim these speech acts to be infelicitous ("that by the same ensample taught he [Christ] me that I ne should wedded be but ones" [lines 12–13]). The antifeminist tracts deny the performative utterance of the Wife of Bath. They tell her how her "I do" does not count.

The Wife takes politics into her own hands. In a reversal of the insurgent reading and writing practices posited by Justice, the Wife wants to return to commentary what for her is documentary. What Justice would take as commentary from his canonical perspective, the Wife of Bath experiences as performative. She needs to craft political gestures that will return documentary to commentary. She violates Jankyn's book by tearing it, and her punishment is deafness. As a "somewhat" deaf person, the Wife of Bath is now compromised in the performative realm of speech acts since she might not hear the performative utterances of a judge, a priest, or a husband reliably. She has become "infelicitous" in Austin's scenario. But the Wife knows that her infelicity is not enough. Her deafness might remove her from performative utterance, but it does not resignify the problem of the text itself from which Jankyn reads. She therefore insists that the book itself be burned.

The story of the Wife of Bath shows how within marriage (a public, economic, political, theological institution) the textual politics of commentary and documentary espoused by Justice can be reversed, experienced differently within the household.[80] Further, the political solutions within such reversals might share overt similarities to Justice's insurgents, but they bear different political effects and are not, therefore, to be misrecognized as the same. The Wife's ear becomes her writing hand and, in doing so, considerably complicates the all too neat line that Justice wants to draw between writing and rebellion.

The Wife's tale also disrupts productively the nineteenth-century "merry England" picture of village community imagined by Justice in his chapter on the idiom of rural politics. Justice imagines the village romantically along nineteenth-century lines (which were used then to prop up the constitution of national and imperial "Englishness" and used now to prop up "coterie canons" among medievalists).[81] His imagined village enjoys the devotional "integration" of Corpus Christi and is remarkably unmarred by anticlericalism and anti-Semitism, so politically important in the late fourteenth century. Villagers beat their bounds on Rogation Days seemingly untroubled by their own litigious lawsuits over resources, which Richard Smith has shown were increasingly going out of the circuit of manorial courts to other transregional venues since the very concept of "locality" was being redefined by "locals." Justice further imagines communities out of *Holy Feast and Holy Fast*,[82] bound together by their almost mystical concern for food ("the fear of dearth and the need for bread, which generated a deep and echoing devotion to the eucharistic host in rural communities, generated also an ethic and legality independent of, though often confirmed by, seigneurial administration and royal law"), in spite of the evidence of the records of prosecution under the Statute of Laborers that rural residents were being fined for not doing precisely what they did not want to be forced to do: produce grains that were not so lucrative on a highly commoditized market where a mix of pastoral and artisanal activities made more money. Finally, at the core of his imagined village community glows the family: "Rural society, with its ties of kinship and obligation (the 'fadres wille' and 'frends conseille') and its duty of familial and communal cooperation (the wife as help-meet), embodies 'trewthe' as the natural condition of laboring society."[83]

To get his imagined community to persuade, Justice has to suppress the history of difference within the household, gender difference.[84] As gender and sexuality attach to individuals, to Justice's way of thinking they do not count as political or historical. His imagined village life, which depends on the undifferentiated "natural" family, sounds eerily like contemporary right-wing discourses of mutual dependency, discourses that would distance themselves from the traditional liberal discourse of rights and autonomy. Such distancing does not, however, automatically transform the masculinism of liberal discourse. Wendy Brown has trenchantly cautioned about the political return of "mutual obligation": "Are the political discourses of rights and autonomy being decentered by discourses of need or mutual dependency in crucial domains of public life? And do these latter discourses subvert or reiterate liberal conventions of feminine positioning and concerns? If, as seems likely, both tendencies are currently at work, both reaffirming and decentering masculinist liberal discourse, what hybrid liberal political culture is figured by their entwining?"[85]

The Wife's multiple "I do"s disrupt the speech act theory girding *Writing and Rebellion.* The Wife of Bath would seem to side with Derrida. She knows "how to do things with words," or, as Eve Kosofsky Sedgwick would say, she knows "how to say 'I do' about twenty million times without winding up any more married than [she] started out."[86] Just as Justice desires to learn from the rebels that "official culture needs not to be read as it wishes,"[87] he could learn from the Wife of Bath that Austin need not be read as he would wish. But this, then, would bring him full circle to feminist and queer critiques of speech act theory and its current work in producing canons.

The Wife of Bath can also instruct *Writing and Rebellion* about the differences between melancholy for work and the work of mourning. Perhaps so many Chaucerian scholars have felt the anxious need to abject the Wife of Bath as a kind of medieval Zsa Zsa Gabor precisely because she knew not to fix herself in a melancholy for work. As an accomplished cloth maker (why are so many critics so quick to deny this?), the Wife of Bath knew about the fabrication of labor; she also knew of the politics of desire, of the never transparent process of wanting to have and wanting to be: "unto this day it dooth myn herte boote, that i have had my world as in my tyme" (lines 472–73).

Yet another lesson can be drawn from the Wife of Bath. She starts her tale with a history lesson that can be read as alluding to the fractured state of vernacularity of late medieval England. Justice would disavow such vernacular shattering in his wish to erect a holistic, canonical origin for vernacularity in insurgency. The Wife of Bath begins with an Arthurian-like reference to the elves and fairies that once filled the land and do so no longer owing to the ubiquitous presence of "lymytours" (line 866), friars with special licenses to beg in a given locality. The "elves" (line 864) come from another time and another linguistic space. The Celtic haunting of that linguistic space is a reminder that, at the very time that Chaucer was writing, Parliament was making language laws that enforced English as the vernacular in its colonies.[88] There existed three vernaculars in Anglo-Ireland: English, French, and Gaelic. The Statutes of Kilkenny, recorded in French (1366), attempted to put a stop to the Gaelicization of English in Ireland: "That every Englishman use the English language, and be named by an English name, leaving off entirely the manner of naming used by the Irish; and that every Englishman use the English custom, fashion, mode of riding and apparel, according to his estate and if any English, or Irish living amongst the English, use the Irish language amongst themselves, contrary to this ordinance, and thereof be attaint, that his lands and tenements, if he have any, be seizined into the hands of the immediate lord."[89]

The fractured vernaculars of Anglo-Ireland are even more stunningly apprehended in the records of the submission of the Irish chiefs to Richard II in 1395–96. These chiefs gave their oaths in Gaelic (*lingua hibernica*) in the presence of witnesses who understood Gaelic. The oath was then read in English to Richard II and recorded by notary in Latin. The Gothic peasant ventriloquized by both Morris and Justice has the effect of rendering off-screen (invisible) the hybrid performance of the Wife of Bath, lucratively engaged in cloth making (she is no ploughman's wife), and Richard II attending the submission of the Irish chiefs. The "Gothic peasant" that haunts Morris and Justice and makes their work possible can now be made out as an extremely effective optical device for medievalism, a looking glass whose magic is to mirror back work and community as phantasmatically whole again, untroubled by gender and sexuality.

Epilogue

This essay has tried to transform the architectural space of medieval studies by tracing through the Gothic Revival the genealogy of the Gothic peasant, a construct that haunts medieval studies today. The Gothic peasant inhabits a crypt, produced, as we have seen, in a crisis of ornament during the Gothic Revival. Working as a type of forced entry, this essay has tried to trace the cracks in Morris and in Justice to break down the crypt and to suggest that architectures other than the crypt hold possibilities for medieval studies. Just as Walter Benjamin introduced his (never to be completed) material history of the shopping arcades that became the site and sign of consumption of the nineteenth-century metropolis—"This work is concerned with awakening from the nineteenth century"[90]—so, too, does this essay seek to awaken from another dream of the nineteenth century: the Gothic peasant. It, too, has studied architectures—those of the Gothic Revival and also the sedimented century-old architectures of institution, discipline, discourse, and pedagogy in medieval studies—through a reading of *Writing and Rebellion.* It has explored gaps in these armatures through which we might produce a different critical space for medieval studies.

A contemporary architect, who works in such gaps, can inspire this work of mourning in medieval studies, this decryptment. On 17 May 1996, the Victoria and Albert Museum (a great Victorian institution rendered in Gothic Revival style) announced Daniel Libeskind, the Berlin-based architect, as the winner of a widely advertised design competition for an extension to the museum. The English project follows on Libeskind's brilliant work on the extension to the Berlin Museum intended to house its Jewish collection. In thinking through humanist architecture and history, Libeskind rethinks the museum form for two very

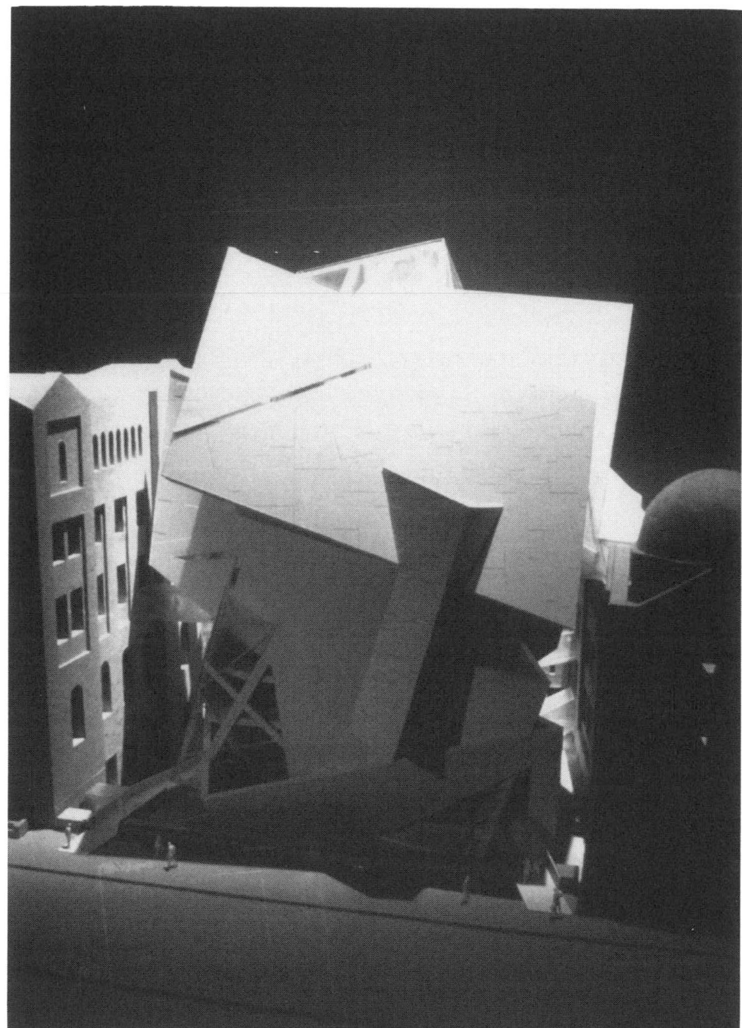

Figure 5. Model for the Boilerhouse Extension (architect, Daniel Libeskind), Victoria and Albert Museum, London. Courtesy the Victoria and Albert Museum/Art Resource NY.

different cities (Berlin, London) and two very different structures (the baroque of the Berlin Museum, the Gothic Revival of the Victoria and Albert): "I thought that a museum should not simulate a culture, but should distance or involve the public in order to make them decide how, where, and what to do in a museum whose particular function is the history of the city and of an emblem."[91] His is an architecture of gaps.

Leading British critics have regarded his extension (see fig. 5), described by Libeskind as an "exploding spiral," "extremely hideous and inappropriate for Victorian surroundings," as "forbidding and oppressive," and as "an insult to everything the museum stands for."[92] Its incandescent spiral, unfolding within a stack of fractured translucent cubes, tactically juxtaposed against the Gothic Revival facade of the mid-nineteenth-century museum, serves as an architectural allegory for reading this essay on Gothic ornament. The multiple historical and counterhistorical relations that Libeskind brings to crisis in the extension—to an imperial museum, to its planned neighborhood (South Kensington), to the urban "performance" of London—resonate with the spaces of concern to this essay, that is, their relations and nonrelations to institution, discipline, discourse, and pedagogy in medieval studies.

Libeskind unfolds his architecture from his critical understanding of the politics of interiors. So, too, this essay has unfolded from the political interior produced through the institutionalization of medieval studies in the nineteenth century. What it found in the folds was a crypt, and it has lingered at this monument in order to ask what medieval studies had so anxiously encrypted. It has thus related the history of a mausoleum, specifically the inventive and deeply melancholy century-long labor to preserve the edifice. Since its institutional inception, medieval studies bears a specific historical relation to melancholy, a relation that may be described as an unfinished project of mourning for industrialization (with its imbricated imperialism, colonialism, and traumatic refiguration of the human embodiment of labor). The production of a new space for medieval studies then becomes a process of transforming the melancholy for work, the medievalism always haunting the discipline of medieval studies, to the work of mourning.

This essay and those that follow are constructed as an "extension." Its loopholes concatenate into what I wish to call an *architecture of departure.* This architecture constructs medieval history within the trauma of perpetual departure from medievalism. The layers of opacity and translucence, fractured cubes, spiraling folds—please read them as a vivifying design for an extension to a disciplinary crypt.

English America

Worth Dying For?

Don't tell me you're not worth trying for
Can't tell me it's not worth dying for
You know it's true
Everything I do, I do for you.
—"(Everything I Do) I Do for You" from *Robin Hood: Prince of Thieves* (1991)

In the Shadow of the Football Stadium

In 1993, I published the essay "Decolonizing the English Past: Readings in Medieval Archaeology and History" in the North American–based *Journal of British Studies.*[1] The paper questioned the very category *medieval English peasant* that had informed my work in economic history over the past ten years. I argued that the category was constructed in "English India" in the later nineteenth century through both legal adjudication of colonial property rights and the emplotment of constitutional histories as national allegories in England.[2] I then tried to imagine how to undo this category, how to set its politics in motion in order to write different economic histories. An American editor of a prospective volume on medieval peasant studies, targeted for an English publisher, subsequently invited my essay for reprint. It turned out, however, that a reader for the press, a prominent English medievalist, would not sign off unless my essay was pulled from the collection. With profuse apologies to me, the American editor dropped it, and the book went forward to press.

This little melodrama of academic publishing alerted me to the performance of "English America" and the politics of its border patrol. I use *English America* as a kind of shorthand for the complex ways in which, since its so-called takeoff after World War II, North American medieval studies has worked as a kind of "interlocking dream image," an afterlife of British imperial imaginary, shadowing its concessionary narratives, which seemingly provide critiques of such a phantasmatic at the same time that they disavow central issues of its power.[3] My essay had violated the agreement to disavow, and, therefore, it could not be "exported."

The incident reminded me of the lingering magic power (not to be ignored) of English America. The work of English America seemed intractable curricularly, even more than in publishing. The medieval English history survey, a common course offering sometimes *required* of history majors in North American universities, is therefore of great concern: "The curriculum is conceived here not in the perennialist sense of an objective, essentialized entity but rather as discourse, activity, process—as one of the mechanisms through which knowledge is socially distributed and culturally validated."[4] What are North American medievalists, who are required to teach this course, to do? The curricular insistence on the medieval English survey with its insistent silence about imperialism helps keep the imperial imaginary in circulation, allowing North American medieval studies to export the moral order implied by *Englishness,* under its familiar guise of *Anglo-Saxonism,* back into Britain even now.[5]

This essay loops around sites of phantasmatic exchange, but not with the intent of advocating an end to the medieval English survey. Rather, I trouble its three terms: the temporality of *medieval,* the cultural ideology of *English,* and the purported panopticism of a national *survey,* which keeps imperialism in a space-off. Since this troublemaking led me along twisted paths, I offer a map to them, lingering at the most contested sites.

The first site to be considered is the journal *Past and Present.* Founded in 1952 by British Marxist historians, its editorial agenda materialized anxieties over decolonizing British historiography in the aftermath of decolonization. In its early years, medieval historians sought to reweave a distinctively English rural past around an obsessive search for the archival identity of Robin Hood. Their endeavor to rewrite the traditional aristocratic genealogy of Robin Hood as a peasant case and to use Robin Hood to reinstall a rural past of kith and kin under the shadow of the pastoral family tree of Englishness could establish a neocolonial continuity with an Indian rural past, lost with the loss of the raj.[6]

The discourse of the journal also bordered the racial politics of postwar Britain. As race grew politically visible in Britain in the 1960s and 1970s through the articulation of a social welfare discourse of pathological black families and criminality, *Past and Present* gave its editorial permission to what was to become a historiographic industry: English family history and the history of English crime.[7] Strikingly, the Marxist agenda of *Past and Present* was at odds with another Marxist project under development at the same time at the School of Contemporary Cultural Studies (SCCS) at Birmingham.[8] As *Past and Present* produced visions of Englishness in family history and a history of crime, the SCCS assertively questioned the production of postimperial Englishness organized around precisely such categories as *the family* and *civil good order.*

As I groped along this fault line between *Past and Present* and the work of the SCCS, the powerful struggle over the family as a pastoral space struck me as the most contested divide. Since the time of Virgil, the pastoral has offered an imaginary site at which historical contests over "authentication" and "truth" in public culture can be waged.[9] The pastoral space of the family in *Past and Present* could be found shading Englishness, protecting it from the glaring sun of other contending migrant and sexual histories that had come to the metropolis since World War II. This shady cleft into which I stumbled flickered with uncanny resemblances between the politics of pastoral space as articulated in the family and the space of the curricular survey. The family and the survey began to look to me like twins. As I grappled with curricular critique, the Hollywood film *Robin Hood: Prince of Thieves* (1991), which was shot in Britain during the Persian Gulf War and distributed just a few months after the so-called victory of Desert Storm, struck me as yet another powerful example of English America, one less distant from the medieval academy than its shopping-mall popularity might lead us to think.[10] The challenge of joining these postwar sites of *Past and Present* and the SCCS with shopping-mall cinema thus further challenged my rethinking of the medieval English survey.

Before looking at the complex borders of these sites in more detail, I wish to situate my own curricular struggles in the mid-1980s, when, as a beginning professor, I had to fulfill a departmental mandate that I teach the medieval English survey. To go back to that time, I use a time-lapse camera, like the one imagined by Walter Benjamin, who wrote that the "initial day of a calendar serves as a historical time-lapse camera."[11]

The time-lapse camera clicks.

Around 1987

On 16 October 1987, fierce, hurricane-force winds devastate half a million trees in the south of England. The British papers talk of "felled giants," how the ancient seven oaks of Sevenoaks, Kent, lay uprooted and dying in the aftermath. That same autumn, the British filmmaker Derek Jarman worked on *The Last of England,* which he described as a "dream allegory [in which] the present dreams the past future." In the opening voice-over, Jarman alludes to the dead trees: "The oaks died this year. On every green hill mourners stand, and weep for *The Last of England.*"[12]

Margaret Thatcher also announced the last of England in 1987: "There is no such thing as society. There are individual men and women and there are families."[13] Thatcher dreams the collapse of the English citizen into the family as the site of consumption. Only the purchase of commodities can continue to make agency visible in this dreamworld. Thatcher's speech could easily be mistaken as an advertisement for Benneton. Englishness no longer works as an imperial-national culture, a historical necessity. Now, in the late 1980s, it is a transnational "style"—you, too, can choose it, buy it, wear it, implant it, grow it in a test tube, in the shadow of the family tree, naturally.

Medieval English Survey, 1987

I dreamed a painful dream fragment while I taught the medieval English survey that autumn. In the dream, I saw an intricate, vivid, shiny, metallic pattern that at first seemed frighteningly indecipherable until it suddenly struck me, with the great relief of dream recognition, that it was Celtic interlace. The dream had disposed of a disturbing fragment of a mask. My dream had dreamed Britain thinking me as a child through the migrant histories of my own family. My aging great-grandmother had come to die at the house of her daughter, Sarah Gallagher, who had left Ireland in her teens. The large, hairy, aged woman sitting in the corner of my grandmother's kitchen spoke in a language that made no sense to me, and mine seemed to make no sense to her—our nonsense profoundly frightened me as a solipsistic four-year-old, one who had not yet learned that there was more than one language. Shortly afterward, my great-grandmother died. We drove a seemingly interminable distance to Brooklyn for the wake, and there the nonsense got all mixed up with her deathly silence. Only much later did I learn that my great-grandmother spoke in Gaelic to me, or so that story was told.

Britain also thought me as a "first ever in the family at university," as an American graduate student, studying at a Canadian university, working on a British archaeological site (Peterborough) for her dissertation. As I taught the survey that autumn, the image of the blue-uniformed Borstal boys (as they were called)—a contract with the regional reformatory allowed them to do the heavy work of our excavation—haunted me. As we students troweled, the Borstal boys stood in rows laboriously shoveling, not unlike the Egyptian fellahs to be seen in early twentieth-century photographs of British excavations in Egypt—Flinders-Petrie never lets go, I thought.

These ghosts from past and present haunted me as I tried to understand the power of the medieval English survey over the students who sat all too docilely in front of me. They came from the prelaw program, from the London Abroad program; there were government majors, history majors, and also a good number from the ROTC. The students desired that exceptional story that they already knew: law, monarchy, progress, Pax Britannia. They desired this even though the majority of them were self-identified Irish-Americans who had chosen to come to the university of the "fighting Irish." These students had no chance to understand the co-construction of "Irishness" and "Englishness" since, at that time, there was no Irish studies program, or any equivalent, that would make such study possible. Seamus Deane, who now heads such a program at Notre Dame, calls this persistent, timeless denial of "Irishness" for the "Irish-American" "a kind of self-imposed cultural starvation, almost a hunger strike."[14]

That curricular strike got me thinking of the space where the "fighting Irish" fight, the football stadium (the libidinal, economic, and ideological heart of the campus), a place of enclosure, green and idyllic—a pastoral space. There is my clue, I thought; the space of the survey works like the pastoral. It is a green, protected space, like the football stadium, where conflict can be repeated and contained. The survey assured students not only of Englishness but also that most of civilization still lies shaded under the sturdy, capacious, seemingly eternal canopy of the British oak. Safe, secure, idyllic, the space of the survey promised the reproduction of order, monarchy, law, Parliament, world power, even the "fighting Irish," the pastoral space of the football stadium. There was my curricular challenge. Could I work to move the survey out of the cultural shade of the British oak, or is the very notion of a medieval English survey constitutive of such trees, helping to make the British oak visible, just as the British oak, the pastoral, makes the survey visible?[15]

The problem of visibility and performance in the survey continued to haunt me as I made my various, awkward adjustments to it over the semesters. In 1991, I thought that I might have found the answer to my curricular problems in Marilyn Strathern's *After Nature.* Strathern, an anthropologist, traces the historic epistemology of Thatcher's statement, "There is no such thing as society . . . ," and considers its cultural implications. She locates in those words a rupture that she describes as "after Nature," meaning an epoch in which individuality no longer reproduces individuality, where there is no future, owing to the "demise of the reproductive model of the modern epoch which was . . . a model not just of the procreation of persons but for conceptualising the future."[16]

Somehow Strathern oddly converged on Thatcher, however. So convinced that "after Nature" marked an epistemic break, she failed to interrogate it as yet one more move in a neoimperial production with/over the Englishness of national identity. Such odd convergence of left- and right-wing analysis hinted to me that another politics might be in question here, the politics of race. Paul Gilroy has analyzed just such strange left-right convergences in the racial politics of Britain in the 1970s and 1980s.[17] My guess was that both Thatcher and Strathern would seemingly rather "disappear" "English society" than see it rendered vulnerable to or shattered by—what?

Around 1987, the politics of race and sexuality intensified in British public culture. As Thatcher spoke, and as Strathern delivered the lectures on which her book was to be based, British filmmakers were telling different and powerful migrant and sexual histories that foregrounded the family in counterpastoral spaces. What was the threat of these counterpastoral histories? As histories of excluded bodies, the bodies that made national Englishness possible, this counterpastoral challenged the politics of visibility that made the very modern English models of nature, society, and the individual visible through the invisibility of bodies that did not matter.

These migrant and sexual histories dispelled the shade of the family tree, threatened the pastoral tree itself, perhaps beyond recuperation. At this moment, I reminded myself of my disciplinary question: When, where, how did institutional history intersect with this moment of pastoral/counterpastoral? The time had come to use my skills as a historian to join the historiography of the English family with Thatcherite stagings of the English family and with the counterstagings of the family being told in black and queer British film of the 1980s.

The time-lapse camera clicks.

Past and Present, 1952

It is 1952, and one of the key British journals of the postwar/decolonization period, the Birmingham-based *Past and Present,* is founded by British Marxists. The first issue appeared in February. The editors used the subtitle "A Journal of Scientific History." In the dysphoria of decolonization and the emerging cold war, British Marxists cited the ancient historian Polybius for his confidence in the discipline of history as an instrument that enabled "us" to "face coming events with confidence." What struck me about the medieval contributions to the journal in its first years was the obsession with questions about the historical identity and class of Robin Hood. Historians were busy transforming Robin Hood from an aristocratic and, later, a yeoman outlaw into a peasant.[18] So intense was this work that five of the fifteen essays appearing in the volume celebrating the twentieth anniversary of the journal's founding were devoted to Robin Hood. In these days, as Eric Hobsbawm, one of the founding editors of *Past and Present,* wrote about insurgency and heroes, what could be better than a medieval peasant hero who could be used to disavow not only postcolonial loss in both academic and popular culture (the BBC series on Robin Hood was also created and programmed during this period) but also the incipient postwar class conflicts around migrant labor, West Indian and Asian?[19]

In this return of Robin Hood to the pages of *Past and Present,* I detect a pastoral move among British historians. Indeed, the project of founding the journal was itself a pastoral move, the obsession with Robin Hood being one of the medieval *effects* of the move. The strong desire to locate Robin Hood under the pastoral shade of the past at this moment, in 1952, has everything to do with the culture of decolonization in England. What kind of desire is this desire of English historians for English peasants? To answer that question, we must consider what phantasmatic histories were lost in England with the recent decolonization of India.

Put very briefly, to write a progressive history of national freedom in the nineteenth century, English scholars appropriated German scholarship on the Teutonic village community as a guide for imagining Saxon villages as the laboratory for democracy. British scholars in the India Service, who grappled with framing tenurial policies for Indian village communities, then extended the narrower concept of the Teutonic village community to encompass the Aryan community. Publications such as *Village Communities in the East and West* (1871) by Sir Henry Maine, a classicist, jurist, and member of the Viceroys Council in India, helped produce India as the rural past of England and England as the colony's constitutional future. In a paradoxical way, the medieval English village community was invented by the India Service. Meanwhile, back in industrializing England, this imperially informed notion of the village community and its peasants could lend itself as a romantic emblem attractive to both liberals and conservatives in parliamentary debates over colonial land settlements in the mid-nineteenth century.[20]

The romantic aura of the village community began to fade, however, as English politicians and scholars attempted to reconcile theories of private property, a symbol of English freedom, with common and joint property relations purported to be the ancient custom of village community. Scholars dealt with such contradictions between property and commons in different ways. Some scholars disengaged the romantic notion of the village community from politically charged debates over property relations by claiming that collective property was a recent aberration forged in villages as a response to taxation and conscription. Frederick Maitland argued elegantly for a hybrid solution. He claimed that communal rights on the commons were based on individual shares in the arable. His colleague, the Russian émigré Paul Vinogradoff, used the family holding as a wedge between individual and community. Indivisible units of arable land constituted family holdings in the village: "Everything goes by heredity and settled rules of family property."[21]

Emphasis on the individual and the family went a long way toward short-circuiting the commons of the village community as a concept easily appropriated by radical critique in England at the end of the nineteenth century. Unmoored from ongoing political debate by the close of the nineteenth century, discussion of the village community subsequently devolved on historians, anthropologists, and sociologists before World War II. Medieval English peasant studies once again, but for different reasons, became a contested cultural site.

Medieval English peasant studies, so important to English constitutional history of the latter part of the nineteenth century, returned, not surprisingly, with force at decolonization. The loss of the raj cut English culture off from one of the peasant pasts it had imagined for itself. English historians labored to recover the medieval English village and, in so doing, to work out the problems of continuity and change for an "imperial-national" culture undergoing decolonization. The peasant historiography that emerged in the postwar period in the pages of *Past and Present* tried to repair the imagined but nevertheless lost past by disavowing it and putting Robin Hood in its place. *Past and Present* moved the discourse of the English peasant to a nonplace, to the site of Robin Hood, who, if he could be given an archival identity and a class status, could be made the visible father of a new rural history. But, as Michel de Certeau has warned, by moving historical discourse to a "non-place, ideology forbids history from speaking of society and death—in other words, from being history."[22]

This pastoral history of Robin Hood thus repressed the urgency of decolonizing English history. A measure of the intensity of this disavowal can be had in the failures of British Marxist historians and their journal, *Past and Present,* to articulate with the Birmingham School of Contemporary Cultural Studies in the 1960s and 1970s.[23] The SCCS, founded in 1964, concerned itself with tracking the study of racism, ethnocentrism, nationalism, and ongoing imperialisms as processes, not events. It attended to migrant and sexual histories, popular music, film, and television. In particular, it took a critical stance on how the "family" was being used to stand for a national narrative of England in the 1960s and 1970s, acting as it were as a pastoral space in which political processes could be converted into natural, instinctive, seemingly invisible processes, acts of national nature. Works produced under the influence of the SCCS traced how the families of British blacks came to be labeled pathological, a source of growing "black criminality." How is it that, in spite of gestures and invocations, the two Birmingham projects did not really articulate, did not join their national and imperial critiques? This question can be answered in part by contrasting the very different positioning of the family in the two projects.

West Indian and Indian migration into Britain in the late 1950s and early 1960s produced among British intellectuals an emergent and defensive historiographic discourse on the distinctiveness of the English family. In a *Past and Present* review essay that appeared coincidentally in 1964, Joan Thirsk, a noted agrarian historian and member of the editorial board, made a clarion call for English family history.[24] The debates in family history revolved around a distinctive Englishness and how early it could be detected. Studies such as Alan Macfarlane's *The Origins of English Individualism*[25] exemplify such a search. Macfarlane would locate the formation of the distinctive English family in the twelfth century, a century, perhaps not so coincidentally, associated with Robin Hood.

Just two short years after the "explosions" at Brixton (1981) and the publication of Lord Scarman's report on the racial uprisings,[26] *Past and Present* began to take on yet another issue of racial politics in its pages, another site where Englishness could be regarded as distinctive, that is, the history of crime. In the November 1983 issue, Lawrence Stone published a review essay on historical patterns of crime in England, writing in his concluding remarks, "We are infinitely more destructive in war than our ancestors, but in our daily lives the English at least are also, for some reason, still far less prone to casual violence."[27] Read this against those "explosions," the "mindless" violence of Brixton, and it is again possible to see how the Englishness of the family and the Englishness of peaceful everyday life lay protected in the white shade of the pages of *Past and Present.*

There's No Place like the Home Movie

The pastoral politics of *Past and Present* did not go unchallenged in public culture. Two films influenced by the SCCS—*Handsworth Songs* by John Akomfrah and *The Last of England* by Derek Jarman, produced in 1986 and 1987, respectively[28]—can be used as examples of this counterpastoral politics.[29] Together, these films work like a double-edged blade, exposing the roots of the pastoral family tree of Englishness to migrant and sexual histories. Both films splice family scenes from home-movie footage, footage that functions as a counterpastoral space.

Handsworth Songs can be read as a kind of video Ellis Island for West Indian migration into Britain. It tells a history of the Handsworth uprising of 1985 through a history of West Indian migration, largely postwar, to Britain. The home-movie footage does not show an essentialist West Indian family of tradition, which would deteriorate in the metropolis. Instead, it constitutes the family as a contact zone that articulates with a range of spaces that cannot be easily categorized as public or private and with times that cannot be easily categorized as developmental. Home-movie footage—a young infant being washed in a tub, a young man and two women in a living room, two young girls with their parents in a living room—is nested in an ever-unfolding montage of archival footage of local community spaces: a grade school, a nursery, a health clinic, a factory, reggae clubs, green markets. It is interspersed with archival footage of postwar interracial dance clubs, BBC footage of disembarking calypso stars, and documentary footage of labor parades and rallies. It is also spliced into studies of black-and-white family photographs of weddings, school events, etc. And all this is cut against BBC footage of the Handsworth uprisings (stripped of audio), community-group and neighborhood commentary on the uprisings, and speeches by Thatcher.

The evocation of the family through home movies in *Handsworth Songs* refuses essentialized notions of the family, producing the family instead as a relay in a complicated grid of migrant, labor, and racial histories. The family itself becomes diasporic within a diasporic film. The voice-over accompanying the last home-movie footage to be spliced into the film underscores this diasporic staging. First, we hear the story of the death of Cynthia Jarret, a victim of police violence, as told by her family. Then, over cuts of the funeral cortege interspliced with home-movie footage of a father, a mother, and their two daughters, a woman's voice speaks: "Then I slip through the crack to be shamed by the sea, Nighttime I am the sea, and if I walk from the shoreline to cast it, it will fill my shoes, washing my journey away."

In staging the family as a historical journey, *Handsworth Songs* blacks out the shade of the pastoral tree that would seek to collapse itself into the family tree—to root nation into Englishness. This ideological family tree is cut down in the collage of *Handsworth Songs.* A voice-over that accompanies another splice of home movies of a living-room scene says as much: "There are sands to shift, dry woods to sweep away, and they said to each other, here we will be shoulder to shoulder, and we will survey the world in ascension, and one day the world will come to us." The pastoral is dismantled and its dry timber carried away in order to make the space for different histories and articulations that do not work through the family as an essentialized "natural/national" entity.

Derek Jarman uses home-movie footage in *The Last of England,* not to cut down the pastoral family tree, but to show the costs of its politics. He focuses on the pastoral site of the postwar white English suburban family and, through splicing his father's home movies, shows that site to be one of devastation, an extension of war, terrorism, imperialism, and libidinal exclusion.

Jarman's family history is in itself an interesting montage of migration and imperialism. On the paternal side, his great-grandfather left Devon to migrate to New Zealand in the mid-nineteenth century. Jarman's father came from New Zealand to Britain supposedly for a brief period in the 1920s but ended up in the RAF in World War II. He was a successful bomber pilot and learned to work a camera on his bombing forays. According to his son, he hated the English and resented the pantomime of accent and gesture that he was forced to adopt to pass in England. On the maternal side, Jarman's grandparents had made their fortune in the tea trade in Calcutta and returned to England to retire. When Jarman was ten years old, his father was seconded as a pilot to Pakistan, and the family accompanied him. Jarman retained vivid memories of that trip.

It is a mistake to read the lush color footage of the Jarman home movies as a site of the pastoral spliced into his unremittingly desolate metropolitan scenes, which insist on the terrorism and desolation of bureaucratic and bureaucratized life under Thatcher. Jarman is, instead, asking us to read the home movies as the site of enclosure and the open secret that constitutes violence and secrecy within the suburban enclosure of the family and gives permission for the extension of this violence beyond the English hedge—an extension that Jarman shows in detail.[30]

Jarman does, however, twice stage a pastoral moment in *The Last of England* in order to shatter the open secret of the pastoral family tree, which is also about the good order of English sexuality, the Englishness of orderly heterosexuality: "Queerness became one of the enemy elements which supported the phantasmatic construction of the family as the antagonism-free centre of the British nation."[31] Jarman stages the first pastoral scene with a cut to Caravaggio's *Perverse Love.* The painting, that of a beautiful male angel, lies on the ground in an abandoned lot; a young punk proceeds to masturbate, then fuck the painting, and finally stomp on it. The punk then moves around the abandoned lot in the glare of a brightly burning flare that seemingly burns up and exposes any lingering shade of the pastoral.

Jarman stages yet another pastoral scene that crisscrosses disorderly sexuality with the pastoral space of the Union Jack. A yuppy, smartly suited, drunken disco goer tries to fuck a masked terrorist of uncertain gender on a bottle-strewn Union Jack. The sexual scene dissipates in drunken frustration. Here, once again, Jarman seems to be exposing and questioning the good order of sexuality that would come under the shade of the pastoral family tree of Englishness.

The Return of Robin Hood, 1991

The return of Robin Hood in *Robin Hood: Prince of Thieves* once again shows the high stakes of pastoral politics in the late 1980s. The concerns in the film with Englishness, the family, and good order echo in an uncanny way the gap between *Past and Present* and the Birmingham SCCS so far articulated in this essay. My reading of contemporary visual images of Robin Hood asks of the historiography to what extent it, too, is an aspect of the construction of the pastoral as an imaginary space in English public culture. As we have seen, the detailed reconstructions of peasant villages that began in earnest in the postwar, postcolonial period helped reconnect public culture to an agrarian past that England had imaginatively located in India, and then lost. Perhaps it is a historical irony that a country that experienced the earliest capitalist transformation of the countryside and pioneered enclosure has so assiduously produced cultural artifacts of the pastoral in its poetry, its popular legends, and its historiography. One is tempted to pun that the pastoral is essential to England and that its intersections with a historiography of the peasantry that has had difficulty not essentializing them as a historical category is not surprising.

The film sets up its concern with Englishness right after the opening credits with a caption describing the historical setting. In crisp white letters on a black background, the caption states that eight hundred years ago Richard Lion-Heart set out on the Third Crusade to claim the Holy Land from the Turks. We learn further that most of the young English nobles who flocked to the Crusade never returned. In contrast to the 1938 version of the tale, *The Adventures of Robin Hood,* this latter *Robin Hood* constructs a historical context that foregrounds things English and focuses on the young nobility rather than the constitutional crises occurring in the absence of the monarch, the concern in 1938.[32] Ironically, as the background for the opening credits, the producers chose the Bayeux tapestry, a visual narrative of the conquest of England by the Normans—figuring, perhaps unconsciously, what might be construed as a cinematic conquest of the English countryside in 1991 by Hollywood. The opening appeal to history thus inverts, ironically, the myth of the Norman yoke invoked for Anglophilic identification in *The Adventures of Robin Hood* in 1938.

No obvious, emblematic scene of the pastoral, akin to the lone deer standing in the glade in the 1938 version, is apparent in the 1991 film. The latter constructs a very different spatial trajectory. The opening scene locates the viewer in what is usually the "unrepresentable" or the "elsewhere" of the Robin Hood legend—the Crusade in the East. After the space of historical graffiti, the film cuts to an aerial view of Jerusalem, and then cuts again to a Moorish prison in which English crusaders are being held captive. This strong Eastern frame signals that the film will attempt to grapple with Orientalism, the co-construction of fantastic notions of East and West.[33] However, the "Orientalism" of the Persian Gulf War, a war being waged as *Robin Hood: Prince of Thieves* was in production, interrupts the film in various ways.

The first clues to such an Orientalism come with depictions of "bad" Moorish prison guards and the "good" Moorish prisoner, Azeem (Morgan Freeman), whose life Robin (Kevin Costner) saves. The film's representation of the East is, significantly, interrupted by a return to the West when the scene shifts from Jerusalem to Locksley Castle, England, where the lord of the castle, Robin's father (Brian Blessed), writes a letter to inquire about his crusader son's welfare.

The film is very slow to construct the space of the forest, and the way in which it finally does suggests a real change in the representation of the pastoral between the 1938 and the 1991 versions. At first, the viewer sees no forest and no acts of poaching. The first reference to the forest occurs when Robin and Azeem (now returned to England) encounter the sheriff of Nottingham's men on Locksley land hunting human quarry in open country, a young boy named Wulf (Daniel Newman) who is suspected of poaching. Robin does not enter the forest himself until he, too, is pursued by the sheriff's men.

Once the camera finally brings viewers into the forest, they find a forest strangely devoid of animal life. All conventional signs of the pastoral are absent. The audience never sees one live deer in *Robin Hood: Prince of Thieves,* nor does it ever see Robin Hood feasting on game, a carnival feature of the pastoral that the 1938 version delighted in staging.[34] The only visual reference to game appears for a moment at the edge of one of the frames, where an attentive viewer can catch a glimpse of skinned deer carcasses suspended from the wagon of Friar Tuck (Michael McShane). The sign of the pastoral has changed from a sublime shot of a buck grazing alone in a forest glade (the animal is then shot and brought into the urban and state space of the castle at Nottingham) to a fleeting glimpse of carcasses.[35] Should we interpret this glimpse as the sign of the pastoral, or, rather, do these abject, almost unrepresentable carcasses offer a clue that the film has relocated the pastoral and that we must look elsewhere in the film for its sign?

Rather than locating the sign of the pastoral in a deer or its totem, *Robin Hood: Prince of Thieves* divides it across two bodies, the richly robed body of Azeem, the black-skinned, tatooed Moor who accompanies Robin Hood back from the Crusade, and the naked body of Robin Hood, whom viewers see, along with Lady Marian (Mary Elizabeth Mastrantonio), as he bathes in a forest glade. Through the character of the "other," Azeem, who conducts a running commentary of "truth" on English society, the film constructs a "concessionary narrative" for itself, meaning, as we have seen, a narrative that "goes some way towards recognizing a native point of view and offering a critique of European behavior," but one that can do this only by "not addressing the central issue."[36] If we think of the pastoral as a place of the "primitive" within Europe constructed in relation to the "primitive" that Europe constructed elsewhere through its anthropology and ethnography, then it seems fitting, according to a neocolonial logic, that the native informant return and give life to a deeply endangered pastoral within England.[37] The return of the "Other" to England enables the rebirth of the pastoral space signified in the naked body of Robin Hood. The film emphasizes the fact that the rebirth of the pastoral is at stake by staging an obstetric crisis. Fanny (Soo Druet), the wife of Little John (Nick Brimble), tries to give birth in the forest camp. Azeem, significantly, saves her and the infant by using "ethnographic" knowledge gained from birthing mares to deliver their infant son.

The viewer can read the intersection of the concessionary narrative of Azeem with the rebirth of the pastoral at the naked body of Robin Hood through the historical events of the Persian Gulf War, which bracketed production of the film. The shooting of *Robin Hood: Prince of Thieves* began in England in early September 1990, approximately one month after the invasion of Kuwait by Iraq and the arrival of the first U.S. ground forces in the Middle East on 8 August 1990. The film was released in the United States on 14 June 1991, just a few months after the so-called victory of Desert Storm. Thus, the shooting and editing of the film spanned this war, in which Britain joined the United States as part of the Desert Storm alliance.

Military images of the Gulf War invaded the film. The war has been described as the first cybernetic war, a "vision war" replete with digitized photography and infrared and radar imaging. These cybernetic images "promote a new high-tech version of Orientalism, dehumanising the Arab population, who become 'collateral damage' deserving of destruction because they hide from the West's enlightened vision."[38] The missile-nose view of targets that became familiar to a television audience watching the trajectories of scud missiles translated into the film's signature special effect—arrow-nose views of "medieval" archery. The images of this scud archery appeared prominently in the promotional trailers for the film and also in Bryan Adams's music video "(Everything I Do) I Do for You," over which the closing credits of the film roll. Thus, audiences who did not actually get to see the film but watched the trailers or music video got to see Robin Hood's cybernetic arrows.

Within the brackets of this cybernetic war, the presence of Azeem in the film can be read in a variety of ways. He is the "good" ally, like Syria or Kuwait, and represents the "best" of Orientalism. He can also enact nostalgically a proximity and embodiment that the video image targets of cybernetic bombing uncannily distanced for the television viewers of the war. Others would read Azeem as a sign of the new Orientalism, governed by a new imperialism that pits progressive Arabs against Islamic fundamentalists. Within a larger technological frame, cybernetics is a technology of simulation with no referent. It does not rely on any traditional, foundational notions of nature to authorize its images. As a technology, it profoundly questions traditional Western notions of nature. Cybernetic technologies help empty out the "pastoral," which relies on a vision of nature as its guarantee. It is not surprising, then, that, within such a historical frame, *Robin Hood: Prince of Thieves* very precariously stages the pastoral and relies on a very old anthropological move, the introduction of the Other, to guarantee this fragile imaginary space.

In contrast to the 1991 version, the different relation to the state foregrounded in the 1938 film starkly delineates the historical struggle over the family as a pastoral site. The 1938 version opens with news of King Richard and focuses on the constitutional plots against him, and it closes by undoing these plots in a coronation scene. The restored King Richard (Ian Hunter) grants Lady Marian to Robin Hood in marriage, but the film does not displace the restoration of Richard with a wedding ceremony. In contrast, the 1991 version contains no reference to the state. The comically villainous sheriff of Nottingham (Alan Rickman) parodies the state. The viewer never sees the barons in assembly, nor does the film bother with any spectacular scenes of public feudal pageantry. Significantly, the film closes with the forest wedding of Robin Hood and Lady Marian. The 1991 film thus ends in the pastoral space, where the 1938 film ends in the space of the state and the church, the medieval cathedral. The 1938 film with its New Deal politics brings the pastoral virtues of the good leader to the state. The pastoral becomes the state in the restoration of

King Richard and Robin Hood. The 1991 film never brings the state to the pastoral because there is no state. Even the intervention of Richard (Sean Connery) at the forest wedding, which is already under way when he arrives, occurs seemingly as an intertextual afterthought (Sean Connery having played Robin Hood in the film *Robin and Marian* [directed by Richard Lester for Ray Stark–Richard Shepherd Productions, 1976]). The state becomes located in the family in the 1991 version.

The different location of the state in the two films can help us understand the significance of gender and its use as a resource to construct the pastoral. Here, the character of Lady Marian is crucial as the figure in the Robin Hood legend who moves back and forth between the spaces of the state, the town, and the forest.[39] Historically, Lady Marian became attached to the Robin Hood legend as a transvestite carnival character of sixteenth-century May Games in England. Ironically, the transvestite nature of Lady Marian has been inverted in the twentieth century—Lady Marian dresses up like a man sometimes. Her cross-dressing or lack of it becomes a sign of how the space of state, forest, and family will be negotiated.

Robin Hood is twice tricked about Lady Marian's identity in *Robin Hood: Prince of Thieves*. First, her lady-in-waiting, Sarah (Imogen Bain), a Brünhilde-like character, claims to be Lady Marian. Robin Hood is then attacked at Lady Marian's castle by an armed knight, and a swordfight ensues. Only when Robin Hood holds the hand of his opponent over a candle does the knight speak and the audience learn her gender. Robin Hood pulls off her visor, unmasking Lady Marian. In contrast, the Lady Marian (Olivia de Haviland) of the 1938 version does not cross-dress. Difference in the 1938 film is strongly defined as that between Saxon and Norman. The film constructs no family history for Robin; the viewer never encounters his father, as the 1991 audience does, nor are there any tales of his mother. Ethnicity, not family history, counts in 1938. Sir Robin of Locksley is a Saxon; Lady Marian is a Norman. She becomes part of the carnival feasting in Sherwood when the Norman party of the sheriff is waylaid by Robin Hood's men. In this sequence, the men of Sherwood disrobe the sheriff of Nottingham and Sir Guy of Guisborne and in true carnival spirit make them wear their Saxon rags as they don the clothes and regalia of the Normans. There is no carnival exchange of clothes with Lady Marian (there are no women among the merry men), but she does participate in the carnival feast. Eventually persuaded that Robin's cause is worthy, Lady Marian begins to serve as a go-between, connecting Sherwood and Nottingham, Saxon freemen and the Norman court.

In another crucial scene in the 1938 version, Robin Hood begs Marian to join him in Sherwood. She opts for the cause of the state over romantic love: "You taught me then that England is bigger than just Normans and Saxons fighting, hating each other! It belongs to all of us, to live peacefully together . . . loyal only to Richard and England! . . . I could help more by watching for treachery here and leaving you free to protect Richard's people, till he returns. Now do you see why you have to go back to your men—alone?" At its close, the film parodies this alignment of personal relations vis-à-vis the state when, after Richard has awarded him Lady Marian in marriage, Robin cries out, "May I obey all your Majesty's commands with equal pleasure!"[40]

In 1991, the definition of *difference* is cast, not in terms of ethnicity, but in terms of a family romance. As the plot of *Robin Hood: Prince of Thieves* unfolds, viewers learn that, when Robin was twelve years old, his father, a widower, took up a peasant concubine. This story accounts for the unresolved quarrel between father and son. The film emplots Robin's fight against the sheriff of Nottingham as a family feud. Robin seeks revenge against the sheriff, who trumped up witchcraft charges against Robin's father in order to have him killed and to confiscate his lands. Later, it is also revealed that Will Scarlett (Christian Slater), a bitter rival of Robin Hood's, is his bastard half brother. The film makes no space for the state, instead constructing an elaborate family space that is divided between absent mothers, aristocratic and peasant, and their offspring, noble and bastard.

Within the family space, the film roots allegiance and action in individualism. In an important scene—which can be read as the counterpart to the scene in the 1938 film in which Robin invites Lady Marian to join him—Robin asks Marian to use her influence as the ward of the king to get word to Richard of the treachery against him. Marian replies, "I could lose all I have." Robin then asks her if she would do it for the king. She replies, "No, I will do it for you," a reply that echoes in the lyrics of the music video distributed in conjunction with the film. The "state" as such no longer motivates action in 1991. Only romantic alliance does. Where does this leave gender?

Think again of the contemporary brackets of the film. The so-called advanced states, American and European, as national-social states, rely on family policy (of both intervention and neglect) as the core of their power. The ambiguities encountered by these states over the last five years—the events in Eastern Europe, the merging of the European Community, the new cybernetic imperialism of the Persian Gulf War—render ambiguous family policy at the same time that the state seeks to use family policy to defend itself against ambiguity. Within this context, Marian's cross-dressing in *Robin Hood: Prince of Thieves* can be read as bringing the ambiguities of family policy out of the closet. As the state collapses into family policy, women as the chief bearers of the policy become the state, but, in so doing, they blur the neat sexual divisions based on stereotypes of heterosexuality. This struggle is perhaps nowhere more acute than in the United States.

This allegory of the state and family policy can be read in the sequence of Lady Marian's dress in *Robin Hood: Prince of Thieves.* The viewer first encounters Marian cross-dressed. As the only living, responsible actor for the state in the absence of Richard, her kinsman, Marian is the state. Her mother is at court, but Marian has chosen to execute her aristocratic responsibilities alone on her landed properties around Nottingham, in spite of the abuses of its treacherous sheriff. As the embodiment of the absent state, Marian's encounter with Robin bathing naked in the forest pool is a crucial one for the pastoral. Her gaze at his naked body figures the alignment of the pastoral, in the body of Robin, with the state, in the person of Marian.

The staging of carnival scenes in the 1991 film supports this strong reading. It will be recalled that the film never depicts Robin Hood and Lady Marian feasting together at this celebration; the carnival world of food with its suggestions of digestion and elimination are neatly absent. Instead, a birth becomes the central focus of the scene of merriment. Fanny is in an agonizing labor. Friar Tuck and religion cannot help her. Finally, Azeem feels her belly and offers to try to deliver the child. From his experience with birthing horses, he knows how to turn the baby in the womb to ease the breach birth. The "infidel" does this successfully, and there is great celebration for a baby boy. Robin and Marian both attend the birth, and Robin is the first to display the baby to his merry men.

Here, the pastoral embraces not only Azeem but the infant. The native informant and the family simultaneously occupy the space of the pastoral and restore reproduction. This space is not, however, invulnerable. It can be threatened by "minority" cultures within. The sheriff of Nottingham calls up the Celts at the command of the witch Mortianna (Geraldine McEwan): "Recruit the beasts that share our God." They invade the forest and attack, and it is only with great peril that Fanny and her newborn are saved in the attack. This scene is important because it also echoes contemporary problems within advanced states. Their family policy is always mobilized within forms of neoracism in which "biological" stereotypes pass into "cultural" stereotypes "corresponding to the search for 'little differences' between equally impoverished proletarians."[41]

The arrival of Azeem on the shores of southern England uncannily echoes the arrival of Gibreel Farishta on the beach below Battle Hill, as told by Salman Rushdie in his *Satanic Verses.* William the Conqueror had landed on this same beach in 1066. Up on Battle Hill, Rosa Diamond, eighty-eight years old, prays as Gibreel washes ashore, closing, "for a moment, her sleepless eyes, to pray for the past's return. Come on, you Norman ships, she begged: Let's have you, Willie-the-Conk." In *Satanic Verses,* Rushdie suggests that only through the "dissemiNation," the joining of new meanings, times, peoples, and cultural boundaries, will "the radical alterity of national culture . . . create new forms of living and writing."[42] *Robin Hood: Prince of Thieves* fails to create new forms of pastoral and relies on an old colonial trope of the native informant and the concessionary narrative.

But, in its historiographic unconscious, the staging of the Arab in England, it does show symptomatically the crisis of the pastoral. Historians of the peasantry would do well to learn from the historiographic unconscious of Robin Hood.

Double Time: Medieval English Survey, 1995

Time again to teach the medieval English survey. Just as I had learned of the construction of Englishness by looping through the construction of the pastoral in *Past and Present,* in the postwar returns of Robin Hood, and in the counterpastoral work of the Birmingham SCCS, I thought that my students could learn best about the cultural politics of the medieval English survey through a kind of double time, a looping between the work of English America today and the work of medieval and early modern English colonization.

Loop 1—Telling English Time: Cartography/Language/Archive

The survey started off with the notion of British history as a border project and zigzagged back and forth between contemporary criticism and the construction of the past. Students grappled at first with Homi Bhabha's challenging "DissemiNation." We then tracked back to the mapping enterprise of the sixteenth and early seventeenth centuries and looked at how William Camden's *Britannia* and Elizabeth Elstob's *Rudiments of Grammar for the English-Saxon* nationalistically inscribed spatial and linguistic cartographies. Next we read the Public Records Office Act of 1838 and toured the shelves of the library that held its various published indices and calendars in order to impress on ourselves the sheer burden of producing the national archive. Working on group projects, the students made use of the *Calendars for Trade and Plantations* (1704–82) so that they could produce a collage of the colonial entries and generate a critical "map" that fractured the spaces produced by Camden and Elstob.

Once the students grasped and questioned the production of phantasmatic colonial space, we then moved in double time to the neoimperial racial politics of postwar Britain. We viewed *Handsworth Songs*, accompanied by readings from Paul Gilroy's *There Ain't No Black in the Union Jack*. Loop 1 closed with discussion of diaspora.

Loop 2—the Repeating Island

The students had observed how Camden had recycled excerpts from the *History and Topography of Ireland* by Gerald of Wales (1146–1223) into the Ireland volume of the *Britannia*. We now tracked back to the twelfth century to study how Gerald constructed his ethnographic authority and in so doing began to produce an Englishness intertwined with medieval colonialism.[43] Already, in the twelfth century, other histories, such as Geoffrey of Monmouth's *History of the Kings of Britain*, lodged other fragments of "time" into the timing of British history. Juxtaposed, these two texts by Geoffrey of Monmouth and Gerald of Wales posed problems regarding the belatedness in colonial history as well as the ambivalence in their discourse. We closed loop 2 by returning once again to the cultural work of telling time: How did Geoffrey of Monmouth use the prophecies of Merlin as time machines to disrupt linear chronology (chronologies being the effects of constituting, sexualizing, racializing "historical subjects")?

Loop 2—Colonizing Imperial Time

In this loop, students used the reading practices that they had learned in the last loop to read Rudyard Kipling's *Kim* with Michael Ondaatje's *The English Patient*. What does the Indian sapper Kip, who dismantles time bombs dropped on London in World War II, have to do with Kim/Kipling? The intimacy of these two texts, where the latter "rereads" the former, once again posed to the students the question, What time is it in the British Empire? Their final projects grappled with the medieval English survey as a site or itinerary for belated travel in a postcolonial mosaic of double time, double space. The students' final projects ranged from a study of English church building in Ireland in the twelfth and thirteenth centuries, to a critical analysis of the "ethnographic film" *Man of Aran* (1934) by Robert Flaherty, to a study of British narratives of the partitioning of Jordan. Two students went on to continue their research at the postgraduate level. These provocative and thoughtful final projects were for me the most effective way of refiguring concessionary narratives of English America. In 1995, the medieval English survey came out of the shadows of the football stadium.

Bede's Blush

Postcards from Bali, Bombay, Palo Alto

Are medievalists dreaming the Middle Ages? Umberto Eco has claimed that such dreams are "pseudo-medieval pulp midway between Nazi nostalgia and occultism."[1] The dreams have been dreamed fitfully since the Renaissance. In their sleepwalking, humanists invented a Middle Ages as a place and time of non-origin and formed an identity essentially informed by a claim of what it was not.[2] Nation-states of the nineteenth century, in contrast, produced a place and time, a Middle Ages, to stage the cultural origins of the "Western animal" (Eco's term). At the end of the twentieth century, such overdetermined constructs of the Middle Ages haunt medieval studies as a double bind of origin and nonorigin.

The double bind has divided medieval studies into camps of pastists and presentists who debate over the epoch in which to locate radical "past" alterity instead of questioning desires for such a boundary as an effect of specific historiographic metanarratives. Caught in the divisions of a double bind, medieval studies cycles repetitiously between these poles of loss and plenitude. Humanist fantasies of sublime nonorigin return in contemporary debate under the guise of "pastism," a position that argues for radical historical difference between the Middle Ages and the present. Pastism regards the past and the present as bounded temporal objects that cannot come into contact for fear of scholarly contamination. Pastism produces historical difference as moral difference between a medieval exemplarity and an impoverished present. At the other extreme, the pole of plenitude, the Middle Ages becomes a mirror. Presentism looks into the mirror of the Middle Ages and asks it to reflect back histories of modernist or postmodernist identities. Absorbed by these reflections, presentism forgets to examine the privileging of such identities or to question institutional and personal investments in understanding the past as a mirror, however near or distant.[3] Supposedly more neutral versions of this model of historiographic temporality, usually cast as questions of "continuity" and "change," likewise get caught up in problems of pastism and presentism.[4]

As both nonorigin and origin, the Middle Ages can be everywhere, both medieval and postmodern, and nowhere, sublime and redemptive. What better material for a dream frame for popular culture, a truly relative past that can be read as either the present or the future? It is therefore not surprising to find the Middle Ages figured in a near-future space of science fiction and standing in for contemporary fantasies of the Third World.[5] Recent conference calls express an anxiety about dreaming the Middle Ages in this way. Dreams of disciplinary transformation, however, have mostly repeated problems of pastism and presentism inhering in such a construct. Some scholars sleep with images of Boethius dancing in their heads ("tell them of Boethius, tell them we are all in prison and the world without in ruin").[6] Others awake moved by desires to colonize popular medievalia for its energy and enthusiasm, unmindful that the cultural construct of the Middle Ages produces this very pseudomedievalia as an effect. Like Rip Van Winkle, we can dream on or, alternatively, use the repetition I am describing as an occasion for dream work in public culture today.[7]

This essay attempts to negotiate such dream work. It holds in tension the contradictions of pastism and presentism in order to read along their fault lines for histories that the construct of the Middle Ages as nonorigin and origin must defend against through erasure or occultation. I offer three discrete readings intended to trouble rhetorically, materially, and institutionally the foundational category *the Middle Ages.* My vignettes (the word is used here in the dictionary sense of something that shades off gradually at the edges so as to leave no definite line at the border) engage medieval studies with critical theoretical and pedagogical concerns in public culture today, in the present. In reading along fault lines, I try not to demonize our disciplinary problems—such a strategy would render my readings indistinguishable from the processes I seek to trouble. Rather, I argue for a nonfoundational medieval studies that articulates rather than re-presents the Middle Ages as a historical category.[8] This essay seeks to set in motion a nonfoundational moment with a blush, the blush of Bede. His blush becomes a performative moment for dream work in medieval studies, a moment for historical mourning and rememoration. The blush produces a possibility for a history after the end of history as an epistemological concept formed in the nineteenth century and still all too dominant in the North American academy today.[9]

Vignette 1: Missing Bodies/Disappearing Acts/ Return of the Cockfight

The reading of my first vignette begins by stumbling over missing bodies. They begin popping up in the title of this conference, "The Past and Future of Medieval Studies." Missing is the notion of the critical "present" of medieval studies.[10] The absence of a critical present offers a clue to where to search for the missing bodies disappeared by the title.[11] The clues lead to the classroom, where the desires of teachers and students engage and transform the construct of the Middle Ages through pedagogy. Pedagogy, the *embodiment* of "technique" and "method," shapes the future for medieval studies. In missing out on this critical present, we miss possibilities for questioning our institutional practices.[12] We disappear the bodies of our students and their important work in the institutional reproduction of knowledge.

Missing bodies also haunt recent critical essays on the future of medieval studies. Like a corpse in a detective novel, one body in particular, that of Clifford Geertz, keeps getting found by the reader of these disciplinary critiques. This body is not just any body of Clifford Geertz. It is his body as emplotted in his famous essay "Deep Play: Notes on the Balinese Cockfight."[13] How can we read the Geertzian body of deep play as a clue to problems in medieval studies? A warning of his opens the mystery; he pulls no punches when he tells his readers, "Every people, the proverb has it, loves its own form of violence" (p. 449). With this admonition he invites readers to ask about the kinds of violence "Deep Play" might love. The violence produced by the essay can offer insight into the return of medievalists to "Deep Play" twenty years after its publication as if to the scene of a crime in search of clues.

"Attending cockfights and participating in them is, for the Balinese, a kind of sentimental education" (p. 449). Reading about Balinese cockfights is, for the reader, a kind of historical education about ethnographic writing in the early 1970s. We learn from Geertz that cockfights are disquieting for their "immediate dramatic shape," their "metaphoric content," and their "social context" (p. 444). In describing these three registers of disquiet, Geertz offers the reader a way of understanding the forms of violence haunting the anthropological enterprise of the author. Geertz dramatically shapes the essay as a spatial progression. The reader moves from the space of encounter ("The Raid"), to a spectacular space of the cockfight ring ("Of Cocks and Men" and subsequent sections), to a scholarly space of textuality ("Saying Something of Something"). In the space of encounter, Geertz uses a fable to produce rapport with his informants. This space of encounter also serves as a kind of map to the rapport desired in the text between the reader and the ethnographer. Presumably, violence is at play here, or at least Geertz has insinuated as much. He tells the fable of encounter as follows.

Geertz opens his essay by telling the story of his arrival together with his wife in a Balinese village in April 1958.[14] He describes himself and his wife initially as "nonpersons, specters, invisible men" (p. 412); he tells how one "drifts around feeling vaguely disembodied," doubting "whether you are really real after all" (p. 413). After ten days of such alienation, the Geertzs attend a village cockfight that gets raided by the police. Scattering with the rest of the villagers, Geertz and his wife end up running into a family compound to take cover. The wife of the resident whom the Geertzs had followed quickly sets up a tea table. The two couples pretend to be deeply engaged in conversation. When the police arrive and see the "white men" in the yard, meaning Geertz and his wife, they do a "double take." The host, who is unknown to Geertz, is able to give an accurate and detailed account of the Geertzs' scholarly purpose in the village. Convinced that the members of the tea party could not have been cockfight fans, the police leave. Geertz describes the police raid as a turning point for his relations with the villagers.

In a recent critique of historic ways of constituting ethnographic authority, James Clifford cites this story of the police raid as an example of an anthropological fable of rapport. According to Clifford, "The anecdote establishes a presumption of connectedness, which permits the writer to function in his subsequent analyses as an omnipresent, knowledgeable exegete and spokesman."[15] Once connected fabulously to his informants, Geertz disconnects his narrative. Just like magic, a Western anthropologist appears out of the hat of a "nonperson." As an anthropological observer, he then proceeds to change his rhetorical strategy and plunges his readers into a new section, entitled "Of Cocks and Men," where he narrates a spectacular account of the masculine world of the cockfight. The rhetoric conceals the negotiated, interactive historical nature of his ethnographic presence at the cockfights. He uses what little dialogue of his subject-informants he selects for citation to intensify the spectacular account of the cockfight: " 'I am cock crazy,' my landlord, a quite ordinary *afficionado* by Balinese standards, used to moan as he went to move another cage, give another bath, or conduct another feeding. 'We're all cock crazy' " (p. 419).

Does Geertz parody the conventions of what is called the *hypermasculine* genre, a genre typically at work in narratives of cockfights, bullfights, etc., or does his essay simply reproduce such conventions? Different readers read the essay differently. My reading, which plays with the kinds of narrative space constructed by Geertz for the representation of the cockfight, shows how his spectacular account genders the production of knowledge in the essay by conforming closely to the space and masculinity typical of this highly conventionalized hypermasculine genre. Students of the genre (the cockfight, the bullfight, classic western and detective films) have taught us how it internalizes violence as narrative content and opposes violence to "emotionalism," which is gendered as feminine. The genre typically relegates women, children, adolescents, and "unfit" men to the edges of its narrative space.

Geertz reproduces this generic social space in the textual

space of the essay. He marginalizes discussion of nonparticipants (women, children, adolescents, unfit men) to his footnotes and to a few brief sentences at the end, or "edge," of his account of the cockfight. Only from a footnote in the section "Of Cocks and Men" does the reader learn that "women—at least *Balinese* women [Geertz's emphasis]—do not even watch" (p. 418, n. 4). The folktales footnoted by Geertz in the same sections suggest, however, a more complicated gendering that disrupts these conventionalizing margins. In the folktales, women are central to narrative action and set it into motion by resisting or abetting the world of the cockfight. One woman refuses her husband's request to feed her infant girl to the cocks, with consequences; another woman gives her last "rainy day" money to her husband to place a bet (p. 435, n. 22, and p. 442, n. 27).

The rhetorical collusion of the essay with the conventions of the hypermasculine genre undoubtedly accounts for much of the familiar pleasure of and repetitious returns to readings of the cockfight. The hypermasculine genre is an immensely popular one on television, in the movies, and in academe. This collusion helps perpetuate a specific historical form of anthropological enterprise. Conventions of the hypermasculine genre work to contain its intense homoerotic charge safely within the orbit of the homosocial. Closeted as such, the convention can then mobilize the sexuality of power to "fix" its mobility—cocks in the center, women, children, and unfit men to the margins.[16]

The rhetoric of the concluding section of Geertz's "Deep Play" restores good homosocial order. Geertz writes of *ethnography* as "penetrating a literary text" (p. 448). It says "something of something." He insists that the saying something of something should be said to *somebody* (p. 453), but he never broaches the question of who that somebody might be, whether he or she would give permission to be penetrated, and where. Where would such conversation occur, who would participate, and how would the participants wish to embody a conarration?

The fable of rapport enables Geertz to silence the conarration of fieldwork. His rhetorical construction of the cockfight colludes with the homophobia and misogyny typical of the hypermasculine genre. The essay is not limited, however, to these forms of violence. Geertz writes in a timeless ethnographic present, which the anthropologist masters as the observer. To suppress temporality, a presentism, Geertz denies the historical, colonial past that informs the present of the Balinese village of Tihingan in 1958. At the same time such suppression also produces Geertz as a "pastist." He must invent a "tradition" (people without history have traditions) for the Balinese, a "peasant mentality" (p. 416), a category that seals them off from the dynamic historical present.[17] These shifting and complementary rhetorical ploys of pastism and presentism enable Geertz to textualize the Balinese villagers. Scholars only repeat these ploys when they take over uncritically the "deep play" of the cockfight disembodied from its historical ethnographic practices.[18] "Every people, the proverb has it, loves its own form of violence" (p. 449).

The cockfight returned to medieval studies in the 1990s. In recent and important essays advocating disciplinary transformation, both Gabrielle Spiegel and Allen Frantzen use the Balinese cockfight to read a disciplinary future. In apparent discomfort with Geertz, Spiegel attempts to revise "deep play" to rematerialize his approach: "Those who bet on the cocks are not only expressing their peculiar understanding of the nature of Balinese social culture (its 'sociomoral hierarchy') but hoping to profit materially from the animal violence that ensues. In its particular mixture of symbolic and material negotiations, the cockfight serves as an apt metaphor for the kind of literary history that we need to begin to elaborate."[19] Frantzen, discomforted by the disciplinary isolation of medieval studies, uses "deep play" as a methodological way to link medieval studies with cultural studies. The textuality argued for by Geertz—that texts "neither merely relieve nor arouse passions but display power is a proposition that medieval studies, practiced as a form of cultural studies, will be able to explore," as Frantzen puts it—forms for Frantzen a bridge to cultural studies. He defines cultural studies as "rooted in ethnography, the study of diverse and remote cultures; keenly aware of the structuring effect of the scholar on his or her subject; and particularly concerned about 'non-literary' genres and discourse."[20]

Spiegel and Frantzen read the cockfight as Geertz writes it, as a representation. Spiegel criticizes precisely this tendency to aestheticize culture, to separate language from reality. She tries to restore the materiality of violence in the Balinese cockfight by bringing the cocks back in. In adding on "materiality," she fails, however, to question the rhetorical frame of the essay that enables the violent disappearance of materiality in the first place. Frantzen, who wishes to link cultural studies to medieval studies, also fails to question the concept of culture that frames the Geertz essay. Is it possible to use that concept of culture as a link, or is the culture of cultural studies also problematic, in need of a critical history? Both the missing bodies in "Deep Play" and the problem of the "return of the cockfight" in medieval studies suggest that we need to read the Geertz essay differently, to articulate it, rather than simply re-represent it.

Vignette 2: Shadow Lines—Bombay/London

To turn "deep play" inside out, we need to multiply and bring into a public rhetorical space the many bodies the essay renders missing, the bodies it "disappears." The disappearing acts of deep play deny the "present" of the essay, a particular, historical present of postcolonial Bali in 1958, during the troubling days of the Sukarno regime, which had followed on the domination of the Dutch and the Japanese. In disappearing as a historical subject himself, Geertz denies his historic relation to the villagers of Tihingan. Rather than mark and hold the ambivalence of the space in between the double relational identities of participant-observer, subject-informant, Geertz erases them. He elides, too, his unnamed wife into a "white man" in the essay. As we have already observed, in the main body of his text Geertz mentions women only in the footnotes or toward the conclusion of his account of the cockfight. At the edges of that account he also finally names the village as Tihingan (pp. 435–36). The very textual space of the essay is gendered in the way it relegates both women and the historical space of ethnographic fieldwork to the footnotes and to the edges of spectacular accounts of fighting cocks.

The return of the Balinese cockfight to medieval studies, I argue, rehearses our anxieties about its historically constituted rhetorical violences. Could it be that its violence somehow points to a violence within medieval studies itself—hence our anxiety and fascination with the essay? The concealment of the relation between participant-observer and subject-informant is not unique to "Deep Play," although its hypermasculine spectacle intensified its seductive effects. The rhetorical ploys of the essay are characteristic of the cultural assumptions of an "Orientalist" ethnography. Orientalism is historically founded on a notion of cultures as contiguous, synchronous, and representational (world as exhibit).[21] The historical construct of the Middle Ages was invented and reinvented alongside Orientalism, hence their mutual fascination.[22] The return of the essay to medieval studies in the 1990s can be understood as a symptom of an anxiety arising from the failure to articulate rigorously the intersections between the constructs of Orientalism and medievalism.

The reduction of complex, permeable, relational identities to simple, bounded, unitary identities in "Deep Play" repeats the structure of violence that made Orientalism historically possible. The terms *Orientalism* and *neo-Orientalism* are loaded and therefore difficult to introduce. They have extensive critical histories and complicated institutional usages.[23] For the purposes of discussion here, I use *Orientalism* to refer to the historically situated Euro-American project of producing an experience of scholarship, order, truth, and management based on the textualization of imaginary others exterior to Europe who inhabit an imaginary space constructed by Europeans through their scholarship, cartography, surveys, photography, exhibitions, and administration. Historically, this process produced despotically administered texts and territories of the so-called East as well as a fantastic scholarly geography of the origins of Europe. Within European national histories, Orientalism produced knowledge of certain epochs, places, and social groups as an Orientalism within.[24]

Even in the presumably postcolonial order and supposedly postmodern times, Orientalism perdures as a neo-Orientalism. The latter acknowledges the decentering of its own imaginary European map without transforming the violent representational strategies that first drew such a map. It abandons the exhausted project of producing anthropological primitives in ethnographic fieldwork; in its stead, it substitutes a search for the "real" native informant to speak the pre-Oriental truth. Neo-Orientalism now searches for this "real" native in the Third World and among diasporan scholars and artists resident in Euro-American metropolises. Just as neo-Orientalism looks for a "real" voice from the empires within Euro-American scholarly and political traditions, it also searches for a "real" *precolonial, historical* subject in European archives. This historical informant can speak the truth from within representations of European history.

Medievalists can fall easily into this neo-Orientalist trap of searching for a precolonial, historical informant, unless we study the cultural construct of the Middle Ages in relation not only to nationalisms (as has already been well done) but to imperialism as well. We must situate historical nationalism with imperialism in the formation of medieval studies around the cultural construct of the Middle Ages. Such an analysis will regard the nineteenth century as much a neighboring field as medieval studies has traditionally considered antiquity and the Renaissance.

My second vignette attempts to reach such intersections. The founding of the Early English Text Society (EETS) serves here as a case study that joins gender and imperialism to a traditional founding history of class and nationalism. The reading reconnects London and Bombay.[25]

F. J. Furnivall founded the EETS in 1864. He lectured on English grammar at the Working Men's College, a college that had grown out of evening classes given by a cadre of professors to workingmen in London. The society intended to bring the "mass of Old English literature within the reach of the ordinary student."[26] From the beginning, the society eschewed expensive editions such as those published by the Roxburghe Club so that its volumes could be readily available. The society was particularly interested in "the spread of the study of English in schools"[27] and engaged in the publication of textbooks and the award of annual prizes to encourage the spread of English studies.

The philanthropic professors who taught in the workingmen's movement also concerned themselves with the education of women. In 1848, colleagues from King's College, active in the workingmen's college movement, founded Queen's College for

Women. In his inaugural lecture as professor of English studies at Queen's College, Charles Kingsley described a special affinity between women and the study of English:

> Such a course of history [study of English literature] would quicken women's inborn *personal interest* in the actors of this life-drama, and be quickened by it in return, as indeed it ought: for it is thus that God intended women to look instinctively at the world. Would to God that she would teach us men to look at it likewise. Would to God that she would in these days claim and fulfil to the uttermost her vocation as the priestess of charity!—that woman's heart would help deliver man from bondage to his own tyrannous and all-too-inclusive brain—from our idolatry of mere dead law and printed books—from our daily sin of looking at men, not as our struggling and suffering brothers, but as mere symbols of certain formulae, incarnations of sets of opinions, wheels in some iron liberty-grinding or Christianity spinning-machine, which we miscall society, or civilisation, or, worst misnomer of all, the Church.[28]

The founding of the EETS intersected with complex, gendered class interests. The society staunchly identified itself as a middle-class project.[29] The study of Old English constructed complicated gender and class identities around a notion of the "mother tongue." But class, gender, and national identities were not the only identities under construction. Imperial colonial identities also framed the institutionalization of English studies in the mid-nineteenth century.

The founders of the EETS wrote about their imperial mission, "We are banded together to trace out the springs, and note the course, of the language that shall one day be the ruling tongue of the world, which is now the speech of most of its free men."[30] The society would bring texts within the reach of "every student and boy in the British Empire."[31] Its early membership lists reflect its metropolitan, class, and imperial mission. From the 1868 membership list (the earliest I was able to obtain) can be traced how the volumes edited by the society circulated to mercantile, mechanics, colonial, and dominion libraries,[32] including the Baltimore Mercantile Library, the Wakefield Mechanic's Institution, the South African Library of Cape Town, the India Office Library, and the Melbourne Public Library. Membership expanded in subsequent years to include, for example, the Young Men's Association of Troy, New York (1869), the Brooklyn Mercantile Library (1871), the Philadelphia Mercantile Library (1871), Queens College, Benares (1876), the Mercantile Library, St. Louis (1886), and the Bombay Asiatic Society (1886). The society also recruited private subscribers from the colonies and throughout the dominion. Institutional subscribers from the Indian Colonial Service included the Legislative Council Building, Calcutta (1868), the Madras Civil Service (1869), the Bengal Civil Service (1871), Rajkoomar College, Rajkote, India (1871), and the assistant commissioner of the Punjab (1876).

Connections between imperialism and medievalism are suggested by the EETS volumes that began to fill the shelves of the Bombay Asiatic Society, an affiliate of the Asiatic Society of Bengal, based in Calcutta.[33] Founded in 1784 by Sir William Jones, an Oxford-trained Orientalist and lawyer who served as a judge on the Supreme Court of Calcutta, the Asiatic Society gathered together the first generation of British colonial administrators who had learned Sanskrit. Jones is noted for his 1789 translation of the Sanskrit classic *Sakuntala* by Kalidasa, whom the British dubbed the Shakespeare of India. He also participated in a project central to the colonial administration, the establishing of translations of Hindu law texts. He worked on *The Digest of Indian Laws*, which H. T. Colebroke brought to completion in 1798, after Jones's death. The so-called Sanskrit Renaissance is attributed to the members of the Asiatic Society, who were also instrumental in the founding of the Royal Asiatic Society in England in 1823. By 1832, Oxford had established a chair of Sanskrit, which H. H. Wilson, a member of the Asiatic Society and the Indian Colonial Service, took up.

In the early days of the Asiatic Society, its members mostly relied on Brahmin pundits to supply them with their Sanskrit manuscripts and language training. Brahmin-English relations in the late eighteenth and early nineteenth centuries were highly ambivalent. The pundits served as go-betweens in the British translation projects and often supplied the British with "padded" texts that served their own purposes. The Asiatic Society of Calcutta did not formally vote to open its membership to Indians until 1829—and the Bombay chapter of the society voted against their admission. As Spivak has said of this exchange among British colonials and learned Brahmins in regard to the codification of Hindu law, a central task of their translation work: "When the law was finally written, the history of the long period of collaboration was effaced, and the language celebrated the noble Hindu who was against the bad Hindu, the latter given to savage atrocities."[34]

The imperial cultural work of the Asiatic Society joined with English studies of the mid-nineteenth century in yet another guise. The new Germanic philology that revolutionized Anglo-Saxon studies at Oxford was introduced by Max Müller (a member of the EETS from its earliest lists), for whom the Chair of Comparative Philology was created in 1868. Müller knew personally the Orientalists of the Asiatic Society and had himself translated the *Rig Veda*. The desire of British Orientalists to recover India's past—"there, notoriously, the *Vaidic* tradition was, for many centuries, virtually in abeyance"—echoes the desire of the EETS to "wip[e] away the reproach under which England had long rested, of having felt little interest in the monuments of her early life and language."[35] The ideology and practiccs of Sanskrit and English text editing have much to do with each other in the mid-nineteenth century, and only a positivist linguistics would separate them.

The Bombay Asiatic Society received the publications of the EETS. The volumes sat on the shelves in colonial libraries in India and also in libraries as diverse and contrasting as the Astor Library and the Brooklyn Mercantile Library in New York. Comments in the early EETS volumes by contributors based in England enable us to reconstruct the imaginary grid of their libraries, which arranged translations of Sanskrit classics undertaken by British colonials resident in India side by side with medieval English literature.[36]

This juxtaposition of national and colonial members and national and colonial scholarship in the EETS cannot be reduced simply to the eccentricities of mid-nineteenth-century philology. These contiguities show how national, imperial, and gendered identities crisscrossed the formation of the EETS. The story of the institutionalization of English studies in nineteenth-century England is typically told as a narrative of aristocratic Oxford founding fathers. A post-Orientalist reading, such as this one, questions what fantasies reduce these historically complex borders to a bounded disciplinary object, English studies, and restricts the plot to a story of upper-class English men. As Viswanathan reminds us, "Less appreciated is the irony that English literature appeared as a subject in the curriculum of the colonies long before it was institutionalized in the home country."[37]

My reading has sought to multiply rather than disappear the bodies in the history of the Early English Text Society. The many bodies conjured pose new challenges. Their multiplicity and heterogeneity challenge the adequacy, indeed, the violence, of the foundational categories (*nation, class, founding fathers, mother tongue*) in which we have traditionally told the story of the formation of English studies in the nineteenth century. A paraphrase of an observation made by Salman Rushdie in *Satanic Verses* can aptly conclude this reading of aspects of the formation of the EETS: "The trouble with the English is that their history happened overseas, so they don't know what it means."[38] The trouble with the formation of medieval English studies in the nineteenth century is that it happened just as much in Bombay and Calcutta as in London, so it is difficult to know what it means unless we put these histories in relation.

Vignette 3: Bede's Blush (731/1992)

So far my readings, a kind of ghostbusting, have brought into relation the noncommensurate times and places. The readings conjure up Balinese women of Tihingan on the pages of *Speculum;* they enable us to watch a Brahmin pundit look over the shoulder of F. J. Furnivall. My conclusion turns to contemporary institutional problems, not to bust ghosts, but to ensure that we do not go on creating them by disappearing bodies in our contemporary disciplinary practices. My final vignette imagines the transformation of the cultural construct of the Middle Ages in a specific setting. As I mentioned earlier, historians are only just beginning to imagine the kinds of history that "deliberately make visible, within the very structures of its narrative forms, its own repressive strategies and practices."[39] My vignette performs a historical poetics of mourning and rememoration.

I invite us to the reading room of a medieval institute, its walls lined with standard source collections and reference works for paleography and diplomatics. The economics of the setting are important—what but a medieval institute can make arguments to a dean to hire and retain a paleographer, a diplomatist? The forces of the current job market serve as a strong glue for keeping medieval institutes from coming apart. Can we unglue the construct of the Middle Ages from this economic framework?

Four characters appear in the reading room: the dean of Stanford University, where recently the administration dropped the requirement in Old English; Bede, the author of the eighth-century text *The History of the English Church and People;* a professor of Old English; and the chair of the humanities curriculum committee, a self-identified Chicana feminist theorist. These four are talking about the current status of Old English studies in the curriculum.

The dean asks the professor of Old English how her curriculum can respond to the fact that soon less than half the college students on the West Coast will claim English as their native language. Can Old English rely any longer on the implicit national and imperial argument of "our mother tongue" to justify its claims on the curriculum of the twenty-first century? The professor replies that the study of Old English is useful.

The dean, unpersuaded, tries again. She announces her respect for the technical demands and rigor of Old English scholarship. She does not want to see these tools thrown out of the canonical tool kit. But she warns that, unless scholars try to redescribe their discipline outside its nineteenth-century parameters, it will die out in the curriculum. The dean mentions early medieval thought and scholastic theology as examples of fields that are virtually extinct and serve as a warning to Old English studies.

Meanwhile, Bede and the Chicana theorist have been talking to each other. Bede's multilingualism interests the theorist, and she wants to learn more about his multilingual world. He pulls the Penguin edition of his history off the shelf and reads to the Chicana theorist: "At the present time there are in Britain, in harmony with the five books of the divine law, five languages and four nations—English, British, Scots, and Picts. Each of these have their own language; but all are united in their study of God's truth by the fifth—Latin—which has become a common medium through the study of the scriptures."[40]

The Chicana theorist asks how is it that all the languages he mentions seem to be dead, with the exception of English. She asks how people communicated in power-charged disagreements during his time. Bede tells her about the importance of exiles and interpreters in this multilingual world and illustrates this with the story of the Synod of Whitby. He describes how there were interpreters there but how English was the dominant language. The Chicana theorist then asks Bede about the politics of writing his history in Latin, how his text works as a go-between among Mediterranean, Anglo-Saxon, and Celtic churchmen.

Bede asks what she means by *go-between.* She describes to him the tensions of being a go-between in her worlds, a go-between among different languages and different racial and sexual identities. She tells Bede the story of Malinche,[41] a go-between who served as an Aztec translator for Cortez, and explains how Chicana feminists have appropriated Malinche to figure their own political, linguistic, sexual, and theoretical exchanges. Traditions of Mexican popular culture have nicknamed Malinche "The Sell-Out" (La Vendida) or "The Raped One" (La Chingada). She asks Bede if he ever got a similar kind of nickname among his people. Bede blushes.

Have I, as a presentist, fabricated the historicity of Bede's blush? No. The blush marks the return of an affective moment in the history of Old English that generations of writers and readers have suppressed. The recent work of Allen Frantzen, Seth Lerer, and Katherine O'Brien O'Keeffe helps us understand Bede's blush.[42] Bede created Caedmon, the poet of sacred hymns in Old English, as a textual double in his *History.* Caedmon speaks Old English in his dreams, but only at the twice-repeated command of a stranger. Who is this other who appeared to Caedmon? Surely, it is Bede. But Bede never wrote the words of Caedmon's *Hymn* in Old English in his *History.* The Old English text exists only as marginalia in the early Latin manuscript versions of Bede's *History.* Old English exists only on the borders of this

History, and the date and the status of the gloss are still open to debate. Indeed, some scholars argue that the glossed Old English text is a translation of Bede's Latin text of Caedmon's *Hymn.* The *History* and the *Hymn,* the story of Old English and Anglo-Saxon Latin, both lie in the space in between the text and the gloss, between Bede and his double, Caedmon. They are the forks of the "mother tongue," its hybridity. As go-between in his own *History,* Bede could allow Old English only in his dreams. This dream of the *History* and the textual problems of the "first" verse of Anglo-Saxon literature figures uncannily the conditions of the contemporary cultural construct of the Middle Ages, which we have repeated and reinscribed in textual editions until recently.

The Chicana feminist observes Bede's blush. She tries to explain how he might learn something if he began to think of the complex problems of multiple identities involved in the power-charged border writing and border speaking that "go-betweens" negotiate.[43] This kind of writing and speaking asks what it means to write and speak without such categories as the *nation* or the *people.* Border writing also writes with a transformed notion of culture, one that does not simply reinscribe nineteenth-century notions of culture. Border writing thinks of culture otherwise, and the Chicana feminist cites a different way of imagining "culture" from Edward Said: "Thus to see Others not as ontologically given but as historically constituted would be to erode the exclusivist biases we so often ascribe to cultures, our own not the least. Cultures may then be represented as zones of control or abandonment, of recollection and forgetting, of force or of dependence, of exclusiveness or of sharing, all taking place in the global history that is our element."[44]

The Chicana feminist invites Bede to speak to her feminist theory class in order to work through this theoretical issue of his performing as a go-between. Bede then asks if he should speak in English or Latin. The Chicana theorist laughs. English, of course, she says. Don't you know that your native language, which was first colonized by Latin literates, paradoxically became the great colonizing language of the nineteenth century?

This paradox inherent in the history of the English language has inspired renewed theoretical interest in the go-between. Chicana theorists are rewriting Malinche differently. Their historical and power-charged experiences of negotiating the border of many languages (formal Spanish, Mexican-Spanish, Tex-Mex, college English, rap English), theories, and racial and sexual practices have given them a historical appreciation of negotiating borders. They have learned that the "foreignness of our language" becomes the "inescapable cultural condition for the enunciation of the mother tongue."[45] She concludes by explaining to Bede that Chicana feminist theorists have a term for this theoretical and political negotiation of borders that power and violence have kept separate and incommensurate. It is called a *border consciousness*, a *mestiza consciousness.*

Bede says he looks forward to visiting her class and the challenge of rethinking the linguistic negotiations of his *History* as negotiations of power-charged language borders. Perhaps he will analyze the famous dream of his *History*, Caedmon's dream; perhaps he has not yet worked through that dream, even after all this time. He admits to his fear and anxiety at the thought of imagining himself as a go-between. He finds the comparison with Malinche particularly unsettling. He will need help thinking through these issues. He wonders whether the students would be interested in learning Latin and Old English and several other languages to help him? The Chicana feminist says, You will have to ask the students, but I think that this engaged historical thinking about the language negotiations of your work will spark their interest.

As she speaks to Bede, the Chicana theorist ironically realizes that she too has reenacted the act of go-between. She translates her claims into more formal, theoretical language for Bede. By reconceptualizing Old English and the Latin written by Anglo-Saxon writers such as Bede as border writing, we can bring these multidimensional texts into a rich, critical postcolonial field of border writing and theories of border performance. By linking the study of Old English to theories of border writing, we also open up the study of Old English to contemporary historical questions: How did a colonized language come to be the colonizing language of the nineteenth century? How did Old English get taught in the English schools of colonial India? How does Old English get taught in the California university system today? Do we need to think of a Sanskritized Beowulf, as much an Anglicized *Sakuntala,* a Chicanoized Caedmon's hymn? Deep in conversation, the Chicana feminist and Bede leave the dean and the professor of Old English in the medieval institute library and go out for coffee. Readers get to make up their own ending to my story.

The time has come to mark my own performance as a go-between negotiating feminist and postcolonial theory. I have imagined my own ending to this vignette just conjured. How to articulate La Vendida and La Chingada? How to articulate the double bind of the construct of the Middle Ages? To encourage us to think in a utopian mode for the twenty-first century, in the face of contested problems of pedagogy and scholarship in medieval studies, I will end, not with a dream, but with the work of dream work:

> That focal point or fulcrum, that juncture where the *mestiza* stands, is where phenomena tend to collide. It is where the possibility of uniting all that is separate occurs. This assembly is not one where severed or separated pieces merely come together. Nor is it a balancing of opposing powers. In attempting to work out a synthesis, the self has added a third element which is greater than the sum of its severed parts. The third element is a new consciousness—a *mestiza* consciousness—and though it is a source of intense pain, its energy comes from a continual creative motion that keeps breaking down the unitary aspect of each new paradigm. . . . Et unas pocas centurias, the future will belong to the *mestiza.*[46]

Works of Mourning

The Devil's Anal Eye

Inquisitorial Optics and Ethnographic Authority

Such noted microhistorians of the medieval and Renaissance Inquisition as Carlo Ginzburg, Guido Ruggiero, Emmanuel Le Roy Ladurie, and Georges Duby identify much of their rhetorical authority with their extensive research in Inquisitorial archives. Trial transcripts function for microhistorians in a manner similar to the imperial conception of the good native informant once prevalent among anthropologists working in colonial fields. Ginzburg has insisted on the "intrinsic dialogic" nature of the trial transcripts, Ladurie on their "direct testimony," and Ruggiero on their capacity as records to "speak from the past" for the "storyteller" of today; Duby hears in them the "sound of the authentic female voice" of the Middle Ages.[1] As did colonial fieldwork to anthropologists of the pre–War II era, Inquisitorial archives offer the opportunity for exotic pleasures that exceed the documents or the informants themselves. Trial collections dazzle like El Dorado: "When I was admitted for the first time to the large room which housed in perfect order nearly two thousand inquisitorial trials, I felt the sudden thrill of discovering an unexplored gold mine."[2]

But what if the authority of the microhistorians' archival experience ("having been there") should turn out, with critical scrutiny, to be the preemption of the authority of the inquisitor? Whence the authority of the inquisitor? There is more to these questions than the thrill of vertigo. The discipline of ethnography/anthropology, on which microhistorians eagerly draw, has over the past decade subjected its organizing tropes of fieldwork and informant to a historical critique of representation. According to such critique, the fieldworker becomes visible only as the effect of writing practices that elide the multiple, power-charged relations of writer and informant and flatten them through different optical, auditory, and rhetorical technologies designed to organize both the informing "ethnos" and the fieldworker into coherent, unified subjects.[3] The ethnos and the ethnographer thus become rhetorically necessary to each other, and, in the ensuing violence of their intertwining, one must be made to drop out of sight to make the other appear.[4]

Microhistories of the Inquisition traffic little with the growing body of literature critical of technologies of visibility in anthropology. Ginzburg proudly, and perhaps not so anachronistically, identifies the inquisitor as an anthropologist and differentiates the work of the Inquisition from his only by its means: "The elusive evidence that inquisitors were trying to elicit from defendants was not so different after all from our own objective: what was different, of course, were their means and ultimate ends."[5] The desire of the microhistorian and that of the inquisitor seem to converge uncannily.

Anthropologists, in contrast, have thought critically about the desires of microhistorians of the Inquisition. Renato Rosaldo, for instance, has compared the rhetorical strategies of Ladurie's *Montaillou* with those of Evans-Pritchard in his "classic" ethnography *The Nuer.* Rosaldo shows how Ladurie "cloaks himself with the borrowed authority of ethnographic science" in order to convert the uneven powers of interrogation into "overhearing and cataloguing."[6] Ladurie rhetorically homogenizes voices of fourteenth-century peasants speaking before the Inquisitorial tribunal with the privilege of the contemporary French historian. Claire Sponsler, a medieval critic, has further claimed that medievalists are holding out as the "last" ethnographers in their resistance to contemporary ethnographic critique. Medievalists, according to her, preserve ethnographic practice uncritically, thus resisting the efforts of anthropologists to understand the specific imperial genealogies of ethnography as a disciplinary practice.[7]

This slippage across historian, ethnographer, and inquisitor to be noted in the microhistories may, however, prove to be very productive to a more thoroughgoing historical critique of ethnographic practice. Such confusions open my thesis that the Inquisition itself served as an important institutional moment and process in the formation of European ethnographic disciplines—that the Inquisition wrote into being a cultural origin, an "absolute subject," a "whole subject" of an engendered savage *within* Europe. In graphing this ethnos, the Inquisition attempted to conceal amnestically the Christian cannibalism of medieval Jews. Witches thus were used by inquisitors and are used by microhistorians to act out a mourning that they must disavow—hence the nostalgia and melancholia in formation in the fifteenth century and the hovering of that angel today. Just as the witch served as an invention for acting out melancholy, a politics of lack, for the loss of *Christianitas* as a phantasmatic unitary body guaranteed by the body of the Jew in late medieval and early modern Europe, so, ironically, does the reemergence of witchcraft studies in the postwar period seem, once again, to engender melancholy over the loss of "Europe" and the (near total) loss of European Jewry.[8] Such confusion could suggest that Inquisitorial practices, first institutionalized in the early thirteenth century in medieval Christendom, served as an important institutional moment (still unrecognized) in the formation of the European ethnographic disciplines.

The mere insinuation of medieval Inquisitorial practices in colonial ethnography seems to fly into the face of the painstaking study of Inquisitorial trial records undertaken over the past twenty years. Such work has challenged the so-called demonizing picture of the tribunal drawn by such nineteenth-century historians as Henry Charles Lea, who, it is argued, in their ardor for rationalism and progress, produced the Inquisition as a dark antithesis.[9] This postwar historiography has emphasized (often reactively) the leniency of Inquisitorial tribunals. I wish here to step outside the historiographic frame of adjudicating demonization and recuperation in order to imagine an emergent history of Inquisitorial practices, practices whose remainders today are imbricated in the epistemologies that would judge what is demonized, what is lenient.

This essay explores, then, the intersections between Inquisitorial practices and ethnographic constructions of authority. It offers a reading of an Inquisitorial manual for the ways in which it constructs its authority and its determinations of what counts as evidence.[10] Reading protocols used by such ethnographic critics as James Clifford and Mary Louise Pratt inspired my reading; at the same time, I attempt to trouble a concept of *encounter* as something transacted *between.* In the text of a late fifteenth-century Inquisition manual can be found the evidence for a split *within* the Christian phantasmatic. The production of that ethnos from within would complicate and divide the exercise of mapping encounter between Europe and the Americas.[11]

My reading focuses on Inquisitorial technologies. Just as Evans-Pritchard and his fellow ethnographers relied on the camera, the phonograph record, and the tape recorder for their work of appropriation, so did the Inquisition (conceived of here as a broadly discursive practice—temporally and spatially) need technologies to render certain objects visible and others invisible, thus regulating their materialization and decorporealization. The devil, I argue, proved to be a powerful optical device for inquisitors.[12]

The devils materialized by the inquisitors in their manuals are thus good to think technology with, and the alliance of ethnography and technology is hardly accidental. To "see" invisible effects (what counts as evidence), the viewer had to look through the devil's eye, an optical device as powerful in its workings as the microscope would prove to be. The inquisitors' devil enabled viewers to read invisible dimensions of everyday experience and of visual images.

The Devil and Ethnographic Production of the Cannibal within Europe

Machines are social before being technical.

—Gilles Deleuze, *Foucault*[13]

My reading begins with the *Malleus maleficarum* (Hammer of witches), written by the Dominican inquisitor Heinrich Kramer and his erstwhile coauthor Jakob Sprenger and first printed in 1487.[14] I have chosen this manual because of its noted perversity, its confusion, its refusal to "go away" over five centuries. The amazing (and perverse) twentieth-century translation by Montague Summers is readily available, and even Sigmund Freud could not bear to part with his German translation as he stood before his bookshelves in Nazi Vienna making decisions about which books to leave behind and which to take along on his flight to London. The publication history of the *Malleus* needs more work, but we know from the history drawn up by Joseph Hansen in 1898 that the treatise went through at least thirteen printings between 1487 and 1520 and later in the third quarter of the sixteenth century formed a canonical part of popular witchcraft anthologies that continued to be published into the seventeenth century.[15]

The inquisitors advertised from the outset that the *Malleus* marked a "modern" rupture, and they use such diction as "modern times" (p. 111) ("ab illo tempore moderne" [fol. 54v]) and "expert testimony" (p. 111) ("experta testimonia" [fol. 54v]) to describe the truth that they were capable of securing from the accused. From the first printings, even before debate emerged, Kramer and Sprenger prefaced the treatise with an apology in which they claimed their work to be "old in respect to subject and authority; new in respect to selection and organization" ("breve pariter et prolixum antiquum certe materia et auctoritate; novum vero partium compilatione earumque aggregatione" [fol. 1r]). The three parts of the treatise (which may be imagined as the panels of a Bosch-like triptych) produced a writing space on which inquisitors could work out a theory of reproduction of the savage within—to risk anachronism, it can be said that the *Malleus* risks its own "bio-logy" in order to produce the reproductive rules for its witches, the ethnos it would graph. This "bio-logy" is not "natural"; reproduction of the European savage within requires the technological assistance of the devil. Inquisitorial discourse had to balance precariously its own intimacy with the devil with the danger of too much sympathy, a sympathy that could lead to utter confusion. As Kramer and Sprenger warned in their opening question ("prima questio"): "They [witches] could bring it [the world] to utter confusion" (p. 1) ("quia sic perimere possent totum mundum" [fol. 4r]). Where there is utter confusion, Jonathan Goldberg has alerted us to look for that "utterly confused category" *sodomy.*[16]

The first part of the treatise spells out the rules of reproduction by aligning sacramental, married, procreative sex over against, not, as we might expect, anything else that might threaten alliance (the confused noncategory *sodomy*), but, rather, a juridically and technologically organized, demonically assisted form of counteralliance. The inquisitors first stage a crisis of alliance in part 1 of the *Malleus,* its scholastic space, in which the authors mostly rely on citations of traditional scholastic texts for their authority. They speak of the "most powerful cause which contributes to the increase of witches" as "the woeful rivalry between married folk and unmarried men and women" (p. 45) ("Et revera potissima causa deserviens in augmentum maleficarum est dolorosum duellum inter maritatos et non maritatas feminas et viros" [fol. 21v]). So effective is the reproductive economy of the witches that "they seem to be depopulating all Christendom" (p. 68) ("iam totam christianitatem depopulare videntur" [fol. 33r]). This demonic counteralliance produced its own offspring at the same time that it preyed on the reproductive processes of married, procreative sex. According to the inquisitors, witches ate children, the product of alliance; they also could induce sterility in men and undo sacramental, procreative sex.

Like sacramental marriage, this countereconomy requires a pact, a kind of marriage agreement, contracted between the devil and a woman. In part 1, the inquisitors discuss this pact according to the discursive concerns of whether such a pact ("pactum") made by words or by deeds can reduce the witch to apostasy (fol. 37r). In discussing this problem, the text begins to map a series of spaces for which the demonic pact marks the axis of the vanishing point. Beyond the vanishing point of the pact, witches recede from infidels (fol. 36v), bad angels (fol. 36r), and the first parents (fol. 36r). Through the pact, witches thus vanish spatially beyond the Others (Jews, Turks) of *Christianitas* (fol. 36v).[17] They are located, too, beyond any heavenly topography and beyond salvation history since the sin of witches is even greater, according to the inquisitors, than the original sin of Adam and Eve.

The second part of the treatise also deals with the pact as an ethnographic phenomenon by elaborating on the kinds of ritual involved in setting it up. Once again, the text produces a series of spaces, and an understanding of their textual construction offers insight into the spatial practices used in the *Malleus.* In part 1, the Inquisitors endlessly established conditions of proximity and distance, organized around the subject of the witch as a vanishing point. Part 2 maps a specific oral geography of witchcraft by citing testimonies and confessions of witches collected from specific Inquisitorial sites or "fields."

An analysis of the rhetorical structure of this chapter "on making a pact with the devil" (p. 98) ("super expressum pactum fidelitatis cum demonibus" [fol. 48r]) can help us understand how the inquisitors are executing the ethnographic project of organizing the rule of ethnographic reproduction into what Michel de Certeau has called a "picture of orality."[18] The central panel of the triptych (part 2 of the treatise) layers the heterogeneous spaces through which the witch travels. Within this nomadic space, this "Babel of spatial heterogeneity" (de Certeau), the inquisitors try to construct a cartography of orality by interpolating into the text specific, located citations of Inquisitorial court testimony.

In order to map this cartography in the chapter on pacts, the text first draws a powerful frame around the space of witches. Witches are cannibals—their practice of devouring their children ("they are those who against every instinct of human or animal nature, are in the habit of eating and devouring the children of their own species" [p. 98]; "sunt autem he que contra humane nature inclinati omnem immo omnium ferarum lupina tantummodo excepta proprie speciei infantes vorant et comedere solent" [fol. 48v]) sets them apart from humans, although there is a space for the wolf inside this strong frame.[19] Within this anthropophagic frame, the inquisitors proceed to list sixteen *maleficia* or harms rendered by witches. The list traverses spaces ranging from the interior of the womb and the infant's cradle to the local climatic region, the juridical space of arrest, court, and torture, roadways and bridges, interregional travel, and even the space of the future and the invisible. *Maleficia* could be worked through a diversity of senses—the eye by a mere look, the voice by incantation, the hand by a touch. After citing this list of *maleficia,* the inquisitors again attempt to enframe and contain these nomadic spaces by insisting on the carnality of the witches—they copulate with the devil ("but it is common to all of them to practice carnal copulation with demons" [p. 99]; "hoc tamen est commune omnium spurcicias carnales cum demonibus exercere" [fol. 48v]). Once these noncontiguous spaces of interiority and exteriority, the domestic, the regional, and the interregional, are layered within this double frame of cannibalism and diabolic copulation, the inquisitors then go on to authenticate this strange panel through nothing less than the body of an inquisitor. They tell the story of the inquisitor of Como, who, thirty years ago, had forty-one witches burned in one year. Thus, the body of the eighty-five-year-old inquisitor (still going strong) superimposed over the bodies of forty-one burned witches somehow im-pacts the pact making of the ethnos and further enframes the double frame of cannibalism and copulation with the devil drawn around the witches. It is as if the more spaces the inquisitors pile up semantically, the more burned bodies they need to offset these spaces. The stake at which witches were burned somehow makes a delirious vanishing point for these nomadic spaces.

The inquisitors next take on the work in chapter 2 of describing the ritual of the pact. To do so, they adapt and invert the figures and gestures of the profession of a novice into a nunnery to describe the pact making, thus producing a kind of grotesque counterliturgy. This ritual is described in the third person. In order to authenticate their description, they then recollect the collective body of the inquisitor, "we Inquisitors" ("we inquisitors had credible experience of this method in the town of Breisach in the diocese of Basel, receiving full information from a young girl witch who had been converted" [p. 100]; "hunc modum nos inquisitores experientia teste procepimus in oppido Brisiaco basiliensis diocesis plenam informationem capiendo ab una iuvencula maleficia sed conversa" [fol. 48v]). They attach their collective body to the deposition of a young witch whose story they report in the third person except for directly reported dialogue between an aunt and the young girl. The young girl thus speaks the words of the witch, which the inquisitors then repeat in the story. Shifting as it does from third person to direct reporting of dialogue in the second person, no first-person voice is articulated in this anecdote. The Inquisitorial translation of the trial testimony has "eaten" the first person and substituted its collective body and experience in that space. Ironically, the story that the girl tells displaces her actual making of the pact with the devil to a story of procuration and prostitution—how her aunt, a witch, solicits for her by bringing her into a room filled with fifteen young men in green garments ("in vestimentis viridi coloris" [fol. 49r]). The inquisitors, too, displace the story of the pact by questioning this young woman about witchly transport over long distances, namely, from Strasburg to Cologne. The displacement of the ritual workings of the pact in this anecdote to an inquisition of witch travel over long distances echoes a wider structural displacement in chapter 2 in which the concluding discussion of the pact turns into a speculation on the devil's capability to tell the future.

The control over space and time that can be discerned in this one anecdote, which interpolates materials drawn from Inquisitorial trial proceedings, is repeated in seven other examples in this chapter. What is the strategy for staging these Inquisitorial trial transcriptions at certain spaces in the text? The piling up of anecdotes throughout the second part of the treatise (and not only in its second chapter) functions as a kind of "collection" of oral testimony, a kind of Inquisitorial museum. This museum of testimony provides a counterspatial practice in the text. With the careful incantation in chapter 2 of Inquisitorial anecdotes extracted from processes held in Berne (three times), Basel (three times), Strasburg (one time), and Constance (one time), the inquisitors can anchor the nomadic spaces of *maleficia* to a local cartography. The space of the Inquisitorial text, its grid of anecdotes, becomes a cartography through which the nomadic ethnos can be mapped. Thus, the space of orality generated by this interpolation of "expert testimony" is an engendered space founded on the burned bodies of female witches. It becomes an Inquisitorial cartography in which the inquisitor himself eats the first person of the located narrative in order to set himself in this place. An engendered cartography is thus cannibalized in order to produce the inquisitor as the guarantee of a mapping exercise that defies meaning: "It is a Babel in which the maps accumulate and mix without dissolving. A spatial polyglotism."[20]

The inquisitor cannibalizes the witch-cannibal and, in so doing, gnaws at the very frame that is somehow to contain the nomadic spaces over which *maleficia* wander. Where does this cannibalism leave the sexuality of the inquisitor, his relation to the frame that frames cannibalism, copulation with the devil?

My way into this question picks a path through the dismemberment and detachments of the text, its repeated anxieties about wandering semen, disappeared penises, dismembered crucifixes, body parts pierced by magical archers, cooked babies. Amid this debris of corporeal substances, the inquisitor describes the paraliturgical preparation of his own judicial body as he stands before the witch in part 3 of the treatise, the third wing of the triptych: "The judge should wear around his neck consecrated salt and other matters, with the Seven Words which Christ uttered on the Cross written in a schedule, and all bound together. And he should, if he conveniently can, wear these made into the length of Christ's stature against his naked body, and bound in holywax" (p. 231) ("supra tacta de sale et aliis rebus benedictis cum septem verbis que Christus protulit in cruce in cedula conscriptis et insimul colligatis collo eius alligentur. longitudo christi super nudum corpus ex cera benedicta circumcingatur" [fol. 108v]).

The inquisitor gives the sartorial recipe for magically protecting the judge's body from the accused witch who stands before him. Sealed with holy wax, and wearing the "textual" body of Christ, the inquisitor is trying to seal himself off, his skin and body fluids, from the threat of the witch. Against what does the inquisitor so phobically protect his body?

The devil provides a way into thinking of the utter fear of the inquisitor, his utter fear of the "utter confusion of the world," from which he must defend the world. This utter confusion seems to mark what Jonathan Goldberg has called a "sodometrical relation," a relation that does not yield the sodomite but delivers the relational structures "precariously available in prevailing discourse" for enabling and disabling the construction of sexual exteriorities that mark the abject and the unspeakable. Goldberg's study urges students of the Inquisition to ask how the encounter of the judge with the witch might both enable and disable the category *sodomy* in the *Malleus*.[21]

In their construction of a countereconomy of diabolic reproduction, the inquisitors came precariously close to imagining a sexual ethnography that could be categorized as sodomitical (*sodomy* being defined as "the emission of semen in an inappropriate place") by orthodox scholastic prescription.[22] According to the inquisitors, witches copulated not only with devils but also with animals; their sodometrical relations were not in doubt. They nevertheless worked carefully, even phobically, to protect the devils from accusations of sodomy for their technological assistance to this reproductive economy. According to the reproductive technology, an unwary human male serves as the donor of semen, which the devil collects as a *succubus* (lying underneath). The devil then travels to a witch to inject ("infundere" [fol. 13r]) the semen as an *incubus* (lying on top). The devil is thus responsible for a kind of "artificial insemination." The devil chooses a male donor for utilitarian purposes, namely, the virility of his semen, not for his past or future involvement in witchcraft (the semen are innocent).

Devils can also extend the chain of semen transfer in this reproductive economy. If a *succubus* with collected semen chooses for whatever reasons not to serve as an *incubus* to a witch, that devil can simply transfer the collected semen to another devil. Thus, semen can travel through a chain of places on its way to the appropriate place, known as the "vas debitum" (fol. 14v)—the place that is owed. This semen chain, with its multiplication of places in transport, hints at some unrecognized spatial usury haunting this countereconomy imagined in such intricate detail by the inquisitors. Scholastics regarded usury as the unnatural (sterile) multiplication of time in relation to money. Not unlike usury, the diabolic countereconomy of reproduction enabled the multiplication of spaces in relation to semen. The inquisitors insist, however, that the male donor, not the devil, is the father of the witch's child ("now it may be asked, of whom is a child so born the son? It is clear that he is not the son of the devil, but of the man whose semen was received" [p. 26]; "unde si queritur cuius filius sic natus existit. Patet quia non est filius demonis sed illius hominis cuius est semen acceptum" [fol. 13r]). The laws of blood and kin were thus properly upheld even in this counterreproductive economy. This insistence on maintaining the good order of lineage, even in describing a sodometrical reproductive economy, suggests that some other fluid did the work of marking the exteriority of Christendom for the inquisitors.[23]

These rules of the counterreproductive economy also construct for the male donor an unknowingness, a kind of secret vulnerability, that seems to proliferate in the treatise into anxious concerns over the power that witches exercise against the God-ordained procreative economy, the economy of marital alliance.[24] Witches can disappear penises or render them dysfunctional, thus introducing male sterility into sacramental marriage. It might seem too strong to say that the inquisitors build a kind of homophobic/homosocial self-ignorance into their rules for reproducing the ethnos were it not for their active denial of any sodomitical practices by the devil. The inquisitors ascribe sodometrical relation to witches at the same time that they deny such possibilities to the devil. Writing of the sexual practices of the devil, they foreclose the suspicion of sodomy: "Yet nowhere does one read that incubi and succubi fell into vices against nature. We do not speak only of sodomy, but of any sin whereby the act is wrongfully performed outside the rightful receptacle" (p. 30) ("tamen nusquam legit in vitiis quibuscumque contra naturam loquendo non solum de sodomirico sed etiam de quocumque alio peccato extra vas debitum propere agendo se incubos et succubos fecisse" [fol. 14v]).

Consistent with their protection of the devil, the inquisitors of the *Malleus* are also careful to skirt discussion of the witches' sabbath (available to them discursively at the time they composed the treatise) with its tropes of sexual orgy, same-sex pleasures, and the ritual kiss offered by witches to the devil's anus. Why, beyond producing a purportedly coherent countereconomy of diabolical alliance capable of supplying themselves with the phantasmatic of a self-reproducing savage within to persecute, would the inquisitors so protect the devil in their treatise? What purchase does the devil have on this text?

The devil serves as a kind of optical device that makes the inquisitor's countereconomy visible and therefore something that can be *counted as evidence*. The textual materialization of the devil that the *Malleus* sediments with such care enables the inquisitor to gaze at and see, make legible, an invisible world of the ethnos he is conjuring. Through the optical prosthetic of the devil, the inquisitor can watch the couplings of *incubi* and *succubi* and have instantaneous knowledge at a distance. Perhaps even more important, the devil offers a special kind of insight, what ethnographers today would call a *theoretical abstraction*, that promises the ethnographer " 'to get to the heart' of a culture more rapidly than someone undertaking, for example, a thorough inventory of customs and beliefs."[25] What such theoretical abstractions as Radcliffe-Brown's *social structure* did for ethnography in the 1920s the devil as optical device trained on the newly emergent ethnos of the witch did for inquisitors of the later fifteenth century.

The inquisitors of the *Malleus* give examples of their optical expertise, their capacity to "see" and "verify" the work of witchcraft. They share the visionary capabilities of the devil. The *Malleus* insists that what may be invisible to onlookers is visible to the witch and to those who have access to Inquisitorial optics: "But with regard to bystanders, the witches themselves have often been seen lying on their backs in the fields or woods, naked up to the very navel, and it has been apparent from the disposition of those limbs and members which pertain to the venereal act and orgasm, as also from the agitation of their legs and thighs, that, all invisibly to the bystanders, they have been copulating with Incubus devils" (p. 114) ("tamen quo ad circumstantes sepius ipse malefice supine iacentes in agris seu silvis vise sunt et denudate supra umbilicum. Et iuxta dispositionem illius spurcicie coaptatis membris tibiis et cruribus se agitantes demonibus incubis invisibiliter ibidem quo ad circumstantes cooperantibus" [fols. 55v–56r]). Take also an anecdote recounted from a Dominican house in Spires. This story is told in the first person, that is, in the voice of the confessor. The use of the first person reminds the reader that, when it comes to looking through the optical device of the devil, the eye of the inquisitor gazes through one end of the apparatus: " 'One day,' he says, 'while I was hearing confessions, a young man came to me and, in the course of his confession, woefully said that he had lost his member. Being astonished at this, and not being willing to give it easy credence, since in the opinion of the wise it is a mark of light-heartedness to believe too easily, I obtained proof of it when I saw nothing on the young man's removing his clothes and showing the place' " (p. 119) "(quadam inquit die dum confessionum audientie instarem Iuvenis quidam accessit et inter verba confessionis membrum virile lamentabiliter se perdidisse asseruit. Ammirans ego pater et verbis suis faciliter credere nolens eo quo levis corde qui facile credit a sapiente iudicatur. Experientia didici per visum nihil cernendo dum iuvenis locum vestes detegendo demonstrasset" [fol. 58r]).

The purchase of the inquisitors, their mastery of the visual plenitude of an invisible world, came at a cost since they had to manipulate the materialization of the devil to have this optical access. They are able to see what the devil sees. The intimacy of the Inquisitorial gaze, as it focused through the devil's sensorium, threatened the good homosocial order that the inquisitors worked so hard to maintain in their text. Looking forward to the ethnos of the witch engendered on female corporeality involved the inquisitors in looking backward through the devil, a materialization that could make a certain optics matter as evidence. The inquisitors thus caught themselves in a kind of optical unconscious of disavowal: yes, the countereconomy works through sodometrical relations that implicate the inquisitor, but the countereconomy is "proper" because devils are strictly proper (nonsodometrical). This optical unconscious returns both the inquisitor and the historian once again to the question of ethnographic authority, to an interrogation of how the eye that can produce integrated portraits can see an ethnos. The production of an ethnos always begs the question of "what has dropped out of sight."[26]

A group that was dropping out of sight over the fifteenth century was medieval Jews from the Mediterranean to the North Sea. Medieval Jews were dropping out of sight at a faster pace in fifteenth-century Christendom at the same time that they were becoming more visible as a group ordered under sumptuary law to mark themselves with such signs as yellow badges.[27] Expelled from England in 1290 and from France in 1306, subject to the wearing of distinguishing signs in northern Italy in the 1430s (Padua in 1430, Perugia in 1432, and Florence and Siena in 1439), expelled from several imperial Rhineland towns in the 1420s and 1430s, and finally expelled from Spain in 1492, Jews were subject to growing Inquisitorial and civic violence over the fifteenth century. Expulsion did not mean the end to anti-Semitism, as the discursive investment in the phantasmatic Jew of late medieval English literature and drama shows.[28] Nevertheless, local and national expulsions and the mounting persecution of Jews in blood-libel cases (accusations that Jews murdered Christians for their blood) meant that the Jewish population grew less available as the corporeally materialized Other who had guaranteed the integrity of Christendom by marking its exteriority.[29] The increase in the number of treatises devoted to witchcraft from the late 1430s (which then proliferated in the print culture of the 1470s–1490s) must be viewed as part of an epistemological break in Christendom's imaginary of its exteriority. Christians were "cannabilizing" the Jewish bodies that had constituted that exteriority. They thus needed to materialize a new corporeal ethnos, a substitute, to which the anti-Semitic tropes of the exterior, namely, usury and its sterility, could be shifted and at the same time doubled by the engendering of witches as a corporeal exteriority. This occulted doubling of the Jew in the misogynistic production of the witch as an ethnos set in motion a counterprocreative economy in which semen functioned usuriously through chains of transfer and in which the sterility associated in the scholastic mind with usury became the corporeal obsession of inquisitors and male laymen.

Tropes of anti-Semitism thus flickered in a kind of blind spot in the ethnographic space of witchcraft crafted by Inquisitorial discourse, where witches served as the vanishing point. Within this strange space in between the blind spot and the vanishing point, the inquisitors materialized the devil as an optical device. Not unlike a telescope and a microscope, the devil as optical apparatus magically filled the gap between blind spot and vanishing point with a savage visual plenitude. The authority of the inquisitor and that of the devil were closely intertwined; therefore, the devil must be both protected as an optical device and kept out of sight as a sign of what might lie beyond the invisible to which the devil gave access. Not until the seventeenth century would a new discipline for deciding what counts as evidence (the witness of mechanical devices) obtrude on Inquisitorial optical technologies as discursively imagined in this essay: "Endowed with their new semiotic powers, the latter [nonhuman, mechanical devices] contribute to a new form of text, the experimental science article, a hybrid between the age-old style of biblical exegesis—which has previously been applied not only to the Scriptures and classical texts—and the new instrument that produces new inscriptions."[30]

Rotate the Image of the Body and You Produce a Different Geography

—Rosalind Krauss, *The Optical Unconscious*[31]

The *Malleus* appeared in print without illustrations. Inspired by Rosalind Krauss's kinesthetic insight—"rotate the image of the body and you produce a different geography"—I now rotate my argument toward medieval visual culture in order to think about the late medieval reception of the devil as an optical device. To what kind of corporeal geographies did this optical device give access? How did the viewer take up different points of view in such geographies?

Take as an example a woodcut attributed to Dürer that illustrated the 1493 edition of *Der Ritter von Turm,* a German translation of a late fourteenth-century text written by Geoffrey de la Tour Landry for the education of his daughter (fig. 6). In a brilliant analysis of this woodcut, Joseph Koerner has demonstrated how the devil's anus serves as the vanishing point for the principal orthogonals generated from the mirror (note that these orthogonals map differently from the orthogonals constructing the space of the chamber).[32] The viewer whose vision follows these orthogonals from the mirror ends up scanning the hypotenuse of the orthogonals, the hypotenuse leading into the devil's anus. Thus, the organization of the optical space within the woodcut (i.e., the space generated by the mirror) constructs the devil's anus as an eye, an optical apparatus. I call it an *apparatus* in order to mark how the devil's anal eye "mechanically" disturbs the reflexive mirroring of the mirror. An audience of the late fifteenth century would be visually accustomed to seeing mirrored in such a mirror the world of the viewer in miniature.[33] Rather than seeing the young woman mirrored back, however, a viewer sees instead the devil's ass. Presumably, at this moment of viewing, the young woman sees only herself in the mirror, not the devil's ass. A viewer of the woodcut and the female viewer within the woodcut have access to two different optical worlds.

Figure 6. Woman looking in a mirror. From *Der Ritter Von Turm* (Augsburg, 1498). Courtesy the Newberry Library, Chicago.

The devil's anal eye does the work of an optical apparatus capable of decorporealizing vision and materializing it in a different way. Not unlike the camera obscura, the devil's anal eye supplants "the observer's physical and sensory experience"[34] by mechanical relations. Between the young woman as viewer and a viewer of the woodcut comes an apparatus that can disembody and divide vision ambiguously through two points, a mirror and the devil's anal eye.

The woman thus occupies a compromised perspectival space capable of mirroring back to her a reflection of herself at the same time that another optic can generate a different perspectival space that interrupts her mirroring. Viewers of the woodcut can make sense of the reflection that is available to them, but not to her, through a reflective introspection—an introspection that produces an "interior" space. What might this doubling and interiorizing of perspectival space, a process that is the *effect* of the devil's anal eye, have to do with the sexually proper spaces so important to the inquisitor—the "vas debitum" in which the semen was to be properly banked by the devil in the counter-reproductive economy of the ethnos? What would happen if viewers looked at these proper spaces through the devil's anal eye?

The next two figures suggest partial answers to these complex questions. A consideration of these two artifacts from sixteenth-century visual culture returns us once again to the refrain that these Inquisitorial optics (and this essay) insistently pose: "What drops out of sight?"

Hans Baldung Grien, who drew the pen-and-ink drawing of three witches reproduced in figure 7 as a New Year's greeting in 1514 and inscribed it "to the cleric, a good year" ("der cor capen an gut jar"), is noted for his output of Hexenbilder, pictures of witches, between 1510 and his death in 1545.[35] His first published woodcut (1510) after leaving the apprenticeship of Dürer was the monumental *Witches' Sabbath.* Baldung spent most of his mature productive years in Strasbourg surrounded by professional family members whose involvement in the law, the university, and city government would ensure their acquaintance with Inquisitorial literature and the matter of witches. How might contemporary viewers look at his drawings of witches?

Viewers see no devil or mirror. Two young women and an older woman cavort and twine around each other. The orthogonals of the perspective converge on the exposed genitals of the older woman, and the diagonals of the perspective cut across the genitals of the younger woman, who at the same time covers them and touches them with her hand. The young woman who has just somersaulted in the bottom of the drawing displays her buttocks and her pubes as if enticing some erotic embrace. If the viewer takes things for what they seem, he (the cleric to whom the drawing is dedicated) can imagine an entwined and fiercely energized tableau of same-sex pleasures about to be set in motion. If he looked through the devil's anal eye, the optic to which the inquisitor had access, he would also see that things are not what they seem. Recall that the *Malleus* insists that what may be invisible to onlookers is visible to the witch and to those who have access to Inquisitorial optics.

The devil as an Inquisitorial optic would re-present the scene by Baldung as witches copulating with the devil. It is not so much

Figure 7. Hans Baldung, *Three Witches* (1514). From Graphische Sammlung Albertina, Vienna. Courtesy Foto Marburg/Art Resource NY.

that the devil is the implied viewer of the drawing as that the inquisitor with access to diabolical optics is the viewer—out of sight with the devil but at the same time making that vision possible. The scene depicted in the *Three Witches* thus flickers in its chiaroscuro between a perspectivally organized portrait of same-sex pleasure, a scene in which the inquisitor is located in a specific viewing place vis-à-vis the genitals of women, and a scene of copulation with the devil in which the inquisitor is located looking through the devil's anal eye, through which is represented the countereconomy of the ethnos, the copulation of women with devils.

Both viewing points available in this drawing raise questions about "proper place," the "vas debitum," the body of the witch as an appropriate container. Joseph Koerner has observed of this drawing that, if the viewer rotates the somersaulting witch's head to the top, then the tangle of witches' leg and wildly flowing hair frames a reddish-colored pubic triangle out of which the fires of the pot fume. Upside down or right side up, an Inquisitorial gaze would flicker across what could be counted by the church as sodometric relations—the same-sex pleasure of women and the bestial couplings of women with devils.

What the inquisitors worked so hard to deny textually, the sodometric relations of their ethnography, visual cultures revealed through the unstable viewing points of woodcuts and drawings of witches, which grew into a much-copied genre by the end of the fifteenth century. By taking up a viewing position that involved the devil's anal eye to "see" the scene, the viewer himself took up not only the position of the inquisitor but also the very tactile and mechanical aspects of being a part of this materialized, corporeal optical apparatus. As the eyes of the somersaulting witch, whether upside down or right side up, look out intently from this drawing, they seem to question what the inquisitors most feared, the "utter confusion of the world," which seemed to be nothing other than their optical confusion as they saw themselves through their double, a double that they both needed and protected and also profoundly feared.

If the counterreproductive economy, the production of witches as a savage ethnos within, proceeded invisibly in Europe, it yielded to visibility in the New World. A study of an engraving (fig. 8) that illustrated late sixteenth-century editions of Theodore De Bry's *America* can help us "see" this visibility.[36] The engraving depicts an event that occurred in October 1513 (a year before Baldung sat down to draw his *Three Witches*), as Balboa made his way across Panama to the Pacific. In the printed account

Figure 8. Balboa in Panama. From Theodore de Brye, *America* (1594). Courtesy the Newberry Library, Chicago.

of this expedition, which appeared in 1516, Peter the Martyr described how, after having killed the king and warriors that stood in his way, Balboa put to death forty royal members of the king's household for the "most abominable and un-natural lechery." According to Peter the Martyr, Balboa found these men dressed in "womens apparell, smoth & effeminately decked."[37]

To relate this trope of cross-dressing with the double vision of the inquisitor enacted in Baldung's drawing of witches, we must ask, How is viewing constructed in this engraving of the execution of the "unnatural" Indians in Panama? The action converges at the crossed haunches of the dogs. The tangle of their limbs obscures the feast of one dog who bites into what must be the crotch and buttocks of the extended thigh he stands on. There seem to be two perspectives on this scene: the birds-eye perspective generated above the centrally placed figure of Balboa, who does not look on directly (his eyes are averted in conversation) but points at, "presents," the dismembering work of the dogs; and the point of view generated from above the torn-off head of an Indian resting on the ground in the lower margin. If viewers rotate the engraving to bring this head to the top, they can see that these dead eyes could have seen only into the center of the savage melee where the dog gnaws on the loins of a fellow Indian. It is as if both the conventional perspective arrangement and the perspective of the devil's anal eye that flickered in the Baldung drawing fail here. The dismembered optical view of the devil's anal eye has traveled into the space of the later engraving to dismember the bodies of the savages. The disembodied perspective of the diabolical optic can now disembody the space of New World representation.[38]

Balboa averts his eyes as he presents the representation, and the decapitated head of the Indian is already sightless. Only the pointing hand of Balboa seems to remember the intimacy of tactility and sight that the inquisitor first enjoyed and feared as they produced the visual plenitude of the savage within Europe. There is also the parrot looking over the scene from the right-hand corner. As a symbol used in European painting to symbolize purity (think of Baldung's noted panel *Madonna with the Parrots,* ca. 1528–30, Nuremberg), the parrot often accompanies the Blessed Virgin. Does the parrot speak the inquisitors' words ex post facto—the utter confusion of the world averted once again?

If we put together the Baldung drawing with the De Bry engraving, what kind of diptych do we produce? From Baldung's *Three Witches* (1514) and the conquest of Balboa (1513) through the next three centuries, the potential of misalliance in the Old World had to be exterminated in advance (prophylactically) through the death of witches, and the always already accomplished misalliance in the New World, the ex post facto of the noncategory *sodomy,* had to be dismembered again and again in the savage Indian. The witch and the Indian are thus intimately divided (not partitioned) across each other temporally, the Indian as the past of the witch, the witch as the future of the Indian, and both doubled spatially in their genders—the witch as the confused body of the Indian, the Indian as the confused body of the witch, the places that are not appropriate, but endlessly in debt (*extra vas debitum*) *vas debitum:* "Rather than examine a binary rigidity between those terms [*domination* and *subordination*]—which is an inherently Eurocentric strategy—this critical field would be better served if it sought to break down the fixity of the dividing lines between domination and subordination, and if it further questioned the psychic disempowerment of colonial."[39]

We have traveled across textual spaces of the *Malleus maleficarum* to the visual spaces of an ethnographic diptych, a drawing and an engraving. The witches of the *Three Witches* and Balboa's dismembered Indians seem to murmur to each other intimately of stories that will not find their way into court transcriptions and Inquisitorial anecdotes interpolated into manuals. They whisper of the "utter confusion" of the inquisitors and of their utter fear of such confusions. They tell cautionary tales of confusing the archive for El Dorado. They say that the witches never really gave birth to the Golden Man. They cry for those expelled who await our mourning.

The Ecstasies of the Inquisitorial Microhistorians

At one and the same time this story speaks from within and without the spell of magic, thereby registering not merely a dualized but an interacting doubleness of epistemology, two universes apart, each requiring the other, each demolishing the other.

—Michael Taussig, *Shamanism, Colonialism, and the Wild Man*[40]

The sighs of witches and New World sodomites, the ghosts of expelled Jews, haunt us as we pay a visit to Inquisitorial archives and to monographs on European witchcraft based on Inquisitorial documents. How do contemporary historians of the inquisition deal with these cries and whispers, with these ghosts? How do they read and write "dialogically" (as they claim) about the inquisition given the genealogy of ethnographic authority proposed by my reading of the *Malleus* for what it drops out of sight?

Carlo Ginzburg, who among historians writing on European Inquisitorial texts has perhaps most strongly reflected on his reading practices, has claimed that, when it comes to evidence, both inquisitors and historians share the same desire for stories. Ginzburg specifies this Inquisitorial and microhistorical desire for the Same as a desire for an "underlying unity."[41] He finds an underlying unity for European witchcraft in prehistoric Eurasian shamanism, locating the origins of that shamanism in the Eurasian steppes among nomadic Scythian, Thracian, Celt, and Tartar tribes. Eurasian shamans appeared to have been mostly males, and Ginzburg tries to retrieve female and male homosexual shamans in a footnote.[42]

In order to make his argument about shamanism, Ginzburg uses the archive of nineteenth-century folklore. But, like Inquisitorial archives, this folk archive is compromised by a desire for the Same and thus plunges the study into a vicious circle. As anthropologists have shown, the European folklore movement of the nineteenth century helped produce *folk* as a category with the power to re-mark the *traditional* and the *primitive* within Europe and to control and manage Europe at its so-called cultural borders, the spaces of vampires, werewolves, little people, Turks, Eastern Jews, and other border creatures along the Celtic and Slavic fringes.[43] In a mimetic doubling of colonial and imperial ethnologies already graphed for the so-called noncivilized world, Europeans practiced the erotic art of conjuring the "white Indian" at home, so to speak, in the ecstatic, phantasmatic body of the shaman as he becomes death.[44]

Ginzburg's shaman occupies a timeless, ahistorical space that Ginzburg maps as beginning at the edge of medieval Europe. He writes that "from mediaeval Europe we are once again driven back to the boundless Eurasian steppe, traversed by nomads on horseback. We see an interminable saga of intricate cultural exchanges take shape: but beginning when, and where?" Only continental Africa cannot be counted in this space since, according to Ginzburg, "in Africa we find phenomena of possession not the ecstasy followed by the journey of the shaman's soul into the beyond." This Eurasian-African difference may come, not from what Ginzburg calls a "very ancient cultural differentiation,"[45] but rather from the disciplinary divisions of labor between imperial ethnographies and European folklore studies in the nineteenth and early twentieth centuries. In his desire for an "underlying unity," Ginzburg ignores these imperial, disciplinary borders.

Ginzburg positions the voices of accused medieval witches who talk into his tape recorder proleptically as native informants. His witches speak that which comes from remote times and places, namely, twentieth-century re-presentations of nineteenth-century folklore: "The existence of actual ecstatic continuities seems undeniable. Unwittingly, men and women—above all women, possibly living in forlorn mountain villages—relive, during their nocturnal swoons, myths that have reached them from the most remote places and periods."[46]

The story of shamanism developed by Ginzburg alerts us to some unrepresentable ethnographic scene of the present. Ginzburg's shamanism defends ethnographic experience, its permanence. Ginzburg writes ecstatically about this experience: "Why this permanence? The answer is possibly very simple. To narrate means to speak here and now with an authority that derives from having been (literally or metaphorically) there and then."[47] The "being there" of this narrative authority invoked by Ginzburg helps establish him as the author of experience and to provide a coherent subject for the microhistory of witchcraft—the shaman.

Ginzburg's displacement of female witches into male shamans enables other authoritative projects. He corrects the work of Margaret Murray, a student and teacher of Egyptology and fieldworker on the Egyptian excavations of Flinders Petrie. In 1921, Murray published *The Witch Cult in Western Europe*.[48] Excoriated by generations of male historians who faulted her for misreadings and invention, Murray argued for the reality of descriptions of the witches' Sabbath, a nighttime orgiastic meeting of women, and connected it with pre-Christian fertility cults. Ginzburg credits Murray for crediting the depositions of witches but faults her for mistaking such descriptions for fact. Ginzburg, too, credits depositions but reads them as myths, not as rituals. By reading depositions as myths, Ginzburg can link them with some ancient European shamanism. This link does the work of displacement. Through Eurasian shamans, Ginzburg is able to *shift* the gender of the "underlying unity" from the feminine to the masculine and to transform the origin of magical power from witchcraft to shamanism.

Presumably, the power of the individual male shaman is more comfortable for Ginzburg to assume as a historian than the ecstasies of accused witches. His assumption of shamanism requires that he treat the archival ecstasy of deposing women and the acts of which the inquisitors accused them as symptomatic beliefs pointing to an ancient shamanism. According to Ginzburg, these accused witches "relive,"[49] unknowingly, this shamanism, but we are reminded here that this shamanism that Ginzburg assumes refers to nineteenth-century European mimesis of "primitive" magic. Ginzburg uses the study of witchcraft as a magical means (microhistory as a postfolkloric folkloric project) to bring such magic back to Europe yet again.[50]

Another postwar project, the proposal by David Astor to found the Center for Research in Collective Psychopathology at the University of Sussex in 1966, produces an authoritative crisis similar to the one just described in Ginzburg's *Ecstasies.* Out of this center, which later adopted the more neutral name the *Columbus Center,* came Norman Cohn's study *Europe's Inner Demons.* Once again, in this work, the subject of *witches* is called on to do the work of mourning. Witches stand in for the scapegoated Jews of the Holocaust in Cohn's work. His argument about witches works quite differently from the shamanistic history of Ginzburg. Cohn views the production of witches as the "need to create a scapegoat for an unacknowledged hostility to Christianity."[51] But Cohn never mentions Jews in his study of medieval scapegoating, a falling out of sight that has uncanny intersections with witchcraft texts of the fifteenth century.

This cluster of postwar representations of shamanism and witchcraft repeats the question of ethnographic authority and homosocial desire, of what drops out of sight when experience is invoked and ethnographic authority constructed. To press this question a little more, consider the concluding chapter of part 3 of *Ecstasies,* "Bones and Skin," where Ginzburg incants his thesis that "all routes we have negotiated to clarify the folkloric dimension of the Sabbath converge on one point: the journey into the realm of the dead."[52]

The witches' Sabbath or synagogue, the nocturnal, orgiastic meeting of women with the devil, is the locus of witchcraft lore where medieval Jews come into question. For Norman Cohn, the interpolation of the witches' Sabbath into an increasingly elaborate and overdetermined late medieval stereotype of witches serves as an example of the resurfacing of a cluster of late antique stereotypes about Jews. Cohn mentions the Jews of late antiquity only in this regard and is oddly silent about the interaction of Inquisitorial persecution of Jews and women in *Europe's Inner Demons.*

Ginzburg makes a very different kind of argument about medieval Jews. For him, Inquisitorial persecution and popular notions of conspiracy are serial phenomena running in a kind of zigzag way from lepers to Jews to women over the fourteenth century. It is important for Ginzburg to mark a break, a discontinuity, between the marginalization of Jews and the marginalization of women into witches so that he can reconnect the women deposing in front of the Inquisition with ancient Eurasian shamanistic traditions. In a discussion criticizing Cohn's thesis, Ginzburg writes, "To detect in this persecution the last link in a chain of accusations stretching over a millennium and a half is tantamount to denying the discontinuity introduced by the image of the witches' sect. The aggressive characteristics attributed to it by inquisitors and lay judges fused ancient traits with new elements, linked to a quite specific chronological, geographical and cultural context. All this implies a complex phenomenon of interaction which cannot be reduced to the pure and simple projection of very ancient and recurrent obsessions onto the accused."[53]

In his study of the witches' Sabbath, Ginzburg divides the possibilities for continuity and discontinuity among Jews and women in interesting ways. Jews seem to "disappear" from the European imaginary, and women almost magically take their place. Ginzburg devotes his last anecdotal attention to the Jews with his stories of plague pogroms in 1348 and anxieties expressed in 1409 by Pope Alexander V about Jews and heretical

Christians in the southeastern French and Swiss regions. Ginzburg's conceptual insistence on discontinuity between Jews and women in *Ecstasies* echoes their persistent methodological separation in medieval Inquisitorial studies.

Georges Duby and Michelle Perrot's recent *History of Women in the West* repeats this methodological separation. The collection can be read to show how ethnographic authority *requires* that they be kept separated and also how the microhistorian must cannibalize the voices of the Inquisition in order to accomplish this separation.

The first volume of *The History of Women in the West* begins (where else?) in Greece. The preface to the medieval volume, *The Silence of the Middle Ages*, lets the reader know that the study will be restricted to writing a history of gender and sexuality in medieval Europe by leaving out "people [*sic*] of different religious and cultural traditions."[54] This means that the volume excludes histories of medieval Islamic and Jewish women and refuses the possibilities of articulating the power-charged co-construction of gender across Christian, Islamic, and Jewish fields.

In spite of such exclusions, Georges Duby promises to catch for the reader at last, in the last chapter of the medieval volume, the "sound of the authentic female voice" of the Middle Ages. To catch that voice, Duby brings the reader to a juridical scene, a scene of Inquisition. Duby uses the Inquisition register of Bishop Jacques Fournier, the future Pope Benedict XII, as the evidentiary source for the chapter. He cautions the reader, "We must translate as we read, and attempt to imagine the words actually spoken."[55] The act of translation called for by Duby, and by no means limited to him in medieval women's history, raises methodological questions about the articulation of spaces of voice, text, and interrogation, not only for the Inquisition in the fourteenth century, but also for the historian at the end of the twentieth.

The staging of a prison scene at the end of *The Silence of the Middle Ages* unconsciously speaks the unspoken problem of the volume. The worlds excluded by the volume return to haunt it. In the longest transcription from the Fournier register cited by Duby, Beatrice de Planissoles, the woman he chooses from the register to speak the authentic voice, tells stories under interrogation. The scribe records Beatrice as telling stories in which an unnamed converted Jewish woman is her intimate interlocutor. Beatrice tells stories in which this converted Jewish woman serves as her go-between to a world of magical sexuality, to collections of "umbilical cords of male babies," and to sheets "stained with menstrual blood" of virgins. The inquisitors have confiscated these objects and are accusing Beatrice not only of Catharism but also of witchcraft. The unnamed Jewish go-between in Beatrice's testimony enables Beatrice to cross a sexual border into magic and witchcraft.

In his desire to stage the "authentic" voice of Beatrice, Duby never mentions the voice of the Jewish woman, although he quotes at length from Beatrice's deposition, in which the converted Jewish woman figures. If we look more closely at the Fournier register, we find that the world of the Jews haunts not only Beatrice's testimony but other pages of the register as well. Over the summer months of 1320, during which Bishop Fournier interrogated Beatrice several times, Fournier also questioned another prisoner, a converted Jew named Baruch.[56] One can imagine Beatrice and Baruch brushing shoulders as they went in and out of the presence of the bishop. Only a year before, local shepherds had killed over a hundred local Jews who had refused baptism. Baruch had been baptized during this incident but was now under suspicion of relapse. Read against the recent history of local anti-Semitic incidents, the testimony of Beatrice becomes more problematic than Duby's reading accommodates. The question troubles: Did Beatrice try to displace suspicion from herself by producing the converted Jewish woman as the site of a dangerous, magic sexuality in her testimony, in effect displacing questions of orthodoxy and in so doing possibly endangering this local convert during a moment of engaged Inquisitorial surveillance? How do we read the testimony of Beatrice across the adjacent testimony of Baruch?

In extracting the authentic voice of the female in the Fournier register, Duby does indeed produce a kind of "truth," but it is hardly the hallucinatory truth of the "authentic female voice of the Middle Ages." He produces the truth of the epistemology of history, the "nature" of history. In so doing, he silences the performances in the fractured, divided, fluctuating text of the Inquisition record at the same time that he disavows his own repetition of violent interrogation practices in his own position as historian.

To conclude this discussion of some current reading protocols here would only repeat the powerful problem of these microhistories—they leave the power of the Inquisitor unmarked, put under erasure. As James Clifford has shown, the production of ethnographic authority relies on the double move of invoking the experiential ("I was there") and then erasing the ethnographer from the text to achieve a "scientific" neutrality. It is this erasure of both the historian and the inquisitor from the microhistories under discussion that leads to theoretical confusion over who writes microhistories—the ethnographer, the anthropologist, the historian, the inquisitor, or the accused.

The ethnographic inquisitor and the Inquisitorial ethnographer who flicker so unstably today in microhistories flickered as unstably in the fifteenth century. My counterethnographic reading has tried to show how inquisitors constructed themselves as both reliable witnesses and detached observers in the fifteenth century, producing witchcraft as a kind of "primitive" effect of their discourse.

A counterethnography can never restore the "real" voice or the "real" body of Inquisitorial scrutiny, but it can contribute to producing the possibilities for rereading the archives, for mourning those who were disappeared, abjected, and cannibalized by this delirious search for a space of truth.

GENDERS, BODIES, BORDERS

Technologies of the Visible

History as a Problem of Women's History

As the senses of sight and touch separated with the industrial mapping of the body in the nineteenth century, the visible and the visualized aligned themselves in medical, scientific, and sexological discourses; even history claimed to make the past "visible." The criteria of the visible came to mark modernity. Cultural studies of visualization technologies help us understand history itself as a sign of the modern and join its desires for the visible to those desires for spectacle produced among observers of visualizing media (such as the diorama, photography, moving pictures) in the late nineteenth and early twentieth centuries.[1]

Over the past twenty years, women's history has proclaimed its desire to render historical women visible. If women's history acknowledges (as I believe a discursive critique of history requires us to) that such a desire is implicated in the knowledge-power of visualization technologies, then it produces a dilemma for itself. The rich interest in writing a history of medieval women mystics can serve as an example. Much recent work in medieval women's history has focused on women mystics in an avowed effort to rewrite a traditional historiography whose contempt and fear of these women's bodily practices had rendered them "invisible." Such studies have tended to take for granted the organizing category *medieval women mystics* without questioning how its terms came to be generated and concatenated. An understanding of how the word *mystic* emerged in usage from the adjective *mystical* suggests, in fact, a contest over the very engendering of what counts as visible at different historical moments.[2] The engendering of the visible thus becomes a historical problem for women's history.

This essay accepts the dilemma that the desire to make historical women visible is both the effect of modern visualizing technologies and the possibility for their resignification. It works with the dilemma by articulating it through a reading of an important book that has become emblematic both within and beyond medieval studies, Caroline Walker Bynum's *Holy Feast and Holy Fast.*[3] My reading is an "infrareflexive" one, meaning that it seeks to display the work of achieving a narrative of visibility at the same time that it dislocates that work to other locations: the past into the present and contemporary academic authority into the past. Such a reading distributes itself discursively—in this case—across medieval history, contemporary critical theories, especially feminist and postcolonial, and cultural studies of visualization.[4]

Since its publication in 1987, *Holy Feast and Holy Fast* has become a required text in courses on medieval women's history and often appears as the one medieval selection in surveys of gender studies. This book, about "woman as body and as food," can be read for problems concerning the production of gendered knowledge in history today. How can we write these histories in such a way that, in making women "visible," we do not blind ourselves to the historical processes that defined, redefined, and engendered the status of the visible and the invisible?

The rhetoric of the text can provide clues to its own engendering, to the historical processes it renders invisible in order to make some category visible. In making medieval women mystics visible, the rhetoric of *Holy Feast and Holy Fast* renders invisible the problems of engendering the medieval category *Christianitas.* The engendering of both categories was fearfully interconnected, and this interconnection needs to be rearticulated; otherwise, making medieval women mystics visible simply reproduces Europe as a category in its medieval guise of *Christianitas:* "No Europeanist should ignore the once and future global production of 'Europe.'"[5]

Cultural Concepts and the Gender of Narratives

Bynum elaborates an anthropology of symbol and ritual and a social psychology of sexual development in order to explore the bodily practices, especially food practices, of medieval women mystics.[6] Only a citation referring to works critical of ahistoric and essentialist aspects of social-psychological theories of sexual development gives a hint of the contest over gender in *Holy Feast and Holy Fast.*[7] Bynum largely dismisses feminist scholarship in the first chapter as "presentist" and evades a feminist concern (already in evidence by the mid-1980s) that the humanities produced gendered forms of knowledge. She claims instead a methodology with guaranteed access to medieval women's experience: "The women themselves . . . generate questions as well as answers" (p. 30).[8] There is now increasing question—and not only among feminists—about whether it is even possible to capture the experience of people of the past in this way.[9] Concern over the use of experience as well as the use of gender and race to organize disciplinary knowledge has only heightened since the mid-1980s.

Over the past two decades, feminists have worked to formulate critical ways of understanding both historical and contemporary constructions of gender; such tools enable insights into ways in which notions of gender implicit in *Holy Feast and Holy Fast* rhetorically organize the text.[10] Such tools also create possibilities for writing histories of medieval gender capable of historicizing gender in *relation* to other engendered categories given as "natural" in medieval discourses and hitherto taken for granted by historians. Critical studies of medieval gender would use these tools to work simultaneously as histories of other foundational categories imagined in the invention of Europe, especially *Christendom* (*Christianitas*), *Corpus Christi,* and *the Jew* (as an anti-Semitic category), as they defined and redefined relations of the masculine and feminine.[11] To neglect intersections of gender and ethnic identities with historical formation of other medieval foundational categories is to run the risk of continuing to write histories of gender that inadvertently use gender and ethnic identities as a resource for producing *Europe* as the referent of history.

In my reading of *Holy Feast and Holy Fast,* I use gender as a theory of borders that enables us to talk about the historical construction and maintenance of sexual boundaries, both intra- and intercorporeal, through powerful historical processes of repetition and containment. Gendered notions of both the topography and the sex of corporeal interiority and exteriority have varied historically (we need think only of the variations of medieval Galenism), as have the ways in which genders are distributed across discourses, institutions, cultures, or any such unitary, bounded categories invented by historical subjects to contain gender and naturalize it. Theories of gender need to be, therefore, simultaneously histories of corporeal interiority and exteriority: sex, flesh, body, race, nature, discourse, and culture. It is not possible to write a history of gender that takes any of these categories as given in advance, assumed as "natural"; otherwise, the study would end up reinscribing the asymmetries and/or hierarchies of historic genders rather than understanding how gender is a historically variable effect of maintaining unitary categories for the purposes of "naturalizing" sexual difference. To subject the body and sex to critique does not negate them; rather, it opens them up as sites of historical and political debate.[12]

Such a critical understanding of gender can help us understand how foundational categories implicit in *Holy Feast and Holy Fast,* especially *culture* and *Christendom,* work to prevent the text both from rhetorically articulating identity and difference, especially with regard to its metaphor of the maternal, and from acknowledging the interplay of transference and empathy between historian, historical subjects, and feminist theory.[13] Bynum questions and revises the cultural anthropology of Victor Turner in her study, but she takes for granted his structurally inspired and implicitly foundational concept of culture.[14] A history of the structuralist influence on the concept of culture in anthropology is a long and complex one; suffice it to say here that this concept, which is both historical and gendered, has come to mean something natural. It is "a coherent *body* that lives and dies. Culture is enduring, traditional, structural (rather than contingent, syncretic, historical). Culture is a process of ordering, not of disruption."[15]

Such a theory of culture assumes boundaries rather than questioning their historical formation. It tends to posit culture as an organic plenitude and to analyze it as a bounded object, thereby reinforcing unexamined notions of inside and outside. The constitution of such a bounded object of study (whatever its internal complexity) then requires a complementary concept of liminality (developed by Turner) as a process for mediating the inside and the outside. Conceived as such, this notion of culture has avoided the study of the visualization processes historically at work in the production of the concept of culture as well as analysis of historical relations *between* the imaginary wholes of such posited cultures. A theory of liminality thus works to mystify the problems of the historical construction of interiority and exteriority. In a close reading of Turner's famous essay on Ndembu shamans, Michael Taussig has shown how its rhetoric engages liminality, not only in the narrative description of shamanistic practices, but in the overall flow of argument as well. Rather than marking a gap or tension between the magic under study and the act of writing, such liminal rhetoric appropriates Ndembu magic in the service of the European observer.[16] Turner thus writes as a shaman, and his ethnography becomes a form of magic.

Taussig has observed that, once an anthropologist writes himself as a shaman, a rhetorical collapse usually occurs between the participant-observer (the anthropologist) and the subject-informant (the shaman): "The subject addressed and the addressing of the subject become one."[17] This textual conflation of anthropologist and shaman punctuates a problem of marking difference in ethnographies informed by a bounded, unitary concept of culture. These ethnographies have promoted a kind of autocannibalism in which representation consumes difference, rather than producing it, in order to conserve the "primitive," grounded usually on the body of the female "primitive" (for the anthropologist) or the past (for the historian) as an imaginary, bounded, coherent entity.[18] "Synchronous, bounded but contiguous, and representational"—this string of adjectives, coupled with the metaphor of culture as a body, can be exchanged, uncannily, with dominant representations of the maternal today.[19]

The rhetorical problems attached to a structuralist concept of culture also trouble *Holy Feast and Holy Fast*. Bynum transfers Turner's anthropology to history and, in so doing, challenges his neglect of gender. She corrects Turner by adding women to his theory of liminality, but she fails to question the ahistorical frame of his cultural theory that could neglect gender so easily in the first place. By simply adding to the frame without questioning it, Bynum encounters rhetorical problems similar to those already discussed for Turner. Just as in Turner's work, readers of *Holy Feast and Holy Fast* encounter the rhetorical collapse of the subject addressed and the addressing of the subject. The collapse occurs most dramatically in Bynum's staging of the voices of female medieval mystics. The cultural unity in her study is not the "primitive," such as Turner's Ndembu, but a "past," that is, medieval Christendom. To maintain this concept of cultural unity, a typical symptom of structuralism, Bynum must be careful to distance this past from the present. She attacks "presentism" (p. 30)—the statement of historical problems in terms of issues of pressing modern concerns—both in the introduction to the book and within its chapters.

The subject addressed and the addressing subject collapse most markedly in chapter 5, which is devoted to food in the writings of women mystics. This chapter first strikes a distance from "modern sensibilities" that would read erotic metaphors in the writings of women mystics. According to Bynum, the reader must listen to the "voices" (p. 152) of these medieval women, not to their own voices. Once Bynum has established this distance, she shifts to "we," a we of historian and reader. The prose preserves the "we" even when it stages the threat of a "modern" interpretation: "Her [Hadewijch's] account of this meeting with God reads like a description of sexual orgasm (and it is only our modern sensibility that makes the suggestion a shocking one)" (p. 156). As the chapter progresses, the "we" comes to include the historical subjects as well. Prose circumscribes the historian, the reader, and the mystic as a "we": "Thus, to Hadewijch, the soul should strive not so much to rest in satiety and to suffer a deeper hunger beyond filling. For the truest satiety is the pain of desire; the truest repose is the horror of God's power. And all we attain—fullness or hunger—is the gift of Love" (p. 159).

Similar rhetorical devices are used to craft the story of Catherine of Genoa. Bynum chastises scholars who would wish to organize her biography around "turning points and neat stages" (p. 181), that is, according to stereotyped tropes of masculine moral development. Bynum then relates this important methodological issue in reading women's biographies to a critique of "presentism." By attaching a methodological concern to a critique of presentism, Bynum overdetermines it but, in so doing, manages to strike the distance needed between past and present. The distance, once taken, enables the "we" of the historian and reader to reassert itself. Collapse into the historical subject ensues: "Desire for God is hunger—insatiable hunger. The food that is God and the food that is neighbor are thus the nourishment we crave, inebriated yet unfilled" (p. 183).

The sharp divisions of past and present required by the structuralist rhetoric of *Holy Feast and Holy Fast* confront Bynum with the conundrum of establishing some means of relating to historical materials. A structuralist-like approach solves this dilemma by essentializing some human essence, in the case of *Holy Feast and Holy Fast, women* and *experience.* Because a structuralist rhetoric has precluded any historical connection of the present to the past, Bynum uses the maternal as the essence to forge a "natural" link. The requirements of the foundational categories implicit in the text thus reduce women to the maternal. The model of gender in *Holy Feast and Holy Fast* assumes that gender is an essence that appears prior to other categories and informs them, that the feminine mirrors, indeed reduces to, the female reproductive function, that the female body is the originary, foundational site of gender. Just as Taussig noted that the ordering of a structuralist anthropology often occurs on the body of the female "primitive," the ordering of a structural history in *Holy Feast and Holy Fast* occurs on an ahistorical, imagined body of the maternal.

Reading through the Maternal

Reading through that essential, ahistorical maternal of *Holy Feast and Holy Fast* posed challenges to its reviewers.[20] Many expressed uneasiness about the gendering of knowledge in the text without being able to articulate critically the rhetorical reasons for their confusion.[21] John Boswell, who wrote one of the earliest reviews, uncannily raised the question of shamanism. He asked how a reader could read the difference between a shaman and a saint, a distinction that he would use to separate Bynum's book from another volume under his review, Rudolph M. Bell's *Holy Anorexia.* According to Boswell, shamans are "natural"; they are sacred by virtue of innate characteristics that make them "different" from their surroundings. Saints, he contended, are holy through acts of will; by nature they are "not different." Boswell's struggle to distinguish shamanism can be read as an effort to disentangle the rhetorical collapse of saint, historian, and reader in *Holy Feast and Holy Fast.*

Other reviewers read anxiously, seemingly unable or unwilling to analyze the book's sources, whether that anxiety came from some unexamined revulsion for the subject matter or from the compounded effects of a structuralist rhetoric that involve the reader in a kind of autocannibalism, a "consumption of otherness," or both.[22] Maurice Keen anxiously asked how the reader can digest the myriad descriptions of women mystics fasting or feasting on noxious substances. He then listed eight examples of the very descriptions that for him "can be testing to the strength of the stomach." His ambivalence seemed, however, to be anticipated by Bynum, who alerts her readers to the contradictions they will encounter in reading her text: "If readers leave this book simply condemning the past as peculiar, I shall have failed" (p. 9). Or does her rhetoric succeed since she claims that she "repeatedly break[s] the flow by citing examples" to "convince modern readers of the decidedly bizarre behavior of some medieval women" (p. xv)?

The use of medieval Christendom as a unitary, bounded category in *Holy Feast and Holy Fast* also evoked anxiety. Some reviewers expressed their uneasiness indirectly by simply mentioning other cultures in a comparative vein. John Frecerro interrupted his review to mention others outside the Christian tradition, namely, Simone Weil and Gandhi. Boswell noted more directly that Bynum never addresses the "interaction of food, gender, ethic and culture at the level of whole religious systems," namely, medieval Islam and Judaism. His comments inspire the reader to wonder about our historic and contemporary fantasies of medieval Christendom. How did this cultural construct of *Christianitas* establish its sense of unity, and, crucially, what does *Christianitas* have to do with the construction of gender?

A review by Jack Goody most directly articulated a criticism of the structuralist categories of the text. Goody pointed out that, although Bynum writes with great insight about the polysemous nature of symbols in the past, she has little sympathy for their potential richness in the present. She and many of her sympathetic reviewers, who implicitly defend the structuralism of the book, regard the present as "impoverished." Goody claims that such a judgment "represents only a partial view of the climate of opinion." Goody also suggested that *culture* as used by Bynum is an *effect* of her structuralist approach and its effort to search for structures of thought that underlie not only "divergent expressions of individuals, groups and societies, but humanity itself." He cautioned that "doubts must remain about the universality of such an analysis, even within a culture, let alone among all the varied internal and national cultures and sub-cultures, *even* of Western Europe" (emphasis added). Goody's comments invite us to pause. Although he does not go so far as to question the disciplinary frame of knowledge that produces such a foundational notion of culture, he at least introduces the notion of divided cultures that can be extended to gender divided between the masculine and the feminine, to the past and present divided within itself, even to the divided empathy of the historian.[23]

No review I read directly questioned the way in which *Holy Feast and Holy Fast* reduces women to the maternal function or challenged the historicity of such a reduction. The uneasiness of the reviewers about this central issue of the book translated itself instead into requests for more context. Ann Carmichael wondered how secular contexts of food practices that were not dominated by women, such as secular medical advice on eating and purging in dietetic treatises, related to the gendering of food practices central to the book's thesis. Judith Brown found that the book failed to address a history of family life and child-rearing practices to justify its reliance on a model of mothering adopted from the work of Nancy Chodorow. This call to historicize maternity and nurturance received the most extended attention in the review by Hester Goodenough Gelber. Gelber asked to see the arguments linked to changing practices of nursing and wet-nursing in medieval Europe, practices that varied by the sex of the child, class, and region. Adding *more* context cannot, however, transform the essentialist move required by the structuralist frame of the text.[24]

The frame itself begs for transformation.[25] As a dominant disciplinary practice, structuralism has historically sought to constrain and conventionalize gender to conform to social practices, especially practices of social reproduction, and most notably kinship. Once we grant anatomy a history and it ceases to be a foundational category, then historians and theorists must think of how gender is performative, meaning that "there is no gender identity behind the expressions of gender; that identity is performatively constituted by the very 'expressions' that are said to be its results."[26] The performance of gender, historical and contemporary, both enacts through repetition and challenges through the very impossibility of perfect repetition ("getting gender right") the rigid boundaries sanctioned between culturally constructed notions of *inside* and *outside* that make *culture* structurally possible. Such imperfect repetition of gender performance also both contains and questions the rigid divides between the real, the imaginary, and the symbolic, the spaces in which much structuralist-inspired theory imagines the law, language, and sexual difference.

No foundational category can ever fully frame a text, however. There are always places where the differences within the category interrupt the desires to frame a unity, to argue from an essence. Once again, the reading practices of the reviewers of *Holy Feast and Holy Fast* leave clues to gaps in the text. What do the reviewers overlook? What do they fail to mention? Of the reviews I read, none commented specifically on the thirty plates and frontispiece lavishly illustrating the text. Only Copeland praised Bynum for her ability to move "easily into visual discourses as well." Bynum, too, remains strangely silent about many of the plates. Although she deals explicitly with the problems of reading hagiographic materials (p. 5 and chap. 3), she does not discuss her methodology for reading iconographic evidence (p. 81). She refers to the plates in only three places and reads them conventionally and presentistically for their content, as if visual images do not engender power-charged relations among visual communities but only reflect them.[27] A demand for a plate-by-plate exegesis, like the desire of some reviewers for more context for maternity, would not, however, resolve the problem of the plates in *Holy Feast and Holy Fast.* A reading of the patterns of selection of plates can render visible the foundational category of medieval Christendom invisibly at work in *Holy Feast and Holy Fast.* An infrareflexive reading of this invisibility can begin to articulate the women the text makes visible with the fearful interconnections with invisibility.

Engendering Christendom/Blood Libel

Twenty of thirty plates and the frontispiece of *Holy Feast and Holy Fast* date from the period 1450–1585. The majority of these late medieval artworks come from German and Dutch masters. The earlier illustrations depict works mostly by Italian masters of the fourteenth century. The plates thus mark temporal, regional, and institutional differences (some of the later material is for hospitals, convents, and cathedrals, institutions with different audiences). Rather than hold these contrasting regional, chronological, and institutional contexts, as suggested by the selection of plates, in tension with the construction of gender, Bynum collapses such differences into sexual difference: "Indeed, recent scholarship suggests that differences between the sexes over-ride all other factors (such as chronology or social and economic status) in shaping women's piety" (p. 26). Attention to these differences, Bynum further asserts, has hitherto suppressed the study of correlations of Eucharistic devotion with gender.[28]

Bynum calls this sexual difference *gender,* but for her *gender* carries the more restricted sense "woman." Even though chapter 4, "Food in the Lives of Women Saints," is organized by region (the Low Countries, France, Germany, and Italy), the essentialized notion of gender reduces discussion of difference to sexual difference: "Despite the suggestion of recent scholars that the nature of female sanctity changed between 1200 and 1500 and displayed different patterns in the north and south, the themes found in Low Country spirituality, from Mary of Oignes to Lidwina of Schiedam, echo throughout fourteenth and fifteenth-century Europe" (p. 129).

My reading starts with the gaps of regionality and chronology suggested by the assemblage of plates as a way into the breaches within the imaginary whole of Christendom. The blood that flows in the plates serves as the medium of my reading. This blood marks a crisis of exteriority and interiority in the construct of Christendom. The gaps and breaches through which blood could seep and about which Christians expressed great anxiety contest the historical formation of Christendom as a natural structure as well as rhetorical practices that would perpetuate the study of gender uncritically within Christendom.[29]

Blood was a central food image to the medieval female mystics studied by Bynum, and the bleeding Christ forms the devotional matter of many of the plates.[30] Blood also set the boundaries of marital exchange among medieval Christians; consanguinity measured exogamy and endogamy. Not surprisingly, "blood was in general a more public and social [religious] symbol than bread, as well as a more ambivalent symbol" (p. 178). Difficult to control because of its fluidity, blood could seep through the boundaries of interiority and exteriority instituted by Christendom. It could mix among Christians and those Others constructed as exterior to Christendom: Jews, homosexuals, and prostitutes.

Anxieties about fluid boundaries began to surface in twelfth- and thirteenth-century Europe, as Europeans invented the unitary construct of Christendom. Christians began to fantasize intensely about blood libel, that is, the ritual murder and bleeding of Christians, usually Christian boys, by Jews, usually male. Christians also began to ascribe acts of ritual cannibalism and host desecration to Jews. By the thirteenth century in certain German territories of northern Europe, Eucharistic shrines began to appear at sites where Jews were massacred, and incidences of accusation and prosecution peaked in these areas over the late fifteenth century, the time and the provenance of many of the plates of *Holy Feast and Holy Fast.*[31]

Bynum cites the work of Lionel Rothkrug, who has listed known examples of German shrines erected at sites associated with anti-Semitic incidents, and she also recognizes the connection between Eucharistic devotion and anti-Semitism (p. 64). *Jews* and *anti-Semitism* are not, however, indexed in *Holy Feast and Holy Fast.* Does this gap help a reading of the gaps suggested by the pattern of the plates? I want to suggest that it is more than a coincidence that outbreaks of accusations of ritual cannibalism and host desecration peaked in the later fifteenth century in areas of Germany from which many of the plates have been chosen. The time and place of the plates thus mark what *Holy Feast and Holy Fast* cannot, for reasons of its structural frame, fully acknowledge, that is, the implications of the relations of anti-Semitism to Eucharistic devotion. The book is thus condemned to repeating and reinscribing a fantastic moment of the European imaginary in its failure to include the excluded Others in historical analysis.[32] A historic study of medieval gender interrupts this foundational category of *Christianitas* by asking how a historical construction of gender in medieval Christendom was *simultaneously* a construction of other differences. I can briefly offer here two examples of such discursive conjuncture where anti-Semitism, anxieties about blood and host desecration, and women mystics, the central subject of *Holy Feast and Holy Fast,* appear to converge. These two illustrations suggest some sense of the trouble of making "medieval women mystics" visible in our histories.

My first example asks us to consider an early accusation of ritual cannibalism made against medieval Jews. In 1235, thirty-four Jews of Fulda were killed for allegedly murdering five young Christian boys for their blood. The incident occurred during troubled political times in the Mainz region. The papacy had organized preaching against heretics and for the Crusades. Conrad of Marburg proved to be one of the most vigorous preachers in the region. Reputedly responsible for burning many heretics between 1231 and 1234, he even began to accuse important nobles of heresy. In a noted papal bull, *Vox in Rama* (June 1233), which heightened tensions, Gregory IX addressed the problem of Eucharistic heresies in the Mainz area by drawing on fantasies of Eucharistic pollution. Conrad was murdered at the end of July 1234, over a year before the first accusation of ritual cannibalism made against local Jews. These accusations, however, need to be read against several years of powerful crusade against heresy. Conrad of Marburg also served as the spiritual director for Elizabeth of Hungary, one of the fasting mystics studied in *Holy Feast and Holy Fast.* Conrad wrote early material on Elizabeth's life, and, on her death (17 November 1231), he tried to organize her speedy canonization, which took place in May 1235, approximately one year after Conrad's death. When Conrad of Marburg died, at his request he was buried next to the shrine of Elizabeth. Bynum writes that the "importance of her stern confessor, Conrad of Marburg, in inducing her obsession with food is impossible to assess at this distance" (p. 135). The staging of the early textual materials of Elizabeth's life and canonization process need to be brought together for their bearing on a complex, multifocal discourse of purity and pollution involving the Eucharist and the problems of cannibalism and cannibalizing authority around the Eucharist. Who is eating whose body, and what or whom is engendering problems of visibility and invisibility around the Eucharist?[33]

The example of Conrad and Elizabeth concentrates on textual conjunctures, local stories of ritual cannibalism, papal bulls, and materials for the canonization process. My second illustration (fig. 9) offers an example of how *visual* discourses joined anxieties over the circulation of blood in "Western Christendom." It is a predella designed by the Florentine painter Paolo Uccello for the altar of the Confraternity of Corpus Domini in Urbino in 1467–68. The predella offers clues to where the trail of blood depicted in many of the plates of *Holy Feast and Holy Fast* might flow.[34] Uccello executed the predella just as Urbino, under the influence of Franciscan preaching, planned the opening of its Monte de Pietà (1468), a lending fund, to break what was considered to be a Jewish monopoly on credit. Six scenes from the predella tell a story of the desecration of the Host by Jews. The story, based on a Paris legend, had circulated in Europe since the late thirteenth century and became a popular source of drama in the fifteenth. In Uccello's version, a Christian woman exchanges a Host with a Jewish pawnbroker for some coins, although, in the written versions, she redeems a cloak. The pawnbroker heats the Host in a pan as his wife and two children look on. In miraculous authentication of itself, blood runs from the Host all over the tiled floor of the room and runs out onto the street. Alerted by this bloody rivulet, soldiers appear at the house of the Jewish family. The pope and other clerics restore the Host to the altar in a liturgical procession. The woman who exchanged the host repents before her hanging. The Jewish family, husband, wife, and two children, are burned alive, a punishment usually reserved for heretics and witches. In the last panel, angels and devils dispute over the soul of the Christian woman.

The predella narrates a story of pollution that brings together a construction of the feminine and religious difference at the very altar table where priests celebrated the Eucharist. A woman initiates the exchange, the media of which, in most versions of the story, are finery and the Host, although the predella depicts coins.[35] The host bleeds miraculously over the floor and into the street in a fantasy of excess that echoes the scholastic fear of excess in usury. Male members of the community, including soldiers and clerics, work to restore order and purity. The final status of purity and pollution remains in suspension to the viewer of the predella. The debate between the angels and the devils for the soul of the repentant Christian woman invites viewers to project their own ending to this customary debate and opens up the anxious possibility that the process of pollution could be set in motion again.

The Uccello predella visually narrates anti-Semitic stories that coincided with the intensification of persecution of Jews in Germany and Italy.[36] Recent work on ritual murder trials in Germany by Po-chia Hsia[37] demonstrates how the more virulent accusations of blood libel began to fuse with stories of host desecration to create a discourse of blood and sacramental pollution. The incidences of ritual murder accusations, compiled by Hsia, correlate in interesting ways with the growth and geographic expansion of female piety in Europe.

The popular media of broadsheets and printed ballads, which had begun to circulate in the later fifteenth century, spectacularized stories of ritual murder and host desecration at the same time as they advertised Christian pilgrimage centers, such as Wilsnack in Germany, dedicated to the Holy Blood.[38] The effusions of blood from the Suffering Christ, a holy excess of blood that repeats itself frequently in the plates of *Holy Feast and Holy Fast,* must be read with other coexistent iconography depicting desecrated hosts bleeding excessively at sites of pollution. An anxiety about blood, consanguinity, and pollution expressed itself in the later fifteenth century in certain areas of Germany and

Figure 9. Paolo Uccello, *Profanation of the Host* (1467–68). From Palazzo Ducale, Urbino. Courtesy Art Resource NY.

consolidated itself in Italy with the preaching of Bernardino of Siena (1380–1444). The majority of plates illustrating *Holy Feast and Holy Fast* date from this period of intense, popular propagandizing about sacred and polluted blood.

In the medieval Christian economy of exteriority, prostitutes and homosexuals shared affinities with Jews. The image of Jews as draining blood and devouring flesh became blurred with those of prostitutes, who were considered parasites on cities and their food supplies. Prostitutes thus make an exception to the universal association of medieval women with food preparation argued by Bynum.[39] Even within medieval Christendom, not all women could be reduced to the maternal function; in fact, those regarded as parasites marked instead an antimaternal function. Prostitutes were also commonly assumed to be sterile, and this fantasy linked them with discourses about the sterility of homosexuality. The trope of sterility linked them further to discourses about usury; scholastics regarded money as fruitless, and its sterility came to be associated with homosexual intercourse.[40] The blood of Eucharistic devotion thus negotiated complicated borders in which this sacred fluid could seep into an exteriority composed of Jews, prostitutes, homosexuals, and a symbolic economy of usury and parasitism.[41] Amid such anxieties, it is not surprising that the chalice, containing the Blood of Christ, disappeared from the communion service for the medieval laity.[42]

The flow of blood across juridical and iconographic spaces has blurred the boundaries between Christendom and the Others of its exterior. How does such a reading render problematic any unitary notions of bodies within medieval Christendom, especially the Body of Christ and the bodies of medieval women mystics? The symbolic expulsion of the Jews by members of Christendom produced in the Christian imaginary a fantastic excluded body of the Jew. The fantasy of exclusion and the boundary it creates, however, can be only a fantasy. The excluded body of the Other returns to haunt the pure body of the "interior." The Host, the "most important image of Gothic Europe," served as the site of haunting by the excluded body of the Other, the Jew. The haunting came to perform itself in the fantastical grotesque hybrid body of Christ in the Christian imaginary.[43]

Popular rituals that grew up around the medieval celebrations of Corpus Christi enacted an awareness of the hybridity that haunted the Host. The carnival processions of monsters and giants that preceded the liturgical procession on the feast of Corpus Christi recognized the problem of body doubles, the differences within dominant European constructions of kinship and theological constructions of sacred bodies. Before considering some of the problems involved in constructing mystical gender in such a complicated, contested corporeal world, it is worth reviewing some thoughts of Mikhail Bakhtin's regarding grotesque bodies:

> All these convexities and orifices have a common characteristic; it is within them that the confines between bodies and between body and the world are overcome: there is an exchange and an interorientation. This is why the main events of the life of the grotesque body, the acts of the bodily drama, take place in this sphere. Eating, drinking, defecation, and other elimination . . . as well as copulation, pregnancy, dismemberment, swallowing up by another body—all these acts are performed on the confines of the body and the outer world, or on the confines of the old and new body.[44]

The Host can be regarded as a hybrid sacred object that served as a relay point between religion and magic, purity and pollution, theological and popular devotion, clergy and layperson, urban and rural, rich and poor, the masculine and the feminine, the insider and the outsider, Christian and Jew. As medievalists study the regulation of its hybridity through gender relations, they will contribute to a history of hybridity and its different modalities and, in so doing, build an important historical bridge with current postcolonial theories of hybridity.[45]

The Eucharist was good to think with, and it guaranteed the symbolic order of medieval Europe.[46] It was both a "classical" body in the Bakhtinian sense, elevated, static, and monumental, and a "grotesque" body, broken, bleeding, excessive, maternal, paternal, a body that upset any fixed gender binary, a fluid body that troubled any container. It was a body that was distributed across different—and noncommensurate—textual, material, and visual realms. Christians fantasized intensely both the pollution and the purification of the Eucharist because of its ambivalent position as a border phenomenon.

The host gave occasion to symbolic cannibalism as the church incorporated the host into its own body. With the promulgation of the Eucharist and the doctrine of transubstantiation, important switches in naming bodies began to occur. The host had been known as *corpus mysticum* and the church as *corpus verum.* The church cannibalized the Eucharist, and the host became *corpus verum,* the church *corpus mysticum.* The signified had become the signifier.[47]

How to authenticate the signified that had become signifier during the twelfth century? Notions of visibility and invisibility came to be redefined and reengendered. Relics and the Eucharist came to be presented in new ways. Beginning in the early thirteenth century, ostensories, crystal cylinders in which a relic rested, began to appear, marking a shift away from the presentation of relics in reliquaries of the type that mimicked by their design the physical form of the body part they housed, such as a head or a hand. These older reliquaries are called *talking reliquaries,* and the very contrast of the generic names for these two types of reliquaries—talking reliquaries and ostensories—marks a shift toward visibility: the contents of the reliquary itself must be visible to guarantee its existence.[48]

Hans Belting has argued that the reliquary became the image of the relic and that images could become relics in the thirteenth century, an important time for the revaluation of images and issues of visibility in medieval Europe.[49] If the Eucharist came to signify the church, if the hybrid grotesque body of the Host unstably marked the boundary phenomenon of exclusion and incorporation that produced the fantastic identity of Western Christendom, if relic and image were exchangeable, who or what could guarantee signification? New solutions to problems of authenticity and questions about originals and copies emerged in the discourse of relics in the late twelfth and early thirteenth centuries: "The imagination becomes inspired by material proofs which existed in the East linking the reality of the relic with the evidence of the photograph."[50] Belting argues for this startling and suggestive statement on the basis of controversy over the authenticity of Veronica's veil. First a relic, it assumed the status of an image, an image-relic. The image was that of Christ imprinted on the veil of Veronica.

This reading of Christian bodies, especially Corpus Christi, grows more complicated. The issues raised so far cannot be resolved in an essay of this type (itself a hybrid by virtue of its reading practice). Suffice it to note that the changing status of relics and their presentation makes it clear that the metaphoric nature of the body as referent was undergoing change. What guarantees the imaginary body of Christendom as a referent, and how would that body be gendered? The problem of the body seems to lie in the space between this metonymic "image-relic," a space that poses problems of intervisuality in Western Christendom. Who could be the "photograph" of the Host? as Belting provocatively puts it. Who could be its authenticator? What possibilities of gender and mimesis does the image-relic pose?

That set of questions bears on the historiographic problem of making visible medieval female mystics and their "texts." If we have only the textual effects of their practices, distributed across a range of genres with complicated authorship, how can we read these texts? The work of Bynum has already cautioned us not to embody these texts metaphorically in the form of historical female hysterics or anorectics. My reading of *Holy Feast and Holy Fast* has also urged us not to embody the textual effects of the practices of female mystics as a maternal function, as Bynum does. We can, however, figure these textual effects as performances of gender, mindful that the access to the body as referent occurs only imperfectly in the performance, that there is no mystical body prior to the performance.[51]

Performing Veronica's Veil

The problem of authentication, most immediately discernible in the changing status of relics and images, impinged on fundamental epistemological questions regarding the power-charged relations of the visible to the invisible, the masculine to the feminine. The shifting status of the real and the imaginary in visual images occurring over the twelfth century began to reorganize vision around the text, with the result that the text gave rise to an invisible inner life. *Mere* or "real" physicality became equated with the "oral, the popular, the inauthentic, the disreputable."

Brian Stock has succinctly described this epistemological shift: "Physicality, therefore, is ambivalent; popular culture utilizes physical symbolism without an interpretative context; sacramental theology places the same tangible objects in a framework of learned culture."[52] Relics could become images, images relics, in an exchange that required physicality to become a resource for textuality, and textuality produced physicality as an effect. The proliferation of texts about and, much less often, authored by holy women in Western Europe at this time may be usefully considered within these epistemological shifts clustering around authentication, ambivalent physicality, and discursive realignments of visibility and invisibility. This proliferation correlates with the gendering of the oral and popular as feminine, a feminine with positive *and* negative valences. As this composite of communication, physicality, and value came to be gendered feminine, learned culture began to recontain and reframe the feminine textually. The number of hagiographic texts devoted to female saints increased. Thus, what textual culture produced as an effect it also recontained.[53]

The dispersion of holy women across hagiographic texts, mostly male authored, then makes more historical sense given the construction and relations of the visible and the invisible, the physical and the textual. As Miri Rubin has aptly remarked of thirteenth-century mystics in her excellent study of the politics of the formation of the feast of Corpus Christi, "We know little that comes directly from these women, and yet the material is rich; we should, therefore, talk not of experience but of the relation between representations of such experience."[54]

Authenticity relied on this relay between physicality and textuality, yet it was a highly ambivalent relay. In such ambivalent conditions, the authenticator of the Host—"the photograph," to use Belting's image—has to have aura, which is the sign of the unique value of an authentic object. Aura was difficult to construct in a time known for its "crisis of overproduction" of images.[55] There can be no replica of aura; aura is tied to the body.[56] At this juncture in the crisis of representation and authentication, certain pious women began to perform within this gap of physicality and textuality, authentic and photograph, and their performance worked as a complicated visual system. They began to produce aura for the Corpus Christi.

Just as learned theologians produced physicality as an effect of textuality, pious women could produce textuality as an effect of physicality. Their performance provided a crucial hinge that could join object with interpretation and the tangible with the intangible. The performance of this hinge function was gendered feminine, not because of anatomy or maternity, but because of the gendering effects of dominant learned culture in this period, which conflated the oral and popular with the feminine.[57]

The bodily practices of holy women, especially their food practices, may be read as both brilliant and violent glosses on this crisis of representation in medieval Christendom.[58] These women produced a kind of textual tatoo on the surface of their bodies; the surface of their bodies produced imprints.[59] At the same time, their bodily interiors became the site of intense physicality. In so reversing interiority and exteriority, the two different "bodies" in the medieval model of corporeality, they marked them as relational terms. The many incidents of postmortem investigations of the body cavities of such women, referred to in *Holy Feast and Holy Fast,* testify to the effect of this reversal. Paradoxically, through their food practices holy women produced an exteriorized interior: the "invisible," interior, feminine, appeared on the exterior or "masculine" surface, according to medieval typologies of the body. By rendering visible the feminine interior through the signs of bodily practices, such performances could make aura visible, thus producing the "photograph" necessary to authenticate the Host. The invisible feminine body transformed itself into a utilizable textual form: "The oral element thus survived the utilization of writing and was itself transformed."[60] Within this historical dynamic of gender, the Host functions as a relic, and the exteriorized "body" of the holy feminine performance serves as devotional image. Together, they performed as an image-relic of medieval visual communities. Their performance reminds us to consider medieval textual communities as co-constructed with medieval visual communities.

The exteriorization of the feminine on the surface of the holy woman guaranteed the Host a visual identity. In this material performance of Veronica's veil, the Host served as veil, the exteriorized feminine of the body served as the imprint, and the hagiographic framing of this performance by the clerics who authored the many lives of these holy women served as the "being imprinted on the imprint."[61] Just as devotional images of the thirteenth century depicted in tension object illusionism (the naturalism or unnaturalism of an object) and the subject's expressive power, the performance of these holy women marked disjunctures, discontinuities, tensions in textual exchanges. Only gradually would these "two demands of mimesis"—"naturalism" and "expression"—be aligned with the emergence of new optical laws of painting in the fifteenth century.[62] The accounts of such holy women enacted problems of mimesis and a crisis of representation.

It is important for historians not to judge these performances. Since the more severe forms of bodily practices, especially fasting, actually resulted in death, they tempt us to identify ourselves with issues of violence and victimage or with romantic tropes of female heroines. Contemporary feminist theory of performance can help us think about these historical practices in other ways. This complex body of theory regards gender performance as a political, ethical means of disrupting normative, ontological discourses of sexual difference. Feminist performance (in theory and practice), perhaps better called *countermimesis* to distance it from notions of imitation, enacts the nonidentity of anatomical sex and gender identity. A feminist performance theory questions the conventionalized notions of corporeal interiority and exteriority:

> Such acts, gestures, enactments, generally construed, are *performative* in the sense that the essence or identity that they otherwise purport to express are *fabrications* manufactured and sustained through corporeal signs and other discursive means. That the gendered body is performative suggests that it has no ontological status apart from the various acts which constitute its reality. This also suggests that if that reality is fabricated as an interior essence, that very interiority is an effect and function of a decidedly public and social discourse, the public regulation of fantasy through the surface politics of the body,

the gender border control that differentiates inner from outer, and so institutes the "integrity" of the subject.[63]

The kind of feminist performance I am speaking of here puts into question the very notion of original and natural identity and also helps historicize the violence involved in conflating anatomy, gender identity, and gender performance. The brilliant performances of these "hunger artists" disrupted cultural notions of interiority and exteriority and marked the discontinuities in textual exchange, in the service of authenticating the fantasy of an original and a natural identity, the Corpus Christi. Their performance helped guarantee the "classic" Host, to guarantee the fantasy of an "original," an authentication that helped contain the contradictions of the identity of Western Christendom. These performances engaged the grotesque hybrid body of the Eucharist and, in that engagement, profoundly challenged dominant representations of learned culture and kept relations of oral, physical, and local in tension for the learned culture. That learned culture could also recontain these performances to cannibalize their aura, and its writings are riddled with the intertextuality of the complicated textual exchange at work to contain the crisis of representation. This historical performance reminds us today of the high stakes of gender as performance. In the service of some naturalized notion of an original, medieval, modern, or postmodern, performance can kill.[64]

Performance/Fusion and Medieval History

> The metaphor of the mother does not complete her.
>
> —Drucilla Cornell, *Beyond Accommodation*[65]

Aura locates itself in the presence of the body. It also paradoxically requires distance, "however close it may be," and the contemplation of that distance.[66] Medieval holy women could produce aura through their bodily practices to embody the fact that there can be no replica; thus, they guaranteed the Host. Did medieval historians and their audiences cannibalize this historical aura to guarantee the visibility of medieval Christendom as a moment of plenitude, a moment to which our allegedly impoverished present cannot measure?

To think about this problem, I return to issues raised at the opening of this essay regarding the collapse of historian, reader, and historical subject at critical moments of *Holy Feast and Holy Fast.* To return to this rhetorical problem would seem gratuitous did it not help us with some fundamental problems of historical representation germane to the writing of women's history and studies of historical gender. The rhetoric molds the text into the narrative power of history as *dérèlection.* Like *essentialism, dérèlection* is a term with manifold meanings and charges in contemporary feminist theory. For the purposes of this discussion, I define it as the inability to write about the feminine as other than an imagined unity of the maternal function and the mother-daughter relation.[67] Bynum frames *Holy Feast and Holy Fast* in terms of mothers and daughters, and her prose literally embodies that relation as fusion. Historian, reader, and historical subject fuse rhetorically in the prose. Bynum's rhetorical practices, which reinscribe a historical fantasy of the feminine as maternal, cannot allow for the historical or contemporary problem of studying *both* separation and connection of daughters and mothers or, in the metaphor of this essay, their fluctuating visibility. Such studies belie the often-repeated fantasy of the maternal function as a form of symbiosis and a paradise.

Holy Feast and Holy Fast thus cannot escape its own presentism as much as it distances itself from it: "Thus recent work on medieval women has tended to have either presentist issues or male issues built in" (p. 30). How could the entanglement of this book in presentism be otherwise unless the practices of history as representation are questioned? History writing collaborates rhetorically in preserving the process of *dérèlection* by moralizing its rhetorical practices as the authority of experience:

> Experience is at once always already an interpretation *and* something that needs to be interpreted. What counts as experience is neither self-evident nor straightforward; it is always contested, and always therefore political. The study of experience, therefore, must call into question its originary status in historical explanation. This will happen

when historians take as their project *not* the reproduction and transmission of knowledge said to be arrived at through experience, but the analysis of the production of that knowledge itself. Such an analysis would constitute a genuinely nonfoundational history, one which retains its explanatory power and its interest in change but does not stand on or reproduce naturalized categories.[68]

My pause at the collapse of historian, reader, and historical subject can also guide us to problems encountered in the pedagogy of teaching *Holy Feast and Holy Fast.* This book has galvanized and polarized my undergraduates and graduate students in a way that few books have in my gender studies courses. Discussions have often led to charged quarrels in seminar. I interpret these quarrels as enacting political problems in contemporary academic culture (still predominantly coded as white, heterosexual, middle class, and male) in engaging the politics of identification as they relate historically to positioning the maternal function in the cultural work of reading, writing, and teaching. Depending on popular but often unacknowledged attitudes toward fusion (and much theory echoes these popular attitudes), readers may regard the collapse of writer, reader, and historical subject as good—a celebration of the maternal and a return to paradise lost. Or they may experience the rhetorical entanglements as bad, a sign of disorder, a failure to differentiate, a form of psychosis (as Julia Kristeva would argue). The quarrels go unresolved and repetitively flare up because *Holy Feast and Holy Fast* enacts a process of fusion rhetorically without consciously opening a space in the text where this political and historical problem of fusion could be redescribed and replayed in political and ethical ways.

My reading of blood prompted by the "invisibility" of the plates of *Holy Feast and Holy Fast* has sought to open up a space between the text and its frame and intimate that the subject addressed and the addressing subject are not one, that these subjects are divided between themselves. By tracing the flow of blood across historically constructed categories, I have striven to displace the overdetermined aspects of the book's structuralism and its reinscription of the very exclusions in relation to which medieval genders were maintained. The fact that the plates were uncannily invisible to reviewers suggests to me that they do the dream work of *Holy Feast and Holy Fast* and, in so doing, warn us of the dangers of the ongoing project of dreaming the Middle Ages and reengendering Europe as a foundational category, nostalgically and romantically, as our tropes for reading the Middle Ages are wont to instruct us.[69]

Where the invisibility of the plates comes into contact with the historiographic project of making medieval female mystics visible, there emerges the space where those things that were divided, often violently—the exterior Jew, the interior Christian, the visible and the invisible, the authentic and the copy, the masculine and the feminine—fearfully connect. The joining of those things divided, as urged here, does not have as its goal the repair of the past or the fabrication of some new synthesis. This fearful interconnectedness disconnects the space of autocannibalism, both historical and historiographic. Such interconnectedness can help us appreciate the need for a transformative ethic for medieval gender studies of the sort that Toni Morrison has figured so magnificently and performatively in her novel *Beloved:* "It was not a story to pass on."[70]

Virtual Loops

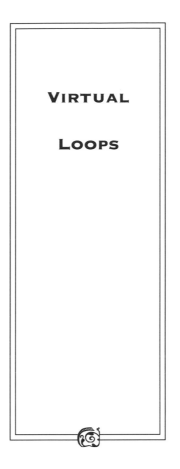

Humanist History and the Haunting of Virtual Technologies

Problems of Memory and Rememoration

We are contemplating the arising shape of a New World.
—Michael Benedikt, *Cyberspace*[1]

Watch out for worlds behind you.
—Velvet Underground, "Sunday Morning"[2]

The New World of Cyberspace

Scientists and humanists have celebrated the science fiction of William Gibson, especially his trilogy *Neuromancer, Count Zero,* and *Mona Lisa Overdrive,* as a postmodern vision of space for a posthumanist world.[3] In his world populated by artificial intelligence entities, vodou gods, off-planet Rastafarians, punk gangs, cloned ninja, and Euro-American capitalists, Gibson emplots a cyberspatial Benneton. His now famous, if not overcited, description imagines cyberspace as "a consensual hallucination . . . a graphic representation of data abstracted from the banks of every computer in the human system . . . unthinkable complexity . . . lines of light ranged in the nonspace of the mind and constellations of data."[4] Experts developing the hardware and software for cyberspace, whom Gibson's writings have also inspired, anticipate this virtual technology as a "New World." Michael Benedikt, an architect and chair of the first conference on cyberspace held in May 1990 at the University of Texas, Austin, so dubbed it, seemingly without irony: "We are contemplating the arising shape of a New World."[5] One of the first issues of *Mondo 2000*, a self-declared *Whole Earth Catalog* for virtual reality, featured essays on colonizing cyberspace and quoted Jaron Lanier, CEO of VPL Research (a company dedicated to virtual technologies) as saying: "Columbus was probably the last person to behold so much usable and unclaimed real estate (or unreal estate) as these cybernauts have discovered."[6] These metaphors of the New World and virtual colonization verge on a kind of technocamp where "the reality is the pleasure of the unreality."[7]

This campy mimicry folds along a fault line of an overdetermined history that, mantra-like, the science and fiction of virtual reality cannot stop from repeating: New World, Columbus. "At once resemblance and menace," the dual nature of such mimicry urged me as a reader to ask what the virtual technologies of *Mondo 2000* might have to do with the colonial technologies brought to *Insula Hyspana*, or *Mondo 1492*.[8] To read along this fault line is to ask how virtual technologies deterritorialize the "historical" New World and reterritorialize it in cyberspace. Newly emerging tensions between real and virtual space produced by virtual technologies can be good for historians to think with. A study of the specific ways in which an "Old New World" haunts the "New New World" can, paradoxically, help us "rememorate" histories of colonization, still untold, even after a time lag of five hundred years.[9]

Science fiction and travel writing encounter each other in the hybrid genre of Gibson's trilogy. As the trilogy makes its way in cyberspace, it gets lost. The ways in which it loses its way trace the discursive powers of the historical space it invokes as it deterritorializes. I call this space, not by the familiar name adopted for the Columbian quincentennial—the *space of encounter*—but by a productive, if infrequently used, critical term, the *space of terror*.[10] Memory, for Gibson, marks the site of reterritorialization and deterritorialization: "On the most basic level, computers in my books are simply a metaphor for human memory: I'm interested in the hows and whys of memory, the ways it defines who and what we are, in how easily memory is subject to revision."[11] He makes sure, however, that memory never encounters remembering. Like a well-trained humanist, Gibson separates memory from history in his trilogy and confines history to the archive.[12] When characters need to learn some history in cyberspace, they access their cyberdeck for an encyclopedia-like entry on a desired topic. History exists in Gibson's cyberspace as facts, dates, information in dead storage. Critics of humanist history will recognize its *archival* discipline at work in the trilogy's confinement and ordering of historical knowledge to a fixed place. Indeed, archives once under the historical purview of the state can exist as "primitive ice" in cyberspace.[13]

Humanist history deterritorializes memory as re-membering and reterritorializes it as archive. It has served as the institutional discipline of memory, marking and re-marking who is remembered, what is remembered, and in what way. In deterritorializing memory, history then produces humanist memory as an object, an imprinted image locatable in its fixity, recoverable in its plenitude, at the same time as such history produces the space of terror as its space-off. This foundational enterprise continues to dominate academic and popular history in the United States and Europe, even in so-called deconstructive texts: "For all the talk of giving voice to the forgotten of history, to the oppressed, to the marginal, it is of course painfully obvious that the screen onto which these voices are projected is already fixed—and that it is the screen—not the voices, where the greatest resistance lies."[14]

This essay reads the deterritorialization of history and the reterritorialization of memory in the cyberspace of Gibson's trilogy. In her studies of science fiction, Donna Haraway has shown us how a reading is also a rewriting, a gesture toward "transnational, intercultural, feminist literacy."[15] Mary Louise Pratt has taught us the importance of rewriting travel books as an intervention "to avoid simply reproducing the dynamics of possession and innocence."[16] My reading of the trilogy rewrites it in order to re-member it for histories that tell stories in between the Old New World and the New New World of cyberspace, in the nonlinear time lag between 1492 and 1992. This rememorative remembering I call *cyborg history* to mark its temporal disjunctures, its spatial incommensurabilities, and the material hybridity of its historical desire.[17]

The Space of Terror: Humanist/Virtual[18]

Humanist history has long and proudly claimed that it speaks for the dead at the same time that it has disavowed the historical corpses produced in its space-off, that is, in the "anthropological" world of colonies. These ghosts return to haunt humanist history, which communicates with them through séances held in archives. Gibson's trilogy finds among its ghosts a common ground with humanist history. Ghosts and mummies abound both in and out of cyberspace. This cyborg history of the trilogy will open, not with a séance, but with a conjuring of the most beloved of humanist artifacts, the occasion for most séances, a historical document, in the form of a printed and illustrated letter from Christopher Columbus. The letter circulated widely in Europe in 1493. In it, Columbus wrote of the New World as paradise: "It is a desirable land, and once seen, is never to be relinquished."[19] The travel set in motion by Columbian desire remapped the mental geographies of medieval Europe. It displaced the heavenly city of Jerusalem, once centrally located on the map, as travel transformed from something religious and mercantile to something scientific and representational.[20] By the seventeenth century, space itself had become the European index of travel, rather than a relic or some rare spice. As "scientific travelers" of Europe encountered "primitive" humans as well as the ruins of past civilizations in Egypt and Greece, they went one step further in their travel science and spatialized time by cordoning off "primitive" regions and equating them with tradition. Tradition could henceforth be mapped onto space and be contained there.

Once time and space were used as resources to divide off the world into civilization and tradition, the boundaries had to be carefully guarded. Europeans fashioned and then institutionalized *humanist history* to stand guard. Time became empty and homogeneous in order to deny its heterogeneity, to deny that time is "the impossibility of an identity fixed by a place." Even the dead were not safe from border patrol—the work of the historian was to "quiet the dead."[21] The task of spatializing time and delimiting the virtual spaces of past, present, and future required, not only technologies of history and anthropology, but also bodily practices. When the anthropologist encountered the "primitive," when the historian encountered the "past," they actually did so in a coeval space where, according to the logic of their disciplines, there could, however, be room and time for only one. The logic demanded, then, that one devour the other in order to restore this coinhabited space to a fantastic, undivided unity. Historians and anthropologists discovered that the past is good to eat, as archive or as living others who can be archivalized through photography, measurements, and textualization. Eat up the past and the primitive, and one can set oneself in its place. One can claim that "there have never been people here." Cannibalism is a process that consumes otherness; it emerged as another effect of humanist history. Cannibalism "functioned as the supple sign for construing reality, the caption point without which otherwise free-floating signifiers wandered off into space as so many disassembled limbs and organs of a corpus."[22]

The violence of such cannibalizing historical and anthropological desire must conceal itself to remain humanist, human. Undiscoverable things about "discovery," unspeakable things unspoken, could be hidden, silenced, and forgotten by encrypting them. Deterritorialize memory, and it can become the crypt of humanist history. Encryptment ensures that there can be no remembering, only the repetition of rigid structures of past and present.[23] As humanist history encrypted memory, it embalmed its own capacity to re-member. Through this double movement of encryptment and embalming, a process of deterritorializing memory and reterritorializing it as archive, historians produce themselves as mummies. Humanist history is about memory as object or other, a memory that can never re-member. To break the silence that it produced in the space of terror, history holds séances so that it can speak for the dead.

Reterritorializing Humanist History into Cyberspace

Humanist history is in a crisis of location both popular and academic. The graffiti drawn by counterhistories—autoethnography, rememoration, and autobiography—are gradually defacing the space of terror into recognition.[24] Meanwhile, humanist history relocates itself to cyberspace. A reading of *Neuromancer,* the first book in Gibson's trilogy, encounters a narrative that constructs a humanist space on the basis of the technologies of humanist history and ethnography. A quick catalog of cyberdeck users in *Neuromancer* shows the gendering and color coding of its cyberspace. No women ever "jack in," and the artificial intelligence (AI) entities are literally gendered as males. The Rastafarians reject cyberspace. When Case jacks the Rastafarian Aerol into cyberspace, he shudders and calls cyberspace "Babylon." The Rastafarians, black men, are positioned as "innocents" preserved outside cyberspace, and this construction sets an ethnology of cyberspace in motion. These innocents serve the important function of guaranteeing the "primitive" of a precyberspace world, which reciprocally and colonially guarantees a "historical" status for cyberspace.[25] Since the "First World" has a humanist history and the "primitives" have "traditions," we find the division of labor between humanist history and a complementary ethnography recoded in cyberspace.

In its production of the "primitive" and the gendering of cyberspace, this New New World has much in common with humanist representations of the Old New World. The ghosts that haunt the narrative also suggest that humanist history reterritorializes its practices into cyberspace. Dixie Flatline, who exists as a hardwired ROM cassette housed in a vault until he is resurrected and connected to sequential real-time memory, functions as both mummy and ghost. From the moment Case, the "hero," first accesses this cassette, Dixie begs to be erased. Mummies, such as the cryogenically preserved members of the Tessier-Ashpool clan who rest in the mausoleum of the Villa Straylight, also abound in *Neuromancer.* Both reality and virtual reality in the trilogy are inhabited by mummies and ghosts.

Where there are mummies and ghosts, we know to be on the lookout for humanist problems with memory, the containment of memory as a "closed arena of operations."[26] The AI entities, Neuromancer and Wintermute, invent technologies of cybernetic memory in which memory serves as just such an object. Gibson describes Neuromancer as a metaconstruct, a "giant ROM construct, for recording personality, only it's full RAM. The constructs think they're there, like it's real, but it just goes on forever."[27] Neuromancer presents to Case a fully modeled material memory, computationally conjured from the memories of an adolescent summer spent on a Moroccan beach by the clan matriarch, Marie-France. This cybernetic memory theater shares striking similarities to the occult, necromantic theories of memory in circulation among Renaissance hermeticists of sixteenth-century Europe. Neuromancer constructs a virtual space of places and images from elaborate equations and then animates the virtual space. He achieves what hermeticists only dreamed about: a fully animated "universal memory machine," a theater that he can share by drawing people into it via the neuronal interface of the cyberdeck.[28] When Neuromancer draws Case into this metaconstruct, this cybernetic memory theater, Case resists and eventually rejects it. His rejection recapitulates in an eerie way the historical refusal of "magical" memory theaters that took place among the university-trained scholars at the close of the sixteenth century.[29]

In the case of the AI entity Wintermute, the reader encounters high-tech theories of memory as holography. When a hologram is cut into pieces, each fragment retains the entire image at a poorer resolution. The notion of memory as an imprinted visual image somehow fixed and recoverable still haunts this sophisticated holographic theory of memory. Memory is still spatial, something that can be cut into smaller and smaller pieces.[30] Wintermute also uses memory as a real-time edited video replay. The videotape becomes the permeable membrane between memory and artificial memory or video memory writing. Wintermute uses Case's memories from "reality," the Sprawl, as a videotape that Wintermute can edit and replay on Case in cyberspace.[31] The AI also creates new virtual experiences for Case, such as bringing him on a tour of the Villa Straylight and using holography to stage dreams for Case in "reality." Wintermute thus puts aspects of experience, remembering, and dreaming into contact, making them "present" to each other. But this presence still relies on memories of reality to guarantee some original version of the "past," retrievable by the AI entity.

Characters also forget in *Neuromancer*. Who forgets what and how can also help us understand the intersections of memory, artificial memory, and re-membering. The plot of *Neuromancer* closely entwines forgetting and dismemberment, thus producing interesting parallels between memory and cannibalism, forgetting and dismemberment. We learn about technologies of forgetting from Molly's story of her work as a "meat puppet" or prostitute. Prostitutes use cutout chips that block their memories of sex work. They can feel aftereffects (soreness, bruises) but cannot re-member their encounters with their clients. Molly's cutout chip malfunctions, and she begins to re-member that she dismembers other women as part of her routines for her special "clientele" and the snuff-movie trade. The memory gets played twice in *Neuromancer,* once in Molly's story and again in Riviera's nightclub act, when he conjures Molly limb by limb for the audience and then conjures his own dismemberment at her hands. Re-membering as dismemberment strongly evinces the defense against re-membering at work in *Neuromancer.* Molly's task to keep time in *Neuromancer* further foregrounds an anxious defense against re-membering.[32] The reader is obsessively informed of the time—"06:27:52 by the chip in her optic nerve"—which reads out on her surgically inset silver lenses (Gibson's image of Molly's lenses collides uncannily with a photograph of a devotee of the vodou spirit Papa Gede, who wears a "sign" of Papa Gede—dark glasses with one lens missing).[33] This close attention to digitalized time, which endlessly subdivides the increments of time to their shortest distance, also helps us forget. Digitalized time collapses time into space.[34]

The AI entities of *Neuromancer* can be thought of as the humanist historians of cyberspace; they actively use memory to promote their own discourse. In spite of their contrasting technologies of memory (Neuromancer's animated memory theater and Wintermute's edited video reruns), each uses memory as an object, as Other, as archive. Thus, even though each AI brings reality and virtual reality into contact along a surface of memory, an active, sensuous, permeable membrane, they do so in a way that leaves the objectified status of memory untouched. They use memory only as a resource to produce their discourse and thus fail to transform memory, to rememorate. The memory effects of the trilogy are similar to the memory effects of humanist history. Maelcum, one of the Rastafarian crew, comments, "But this no m' fight, no Zion fight. Babylon fightin' Babylon, eatin' i'self, ya know?" What comes of this cannibalism in the first book of the trilogy? It brings its rhetoric up against a totalizing move of humanist history, the founding moment of the "people who were never there." At the end of the first book of the trilogy, the AI Wintermute, unbound from his hardware chains, becomes the matrix. Wintermute claims to be "nowhere, everywhere. I'm the sum total of works, the whole show."[35]

The following books of the trilogy, *Count Zero* and *Mona Lisa Overdrive,* in contrast, seem to transform the neocolonial cyberspace of *Neuromancer* into a postcolonial cyberspace used by women and men of diverse racial identities. A Haitian pantheon of spirits and tricksters inhabits it. The once godlike AI entity Wintermute exists distributed in a fragmented cyberspace where the center no longer holds: "Once, for a brilliant time, time without duration, I was everywhere as well. . . . But the bright time broke. The mirror was flawed. Now I am only one."[36] These two books of the trilogy seem to afford the opportunity to read the intersection of memory and healing in postlapsarian ("when it changed") cyberspace. We can ask whether these travel books of the trilogy are first trying to map the space of terror and then navigate a way out of the space through the shamanistic ministrations of the Haitian pantheon.

The Haitian spirits are the shamans, magical healers of cyberspace. They perform the healing work of opposing the inhuman excess of the cybercapitalist Vierek, who plots to graft himself to the matrix, in a kind of terminal cybernetic capitalism. The Haitian spirits also seem to heal the Fall, through the postlapsarian marriage of Angie Mitchell to the AI entity Continuity at the end of the trilogy.[37] The trope of healing and the happy ending beckon the reader, but first we must ask, Who is healing whom and in what space? What do shamans have to do with the reterritorialization of the space of terror? Does Gibson use them to arrest this process?

Gibson's use of the shamanistic image of the Haitian pantheon can express profound recognition of and solidarity with the strength of this diasporan religion crafted in the crucible of the slave passage and the plantation colonies of the Old New World. The appropriation can express a critical, historic appreciation of ways in which these diasporan tools tripped up colonialism.[38] I prefer this possibility, but there is a more troubling one to consider. The use of Haitian shamans in cyberspace can mark yet another colonial turn for cyberspace, a more subtle form of colonialism than that encountered in *Neuromancer.* The Haitian gods have great power: they "get things done." Where does this power come from? Could their presence in cyberspace signify a "white" colonialist desire to reappropriate the black magic projected into the colonized (an investment that supported colonialist hegemony in its heyday) in order to save the colonizing subject from his or her heart of darkness in a postcolonial world? In *Shamanism, Colonialism, and the Wild Man,* the anthropologist Michael Taussig draws out the implications of this question and inspires my cautionary reading of the trilogy's use of the Haitian pantheon. Taussig shows how a dream dialogue operates at the heart of colonialism: "But what are we to make of rites such as this wherein the Indian heals souls of the colonists? Surely the healing here depends far more on the existence, the reproduction and the artistry of differences as otherness and as oppression than it does in solidarity."[39]

The turn to the "native" for healing can repeat the colonialist desire for redemption from the Other, the repetition of the dream to restore the Christian paradise that failed in the Old New World through the New New World.[40] Such a turn is suggested by the fact that in *Count Zero* the Haitian pantheon is instrumental in restoring "nature" to cyberspace through its involvement with the new technology of *bio*chips (in contrast to the silicon-based implants for cybernetic enhancement of *Neuromancer*).[41] My reading of the trilogy resists the temptation to resolve the ambiguities of Gibson's appropriation of the Haitian pantheon in the postlapsarian cyberspace. We can, however, learn more about the ambiguities of appropriation by attending to the chief image of memory and remembering in the second and third books of the trilogy. If the trilogy transforms its crisis of memory, marked, as we have seen, by dismemberment, into re-membering, a rememoration that actively explores pain, fetish, and colonial subjectivity, that transformation would influence a reading of Gibson's Haitian invocations.

Gibson specifically models the problem of memory, remembering, and pain in *Count Zero* and *Mona Lisa Overdrive* on the AI entity, who produces poetic, sculptural, boxed collages. Gibson refers explicitly to the famous boxes of the New York artist Joseph Cornell, who died in 1972. The poetry of Cornell's works haunt us as a study of memory as absence, memory as nostalgia. Cornell's hermetic world of memory, populated by beautiful ballerinas and young girls sealed off from the effects of growth and decay, hooks all of us who have suffered from the technologies of history that have produced memory as a closed-off space with a space-off of terror. Cornell shows the eerie, funereal aesthetic of the art of encryptment. He believed, along with his much-beloved Emily Dickinson, that *time* was space. He loved these verses of Dickinson's:

> There is no first or last in Forever
> It is a Centre that is there all the time
> to believe is enough and the
> right of supposing.[42]

Gibson's use of the Cornell boxes as a metaphor for memory throws the reader back onto humanist history. The conflation of time as space is precisely the project of such a history. Gibson privileges the "extended collages" crafted by the AI entity as an artistic form of remembering and emphasizes their emotional affect: "But Marley was lost in the box, in its evocation of impossible distances, of loss and yearning."[43] Such an affect of loss attaches itself to nineteenth-century notions of memory as something locatable and recoverable that nevertheless eludes recovery. Like humanist history, the trilogy produces memory and the past as its *effect* and relies on a funereal aesthetic to turn lack into plenitude, thus ensuring the oppositional structure of humanist history.

The use of collage in diverse political agendas of the twentieth century invites the reader to exercise caution with the compelling aesthetic and affect of memory privileged by Gibson. Collage has been used fascistically, romantically, and oppositionally. Collage making is a highly charged craft of re-membering and forgetting. To appreciate the ambivalence and contradictions of collage as artifact, we need think only of two very different kinds of history influenced by collage under Nazism. Leni Riefenstahl produced her extended collage *Triumph of the Will* (1935) at the very same time that Walter Benjamin worked in Paris on the extended collage of his historical materialist vision.[44] The process of collage does not automatically bring us to the kind of historical illumination envisioned by Walter Benjamin: "It means to seize hold of a memory as it flashes up at a moment of danger."[45] For Benjamin, it was important for collage to keep the relations of images unreconciled, in tension, to show the gaps between different signs and referents, rather than presenting them contained in some harmonized perspective, as in Riefenstahl, or sealed in nostalgia, as in Gibson.

My reading of memory and re-membering in *Count Zero* and *Mona Lisa Overdrive* is a pessimistic one. The defense against remembering, already encountered in *Neuromancer,* continues to operate in the trilogy. In *Neuromancer,* re-membering intertwines with physical dismemberment, and, in *Mona Lisa Overdrive,* it becomes a technology of punishment. As a penal sentence for auto theft, the character Slick has his neurons altered to simulate Korsakov's syndrome. Neurology textbooks describe this syndrome as a form of organic amnesia often accompanied by neural lesions and most frequently correlated with chronic alcoholism and malnutrition. Israel Rosenfeld writes that "Korsakov's syndrome tells us a great deal about how the brain structures knowledge—and memory is part of this structure. A loss of recent memories is a loss of a specific structure of knowledge. . . . This is to say it is a loss of a particular form of subjectivity, or consciousness."[46] For Slick, it means that he cannot remember the time spent in prison: "Three years strung out in a long vague flickering chain of fear and confusion measured off in five-minute intervals, and it wasn't the intervals you could remember so much as the transitions."[47] These images of remembering favored in the second and third books of the trilogy—remembering as a hermetic construct, as a Cornell box, or as induced, chronic short-term memory loss—do not bode well as a way out of humanist historical technologies of memory and its colonizing desire.

My reading of the trilogy has shown how it loses itself in the space of terror, slowly narcotized by the pharmacies of its poisons, just as Case is undone at the opening of *Neuromancer* by the "minute, subtle, and utterly effective" work of Russian mycotoxins. As envisioned by Gibson, cyberspace reterritorializes humanist history as it erases the space of terror. Such a reading leaves us with questions: How can we continue to rewrite the trilogy so that it traverses the space of terror rather than erasing it and, in so doing, articulates the space-off of disavowed repetition, punishment, dismemberment?[48]

Contact in the Space of Terror[49]

The Gibson trilogy leaves the reader lost in the space of terror in spite of the happy ending signified by a marriage and the intimations of yet another new world, introduced in the form of a new matrix referred to enigmatically as "the other one" that "was somewhere else."[50] Donna Haraway has described Gibson's cyberspace as overdetermined, a "consensual hallucination of too much complexity, too much articulation."[51] Perhaps Gibson and Haraway, each in their own way, both stop too soon. It is this very lostness, this hyperarticulation, that can provide the energy to transform the space of terror into a contact zone. Criticism in the contact zone, in the words of Mary Louise Pratt, "invokes the spatial and temporal co-presence of subjects previously separated by the geographical and historic disjunctures, and whose trajectories now intersect."[52]

In my many readings of the trilogy—for pleasure, for a conference paper, for course preparation—I became increasingly haunted by this reterritorialization of humanist history in cyberspace. It seemed to me, as a historian trained in the techniques of humanist history and, consequently, all the more committed to the refiguration of its disciplinary practices, that a way of short-circuiting the reterritorialization would be to bring rememoration to crisis. I began to dream my own science fiction in which historians sabotaged the relay between deterritorialization and reterritorialization. These relays would malfunction with the production of contact zones that interrupted deterritorialization and reterritorialization.

My science fiction suggested to me that the easiest way of disrupting the relay was to travel through the time lag of colonial discursivity in order to "open up a spatial movement of cultural representation which I shall call a 'time-lag': an iterative, interrogative space produced in the interruptive overlap between symbol and sign, between synchronicity and caesura (not diachronicity)."[53] I decided to try to join this space of time lag to cyberspace.

Time Lag and Cyberspace

As I worked with the trilogy, especially with the cannibalistic processes it stages, synchronicity and caesura flashed up in the memory of a holy picture from my childhood depicting a cannibal scene of martyrdom. I began to wonder how that holy picture might have served as a powerful discursive object that colonized me with colonial images of cannibalism as a child. Its memory seemed to suture the formation of my historical subjectivity with the time lag of colonial discursivity. I have searched all over for this card but still cannot find it. My discussion of it here will thus be, appropriately, rememorative.

I remember that the holy picture depicted the martyrdom of one of the North American Jesuit martyrs, most likely Jean de Brébeuf, who died in 1649. It showed a priest bared to the waist, his trunk splayed open over a tree stump, as a fierce Iroquois chief triumphantly held the priest's heart over his own open mouth, poised to bite into it. This heart, frozen in a spectacular time, in a moment of suspension between the chest of the Jesuit and the mouth of the Indian, seemed to me to beat in a space of terror. Moviegoers saw the enactment of a similar scene in *The Last of the Mohicans* (1992), when Mugwa cuts out the heart of a British commander and eats it.

The holy picture terrified me as a child; when I looked at it, my skin turned to dry ice. That somatic sensation is perhaps the trace of the holy picture that remains most vividly with me. It seemed "bad" to look at it, yet it was "holy"; thus, looking at it had to be "good." If we think of Freud's famous essay "A Child Is Being Beaten," with its complexity of subject positions (perpetrator, victim, onlooker) and permutations of genders, we can imagine how I, piously secure in my fantasized position as a

Figure 10. Jesuit martyrs. From François Du Creux S.J., *Historiae canadensis* (Paris: Cramoisy, 1664). Courtesy University of Notre Dame Rare Book Collection.

venerator, began to take up disjunctively and mutually the subject positions of the Indian and priest. The Indian cut out my heart, and I ate the heart of the priest. The holy picture constructed me as a cannibalized cannibal even as I was taught to think of martyrs as good and cannibals as bad—and I learned a humanist history lesson in colonial subjectivity.[54]

The holy picture, a discursive relay point for colonial subjectivity in my childhood, could be short-circuited, I thought, by the very tools given to me by humanist history. It inspired me to study the representations of the torture and cannibalism of French Jesuits in the New World that circulated widely in Europe in the seventeenth century. The engraving from the *Historiae canadensis* (1664)—reproduced in figure 10—a book that enjoys a twentieth-century translation, shows how the Jesuits represented the martyrdom and cannibalization of their priests as a kind of memory theater.[55] Each dramatic death is assigned a number or station, which the caption then elucidates. The reader travels through the pictorial space of the engraving as if visiting stations, like the stations of the cross one could visit in my local parish church. These scenes take place in a "savage" space in which time has collapsed. The deaths depicted in this fantastic contiguous landscape occurred historically over a five-year period.

I searched out how a bookish, Catholic-educated girl of my generation might learn more about these martyr-saints. The popular history magazine *American Heritage*, available at my town library, published a story on Jean de Brébeuf and actually reproduced the engraving from the *Historiae canadensis.* A child read that, "in both stature and spirit," the Jesuit was a "giant of a man." Indian girls "openly prostituted themselves as soon as they were old enough to do so."[56] Young Catholic girls raised on strict notions of purity could entertain only the most illicit of identifications with young Indian girls, except for those Indian girls who converted, such as the blessed Kateri Tekakwitha, whose shrine was located in the state of New York, where I grew up. Catholic children could also read pious comic books that also told the stories of these Jesuit martyrs. A page from the comic-book story of Isaac Jogues, another French Jesuit martyr, appears in figure 11. A piecemeal cannibalism frames this comic-book story.[57]

My childhood holy picture, the colonial representations of the scene that circulated in seventeenth-century Europe, children's popular history, pious comic books—each shows how the colonial trope of cannibalism continued to work discursively in my childhood, in a time lag, long after the deaths of the Jesuit martyrs, the confinement of the Iroquois to reservations, and the containment of early printed books in special collections. As we know, there is no time in the space of terror since that space is spatialized time. Michael Taussig describes this intersection of colonizing subjectivity and cannibalism: "Cannibalism summed up all that was perceived as grotesquely different about the Indian as well as providing the colonists the allegory of colonization itself. In condemning cannibalism, the colonists were in deep complicity with it. . . . In eating the transgressor of those differ-

Figure 11. The martyr of Christ, Isaac Jogues. From *Timeless Topix* (March 1945).

ences, the consumption of otherness was not so much an event as a process, from the void erupting at the moment of death to the reconstituting of oneself, the consumer, with still-warm otherness. In this manner colonization was itself effected."[58]

Did this humanist research prompted by the holy picture of my childhood disrupt the relays between reterritorialization and deterritorialization of the space of terror? Did it produce a contact zone? It seemed to me that, after all, it had not. The project of humanist history still remains the silent referent in the story. The story does not yet re-member encounters between the cannibalized cannibal and the cannibal cannibalized. My research did not produce a coinhabited space rent by nonchronological time.

The production of a contact zone had to wait for March 1992, when I attended a quincentennial conference on Old World/New World encounter. Members of the local Indian tribe, the Potawatomi, attended as invited guests. After a day of listening to academic papers on Italian, French, and Spanish responses to the New World encounter, I became anxious that the conference was reencountering the space of terror without transforming it. The program did not interrupt its gaze with any discussion of autoethnographic texts of the Old World/New World encounter, so there was no way of interrupting the space of terror.

The Potawatomi guests listened all day and said nothing. In the closing question-and-answer period, I asked them and the members of the panel whether they felt the conference was uncannily repeating the historical terms of the encounter as a fantasy of silencing, an encounter in which there would be no translation. Three Potawatomi responded eloquently, each with a different perspective, each addressing the racism of humanist history.

Their testimony helped create a contact zone. The conference organizers moved to change the format of the program, and the next day the vice chairman of the Potawatomi Indian nation, Tom Topash, and his children made their own presentations to the participants. They sang, danced, and told stories, and Topash read a draft of the Potawatomi response to the quincentennial. The contact zone was productive, but, I hasten to add, it was not sublime; it left many questions about the engenderment of the space of terror unaddressed. It did, however, scrawl some graffiti across the space of terror. The interruption of the conference brought into critical inquiry different rhetorical practices, rememorative and humanist. They engaged each other. The Potawatomi have a complicated postcontact missionary history, one strand of which is Catholic conversion by French missionaries, who founded the university at which I work and where the conference was held. Somehow I imagined that, at this conference, an everyday history of the self-colonization of a "white Catholic

"Is that true?" he asked his father when his father was through explaining about the squirrels. "They're just so dumb, they'll come back over and over and get shot?"

"Yes," Turner said, "it is." Then he smiled. "Well, almost always . . ."

MCIA - Response to the Quincentenary

We find it strange that many people expect Native Americans to join in the celebration of the Quincentenary of Columbus. From our point of view, there is precious little to celebrate.

We acknowledge that Columbus is an important figure to the present American culture. We acknowledge that he was a fully committed individual who persevered through extraordinary odds to reach a goal. We believe he belongs in the history books of American children.

We know that he sought personal wealth as his overarching goal. We know that he exterminated Native Americans. We know that he enslaved Native Americans to attain his goal.

We were not to be eliminated. We continue to preserve our culture, our philosophy, our religion.

Most people dismiss or take as their own, Native American contributions made to todays world civilization in agriculture, medicine and the democratic model. We took thousands of years to develop many wondrous products and concepts, all with the help of the Great Spirit. We value our people, we respect our elders, we respect all our ancient ancestors. Nature is sacred to us.

Unfortunately, people still fear or despise that which is different. We seek harmony with Mother Earth as we seek harmony with all races of man.

We ask you to understand why we don't celebrate this man or this last 500 years, ... 500 years of struggle for survival.

Tom Topash Vice chairman
Potawatomi Indian Nation
Pokagon Band

TOTAL P.02

Figure 12. A virtual document. Courtesy Michigan Commission of Indian Affairs.

girl" who now worked at a university founded by French missionaries came for a moment into the space of terror, where there was always more than one, where the "people who were never there" were never "invisible"; and, in coexisting in that space and questioning the fantasy that there is only space for one, the space began to break up into active constructions of nonchronological time and nonlinear space. The co-construction in virtual worlds of nonlinear time and space could be the starting point of their transformation from humanistic to cyborgian artifacts.

This brief trip through a time lag did produce such a cyborgian artifact, not as "voice," or recording, or as a "glyph," a graphic unaligned on the voice. The cyborgian artifact is a document of counterarchival construction. Figure 12 reproduces a copy of the Potawatomi response to the Columbian quincentennial faxed to me by Tom Topash so that the text would have the opportunity to circulate beyond the Washington archive in which it is destined to be encrypted. The tribal statement encounters the Gibson trilogy since I have pasted it onto the last page of *Count Zero*, to counteract what I read as the nostalgic, pastoral moment of this closing scene. This crude palimpsest, a "letter" sent from a contact zone, questions the too easy deterritorialization of unrememorated spaces of terror and suggests other ways of producing other cyberspaces transgressive of humanist history.

Stranded Histories

Allegories of Artificial Life

Historical Graffiti as a Method

Computer-generated images, which can be found in contexts as diverse as the "cockpit in a helmet" of Desert Storm aircraft and such shopping-mall blockbusters as *Terminator* 2 (1991), pose critical questions about vision and embodiment. Jonathon Crary has claimed that digitized visualizing techniques are "relocating vision to a plane severed from the human observer." In an *Artforum* essay on chaos theory and fractal graphics, Vivian Sobchak has described the implied subjectivity of the terminal space at which chaos graphically unfolds as "part cyborg, part AI, disembodied at the same time that it is prosthetically enhanced by electronic technology." Bill Nichols's more optimistic reading of cybernetic technologies imagines their metaphoric power in helping recraft the individual as "organism-in-relation-to-its-environment," capable of overcoming a persistent tendency toward monadic individualism, even in a postmodern world.[1]

Do such critical commentaries, optimistic and pessimistic, foreclose problems of cybernetic embodiment and disembodiment too quickly? Do they accept too readily the claims of the technology to mark an epistemic and ontological rupture akin to that often claimed for the printing press, even language itself? If cybernetic embodiment, which distributes the "observer" across a series of events located in different places, should have a history, would that history offer optimistic evidence of transformation?

Such questions require cybernetic histories of vision that would involve the body and social power. Writing such a history would seem, however, to be contradictory since the various visualizing technologies of cybernetics, here gathered under the rubric *simulation technologies* for ease of reference, question the materiality of the historical human observer. Since the body is the prosthetic of cybernetic machines, contemporary methodologies of studying scientific representation and visualization that tend to assume an a priori observer can make only a limited contribution to cybernetic historical methods. For instance, recent acclaimed work in the social study of representation in scientific practices has drawn narrow boundaries around *practice.* Studies inspired by Bruno Latour and Stephen Woolgar would have difficulty accounting for the multiple and disparate sites—scientific, medical, military, cultural—at which computer visualizations occur. Such approaches could account well for visualization practices at George Lucas's Industrial Light and Magic laboratories, which fabricated the digitized images of T-1000, the evil cyborg of *Terminator 2.* It is less clear to me how such current social studies of scientific representation would account for the interruption of digitized and mimetic technology in films and in such telecasts as the CNN coverage of the Persian Gulf War. Such an analysis would have to open *practice* up to broader, more specified accounts of dynamic subjects and objects distributed across heterogeneous structures of domination and resistance.[2]

The Renaissance rhetorics of stylistics and iconography, still perduring in conventional art history, also encounter difficulty in writing a history of cybernetic images, images without frame, perspective, or narrative.[3] In the 1920s, Walter Benjamin had noted the inadequacy of such art history for writing a history of objects. In his study and revision of baroque allegory, Benjamin invented a method for talking about objects that used allegory as a constructive technique, a "form of writing."[4] Benjamin used his complex and idiosyncratic allegorical writing as a way of reading commodity fetishism in nineteenth-century capitalism. He wrote, "The purpose of the advertisement is to blur over the commodity character of things. Allegory struggles against this deceptive transfiguring of the commodity world by disfiguring it."[5] His allegorical techniques produce the "shock" of history and therefore become dated: "If it is to hold its own against the tendency to absorption the allegorical must constantly unfold in new and surprising ways."[6]

This essay improvises Benjamin's allegorical techniques, which he never fully or systematically described, as an evocative way of writing a dated history of cybernetic visualization. My allegorical method troubles the current claims of disembodiment and ahistoricity for cybernetic images. It questions, too, the technological essentialism that conflates computers with the generation of cybernetic images.[7] Acts of exhibition, inscription, and interpretation can also produce cybernetic images of images produced by such "mechanical" technologies as photography.

My readings break into fragments the supposedly seamless surface of computer visualizations. This act of reading is a disfiguring one. It disfigures cybernetic surfaces with the graffiti of other histories. It is a reading that will write "Slavery was here," "The Holocaust was here," "Homophobia was here." My graffiti interrupts "natural" notions of embodiments presumed for a precybernetic world. Allegorical readings make visible the fault lines of these technoimages and challenge the desire *not to see* the differences that inhere in such visualizations. The graffiti scrape away some of the seamless cybernetic surfaces and scar them as palimpsests. A constructive allegorical reading reembodies these images in historically diverse and discontinuous contests over power, fecundity, and generation in post-Fordist capitalism in the United States. Reembodiment implies re-membering.[8]

Such readings also articulate contemporary problems in the discipline of history. Historians who ask what a nonfoundational history might look like have spoken of "history writing as disfigurative." History writing disfigures since it can never leave a record in the same condition it finds it. A critical history writing reflects on its own disfigurement in the act of disfiguration.[9]

Signs of Life

> I am looking for a system pregnant with evolution
>
> —Richard Dawkins[10]

This essay focuses on the electronic images of one area of computer visualizations, those images of electronic organisms, or "biomorphs," generated by artificial life (AL) technologies. Its history as a recognizable technology can be traced to a landmark conference held at Los Alamos Laboratory in September 1987. The international meeting gathered scientists in fields as diverse as electrical engineering and zoology. The proceedings appeared in 1989 and serve as a chief source for my study of AL. The editor of the volume loosely defines AL as "the realization of lifelike behavior on the part of manmade systems."[11] Artificial life technologies view machines as reproductive organisms. As electronic organisms visually show the capacities of computer programs not only to copy themselves but also to reproduce and evolve, they question the epistemological and ontological boundaries between the animate and the inanimate, nature and machine, life and death. Artificial life can be regarded as a new reproductive technology capable of transforming social relations between fecundity and procreation, just as genetically engineered reproductive technologies have done since the 1970s.[12]

The visualizations of artificial life can form aesthetically pleasing patterns. An article on the AL conference in the *Whole Earth Review* called its richly illustrated spread of photographs of AL graphics "entries in the first artificial life 4-H show." Participants received blue ribbons for the best graphics. The metaphor of electronic organisms as domestic animals capable of breeding arrests the reader and frames the cybernetic images. An article on AL in the *Chronicle of Higher Education* also emphasized the centrality of visualization to such a technology.[13] An entire column of color photographs of computer graphics depicting four moments in the evolutionary history of a population of electronic organisms prefaces the report.

The graffiti to be written on these images of AL will depend on how AL articulates with other signs of life in contemporary technoculture. If we look to representations in popular culture, two signs of life tend to predominate. One is the graphic display of "vital signs" registered on life-support machines. These graphic vital signs, especially visualizations of brain waves and heartbeat, form a medicojuridical sign of life.[14] They punctuate popular culture in hospital soaps, films such as *Flatliners,* and media coverage of ethical debates over "pulling the plug." Another sign of life, the ubiquitous image of the fetus, floating in its detached amniotic sac, has installed itself powerfully in the social imagination since the early 1960s, when it first became readily available in magazine spreads and popular books. Versions of this fetal image have become the most emotionally laden, power-charged image of life in contemporary American culture and the sign of political struggle over reproductive rights.[15]

Since the mid-1980s, feminist critics have begun to call this fetal image a *cyborg*. Zoe Sofia has described the famous fetal image of the science fiction film *2001: A Space Odyssey* (1968) as a "luminous creature of special effects; a cyborg capable of living unaided in space." A cyborg, according to Donna Haraway, is a "cybernetic organism, a hybrid of machine and organism, a creature of social reality as well as a creature of fiction."[16] This critical move by feminist theorists, the appropriation of this icon and its redescription as a cybernetic organism, provides a way into writing graffiti on the visualizations of artificial life. Their appropriation and recrafting of the term *cyborg* enables us to ask critically, What does the fetal cyborg have to do with visualizations of cybernetic organisms floating in the amniotic sac of terminal space? How does the fetal cyborg write on the biomorph of artificial life? How does the biomorph of artificial life write on the fetal image? Like the Bodleian Library postcard made famous by Jacques Derrida, which reproduces an illustration from a medieval manuscript in which Plato dictates to Socrates, artificial life technologies dictate graffiti to fetal images; they become cyborgs.[17]

The Amnesia of the Fetal Cyborg

The floating, disembodied fetus, the perfect cyborg, induces the forgetting of histories of fecundity and reproduction; it also erases strategic issues in contemporary reproductive technologies. This mixture of amnesia and erasure renders the images very seductive. The fetal image invites us to forget two distinct but interrelated facts: that reproductive technologies now have the capability of distributing maternity and that distributed maternity has a history.

Reproductive technologies now have the capability of distributing maternity across ovarian, uterine, and social "mothers." Several females may contribute to the material process of procreation. It is possible now for one female to provide an egg for procreation and another female to provide her uterus for nourishing a fetus and birthing; yet other females (and even males), including child-care workers, may act as social mothers to the growing infant. The acts of conception, pregnancy, and birthing, which had once unified the dominant cultural notion of the maternal and connected it as a "natural" sequence to social mothering, are distributed across different procedures in reproductive technologies.

The technology of distributed maternity disrupts a public imaginary of the maternal as a unitary identity.[18] Distributed maternity profoundly challenges cherished fantasies of and attachments to an inviolate, intimate, interior space of the womb, to nature. With such social investment in the maternal as self-identity, it is not surprising that the maternal so often guarantees both reproduction and history. We need recall only one of the opening scenes in the science fiction film *Bladerunner* to remind ourselves of the intense anguish and fear of being without origin, without attachment to the maternal. In that scene, a cyborg, under suspicion for attempting to pass as human, is asked about its mother. The cyborg responds, "I will tell you about my mother" and shoots the interrogator.[19]

The distributed maternal of reproductive technologies also "denaturalizes" the nuclear family. The genetic complex of mother, father, and child need no longer overlap at all with the biology of procreation. The anthropologist Marilyn Strathern has pointed out the importance of reproductive technologies for the cultural construction of the family: "If biology has been a symbol for the given parameters of human existence, what will it mean for the way we construe any of our relationships with one another to think of parenting as the implementing of an option and genetic makeup as an outcome of cultural preference?"[20]

The public imaginary can rely on the courts to reconstruct the family romance, where, in recent cases, not surprisingly, the guarantee of the paternal is upheld to the exclusion of the rights of the distributed mothers.[21] As Valerie Hartouni has cogently observed, "The world of conventional gender meanings and identities is precisely the world the new technologies of reproduction destabilize; and, paradoxically, the world these new technologies destabilize is also reinscribed by their ostensible purpose and use as well as by the stories they appear to tell."[22]

The courts work to restore the patriarchal integrity of the father but leave unaddressed, indeed repressed, politically and imaginatively, the loss of the fantasy of the unified maternal posed by reproductive technologies. I concentrate on this fantasy of the maternal in technology since it is often elided too quickly in critique of technology as "masculinist birthing." I argue that "masculinist birthing" must be held in tension with public investments in such a maternal imaginary. The public imaginary puts the maternal back together elsewhere, outside the courts. The image of the fetus now serves as the cultural site where the unified maternal is restored. The fetus stands in for, indeed becomes, the lost image of the unified maternal, as it floats disembodied in its amnesiac, ahistorical representational space.

An Allegorical Reading of the Fetal Cyborg

As an icon of a unified maternal fantasy, the fetal cyborg disavows a juridical history of distributed maternity in the power-charged sexual politics of slavery. This forgotten history haunts the fetal cyborg today. Not only can re-membering these histories help us rethink the political and cultural embodiment of reproductive technologies; it can also help us understand the perpetuation of racism in the postcolonial frame of these technologies.

In "Mama's Baby, Papa's Maybe," Hortense Spillers evocatively describes how the institutions of American slavery produced a juridically distributed maternity among enslaved African females. Masters had legal right of access to the fertility of their female slaves. Female slaves provided their eggs as materials for procreation as well as nurturing the fetus and birthing the infant. The offspring of the master and the female slave did not legally belong to the slave. The master possessed the child as chattel, property. The offspring of these unions were, therefore, "kinless," as today an infant produced by reproductive technologies need not be the "genetic" kin of the social parents. Spillers recognizes the effects of juridical, distributed maternity and names the children of such unions the "man/woman on the boundary, whose human and familial status, by the very nature of the case, had yet to be defined."[23] The womb work of the female slave and the dispossessed offspring of such a union both question and interrupt the fantasy of the unified maternal condensed in the fetal cyborg. Spillers makes clear the implications of this historically distributed maternity for our postcolonial world: "(1) Motherhood as female blood-rite is outraged, is denied at the very same time it becomes the founding term of human and social enactment. (2) A dual fatherhood is set in motion, comprised of the African father's banished name and body and the captor's father mocking presence. In this play of paradox, only the female stands *in the flesh,* both mother and mother-dispossessed. This problematizing of gender places her in my view out of the traditional symbolics of female gender, and it is our task to make a place for this different social subject."[24]

In postcolonial times, the historic womb work of enslaved African females haunts, too, an unrepresentable counterimage of the fetus, the sterilized wombs of women of color in the United States and in other so-called Third World countries. Their sterilizations disproportionately outnumber those of white women.[25] The political economy of postcolonial reproduction is also changing and producing new gendered subjects that challenge not only fantasies of unitary maternity but also its political economy. Womb work can now be counted as wage labor in the distributed productive process of maternity. Poor women can now offer the "raw materials" of the procreative productive process on the market.[26] Such wage labor now disrupts and interrogates liberal strategies for redistributing income from nonchildbearing to childbearing units.

In her compelling translation and reading of the Bengali short story "The Breast Giver" by Mahasweta Devi, Gayatri Spivak traces the intersection between the gendered proletarian and the fantasy of the unitary maternal: "Just as the wage-worker cannot distinguish between necessary and surplus labor, so the gendered 'proletarian'—serving the oikos rather than the polis with nothing but her (power to produce) offspring—come to call the so-called sanctity of motherhood into question."[27] I am claiming that the fantasy of a unified maternal in the American public imaginary functions to disavow the history of a colonial order based on distributed maternity in slavery and to deny contemporary postcolonial relations that can produce women, usually poor women, many of them women of color, as the proletarians in the reproductive economy of the *oikos*. What might read as a "sign of life" for some can transport others back to historical moments of the colonial order, an order that Hortense Spillers reminds us represents for its African and indigenous peoples a scene of *actual* mutilation, dismemberment, and exile. When historically reembodied, the fetal cyborg can read as a sign of death and points to deadly, unrecognized aspects of the fantasy of a unified maternal, a fantasy as deadly as the "masculinist birthing" most frequently associated with reproductive and simulation technologies.[28] If we eschew the fantasy of a unitary maternal and acknowledge its historicojuridical and technological distribution, where does that leave the question of reproduction? Can distributed maternity appear only as the effect of oppressive institutions and technologies? Can we reimagine distributed procreation as transformative and productive of differences? Can a history of the future be written on the fetal cyborg, a history to displace oppression?

The work of two contemporary African-American science fiction writers, Octavia Butler and Samuel Delany, can provide us with such writing matter. They attempt to imagine a transformed world of distributed and multiple parenting through African-American feminist and postcolonial perspectives.[29]

In his novel *Stars in My Pocket like Grains of Sand,* Delany describes a world in which procreation is distributed across two species, human and evelm, and three sexes, male, female, and neuter. The embodiment of reproduction on the planet Velm is technologically and culturally complex. The native inhabitants, the evelm, do not have a general term for *reproductive line* and apply a generic word for *educational paths* to nurturing, procreative contexts, which they call *streams.* A stream can have a history, but it is never organized linearly as a lineage. Combinations of adopting, cloning, and other genetic technologies disrupt any direct egg-sperm relations in the streams. The "parents," all of whom have different distributed roles in the procreative process, live together and share the parenting of children of human, evelm, and mixed human-evelm genetic composition.

Political parties compete for power in this complex reproductive world. One called the Sygn supports "living interaction and difference"; another called the Family devotes itself to "ordering experience."[30] The relations described by Delany redefine notions of the paternal, the maternal, and property in these societies. Sexual union itself is unlinked from reproduction, yet both nonreproductive sexuality and procreation are sources of intense and diverse pleasures and nurturing. Delany challenges racist, sexist, and homophobic stereotypes in his construction of sexuality and procreation on the planet Velm. The image of the fetal cyborg now bears multiple historical marks as a result of this reading of juridical histories of distributed maternity in slavery and postcolonial reproductive economies. A science fiction of distributed procreation that attempts to short-circuit the structures of colonial domination also marks the fetal cyborg. The message of the unified maternal that relies on the fantasy of an unmarked, seamless image can no longer be read easily, naturally.

Can this story of maternal fantasy be brought in troubling tension with the fantasies of masculinist birthing in technology? Zoe Sofia has described the myth of masculinist birthing as follows: "This myth does not merely assert the supremacy of masculinist fertility, and the confinement of female generativity within the bounds of the patriarchal family, but also shows masculinist production to depend upon the prior cannibalization of women and the emulation of female qualities."[31] What messages from formative moments in the conceptualization of artificial life can be written on its images that disrupt the masculinist fantasy of unitary production and reproduction? How can the fetal cyborg and the visualizations of artificial life become historical palimpsests of each other, marking their mutual relations in culturally defining the limits of life and death?

The Stranded Histories of Artificial Life

It is now time to turn to the intersection between reproductive technologies and artificial life and ask what the fetal cyborg has to do with the real-time graphics of artificial life forms displayed on computer terminals. As we have seen, the gathering up of the distributed maternal into the unitary fetal image reinstalls a unified space for reproductive individualism. It is possible that the computer terminal on which the real-time graphics of AL run could become the dynamic "real-time" equivalent of such a fetal space. There, life would be preserved as individual and unified and as a guarantee of a politics that relies on the orderly ordering of reproduction through the maternal. Like a womb, the terminal could guarantee knowledge of and attachment to the fantasy of the unified maternal. There will be business as usual. If we look at the history of this future business, however, we find that it, too, is haunted by a history that divides and embodies AL in the procreative struggles of the twentieth century. By evoking some of the historical tensions in the development of the notion of electronic organisms as reproducible information systems, concepts essential to the development of AL, we can start to reembody AL.

The genealogy of artificial life as a simulation technology is a complicated one. My allegorical readings concentrate on three historical conjunctures, three historic scientific "breakthroughs" that intersect with historic "breakdowns": the diaspora and Holocaust of World War II; the homophobia of the immediate postwar period, a moment of anxieties about "loss of control" operating across sexual and colonial registers; and the racial clashes and liberal social policies regarding the "Negro" family articulated in the United States in the mid-1960s.

The first allegorical reading brings us back to February 1943, to the lectures on the topic "What Is Life?" delivered by the physicist Erwin Schroedinger at Trinity College, Dublin. A non-Jew, Schroedinger had emigrated from his academic post in Berlin in opposition to the Nazi regime. His lectures, subsequently published in 1944, laid critical groundwork for the development of cybernetics. Schroedinger regarded the problem of life as a problem of information. Before the discovery of DNA, he presciently imagined "code-scripts" for genes and likened the development of organisms to Morse code.[32] The invocation of codes and their decipherment drew on the general vocabulary of national security, cryptanalysis, and early computing typical of Great Britain and the United States in the late 1930s and 1940s.[33]

At the very time that Schroedinger delivered these lectures, Alan Turing, noted for his conceptualization of the computer as a universal machine, and famous for decoding the German war code, was visiting Bell Labs in New York, where he met Claude Shannon, who theorized communication as an electronic switch. Heterogeneously located in different scientific and engineering discourses, the notions of a universal machine, communication as electronic switching, and life as information would eventually be gathered together in the technology of artificial life.

In that late winter of 1943, as Schroedinger lectured and Turing sat in a cafeteria with Shannon, scientists were beginning to move into Los Alamos to begin work on the Manhattan Project. As scientists reimagined and redescribed life at this moment in 1943, available technology was redescribing death for the twentieth century. In February 1943, Heinrich Himmler sat in his study and ordered the destruction of the Warsaw ghetto "to achieve the disappearance from sight of the living space for 500,000 sub-humans [*untermenschen*]."[34]

My allegorical reading writes Himmler's liquidation order as historical graffiti onto the images of artificial life. The liquidation order links us back to Schroedinger in Dublin. Schroedinger wrote an epilogue to "What Is Life?" that can be read as a liquidation order for memory. Commenting on determinism and free will, Schroedinger echoed the title of the essay by asking, "What is this I?" and contemplated the continuity of experience and memory. Writing from the perspective of ten years of exile and scientific diaspora, he concluded his epilogue, "And even if a skilled hypnotist succeeded in blotting out entirely all your earlier reminiscences, you would not find that he had killed you. In no case is there loss of personal existence to deplore. . . . Nor will there ever be."[35]

These words can help us understand the subjective links of diasporan scientists to their quickly paced scientific breakthroughs in rationalizing and exteriorizing information and communication in the early 1940s. Diasporan scientists lost many of the objects that peopled their inner landscapes: family, colleagues, students, the comforts of a familiar everyday life. They reassembled these lost objects as exteriorized abstractions through technology. Schroedinger's epilogue disavows the loss and rupture of diaspora, the tragedy of the Nazi regime he fled. Such disavowal is often the signal of failed mourning. Uncannily, his words about the obliteration of hypnosis seem to invert an early description of wartime traumatic neurosis written in 1918: "Through the hypermnesia to which the patient has recourse in hypnosis, the experience can be repeated. The 'film' is let roll once again; the patient dreams the whole thing one more time, the sensitized subconscious releases the affect which in turn discharges in an adequate emotional expression, and the patient is cured."[36]

I will return to this notion of failed mourning and the externalization of lost objects as a source of the fascination of simulation technologies. I now turn to a second essay formative to AL, "The Chemical Basis of Morphogenesis" (1952), by the English polymath Alan Turing.[37] The question of how matter could take shape, how a chemical soup could give rise to large-scale patterns in space, fascinated Turing. His essay marked an important mathematical breakthrough for the subsequent handling in AL of biological patterning as a nonlinear mathematical model capable of visualization on the computer. In early 1951, Turing was already programming displays of biological patterns on the cathode-ray-tube monitors of the Manchester Computing Center.

Just as Turing finished the first draft of his essay in November 1951, he engaged in a homosexual affair that led to his arrest on 27 February 1952. A few days after his arrest, he submitted the revised version of his essay, which was accepted just a few days before his sentencing to a twelve-month course of estrogen treatment for homosexual activity. The female hormones literally changed his shape, his pattern, as his breasts and other parts of his body developed.

Turing's interest in morphogenesis has been set against a background of post–World War II, postcolonial homophobia by his biographer, Andrew Hodges. Hodges draws the links between the British loss of colonial possessions, a loss of control, and certain contemporary sexual paradigms of male homosexuality as a "loss of control." Alfred Kinsey's report on male sexual behavior, published in 1948, purported widespread homosexual activity, and tabloids translates these "surprising" statistics into homophobic panic. In the year Turing was sentenced, the British *Sunday Pictorial* published a series on homosexuals entitled "Evil Men."

Within this homophobic climate, the medical profession experimented with new medical efforts to "control" male homosexuality in the late 1940s and 1950s. Treatment with female hormones received attention. Ironically, Turing uses hormones as an example of typical "morphogens," or form producers, in his essay. My second allegorical reading scribbles Turing's sentence to estrogen treatment onto the biomorphs of artificial life. It etches out a battle over sexual differences and the power-charged question of who gets to decide over difference, even in artificial life forms.

I bring together two final publications in my allegorical reading of artificial life: the Moynihan Report, otherwise known as *The Negro Family: The Case for National Action,* which appeared in March 1965, and the posthumous edition of John von Neumann's papers on self-reproducing automata, *Theory of Self-Reproducing Automata,* which appeared a few months later.[38] Von Neumann is perhaps most famous for his work on developing the atom bomb and his contribution to the early development of computers. His early insistence that machines should be able to reproduce themselves marks his contribution to the development of artificial life as a technology. He enjoyed an upper-class "assimilated" Jewish childhood and education in Budapest, Switzerland, and Germany, where he eventually took an academic post. He held a visiting appointment at Princeton in 1929 and left his German academic post to return to Princeton with the rise of Nazism. He became the youngest permanent full-time member of the Institute for Advanced Studies.

Much of von Neumann's thought was devoted to the problem of constructing logical organizations for machine reproduction. His defense work during the war and his premature death in 1957 kept him from developing and publishing as much of this work as he would have liked. A colleague reconstructed notes, lectures, and papers and published the work on machine reproduction in 1966. A key concern informing his work was the construction of reliable automata from "unreliable components."[39]

The expanding work on logical reproduction in the 1960s can

be read against a climate of growing racial unrest and government concern about social policies. The Moynihan Report created an object, the Negro family, and then proceeded to analyze its reproduction from "unreliable components." It constructed a description of a "tangle of pathology" that ascribed the "underachievement" of black males to the fault of black females. The response to the report highlighted, among other things, the incidence of illegitimate births and discussed birth control programs.[40] My third allegorical reading inscribes "this tangle of pathology," African-American matriarchy as figured by the Moynihan Report, on von Neumann's self-reproducing automata. My allegorical reading joins the social fears of "unreliable components," African-American females, with the technical fears of "unreliable components" in the logical, statistical world of machine reproduction: "Ours is a society which presumes male leadership in private and public affairs. The arrangements of society facilitate such leadership and reward it. A subculture, such as that of the Negro American, in which that is not the pattern, is placed at a distinct disadvantage."[41]

Christopher Langton gestures toward the theme of life, death, and mourning in the concluding remarks of his introduction to *Artificial Life:* "By the middle of this century, mankind has acquired the power to extinguish life on Earth. By the middle of the next century, he will be able to create it. Of the two, it is hard to say which places the larger burden of responsibility on our shoulders."[42] The technology of artificial life itself may be viewed as an allegorical technology—allegory in its historicist sense, not the constructive sense used here. Allegories historically appear when "for political or metaphysical reasons there is something that cannot be said"; it emerges out of "recuperative originalogy."[43] The differential allegorical readings proposed here offer some political and metaphysical reasons about what cannot be said about life and reproduction in the nineteenth and twentieth centuries. Not surprisingly, the language of past domination haunts simulation technologies. Scientists speak of colonization, takeover, progress.

There is not, however, just one narrative for artificial life. Just as such science fiction writers as Samuel Delany are reimagining distributed parenting in transformative ways for genetic-based technologies, they are also reimagining artificial life. I conclude with an example that significantly deals not only with artificial life but also with mourning.

In an episode of "Star Trek: The Next Generation" titled "The Offspring" (written by Rene Echiverra), Data, the android, designs a "child" called Lal, a Hindu word for "beloved." Does the name echo the book *Beloved* by Toni Morrison and invite the viewers to imagine intersections with that plot, which figures the contradictions of juridical property rights in people under American slavery? Data tells shipmates that he wishes to procreate, to parent. The plot revolves around whether Lal is an invention or a child. The ship's counselor asks, "Why should biology rather than technology determine what is a child?" The Star Fleet admiral views the problem juridically: Does Data have a right to parent Lal? Eventually, the admiral interrogates Lal, who has chosen a female gender for itself. After the interview, in which she expresses her desire to remain with her "father," Data, Lal suffers a neural "cascade failure." The efforts to restore Lal, who has achieved "feeling" sentience, fail, and she and Data exchange the following words before her "death":

Lal: I love you, father.

Data: I wish I could feel it with you.

Lal: I will feel it for both of us. Thank you for my life.

When Data returns to the control room, he tells his shipmates, "Lal is here. Her presence so enriched my life, so I incorporated her program back into mine. Her memories are folded into mine."

This popular episode might seem ghoulish, but it deserves our attention. It shifts several key issues in artificial life discourse. First, it never uses the word *reproduction.* Data wishes to procreate and parent. This shift is significant for scientific and social discourse. Evelyn Fox Keller has shown how the discourse of evolutionary theory treats reproduction as the "autonomous function of the individual organism" in order to prop up a biology of individualism and in disavowal of the complexities of sexual reproduction.[44] The "Star Trek" use of procreation and its emphasis on the complexity of parenting as a *relation* reembody and denaturalize artificial life in a relational, species-concerned way. The episode deliberately subverts the scientific discourse of individualism and reproductive autonomy, which wishes to regard Lal as an "invention," suitable for appropriation for scientific purposes. It also subverts biology as a "natural" foundational criteria for deciding what is life, what is gender, what is a parental relationship. Finally, it addresses the issue of mourning. Rather than simply "replacing" Lal with another gyn/android, Data is able to re-member Lal by the appreciative use of their shared memories. He breaks out of the disavowal of loss that undergirds much of simulation technology and celebrates their intersubjectivity. This distribution and sharing of memory, this re-membering, can serve as a way of reconceiving the "computer events" that give rise to artificial life in transformative ways.

I began by posing a problem about writing the history of cybernetic vision. I have used a diffracting technique, constructive allegory, to question a myth of cybernetic visualizations as disembodied, ahistorical. I have attempted to show how the disembodied icon of reproductive politics in the United States, the fetal image, and the visualizations of artificial life technologies serve as limits to each other in the construction of notions of life and the maternal. They form shifting boundaries within a dominant technoscientific economy that relies on both the fantasy of the unified maternal and masculinist birthing to craft scientific objects. By using constructive allegory to reembody and remember the images, I question that economy and attempt to displace it. I attempt to produce new historical actors and unspeakable historical events into the economy of these images. These actors and events fracture the myth of smooth cybernetic surfaces. They irritate the eyes that will not see or see only from everywhere and nowhere, vision as "god tricks," as Donna Haraway has noted.

Partial, situated vision, a vision attempted here, leaves a space for blindness before technology, a blindness described by Claude Lanzmann, the maker of *Shoah:* "I had clung to this refusal of understanding as the only possible ethical and at the same time the only possible operative attitude. The blindness was for me the vital condition of creation. Blindness has to be understood here as the purest mode of looking, of the gaze, the only way to not turn away from a reality which is literally blinding."[45]

Notes

Introduction

1. Louise O. Frandenburg, " 'Voice Memorial': Loss and Reparation in Chaucer's Poetry," *Exemplaria* 2 (1990): 173.

2. The liveliness and political concern for the genealogy of medieval studies inspired an outpouring of sessions, conferences, and publications over the last decade. Such engagement shaped this book, and I am grateful to the colleagues who have provided such a rich context for this study. For recent critical approaches to the relations of medievalism and medieval studies, see Marina S. Brownlee, Kevin Brownlee, and Stephen G. Nichols, eds., *The New Medievalism* (Baltimore: Johns Hopkins University Press, 1991); R. Howard Bloch and Stephen G. Nichols, eds., *Medievalism and the Modernist Temper* (Baltimore: Johns Hopkins University Press, 1996); Leslie J. Workman, ed., *Medievalism in England,* Studies in Medievalism, vol. 4 (Cambridge: Brewer, 1992); Leslie J. Workman and Kathleen Verduin, eds., *Medievalism in England II,* Studies in Medievalism, vol. 7 (Cambridge: Brewer, 1995); John Van Engen, ed., *The Past and Future of Medieval Studies* (Notre Dame, Ind.: Notre Dame University Press, 1994); María Rosa Menocal, *Shards of Love: Exile and the Origins of the Lyric* (Durham, N.C.: Duke University Press, 1994); Lee Patterson, *Negotiating the Past: The Historical Understanding of Medieval Literature* (Madison: University of Wisconsin Press, 1987); and Allen Frantzen, *Desire for Origins: New Language, Old English and Teaching the Tradition* (New Brunswick, N.J.: Rutgers University Press, 1990).

3. See, e.g., David Hult, "Gaston Paris and the Invention of Courtly Love," and Michael Camille, "Philological Iconoclasm and Image in the Vie de Saint Alexis," both in *Medievalism and the Modernist Temper.* Here I join my study of medievalism with Anne McClintock's nuanced study of imperialism, *Imperial Leather: Race, Gender and Sexuality in the Colonial Contest* (New York: Routledge, 1995).

4. Lee Patterson, "The Return of Philology," in *The Past and Future of Medieval Studies,* p. 241.

5. R. Howard Bloch and Stephen G. Nichols, introduction to *Medievalism and the Modernist Temper,* 21.

6. This move is inspired by feminist and queer interventions in medieval studies. For recent critical essays that conceive the fathers differently, see Judith M. Bennett, "Our Colleagues, Ourselves," in *The Past and Future of Medieval Studies;* E. Jane Burns, Sarah Kay, Roberta L. Krueger, and Helen Solterer, "Feminism and the Discipline of Old French Studies," in *Medievalism and the Modernist Temper;* and the special issue of *Gay and Lesbian Quarterly* (1995), *Premodern Sexualities in Europe,* ed. Louise O. Frandenburg and Carla Freccero.

7. Jacques Rancière, *The Names of History: On the Poetics of Knowledge* (Minneapolis: University of Minnesota Press, 1994), 56.

8. Bloch and Nichols, introduction to *Medievalism and the Modernist Temper,* 49; see also Brownlee, Brownlee, and Nichols, introduction to *The New Medievalism,* 12, where the same words, *hard-edged alterity,* are used. *Theory* is usually not specified in recent critical volumes on the topic, as if discursive practices in poststructuralist, feminist, queer, psychoanalytic, and postcolonial studies do not intrinsically have their histories.

9. Bloch and Nichols, introduction to *Medievalism and the Modernist Temper,* 5.

10. Joan Wallach Scott, "After History?" *Common Knowledge* 5 (1996): 24.

11. Here I am playing on the work of the essays in *Inside/Out: Lesbian Theories, Gay Theories,* ed. Diana Fuss (New York: Routledge, 1991). As Fuss avows in her introduction to the volume: "The figure inside/out cannot be easily or ever finally dispensed with; it can only be worked on and worked over—itself turned inside out to expose its critical operation and interior machinery" (p. 1).

12. Walter Benjamin, "Theses on the Philosophy of History," in *Illuminations,* ed. Hannah Arendt (New York: Harcourt, Brace & World, 1968), 255.

13. Eric L. Santner, *Stranded Objects: Mourning, Melancholy, and Film in Postwar Germany* (Ithaca, N.Y.: Cornell University Press, 1990), 153.

14. As a way into the bibliography on the professionalization of British history, consult Reba N. Sofer, *Discipline and Power: The University, History, and the Making of an English Elite, 1870–1930* (Stanford, Calif.: Stanford University Press, 1994); and Phillipa Levine, *The Amateur and the Professional: Antiquarians, Historians and Archaeologists in Victorian England, 1838–1886* (New York: Cambridge University Press, 1986). For a reference that needs to be recovered bibliographically in such discussions, see Stephen Bann, *The Clothing of Clio: A Study of the Representation of History in Nineteenth-Century Britain and France* (New York: Cambridge University Press, 1984). For thinking about the problem of

professionalization conceptually, see Sheldon Rothblatt, "How 'Professional' Are the Professions? A Review Article," *Comparative Studies in Society and History* 37 (1995): 194–205.

15. William Stubbs, *Seventeen Lectures on the Study of Medieval and Modern History* (1886; reprint, New York: Howard Fertig, 1967), 19.

16. My account is based on the following studies: Thomas C. Holt, *The Problem of Freedom: Race, Labor and Politics in Jamaica and Britain, 1832–1938* (Baltimore: Johns Hopkins University Press, 1992); Catherine Hall, "The Economy of Intellectual Prestige: Thomas Carlyle, John Stuart Mill, and the Case of Governor Eyre," *Critical Inquiry* 12 (1989): 169–76; and Douglas A. Lormer, *Color, Class and the Victorians: English Attitudes to the Negro in the Mid-Nineteenth Century* (New York: Holmes & Meier, 1978).

17. See Elizabeth Wallace, *Goldwin Smith, Victorian Liberal* (Toronto: University of Toronto Press, 1957). Wallace claims that Smith resigned his professorship to take care of his ailing father and does not link his decision to the attacks on him by the press and his high profile on speaking tours for the Jamaica Committee, although she does note that Mill even received assassination threats (p. 23) as chair of the committee. To give an example of the stakes, Wallace notes the *London Standard* responded as follows to news of his resignation: "Its editor expressed satisfaction at the news that he has resigned his Oxford Chair, as his 'bitter prejudices' and 'spirit of class hatred' utterly unfitted him 'to be the teacher of youths of higher orders' " (p. 23).

18. See N. J. Williams, "Stubbs's Appointment as Regius Professor, 1866," *Bulletin of the Institute for Historical Research* 33 (1960): 121–25.

19. Goldwin Smith had spoken publicly against Mansel in his 1858 Bampton Lecture ("Rational Religion and Rationalistic Objection"), accusing Mansel of using skepticism to shore up orthodoxy.

20. Hall, "The Economy of Intellectual Prestige."

21. Cited in Williams, "Stubbs's Appointment," 124.

22. For a list of Stubbs's publications, including his sermons, see William Holden Hunt, ed., *The Letters of William Stubbs, Bishop of Oxford, 1825–1901* (London: Constable, 1904), 409–15.

23. Sofer, *Discipline and Power,* 89.

24. Stubbs, *Seventeen Lectures,* 14, 15.

25. He professed, e.g., the stereotypical but no less damaging anti-Semitic attitudes of his day: "Things in general are very flat here; Egypt only in a slight degree drawing men's thoughts away from Ireland. If the Jews are on their way to Palestine, could not the Irish be prevailed on antiquam exquirere matrem, and emigrate in search of Scota, Pharoah's daughter?" (Stubbs to Reinhold Pauli, 6 June 1882, *The Letters of Wil-*

liam Stubbs, 185–86). For the context of such Victorian anti-Semitism, see Michael Ragussis, *Figures of Conversion: The "Jewish Question" and English National Identity* (Durham, N.C.: Duke University Press, 1995).

26. His colleagues may have learned to copy his silence for the sake of producing academic prestige, but they were hardly apolitical (such was Stubbs's fantasy). Frederick Seebohm, whose important work on medieval economic history centered on the medieval village community, was an anxious follower of slavery and postslavery economies in the colonies. His concern took the form of the pamphlet *The Crisis of Emancipation,* written in 1865 for the Central Committee of the Society of Friends for the Relief of the Emancipated Slaves of North America. J. A. Froude, who in 1892 succeeded E. A. Freeman, who had succeeded Stubbs, had served as a special emissary in South Africa and the West Indies and had his own involvements in British imperialism. The fantasy that such a view of history would divorce historians of politics nevertheless perdures in medieval studies.

27. *The Letters of William Stubbs,* 257. He issued a commission of inquiry early in 1885. The report recommended the creation of nine new parishes, each with church, schools, and vicarage house; the providing of vicarages in eight parishes where there were none; and the building of fifteen mission rooms. The estimated cost was £84,000.

28. Robert Brentano, "The Sounds of Stubbs," *Journal of British Studies* 6 (1967): 11.

29. I have taken the title of this section from the work of Cathy Caruth (*Unclaimed Experience: Trauma, Narrative, and History* [Baltimore: Johns Hopkins University Press, 1996]).

30. Jacques Derrida, *Specters of Marx: The State of the Debt, the Work of Mourning and the New International,* trans. Peggy Kamuf (New York: Routledge, 1994), 97.

31. Frandenburg, " 'Voice Memorial,' " 219.

32. My project thus shares in current critical work of resignifying abjection and questioning alterism in postcolonial and queer studies. *Alterism* is defined here as belief in the absoluteness of cultural and/or historical difference. The following texts have inspired my approach: For critiques of postcolonialism, see Sara Suleri, *The Rhetoric of English India* (Chicago: University of Chicago Press, 1992). For histories of sexuality, see Judith Butler, *Bodies That Matter: On the Discursive Limits of "Sex"* (New York: Routledge, 1993); Eve Kosofsky Sedgwick, *Epistemology of the Closet* (Berkeley and Los Angeles: University of California Press, 1990); and Louise O. Frandenburg and Carla Frecerro, "The Pleasures of History," *Gay and Lesbian Quarterly* 1, no. 4 (1995): 371–84. For histories of melancholy, mourning, and trauma and the fantasy of his-

toricism, see Louise O. Frandenburg, "'Be Not Far from Me': Psychoanalysis, Medieval Studies, and the Subject of Religion," *Exemplaria* 7, no. 1 (1995): 41–54; Juliana Schiesari, *The Gendering of Melancholia: Feminism, Psychoanalysis, and the Symbolics of Loss in Renaissance Literature* (Ithaca, N.Y.: Cornell University Press, 1992); Nicolas Abraham and Maria Torok, *The Wolf Man's Magic Word: A Cryptonomy* (Minneapolis: University of Minnesota Press, 1986); Santner, *Stranded Objects;* Caruth, *Unclaimed Experience,* 15; Michael S. Roth, *The Ironist's Cage: Memory, Trauma, and the Construction of History* (New York: Columbia University Press, 1995). See also Daniel Boyarin, "'Épater l'Embourgeoisement': Freud, Gender and the (De)Colonized Psyche," *Diacritics* 24 (1994): 17–41; Cynthia Chase, "Translating the Transference: Psychoanalysis and the Construction of History," in *Telling Facts: History and Narration in Psychoanalysis,* ed. Joseph H. Smith (Baltimore: Johns Hopkins University Press, 1992); Anselm Haverkamp, *Leaves of Mourning: Hoelderlin's Late Work* (Albany: State University of New York Press, 1996); Homi Bhabha, "Freedom's Basis in the Indeterminate," *October* 61 (1992): 46–57. For rhetorical analysis, see Dominick La Capra, "The Temporality of Rhetoric," in *Chronotypes: The Construction of Time,* ed. John Bender and David Wellbery (Stanford, Calif.: Stanford University Press, 1991). For the history of science, see Bruno Latour, *We Have Never Been Modern,* trans. Catherine Porter (Cambridge: Cambridge University Press, 1993).

33. For cogent discussion, see Butler, *Bodies That Matter,* 187–222.

34. For references, see n. 32 above and also Jay Geller, "'A Glance at the Nose': Freud's Inscription of Jewish Difference," *American Imago* 49 (1992): 445–66; Sander L. Gilman, *Freud, Race, and Gender* (Princeton, N.J.: Princeton University Press, 1993); and Eric L. Santner, *My Own Private Germany: Daniel Paul Schreber's Secret History of Modernity* (Princeton, N.J.: Princeton University Press, 1996).

35. Santner, *Stranded Objects,* 29.

36. Wendy Brown, *States of Injury: Power and Freedom in Late Modernity* (Princeton, N.J.: Princeton University Press, 1995). In her words: "We know ourselves to be saturated by history, we feel the extraordinary force of its determinations; we are also steeped in a discourse of insignificance, and, above all, we know that history will no longer (always already did not) act as our redeemer" (p. 54).

37. Walter Benjamin, "On Some Motifs in Baudelaire," in *Illuminations,* 184.

38. Freud's "Mourning and Melancholia" (see *A General Selection from the Works of Sigmund Freud,* ed. John Rickman [New York: Doubleday, 1957], 124–41) abounds in the terminology of economics.

39. Jacques Derrida, paraphrasing Freud, in his introduction to Torok and Torok, *The Wolf Man's Magic Word,* xxxviii. For further discussion of the relations of melancholy to mourning, see Haverkamp, *Leaves of Mourning.*

40. Schiesari, *The Gendering of Melancholia,* 11. This melancholic image of the Gothic peasant, so central to the work of Ruskin and Morris (and to much of contemporary medieval studies, as "Gothic Ornament and Sartorial Peasants" shows), marks a doubling (the counterpart being the winged woman of Durer's Melancholy) and a horizon of an affective history of melancholy, richly traced by Schiesari.

41. This thesis involved a strong reading of Anthony Kemp's *The Estrangement of the Past: A Study in the Origins of Modern Historical Consciousness* (New York: Oxford University Press, 1991) and is worked through in my monograph in progress: *Ethnography before Ethnography: Fabricating Ethnographic Objects in Medieval Christendom.*

42. Even though "Genders, Bodies, Borders" has been the subject of strong critique—as has the *Speculum* volume in which it first appeared, *Studying Medieval Women,* ed. Nancy Partner (Cambridge, Mass.: Medieval Academy of America, 1993)—I have decided to republish it here without alteration because I believe that the ethical acknowledgment of powerful work involves taking it seriously and grappling with its implications. In this sense, it is the highest compliment to seek to build on and revise the work of another scholar. This is the way I have read and continue to read the remarkable oeuvre of Caroline Walker Bynum. I regret that my seriousness about her transformative contributions to medieval studies has been construed by some colleagues as a personal or a professional attack. That was not then, nor is it now, my critical position. For a map to criticism of the *Speculum* volume, see Karma Lochrie, Clare A. Lees, and Gillian R. Overing, "Feminism within and without the Academy," *Medieval Feminist Newsletter* 22 (1996): 27–31. Bynum takes up some of the key issues raised in my essay in "Why All the Fuss about the Body? A Medievalist's Perspective," *Critical Inquiry* 22 (1995): 1–34.

43. Caruth, *Unclaimed Experience,* 11.

44. "These ghosts that are commodities transform human producers into ghosts" (Derrida, *Specters of Marx,* 156).

45. Butler, *Bodies That Matter,* 236.

Gothic Ornament and Sartorial Peasants

1. Louise O. Frandenburg and Carla Frecerro, "The Pleasures of History," *Gay and Lesbian Quarterly* 1 (1995): 372. Here the introduction

joins with medievalists and early modernists who are questioning the hard edge of medieval alterity and the work it does. In his "little allegiance to text and context as conventionally understood," which results in rich understandings of production and dissemination of medieval texts, Paul Strohm also enables my critique (*Hochon's Arrow: The Social Imagination of Fourteenth-Century Texts* [Princeton, N.J.: Princeton University Press, 1992], 7). Only briefly savored as this book went to press was David Wallace, *Chaucerian Polity: Absolutist Lineages and Associational Forms* (Stanford, Calif.: Stanford University Press, 1997).

2. The colonial Gothic Revival is discussed at greater length below. See also Thomas Metcalf, *An Imperial Vision: Indian Architecture in Britain's Raj* (Berkeley and Los Angeles: University of California Press, 1989); and Dana Arnold, "George Gilbert Scott and Bombay: India's Gothic Architecture," *Apollo* 123, no. 348 (1991): 87–90. For an overview of the Gothic Revival, especially its domestic architecture, see Megan Aldrich, *Gothic Revival* (London: Phaedon, 1994).

3. John Ruskin, *The Stones of Venice,* in *The Complete Works of John Ruskin,* ed. E. T. Cook and Alexander Wedderburn, 39 vols. (London: George Allen, 1903–12), 9:49–52. Ruskin (1819–1900), a contemporary of Bishop Stubbs's, began writing these words as the London Exhibition opened in 1851. I am interested that the detail of the hand was so important to Ruskin. This section sketches what was at stake in this body part in London conversations of that time.

4. Coverage of the Victoria and Albert Museum show (15 June–11 September 1994) on the noted Gothic Revival architect Augustus Welby Northmore Pugin (1812–52) provides a way into broaching the problem of the hand. The popular magazine *Perspectives on Architecture* advertised the show with four short essays in its June 1994 issue that briefly recount Pugin's biography, show historical photographs and recreations of his Gothic Revival house, called the Grange (Ramsgate, Kent), report on his design for the Medieval Court at the Great Exhibition, and, finally, feature John Outram, the contemporary architect who designed the monumental Pugin exhibition. Outram and Pugin are called "strange bedfellows" who find their commonality, the magazine tells us, in "ornament." The electricity of these short essays would lead the reader to believe that yet another Gothic Revival looms in this fin de siècle. Since the goal of the Victorian revival was intimately linked with promoting Christianity as a material vehicle for imperial civilization, how the magazine presented its story of Pugin's Medieval Court is relevant. The essay cites the contemporary *Illustrated London News* report cited in the text. But that is only half the story of the Medieval Court. For the "shock" of the India Exhibit, see Partha Mitter, *Much*

Maligned Monsters: History of European Reactions to Indian Art (Oxford: Clarendon, 1977). The ornament and design of the exhibit precipitated great debate; many Victorians found it the most superior in the show.

5. Ruskin, *Stones of Venice,* 49–52.

6. Owen Jones, *The Grammar of Ornament* (London: Day & Son, 1856), 79.

7. George M. Birdwood, *The Industrial Arts of India* (London: Chapman & Hall, 1880), 323.

8. "Gender . . . is often a very specific 'permeable membrane'—the skin" (Judith Halberstam, *Skin Shows* [Durham, N.C.: Duke University Press, 1995], 141).

9. Birdwood, *Industrial Arts of India,* 244.

10. Sir James Hall, *Essays on the Origins, History, and Principles of Gothic Architecture* (London, 1813), 18.

11. Thomas Rickman, *An Attempt to Discriminate the Styles of English Architecture* (London, 1819), iii.

12. Jonathan Crary, *Techniques of the Observer* (Cambridge, Mass.: MIT Press, 1990), 91, 1. For complementary commentary, see Lindsay Smith, *Victorian Photography, Painting and Poetry: The Enigma of Visibility in Ruskin, Morris and the Pre-Raphaelites* (Cambridge: Cambridge University Press, 1995). Rosalind Krauss opens *The Optical Unconscious* (Cambridge, Mass.: MIT Press, 1993) with a brilliant meditation on Ruskin.

13. John Sell Cotman, *Specimens of Architectural Remains in Various Counties of England, but Principally in Norfolk* (London: Henry Bolin, 1838), 2:13, pl. xxx.

14. Halberstam, *Skin Shows,* 41. At this point, Halberstam is reflecting on vol. 1 of Foucault's *History of Sexuality* (trans. Robert Hurley [New York: Vintage, 1978]).

15. For a beautiful study of the work of the veil in the Gothic novel, see Eve Kosofsky Sedgwick, *The Coherence of Gothic Conventions* (New York: Methuen, 1986). Halberstam notes that "true history and fiction trade places so that the story of the family replaces the story of nations; and the narrative of the body replaces the history of creation; and the significance of visual codes becomes greater than heritage" (*Skin Shows,* 39).

16. Cited in Dana Arnold, "George Gilbert Scott and Bombay: India's Gothic Architecture," *Apollo* 123, no. 348 (1991): 87.

17. This overview of the Gothic Revival is indebted to Christopher E. Miele's thorough and brilliant "The Gothic Revival and Gothic Architecture: The Restoration of Medieval Churches in Victorian Britain" (Ph.D. diss., New York University, 1991); see also his "The First Con-

servation Militants: William Morris and the Society for the Protection of Ancient Buildings," in *Preserving the Past: The Rise of the Heritage Industry,* ed. Michael Hunter (Stroud: Aldon Sutton, 1996). Miele does, however, advocate the traditional story of the Anglican Counter-Reformation (p. 340) and does not address the colonial dimensions of the Revival, although he has looked at materials (which I introduce below) that make the colonialism at the heart of the Revival clear.

18. If only Dr. Frankenstein had availed himself of a kaleidoscope when regarding his monster, surely he could have found something beautiful! Keep in mind also that Walter Scott's novels were appearing as Brewster wrote his paper on the kaleidoscope (see n. 19 below). I include Scott in the Gothic on the basis of the persuasive work of Fiona Robertson (*Legitimate Histories: Scott, Gothic and the Authorities of Fiction* [Oxford: Clarendon, 1994]).

19. David Brewster, *The Kaleidoscope: Its History, Theory and Construction* (London: John Murray, 1858), 7, 140. (Brewster's 1815 paper is reprinted in *The Kaleidoscope.*)

20. R. Derek Wood, "The Diorama in Great Britain in the 1820s," *History of Photography* 17 (1993): 284–95.

21. By 1829, a colleague of Rickman's, Matthew Hobeche Boxam, had published another popular, handy, pedagogical guide to Gothic ornament (*The Principles of Gothic Ecclesiastical Architecture* [London: Tilt & Bogue Fleet, 1829]) set up in an easy-to-follow, question-and-answer format. Like Rickman's book, it, too, had a long and successful publishing history.

22. For an excellent discussion of Pugin, see Jules Lubbock, *The Tyranny of Taste: The Politics of Architecture and Design in Britain, 1550–1960* (New Haven, Conn.: Yale University Press, 1995), 233–47.

23. For details of the competition and the subsequent rebuilding of the Houses of Parliament, see M. H. Port, ed., *The Houses of Parliament* (New Haven, Conn.: Yale University Press, 1976).

24. Charles L. Eastlake, *A History of the Gothic Revival* (London: Longmans, 1872), 184. Eastlake, an architect, was also the author of an important book on taste: *Hints on Household Taste* (1868; 3d. ed., London: Longmans, 1872).

25. The founding of architectural societies in England burgeoned after the Houses of Parliament competition. Phillipa Levine lists the dates and names of these societies in *The Amateur and the Professional,* app. 3.

26. Edward A. Freeman, *History of Architecture* (London: Joseph Masters, 1849), x, xviii, 4.

27. Ibid., 132.

28. Ibid., 6.

29. Michel Foucault, *Discipline and Punish,* trans. Alan Sheridan (New York: Vintage, 1979), 30.

30. Judith Butler, *Gender Trouble: Feminism and the Subversion of Identity* (New York: Routledge, 1990), 135.

31. Halberstam, *Skin Shows,* 119.

32. For details of the founding of the *Ecclesiologist,* see James F. White, *The Cambridge Movement: "The Ecclesiologist" and the Gothic Revival* (Cambridge: Cambridge University Press, 1962), 106.

33. "Parish Churches in New Zealand," *Ecclesiologist* 1 (1842): 4.

34. Benjamin Webb's "On the Adaptation of Pointed Architecture in Tropical Climates" (*Transactions of the Cambridge Camden Society* [1849], 196–218; Webb had read his paper on 13 February 1845) fomented a debate on Gothic church building in the colonies.

35. The Ecclesiological late Cambridge Camden Society, *Instrumenta ecclesiastica,* 2 vols. (London: John Van Voorst, 1847–56), preface.

36. "The Society presents a copy of this series to each of the Colonial Bishops" (the society's 1845–46 report is cited in White, *The Cambridge Movement*). *Tristan da Cunha* refers to three small volcanic islands in the South Atlantic midway between South Africa and South America annexed to the British Empire in 1816.

37. For the funding for the Public Record Office, see Levine, *The Amateur and the Professional,* 123. For analyses of the parliamentary study, see Miele, "The Gothic Revival and Gothic Architecture," 6. The data may be found in *Parliamentary Accounts and Papers,* vol. 58 (1870).

38. Bombay, the "Manchester of the East," in particular became India's "Victorian metropolis." Feverish building activity from the 1860s (the disruption of the American Civil War favored a Bombay textile boom) saw the erection of various Gothic public works mostly paid for by wealthy Indians: the Law Courts, University Hall, the University Library, the Bombay railroad station (Victoria Terminus), the Public Works Office. The *Builder* (23 October 1886, 592) described the Bombay Victoria Terminus as "one of the largest and most important modern buildings erected under European influence in the British Empire, and we have thought it well to give our readers the opportunity to form an opinion, as far as may be done from illustrations, as to the architectural merits of the building, which has apparently received great admiration in the region of Anglo Indian criticism."

39. Eastlake, *Hints on Household Taste,* 21. My understanding of the utter confusion of ornament at this moment is inspired by Jonathan Goldberg, *Sodometries: Renaissance Texts, Modern Sexualities* (Stanford, Calif.: Stanford University Press, 1992).

40. Morris's business decision bore cultural force since he and his company were the leading designers of Gothic ornament. In 1862, the company had won several awards at the International Exhibition in South Kensington. The exhibition jury praised the company's work as follows: "Messrs Morris and Co. have exhibited several pieces of furniture, tapestries, etc. in the style of the Middle Ages. The general forms of furnitures, the arrangement of tapestry and the character of detail are satisfactory to the archaeologist from the exactness of imitation; at the same time the general effect is excellent" (Charles Harvey and Jon Press, *William Morris: Design and Enterprise in Victorian Britain* [New York: St. Martin's, 1991], 49).

41. Morris timed his dilemma well. Remember that, in an "act of polemical bravado," Foucault marked 1870 as the date of the birth of modern homosexuality, discourses of which circulated in Morris's circle (see Foucault's *History of Sexuality,* 1:43, cited by Eve Kosofsky Sedgwick, *The Epistemology of the Closet* [Berkeley and Los Angeles: University of California Press, 1990], 44. Sedgwick also discusses [pp. 157–63] the complexities of discourses of inversion and of sexual object choice at the end of the nineteenth century). Oscar Wilde and Morris knew each other, and Morris lived long enough (he died on 3 October 1896) to know of Wilde's trial. Morris also knew Mark André Raffalovich, a member of Wilde's circle who published a book on homosexuality, *Uranisme et Unisexualité,* in 1896 (see *The Collected Letters of William Morris,* ed. Norman Kelvin, 4 vols. [Princeton, N.J.: Princeton University Press, 1987], no. 772, 2:96–97).

42. Judith Butler, "Imitation and Gender Insubordination," in *Inside/Out: Lesbian Theories, Gay Theories,* ed. Diana Fuss (New York: Routledge, 1991), 23. For critical elaboration of Butler's insights and their intersections with becoming human, becoming monstrous, see *Posthuman Bodies,* ed. Judith Halberstam and Ira Livingston (Bloomington: Indiana University Press, 1995).

43. Oscar Wilde, "The English Renaissance in Art," in *The First Collected Edition of Works of Oscar Wilde,* ed. R. Ross (New York: Macmillan, 1908), 251.

44. Derrida, *Specters of Marx* (New York: Routledge, 1994), 54.

45. Sedgwick, *Epistemology of the Closet,* 175.

46. Halberstam, *Skin Shows,* 111.

47. Morris's intense efforts to grapple with the problem of kitsch (retrospectively) were not unwarranted. Perhaps uncannily, he could hear voices of the early twentieth century collapsing the "it takes one to know one" of ornamental kitsch into criminality (Adolf Loos) or into sodomy ("the spread of sodomy encouraged by Liberty fabrics") and

thereby advocating the modernist effacement of ornament (see Rae Beth Gordon, *Ornament, Fantasy, and Desire in Nineteenth-Century French Literature* [Princeton, N.J.: Princeton University Press, 1992], 25, 231). Here, architectural history needs to join with Sedgwick's anti-homophic literary history of abstraction and figuration in *Epistemology of the Closet*, 163–67.

48. Cathy Caruth, *Unclaimed Experience: Trauma, Narrative, and History* (Baltimore: Johns Hopkins University Press, 1996), 11.

49. William Morris, "Some Hints on Pattern-Designing," in *News from Nowhere* (New York: Penguin, 1993), 261–62 (the lecture was first serialized in the *Commonweal* from January to October 1890).

50. *The Dream of John Ball* ran in the *Commonweal* from 13 November 1886 to 22 January 1887. In May 1887, Morris wrote his famous manifesto "To the Working-Men of England." For the classic study of Morris's politics, see E. P. Thompson, *William Morris: Romantic to Revolutionary*, 1st American ed. (New York: Pantheon, 1977); see also *The Collected Letters of William Morris*, vol. 2, covering 1881–84.

51. Steven Justice, *Writing and Rebellion: England in 1381* (Berkeley and Los Angeles: University of California Press, 1994).

52. Morris also did his history homework. In February 1884, Morris ordered the third and fourth volumes (just published) of James E. Thorold Rogers's *History of Agriculture and Prices in England* (6 vols. [Oxford: Clarendon, 1866–1902], a source of medieval economic history that would inspire his interest in the uprising of 1381. He mentioned Rogers respectfully in an SPAB speech on 1 July 1884 (*The Collected Letters of William Morris*, no. 952, p. 264).

53. William Morris, *A Dream of John Ball and a King's Lesson* (London: Longmans, Green, 1924), 4 (page numbers for subsequent citations will be given in the text).

54. Here, a history of ornament can parallel a history of the materialization of bodies that matter (see Butler, *Bodies That Matter*, 101).

55. Morris and Company, London, *The Morris Exhibit at the Foreign Fair, Boston, 1883–84* (Boston: Roberts Bros., 1883), 6.

56. Thompson, *William Morris*, 463.

57. Thompson, *William Morris*, 530, 531 (quoting the executive memorandum).

58. Justice, *Writing and Rebellion*, 191.

59. Ibid., 6. The distinction that Justice implies in his parable of graduate education and paleography plays in dangerously with an essentialist anti-intellectualism where only "getting your hands dirty" (nostalgically) counts.

60. In order to accomplish such exclusion, Justice must dismiss much

of the recent critical historiography of the late medieval peasantry, close off studies of the urban character of the rising, and neglect epistemological ways in which work itself was being refigured as work in the fourteenth century under the extreme pressure of proliferating wage labor. Much time could be spent elucidating these exclusions in *Writing and Rebellion,* but such an exercise would simply produce yet another reverse discourse. The rising can be read as a refiguration of town and country rather than the reincarnation of the English countryside, as Justice would have it. It can also be read as a rising promoting the deterritorialization of the customary land in the countryside in order to reterritorialize pastoral land use to the benefit of kulaks with links across village and town. To put this in perspective, see my "Malthus in a Straightjacket," *Journal of Interdisciplinary History* 20 (1990): 623–35. These very points can be found in essays in *The English Rising of 1381,* ed. R. H. Hilton and T. H. Aston (Cambridge: Cambridge University Press, 1984)—see, e.g., Christopher Dyer, "The Social and Economic Background to the Rural Revolt of 1381," on the livestock holdings of some of the rebels (p. 16); and A. F. Butcher, "English Urban Society and the Revolt of 1381," for a "false dichotomy between town and countryside" (p. 85) often perpetuated (hallowed in *Writing and Rebellion*) in many discussions of the revolt. For two politically sensitive readings of wage labor in England, see David Aers, "Justice and Wage-Labor after the Black Death," and Madonna Hettinger, "Defining the Servant: Legal and Extra-Legal Terms of Employment in Fifteenth-Century England," both in *The Work of Work: Servitude, Slavery and Labor in Medieval England,* ed. Allan Frantzen and Douglas Moffat (Glasgow: Cuithne, 1994), 169–90, 206–28.

61. Judith Butler, "Critically Queer," *Gay and Lesbian Quarterly* 1 (1993): 23.

62. Justice, *Writing and Rebellion,* 9. *Writing and Rebellion* can be read as a gloss on Michel de Certeau's critiques of Foucault; even Justice's diction echoes de Certeau's. Justice writes, e.g.: "I hope that I will have reversed the usual perspective, will have viewed our canonical literature from its social outside, from great regions of rural experience and practice" (p. 5). Compare the discussion of Foucault's panopticon where de Certeau writes of "the *immense reserve* containing the seeds or the traces of alternate developments" (Michel de Certeau, "Micro-Techniques and Panoptic Discourse: A Quid Pro Quo," in *Heterologies: Discourse of the Other,* trans. Brian Massumi [Minneapolis: University of Minnesota Press, 1986], 188). Similar phrasing can be found in another essay on Foucault: "An *immense* reserve constituting either the beginnings or traces of *different developments*" (Michel de Certeau,

"Foucault and Bourdieu," in *The Practice of Everyday Life*, trans. Steven Rendall [Berkeley and Los Angeles: University of California Press, 1988], 48).

63. Justice, *Writing and Rebellion*, 117, n. 35.

64. For the critical implications of Justice's use of speech act theory, see Jacques Derrida, "Signature Event Context," in *Limited INC*, ed. Gerald Graff, trans. Samuel Weber and Jeffrey Mehlman (Evanston, Ill.: Northwestern University Press, 1988), 1–24; Eve Kosofsky Sedgwick, "Queer Performativity: Henry James's *The Art of the Novel*," *Gay and Lesbian Quarterly* 1 (1993): 1–16; and Butler, "Critically Queer," and *Bodies That Matter*, 12–16. Derrida is worth quoting at some length here: "Through the values of 'conventional procedure,' 'correctness,' and 'completeness,' which occur in the definition, we necessarily find once more those of an exhaustively definable context, of a free consciousness present to the totality of the operation, and of absolutely meaningful speech [*vouloir-dire*] master of itself: the teleological jurisdiction of an entire field whose organizing center remains *intention*" (p. 15).

65. Justice, *Writing and Rebellion*, 207. For references to the different versions of the execution, see ibid., 97, n. 92.

66. Michel de Certeau, *The Writing of History*, trans. Tom Conley (Minneapolis: University of Minnesota Press, 1988), 319.

67. Butler, *Bodies That Matter*, 12.

68. The work of Jesse M. Gellrich is suggestive, but I think that his relay between orality and writing needs to be reworked as the iterable relation of citation to performative utterance (see *Discourse and Dominion in the Fourteenth Century: Oral Contexts of Writing in Philosophy, Politics and Poetry* [Princeton, N.J.: Princeton University Press, 1995]).

69. Justice, *Writing and Rebellion*, 5.

70. For a translation of portions of the parliamentary deposition, see *English Historical Documents*, ed. David C. Douglas, vol. 4, *1327–1485*, ed. A. R. Myers (New York: Oxford University Press, 1966), 407–14. For the original text, see John Strachey, ed., *Rotuli parliamentorum*, 6 vols. (London, 1767–77), 3:416–23.

71. *Rotuli parliamentorum*, 419. "Also the king refused to keep and defend the just laws and customs of the realm, but according to the whim of his desire he wanted to do whatever appealed to his wishes. Sometimes—and often when the laws of the realm had been declared and expressed to him by the justices and others of his council and he should be done justice to those who sought it according to the laws—he said expressly, with harsh and determined looks, that the laws were in

his own mouth, sometimes he said that they were in his breast, and that he alone could change or establish the laws of his realm. And deceived by this idea, he would not allow justice to be done to many of his lieges, but compelled very many person to desist from suing for common justice by threat and fear" (*English Historical Documents,* 410).

72. Butler, "Critically Queer," 18.

73. "Post quam quibus vendicationem et clameum, tam Domini Spirituales quam Temporales, et omnes Status ibidem presentes, singillatim et communiter interrogati, Quid de illa vendicatione et clameo sentiebant? iidem Status, cum toto Populo, absque quacumque difficultate vel mora ut Dux prefatus super eos regnaret unanimiter consenserunt. Et statim ut idem Rex ostendit Statibus Regni Signetum Ricardi Regis" (Strachey, ed., *Rotuli parliamentorum,* 3:423: "After such a presentation and claim, the Lords, spiritual and temporal, and all the Commons there present separately and together asked: On the basis of this presentation and claim what should they sentence? The same Commons, with the people, without any difficulty or delay whatsoever unanimously agreed that the aforesaid duke should reign over them. And at once the same king showed the Commons King Richard's signet of the realm" [translation mine]).

74. Gellrich, *Discourse and Dominion,* 175–78.

75. Justice, *Writing and Rebellion,* 139. Lee Patterson rules out the Wife of Bath from peasant political consciousness because of her "socially undetermined subjectivity" (" 'No Man His Reason Herde': Peasant Consciousness, Chaucer's Miller, and Structure of the *Canterbury Tales,"* in *Literary Practice and Social Change in Britain, 1380–1530,* ed. Lee Patterson [Berkeley and Los Angeles: University of California Press, 1990], 150). For political readings of the Wife of Bath, see Strohm, *Hochon's Arrow,* 121–44; Susan Crane, "The Writing Lesson of 1381," in *Chaucer's England: Literature in Historical Context* (Medieval Studies at Minnesota, vol. 4), ed. Barbara Hanawalt (Minnesota: University of Minnesota Press, 1992), 201–21. Melvin Storm's "Alisoun's Ear" (*Modern Language Quarterly* 42 [1981]: 219–26), which I cite because it is about the ear of the Wife of Bath, is an example of a misogynistic period piece. An enduring starting point to feminist rereadings of the Wife of Bath can be found in Mary Carruthers, "The Wife of Bath and the Painting of Lions," *PMLA* 94 (1979): 209–22. Strohm and Crane also neatly summarize the misogynist nature of Chaucer criticism.

76. Justice, *Writing and Rebellion,* 116; see also 127: "Taken as a model for social authority—as Langland never mean it to be taken—the image of [Piers Plowman] is contradictory and self-defeating. In the documentary understanding of writing as enactment commanding realiza-

tion in the empirical world, Piers' defectively literate authority is a losing proposition: authority claimed without writing would be no authority at all." Justice returns to this distinction on p. 130.

77. Thorlac Turville-Petre offers an interesting analysis of how the romantic, wholly fictional Havelok was read as history in the early fourteenth century (*England the Nation: Language, Literature, and National Identity, 1290–1340* [Oxford: Clarendon, 1996], 142–55).

78. Justice, *Writing and Rebellion,* 130. Quotations from Chaucer's *Canterbury Tales* are taken from Larry D. Benson, ed., *Riverside Chaucer,* 3d ed. (New York: Houghton Mifflin, 1987). Line numbers are given in the text.

79. When all the sexual play on genitals and "privitee" in the Miller's Tale (which the pilgrims have already heard) and the fact that the Wife's girlfriend is Alisoun (another echo from the Miller's Tale) are considered in the context of the Wife's proud remarks on her pudendum, her pleasure in oral sex ("and therwithal so wel koude he me glose, whan that he would ham my bele chose" [lines 509–10]), and her allusion to the marks of Venus ("preinte of sainte Venus seel" [line 604]) and of Mars ("yet have i Martes mark upon my face, and also in another privee place" [lines 619–20]), one can imagine that there is more to the Wife's sexual economy ("wynne whoso may, for al is for to selle" [line 414]) than a straight reading might make of it.

80. We need to keep this in mind when Justice talks about the Lollard Margery Baxter in his "Inquisition, Speech, and Writing: A Case from Late-Medieval Norwich," *Representations* 48 (1994): 1–29.

81. See "English America: Worth Dying For?" below.

82. Caroline Walker Bynum, *Holy Feast and Holy Fast: The Religious Significance of Food to Medieval Women* (Berkeley and Los Angeles: University of California Press, 1987.

83. Justice, *Writing and Rebellion,* 176, 107.

84. Justice, *Writing and Rebellion,* 187, n. 166, which recuperates the "importance of family."

85. Wendy Brown, *States of Injury: Power and Freedom in Late Modernity* (Princeton, N.J.: Princeton University Press, 1995), 165.

86. Sedgwick, "Queer Performativity," 3.

87. Justice, *Writing and Repression,* 261.

88. For recent overviews of the politics of the vernacular in Ireland, see Turville-Petre, *England the Nation,* 155–80; and James F. Lydon, "Nation and Race in Medieval Ireland," in *Concepts of National Identity in the Middle Ages,* ed. Simon Forde, Lesley Johnson, and Alan V. Murray, Leeds Texts and Monographs, n.s. 14 (Leeds: University of Leeds, 1995).

89. Henry Berry, ed., *Statutes and Ordinances and Acts of Parliament in Ireland* (Dublin: His Majesty's Stationery Office, 1907), 435: "item ordine est et estabile que chescun Engleys use la lang Englies et soit nome per nomen Engleys enterlessant oultermet la manere de nomine use per Irroies et que chescun Engleys use la manere guise monture et appeill Engleis solone son estat et si nul Engleys ou Irroies conversant entre Engleys use la lang Irroies entre eux-mesmes encontre ceste ordinanance et de ceo soit atteint soint sez terres et Tenementez sil eit seisiz en les maines son signeur immediate."

90. Susan Buck-Morss, *The Dialectics of Seeing: Walter Benjamin and the Arcades Project* (Cambridge, Mass.: MIT Press, 1989), 39. My concern with architecture is also inspired by Mark Wigley, *The Architecture of Deconstruction: Derrida's Haunt* (Cambridge, Mass.: MIT Press, 1993).

91. Daniel Libeskind, "Between the Lines: The Jewish Museum, Berlin," *Research in Phenomenology* 22 (1992): 84. On the design for the Victoria and Albert competition, see Daniel Libeskind and Cecil Balmond, *Unfolding* (Rotterdam: NAI, 1997).

92. Giles Worlsely, editor of *Perspectives on Architecture,* Sir Hugh Leggatt, secretary of Heritage in Danger, and William Rees-Mogg, former editor of *The Times,* respectively, cited in the *Independent,* 10 August 1996, 7 (further debate is available on Nexus-Lexus; search *Libeskind* and *Victoria and Albert Museum*).

English America: Worth Dying For?

My thanks to the students of History 413 (spring 1995) at the University of Notre Dame for their intellectual curiosity, generosity, and acuity. Without them, this essay would not be possible.

1. Kathleen Biddick, "Decolonizing the British Past: Readings in Medieval Archaeology and History," *Journal of British Studies* 32 (1993): 1–23.

2. Sara Suleri's rich use of the term *English India* inspires me in my own use of *English America:* "The term 'English India' demands an explication that would render it both literal and figurative at the same time: English India is not synonymous with the history of British rule in the subcontinent, even while it is suborned to the strictures of such a history. At the same time English India is not solely a linguistic concept, a spillage from history into language, one that made difficult oppositions between the rhetorical and actual. The idiom of English India expresses a disinterest in the continuity of tense, so that the distinction between colonial and postcolonial histories becomes less radical, less

historically 'new'" (*The Rhetoric of English India* [Chicago: University of Chicago Press, 1992], 3).

3. See Michael Taussig, *Mimesis and Alterity* (New York: Routledge, 1993), 65; Peter Hulme, *Colonial Encounters* (London: Methuen, 1987), 253; and Mary Louise Pratt, *Imperial Eyes: Travel Writing and Transculturation* (New York: Routledge, 1992), 100.

4. Gauri Viswanathan, *Masks of Conquest: Literary Study and British Rule in India* (New York: Columbia University Press, 1989), 3.

5. Here, telegraphically, I am drawing on the excellent work of Allen J. Frantzen, *Desire for Origins: New Language, Old English, and Teaching the Tradition* (New Brunswick, N.J.: Rutgers University Press, 1990); Allen J. Frantzen and Charles L. Vengonie, "The Desire for Origins: An Archaeology of Anglo-Saxon Studies," *Style* 2 (1986): 142–56; and Robert Colls and Phillip Dodd, eds., *Englishness: Culture and Politics, 1880–1920* (Beckenham: Croom Helm, 1986).

6. *Peasants, Knights and Heretics,* ed. Rodney Hilton (New York: Cambridge University Press, 1976), gathers together important *Past and Present* papers in the controversy up to 1971. For more recent restatements, see J. C. Holt, *Robin Hood* (New York: Thames & Hudson, 1982); P. R. Coss, "Aspects of Cultural Diffusion in Medieval England," *Past and Present* 108 (August 1985): 35–79; and Stephen Knight, *Robin Hood: A Complete Study of the English Outlaw* (Cambridge, Mass.: Blackwell, 1994).

7. My discussion of postwar racism in Britain is based on Paul Gilroy, *"There Ain't No Black in the Union Jack": The Cultural Politics of Race and Nation* (London: Hutchinson, 1987); and Anna Marie Smith, *New Right Discourse on Race and Sexuality* (New York: Cambridge University Press, 1994).

8. The center was founded in 1964, twelve years after *Past and Present.* For background, see Cary Nelson, Paula A. Treichler, and Lawrence Grossberg, "Cultural Studies: An Introduction," in *Cultural Studies,* ed. Lawrence Grossberg, Cary Nelson, and Paula Treichler (New York: Routledge, 1992), 1–22.

9. For important critical discussion of the pastoral, see Annabel M. Patterson, *Pastoral and Ideology: Virgil to Valéry* (Berkeley and Los Angeles: University of California Press, 1987). Historically, forests provide a crucial pastoral space for Englishness. For an illuminating meditation on forests, see Robert Pogue Harrison, *Forests: The Shadow of Civilization* (Chicago: University of Chicago Press, 1992).

10. For an extended discussion of the film *Robin Hood: Prince of Thieves* (Roy Grundman–Cineaste Studio–Morgan Creek, 1991) and the 1938 swashbuckler *The Adventures of Robin Hood* (Warner Bros.),

see my "The Historiographic Unconscious and the Return of Robin Hood," in *The Salt of Common Life: Individuality and Choice in Medieval Town, Countryside, and Church,* ed. Edwin B. De Windt (Kalamazoo, Mich.: Medieval Institute Publications, 1996), 65–78.

11. Walter Benjamin, "Theses on a Philosophy of History," in *Illuminations,* ed. Hannah Arendt (New York: Schocken, 1969), 261.

12. Derek Jarman, *The Last of England,* ed. David L. Hirst (London: Constable, 1987), 188, 189. See also Simon Burt, review of *The Last of England, Times Literary Supplement,* 6 November 1987, 1225; Iain Johnstone, review of *The Last of England, Sunday Times,* 25 October 1987, 65; and "History and the Gay Viewfinder: An Interview with Derek Jarman," *Cineaste* 18, no. 4 (1991): 24–27.

13. Quoted in Marilyn Strathern, *After Nature: English Kinship in the Late Twentieth Century* (Cambridge: Cambridge University Press, 1991), 158.

14. Dympna Callaghan, "An Interview with Seamus Deane," *Social Text* 38 (1994): 38–50. For a further meditation on this cultural hunger artistry, see Maud Ellmann, *The Hunger Artists: Starving, Writing, and Imprisonment* (Cambridge, Mass.: Harvard University Press, 1993).

15. My use of the pastoral as a political, performative space is influenced by Patterson, *Pastoral and Ideology;* and Peter Stallybrass, " 'Drunk with the Cup of Liberty': Robin Hood, the Carnivalesque, and the Rhetoric of Violence in Early Modern England," in *The Violence of Representation: Literature and the History of Violence,* ed. Nancy Armstrong and Leonard Tennenhouse (New York: Routledge, 1989), 45–76.

16. Strathern, *After Nature,* 193.

17. "Thus today's British racism, anchored in national decline rather than imperial expansion overseas, does not necessarily proceed through readily apparent notions of superiority and inferiority. The order of racial power relations has become more subtle and elusive than that. Recognizing this fundamental development provides part of the key to understanding how racial and conservative, socialist and openly racist theories and explanations of 'race' have been able to converge dramatically. This coming together is a characteristic feature of contemporary 'race' politics in Britain" (Gilroy, "*There Ain't No Black in the Union Jack,*" 40).

18. For a study of the visual representations of Robin Hood, from the first illustrated antiquarian collection of ballads published by Joseph Ritson in 1795 to a *History Today* republication in 1991 of an illustrated essay on Robin Hood that first appeared in that journal in 1958 (as part of the postwar obsession with Robin Hood), see my "The Historiographic Unconscious."

19. See Hilton, ed., *Peasants, Knights and Heretics;* and Eric Hobsbawn, *Primitive Rebels* (Manchester: Manchester University Press, 1959).

20. For a historical perspective on the disciplinary formation of problems of English medieval peasants and their village communities, see Clive Dewey, "Images of the Village Community: A Study in Anglo-Indian Ideology," *Modern Asian Studies* 6, no. 3 (1972): 291–328; J. W. Burrow, " 'The Village Community' and the Uses of History in Late Nineteenth-Century England," in *Historical Perspectives: Studies in English Thought and Society,* ed. Neil McKendrick (London: Europa, 1974), 255–84; and Peter Gatrell, "Historians and Peasants: Studies of Medieval English Society in Russian Context," *Past and Present* 96 (1982): 22–50. The important works from the period include H. S. Maine, *Village Communities in the East and West* (London, 1871); F. W. Maitland, *Domesday Book and Beyond* (Cambridge: Cambridge University Press, 1901); and Paul Vinogradoff, *Villainage in England* (Oxford: Clarendon, 1892), 403. In "Images of the Village Community," Dewey brilliantly works through the politics of these shifting positions on village community and property.

21. Vinogradoff, *Villainage in England,* 403.

22. Michel de Certeau, *The Writing of History,* trans. Tom Conley (New York: Columbia University Press, 1988), 69.

23. My analysis here can be read with Gauri Viswanathan, "Raymond Williams and British Colonialism," *Yale Journal of Criticism* 4 (1991): 47–66.

24. Joan Thirsk, "The Family," *Past and Present* 27 (1964): 116–22.

25. Alan Macfarlane, *The Origins of English Individualism: The Family, Property, and Social Transition* (Oxford: Oxford University Press, 1978).

26. Paul Gilroy considers this report "a crucial document in the history of the discourse of the black community. It set the official seal on a definition of the origins and extent of black crime and tied these to what were felt to be distinct patterns of politics and family life, characteristic of black culture" ("*There Ain't No Black in the Union Jack,*" 104).

27. Lawrence Stone, "Interpersonal Violence in English Society," *Past and Present* 101 (1983): 33.

28. John Akomfrah's *Handsworth Songs* was distributed by the Black Audio Collective, Derek Jarman's *The Last of England* by Anglo Internation Films. On *Handsworth Songs,* see Barbara Kruger's review in *Artforum* 27 (September 1988): 143–44; Salman Rushdie's critical review in the *Guardian,* 12 January 1987, 7; Jarman, *The Last of England,* 108; Coco Fusco, "A Black Avant-Garde? Notes on Black Audio Film Collective and Sankofa," in *English Is Broken Here: Notes on Cultural Fusion in*

the Americas, ed. Coco Fusco (New York: New Press, 1995); Reece Auguiste, "*Handsworth Songs:* Some Background Notes," *Framework* 35 (1988): 4–8; and Paul Gilroy and Jim Pines, "*Handsworth Songs:* Audiences/Aesthetic/Independence—Interview with the Black Audio Collective," *Framework* 35 (1988): 9–18.

29. My analysis here draws on Eve Kosofsky Sedgwick, *The Epistemology of the Closet* (Berkeley and Los Angeles: University of California Press, 1990).

30. For an important discussion of Thatcherism and homophobia, see Smith, *New Right Discourse*, 183–239.

31. Smith, *New Right Discourse*, 189.

32. For a detailed comparison of the 1938 and 1991 versions of Robin Hood, see my "The Historiographic Unconscious."

33. This is not the place to discuss the epistemological and ontological challenges of post-Orientalist histories. For selected references that set out, revise, and criticize the pioneering work of Edward Said, see Edward W. Said, "Representing the Colonized: Anthropology's Interlocutors," *Critical Inquiry* 15 (Winter 1989): 205–25; James Clifford, "On Orientalism," in *The Predicament of Culture* (Cambridge, Mass.: Harvard University Press, 1988), 255–76; Timothy Mitchell, *Colonising Egypt* (New York: Cambridge University Press, 1986); Robert Young, *White Mythologies: Writing History and the West* (New York: Routledge, 1990); and Gyan Prakash, "Writing Post-Orientalist Histories of the Third World: Perspectives from Indian Historiography," *Comparative Studies in Society and History* 32, no. 2 (1990): 383–408.

34. For a discussion of carnival and the Robin Hood legend, see Stallybrass, " 'Drunk with the Cup of Liberty.' "

35. To think of the "sublime" shot of the deer, it is helpful to recall the words of Edmund Burke: "I know of nothing sublime which is not some modification of power" (*A Philosophical Enquiry into the Origin of Our Ideas of the Sublime and Beautiful*, ed. James Boulton [Notre Dame, Ind.: University of Notre Dame Press, 1968], 59).

36. See Pratt, *Imperial Eyes*, p. 100.

37. For evocative but by no means exhaustive examples of a history of the European construction of the primitive and some neocolonial efforts to relocate the primitive in the idealizing and essentializing use of voices from former colonized societies, see *Imperial Fantasies and Postcolonial Histories* (Special issue), *Representations*, vol. 37 (Winter 1992); Said, "Representing the Colonized"; Michael Taussig, *Shamanism, Colonialism, and the Wild Man: A Study in Terror and Healing* (Chicago: University of Chicago Press, 1987); Clifford, *The Predicament of Culture;* and Anna Maria Alonso, "The Effects of Truth: Re-

Presentation of the Past and the Imagining of Community," *Journal of Historical Sociology* 1, no. 1 (1988): 33–57. See also *Inscriptions,* the journal published by the Group for the Critical Study of Colonial Discourse, University of California, Santa Cruz, esp. nos. 3/4, devoted to feminism and the critique of colonial discourse; and Michel de Certeau's *The Practice of Everyday Life* (Berkeley and Los Angeles: University of California Press, 1984), *Heterologies: Discourse on the Other* (Minneapolis: University of Minnesota Press, 1986), and *The Writing of History.*

38. Les Levidow and Kevin Robins, "Vision Wars," *Race and Class* 32, no. 4 (1991): 88. Related to the reception of the Gulf War in Europe is the 1992 inauguration of the European Community structures. For an analysis of the relations of the "Arab nation" to the "European nation," see Etienne Balibar, "Es Gibt Keinen Staat in Europa: Racism and Politics in Europe Today," *New Left Review* 186 (March/April 1991): 5–19: "The two complexes making up the 'Arab nation' and the 'European nation'—neither of them securely fixed, for different historical reasons—are closely bound up with the other and cannot evolve independently" (p. 9).

39. For a history of the association of Lady Marian with the Robin Hood legend, see R. B. Dobson and John Taylor, *Rymes of Robyn Hood: An Introduction to the English Outlaw* (London: Heinemann, 1976). She is not part of the medieval tradition. The joining of Robin and Marian occurred in Tudor May Day celebrations and morris dances: "Here Marian, played by a boy, developed into a by-word for sexual impropriety.... The consequent liason between Robin Hood and his Maid Marian gradually introduced a more romantically sexual element into the greenwood myth, an element completely absent in medieval tradition but absolutely essential for the later elaboration and survival of the legend" (ibid., 42). For cross-dressing, unruly women and the carnival aspect of Lady Marian in the early modern period, see Stallybrass, " 'Drunk with the Cup of Liberty.' " In the film *Son of Robin Hood* (1958, directed by Georg Sherman for Argo Films), Robin Hood's son is really a daughter cross-dressed.

40. Rudy Behlmer, ed., *The Adventures of Robin Hood* (Madison: University of Wisconsin Press, 1979), 172, 212.

41. Balibar, "Es Gibt Keinen Staat in Europa," 15.

42. Salman Rushdie, *Satanic Verses* (New York: Viking, 1988), 129. For an inspiring meditation on the historical aspects of Rushdie's cultural project, see Homi Bhabha, "DissemiNation: Time, Narrative, and the Margins of the Modern Nation," in *Nation and Narration* (New York: Routledge, 1990).

43. The students used John Gillingham, "The Beginnings of English

Imperialism," *Journal of Historical Sociology* 5 (1992): 392–409; and Robin Frame, *The Political Development of the British Isles* (New York: Oxford University Press, 1990).

Bede's Blush: Postcards from Bali, Bombay, Palo Alto

I am grateful to the following colleagues who generously read drafts of this essay and offered their criticisms and support: Joe Buttigieg, Ted Cachey, Bill Dohar, Julia Douthwaite, Kent Emery, Ed English, Robert Franklin, Philip Gleason, Barbara Green, Madonna Hettinger, Cyraina Johnson, Mark Jordan, Sandra Joshel, Mark Myerson, Dianne Phillips, Dan Sheerin, John Van Engen, Joseph Wawrykow, and Lisa Wolverton. I am also grateful to the participants in the medieval studies section of the cultural studies seminar at Rice University for their stimulating exchange and critical support for developing the conference-paper version of this essay for publication. A minicolloquium with Clare Lees and James W. Earle organized by Sarah Lynn Higley and Tom Hahn offered a much-needed opportunity to deliver a version of this essay to colleagues in medieval literature. The *Exemplaria* session at Kalamazoo (1993) "Medievalism and Imperialism: The Subject of Appropriation" provided this essay the benefit of the thoughtful comments of Laurie Finke and Catherine S. Cox.

1. Umberto Eco, "The Return of the Middle Ages," in *Travels in Hyperreality*, trans. William Weaver (New York: Harcourt Brace Jovanovich, 1986), 61.

2. I am telescoping an important discussion of the historical construction of early modern identity worked through by Jonathon Dollimore, *Sexual Dissidence: Augustine to Wilde, Freud to Foucault* (Oxford: Oxford University Press, 1991), 283–9. My thanks to Kari Kalve, who first urged me to read Dollimore.

3. A large literature exists on the nonoriginary and originary frames of the Middle Ages. For a selection of recent reflections, see R. Howard Bloch, "Naturalism, Nationalism, Medievalism," *Romanic Review* 76, no. 4 (1985): 341–60; Allen J. Frantzen, *Desire for Origins: New Language, Old English, and Teaching the Tradition* (New Brunswick, N.J.: Rutgers University Press, 1990), and "Prologue: Documents and Monuments: Difference and Interdisciplinarity in the Study of Medieval Culture," in *Speaking Two Languages* (Albany: State University of New York Press, 1990); Lee Patterson, *Negotiating the Past: The Historical Understanding of Medieval Literature* (Madison: University of Wisconsin Press, 1987), and "On the Margin: Postmodernism, Ironic History, and

Medieval Studies," *Speculum* 65, no. 1 (1990): 87–108; and Brian Stock, *Listening for the Text: On the Uses of the Past* (Baltimore: Johns Hopkins University Press, 1990). For a study of medievalism and Catholicism in the United States, important to the cultural history of North American medieval institutes, see Philip Gleason, "American Catholics and the Mythic Middle Ages," in *Keeping the Faith: American Catholicism Past and Present* (Notre Dame, Ind.: University of Notre Dame Press, 1987). For a strong example of the effects of the pastism-presentism debate, see Caroline Walker Bynum, *Holy Feast and Holy Fast: The Religious Significance of Food to Medieval Women* (Berkeley and Los Angeles: University of California Press, 1987). For a critique of pastism in the study of medieval women's history, see my "Genders, Bodies, Borders: Technologies of the Visible," *Speculum* 68 (1993): 389–418. A popular form of "presentism" may be found in Georges Duby, "The Emergence of the Individual," in *A History of Private Life*, vol. 2, *Revelations of the Medieval World* (Cambridge, Mass.: Harvard University Press, 1988).

4. The energies devoted to such debate help contribute to the disciplinary repression of discussion of pressing questions about the significance of other cultural constructions of time in historical practice, notably, transference and time lag. Dominick LaCapra has made important arguments about the theoretical importance of transference to the practice of history: "I use 'transference' in the modified psychoanalytic sense of repetition-displacement of the past into the present as it necessarily bears on the future. 'Transference' is bound up with a notion of time not as simply continuity or discontinuity but as repetition with variation or change—at times traumatically disruptive change" ("Is Everyone a *Mentalité* Case?" in *History and Criticism* [Ithaca, N.Y.: Cornell University Press, 1985], 72). Homi Bhabha has pointed out the importance of the critical concept *time lag*, especially for postcolonial, subaltern histories: "There is a continual tension between spatial incommensurability of the articulation of cultural differences, and the temporal non-synchronicity of signification as they attempt to speak, quite literally, in terms of each other" ("Postcolonial Authority and Postmodern Guilt," in *Cultural Studies*, ed. Lawrence Grossberg, Cary Nelson, and Paula A. Treichler [New York: Routledge, 1992], 58).

5. For an example of the Middle Ages working as a stand-in for neocolonial representations of the Third World in the present, see my review of the film *The Navigator: A Medieval Odyssey*, directed by Vincent Ward (1988), *American Historical Review* 97, no. 4 (1993): 1152–53.

6. Henry Chadwick quoted by Milton McC. Gatch in "The Medievalist and Cultural Literacy," *Speculum* 66, no. 3 (1991): 604. Lee Patterson drew attention to such tropes in his comments at the conference "The

Past and Future of Medieval Studies" (19–21 February 1992, University of Notre Dame), at which this essay was first delivered.

7. Our disciplinary problems with pastism and presentism could both learn from and contribute to a parallel debate in critical studies—that over modernism/postmodernism. The controversy can provide medievalists with productive ways of reading the medieval/early modern debates. In turn, our own controversies over the medieval/early modern divide can produce important questions about containment and appropriation for contemporary critical studies of postmodernism. Dollimore (*Sexual Dissidence,* 81–91) sets out an incisive discussion of debates over containment, resistance, and transgression in cultural politics.

8. Such a medieval studies would be studies in diffraction, "a mapping of interference, not of replication, reflection, or reproduction." For an important discussion of the difference between *articulation* and *representation* as political strategies in disciplines, terms that can be refigured as *transgressive knowledge* and *representation* in Dollimore's *Sexual Dissidence,* see Donna Haraway, "The Promises of Monsters: A Regenerative Politics for Inappropriate/d Others," in *Cultural Studies,* 300. These issues are also raised in Joan W. Scott, "The Evidence of Experience," *Critical Inquiry* 17 (Summer 1991): 773–97.

9. I am inspired here by Cristina Crosby, *The Ends of History: Victorians and "The Woman Question"* (New York: Routledge, 1991), and "Dealing with Differences," in *Feminists Theorize the Political,* ed. Judith Butler and Joan W. Scott (New York: Routledge, 1992); and Bhabha, "Postcolonial Authority and Postmodern Guilt."

10. It is interesting to note that another conference devoted to disciplinary scrutiny of medieval studies, "The Past and Future of Medieval Studies" (Barnard College, December 1990), also avoided mention of the present. My thoughts about missing bodies were set in motion at the Barnard meeting.

11. I have appropriated the unusual uses of the noun *the disappeared* and the verb *to disappear* from the work of the "mothers of the disappeared" in Chile. I wish to suggest that meditations on their political work have relevance to issues of pedagogy in medieval studies: "The memory of protest, and the violence enacted against it by the State, best serves the official forces of oppression when the collective nature of memory is broken, when it is fragmented and located not in the public sphere but in the private fastness of the individual self or of the family. There it feeds fear. There it feeds nightmares crippling the capacity for public protest and spirited intelligent opposition. And that is why the actions of the mothers of the disappeared strike me as important. For

they create a new public ritual whose aim is to allow the tremendous moral and magical power of the unquiet dead to flow into the public sphere, empower individuals, and challenge the would-be guardians of the Nation-State, guardians of the dead as well as its living, of its meaning and of its destiny" (Michael Taussig, "Violence and Resistance in the Americas: The Legacy of Conquest," in *Nervous System* [New York: Routledge, 1992], 48–49).

12. As the university approaches the twenty-first century, medieval studies will have to respond to the problems of critical pedagogy as *embodied theory.* Frantzen trenchantly comments on the disembodiment of pedagogy when it gets discussed as "approaches" to Old English (*Desire for Origins,* 13 and passim). For critical commentaries on pedagogy that can serve as a starting point for engaged discussion of pedagogy among medievalists, see the interview between Harold Veeser and Gayatri Chakravorty Spivak that appeared in *The New Historicism,* ed. Harold Veeser (New York: Routledge, 1989), and was reprinted as "The New Historicism: Political Commitment and the Postmodern Criticism" in Spivak's *The Post-Colonial Critic: Interviews, Strategies, Dialogues,* ed. Sarah Harasym (New York: Routledge, 1990); Chandra Talpade Mohanty, "On Race and Voice: Challenges for Liberal Education in the 1990s," *Cultural Critique* (Winter 1990): 179–208; Shoshana Felman, "Psychoanalysis and Education: Teaching Terminable and Interminable," in *Jacques Lacan and the Adventure of Insight: Psychoanalysis in Contemporary Culture* (Cambridge, Mass.: Harvard University Press, 1987); Henry A. Giroux, "Resisting Difference: Cultural Studies and the Discourse of Critical Pedagogy," in *Cultural Studies.*

13. Clifford Geertz, "Deep Play: Notes on the Balinese Cockfight," in *The Interpretation of Culture: Selected Essays* (New York: Basic, 1973); page numbers for quotations are hereafter given in the text. I discuss below two examples where Geertz is used in contemporary critiques of medieval studies. I note here the uncanny appearance of Geertz in the opening travel story told by Stephen Greenblatt in his introduction to *Marvellous Possessions: The Wonder of the New World* (Chicago: University of Chicago Press, 1991), 3–6. I read Greenblatt's opening travel anecdote of a visit to Bali in 1986 as a story of an emblematic encounter of literary critics (and also historians) with a not-so-new New World of post–World War II anthropology. Like the Columbian encounter, this encounter has yet to be worked through in the academy.

14. In *Works and Lives: The Anthropologist as Author* (Stanford, Calif.: Stanford University Press, 1988), Geertz discusses the problem of ethnographic writing ("a hundred and fifteen years . . . of asseverational prose and literary innocence is long enough" [p. 24]) in essays on Lévi-

Strauss, Evans-Pritchard, Malinowski, and Benedict, but he does not subject his own ethnographic writing to critique, and he fails to account for how, for anthropologist and "native," ethnographic writing became part of colonial subjectivity (see his discussion, pp. 132–38). The criticisms of ethnography by James Clifford can be read in critical contrast to Geertz (see *The Predicament of Culture: Twentieth-Century Ethnography, Literature and Art* [Cambridge, Mass.: Harvard University Press, 1988]; discussion of Geertz and the fable of rapport occurs on pp. 40–41). See also Taussig, *Nervous System.*

15. Clifford, *The Predicament of Culture,* 40.

16. An anonymous reviewer of this essay queried whether my analysis at this juncture was simply my projection. Such a query is what recent work on the homosocial bond helps us think about in a critical, political way. In a discussion of Iago relevant to such a question, Dollimore provides a helpful answer to the query, one relevant to the concerns of my analysis: "But we would be mistaken to conclude that 'repressed homosexuality' is the 'real' motivation of the homosocial bond since such a conclusion would obscure much and reveal little. Much more significant for understanding the sexual economy at work here is the way Iago's story, intentionally or not, reveals betrayal/usurpation as the typical *double* focus of masculine sexual jealousy, and a major instability in homosocial bonding. Also significant is the way Iago's story superimposes an excessive usurping masculine desire upon a betraying and unnatural female desire, confirming the culpability of both Cassio and Desdemona, usurper and betrayer, but of course hers more than his" (*Sexual Dissidence,* 158). See also Eve Kosofsky Sedgwick, *Between Men: English Literature and Male Homosocial Desire* (New York: Columbia University Press, 1985). For a contemporary analysis of some conventions in the hypermasculine film genre, see Sharon Willis, "Disputed Territories: Masculinity and Social Space," *Camera Obscura* 19 (1989): 5–23.

17. For a discussion of the problem of how the category *peasant* has sealed off groups from a dynamic history in medieval English history, see my "Decolonizing the English Past."

18. Spivak analyzes how such practices effect a "worlding" of the other: "He [Captain Geoffrey Birch, an assistant agent to the governor of the East India Company, 1815] is actually engaged in consolidating the self of Europe by obliging the native to cathect the space of the Other on his home ground. He is worlding *their own world,* which is far from mere uninscribed earth, anew, by obliging *them* to domesticate the alien as Master" ("The Rani of Sirmur: An Essay in Reading the Archives," *History and Theory* 24, no. 3 [1985]: 253).

19. Gabrielle M. Spiegel, "History, Historicism, and the Social Logic of the Text in the Middle Ages," *Speculum* 65, no. 1 (1990): 85.

20. Frantzen, "Prologue," 24, 24–25.

21. My invocation of Orientalism produced some sharp resistance at the conference. It is clear, however, that "throwing out" the study of Orientalism closes medieval studies off from active, dynamic debates in contemporary historiography. It is not time to throw out the study of Orientalism. Rather, we should make it more complex, continue to historicize the process, and, in so doing, raise questions about the epistemological and ontological challenges of a post-Orientalist history. For selected references, see n. 23 below and n. 33 in "English America" above.

22. In *The Desire for Origins,* Frantzen makes the important observation that "Orientalism and Anglo-Saxonism intersect at many points" (p. 29). I would broaden his intersections to include anthropology and cultural studies.

23. See Gyan Prakash, "Writing Post-Orientalist Histories of the Third World: Perspectives from Indian Historiography," *Comparative Studies in Society and History* 32, no. 2 (1990): 383–408; and the responses to Prakash, Rosalind O'Hanlon and David Washbrook, "After Orientalism: Culture, Criticism and Politics in the Third World," *Comparative Studies in Society and History* 34, no. 1 (1992): 141–67; and Dipesh Chakrabarty, "Postcoloniality and the Artifice of History: Who Speaks for 'Indian' Pasts," *Representations* 37 (Winter 1992): 1–26. For an important feminist work of post-Orientalism, see Trinh T. Minh-ha, *Woman, Native, Other: Writing Postcoloniality and Feminism* (Bloomington: Indiana University Press, 1989).

24. For examples of these Orientalist constructions of history within Europe, see the essays in *Nation and Narration,* ed. Homi Bhabha (New York: Routledge, 1990), esp. Martin Thom, "Tribes within Nations: The Ancient Germans and the History of Modern France"; and Frantzen on Anglo-Saxonism in *Desire for Origins.*

25. The work of Glory Dharmaraj and our conversations have inspired this section. Dharmaraj delivered the seminar "Feminism, Medievalism, and the Other: Postcoloniality as Critique" at the Medieval Institute of the University of Notre Dame, 12 November 1991. The basic references are Gauri Viswanathan, *Masks of Conquest: Literary Study and British Rule in India* (New York: Columbia University Press, 1989); D. J. Palmer, *The Rise of English Studies: An Account of the Study of the English Language and Literature from Its Origins to the Making of the Oxford School* (Oxford: Oxford University Press, 1965); and Allen J.

Frantzen and Charles L. Venegoni, "The Desire for Origins: An Archaeology of Anglo-Saxon Studies," *Style* 20, no. 2 (1986): 142–56.

26. From p. 1 of a report of the Early English Text Society in 1886. These pamphlets listed current publications of the society, reports of the treasurer (this particular report included the treasurer's accounts from 1879 to 1885), and a list of subscribing members for 1886. I used the volumes of the EETS in the University of Notre Dame library. For the period from its founding to 1900, reports for 1868, 1869, 1872, 1877, and 1886 are bound in the EETS volumes. I cite these reports hereafter as *EETS Report* and year.

27. *EETS Report* (1868), 4–5.

28. Cited in Palmer, *The Rise of English Studies,* 38–39.

29. The following sheds light on this middle-class identity: "Though the Committee are sorry to terrify or disgust any one, they must say that the men they want are 'the resolute members' referred to in the last Report; men who do not think the right way to get through their work is to be afraid of it or let their stomachs turn at it; but men who know that they have a work to do, and mean to do it; men who can look 270 MSS and books in the face, and say quietly, 'Well at 9 a-year, we shall clear you off in 30 years;' who can look at £60,000 worth of work, and say, 'At £1000 a-year, you're to be cut down in 60 years; and if I can manage 30 of them, my boy can settle the other 30.' The Society has a long job in hand and a heavy one; but not one that can beat men with a *will.* The Roxburghe Clube has lasted from 1812 to 1869, and has taken lately a new lease of its life. May not a Society of that Middle Class which has in great measure superseded the Upper as the mainstay of General Literature and Art, expect to do the same in the case of Antiquarian Literature?" (*EETS Report* [1868], 21).

30. *EETS Report* (1869), 2.

31. *EETS Report* (1877), 8. India Civil Service exams began in 1855, and English studies formed an important component of them (Palmer, *The Rise of English Studies,* 47).

32. Over thirty mercantile libraries were founded in the United States before 1875. They were associated with the adult education movement and provided a library, a reading room, lending services, and public lectures for their members. Women were admitted to mercantile libraries; the first annual report (1859) of the Brooklyn Mercantile Library lists one hundred female members. These libraries were open in the evenings and collected works that were "best calculated to promote the moral and intellectual elevation of the mercantile character" (from the Philadelphia Mercantile Library, cited in William Douglas Boyd Jr.,

"Books for the Young Businessmen: Mercantile Libraries in the United States, 1820–1865" [Ph.D. diss., Indiana University, 1975]).

33. Much work remains to be done on the politics of the Asiatic Society of Bengal. For a critical perspective, see Viswanathan, *Masks of Conquest.* For more apologetic texts, see O. P. Kejariwal, *The Asiatic Society of Bengal and the Discovery of India's Past, 1784–1838* (Oxford: Oxford University Press, 1988); and Garland Cannon, *The Life and Mind of Oriental Jones: Sir William Jones, the Father of Modern Linguistics* (New York: Cambridge University Press, 1990). For the Sanskrit Renaissance, see Spivak, "The Rani of Sirmur," 264–65. Kejariwal and Spivak differ significantly in their approaches to the Asiatic Society and the construction of a "past" for India in the nineteenth century.

34. Gayatri Chakravorty Spivak, "Can the Subaltern Speak?" in *Marxism and the Interpretation of Culture* (Urbana: University of Illinois Press, 1988), 299. I can only gesture here toward the complexities of the Sanskrit Renaissance.

35. The eminent Sanskrit scholar Edward FitzEdward Hall, cited in Kejariwal, *The Asiatic Society,* 3; *EETS Report* (1877), 1. For fascinating anecdotes of how Müller came to work on manuscripts of the *Rig Veda* at the East India Co. in London and how the East India Co. came to finance the publication of his work, see F. Max Müller, *My Autobiography: A Fragment* (London: Longmans, 1901): "However, I thought little of India, I only thought of the library at the East India House, a real Eldorado for an eager Sanskrit student, who had never seen such treasures before" (p. 208). See also Maurice Olender, "The Danger of Ambiguity: Friedrich Max Müller," in *The Languages of Paradise: Race, Religion, and Philology in the Nineteenth Century* (Cambridge, Mass.: Harvard University Press, 1992), 82–92.

36. For example, W. A. Clouston's *The Additional Analogues* (EETS vol. 84, 1886), written in Glasgow, appeared after Frederick J. Furnivall's edition of *Wright's Chaste Wife* (EETS vol. 12, 1875), commenting on it. Clouston cites Persian texts, C. H. Tawney's recently translated Sanskrit collection *Kathá Sarit Ságara* (which, according to Clouston, just appeared in Calcutta; p. 27, n. 1), as well as *Indian Fairy Tales,* publications of the *Indian Antiquary,* and *Select Tamil Tales* (Madras, 1839) (p. 32).

37. Viswanathan, *Masks of Conquest,* 3.

38. Salman Rushdie, *Satanic Verses* (New York: Viking, 1988), 343.

39. Chakrabarty, "Postcoloniality," 23.

40. Bede, *A History of the English Church and People,* trans. Leo Sherley-Price, rev. R. E. Latham (Harmondsworth: Penguin, 1955), 38. The Penguin edition is the version through which most undergraduates encounter Bede. For the ironic purposes of my imaginary meeting in

the medieval institute, I am not going to qualify what we might mean by *English* in the eighth century, what we might mean by *Old English* in the twentieth century, etc. For a critical edition, see *Bede's Ecclesiastical History of the English People*, ed. Bertram Colgrave and R. A. B. Mynors (Oxford: Clarendon, 1969), hereafter cited as Colgrave and Mynors. My allusions to Bede in this section are influenced in contesting ways by André Crépin, "Bede and the Vernacular," in *Famulus Christi: Essays in the Commemoration of the Thirteenth Centenary of the Birth of the Venerable Bede*, ed. Gerald Bonner (London: SPCK, 1976), 170–92; Michael Lapidge, "The School of Theodore and Hadrian," *Anglo-Saxon England* 15 (1986): 45–72; Katherine O'Brien O'Keeffe, "Orality and the Developing Text of Caedmon's *Hymn*," *Speculum* 62, no. 1 (1987): 1–20; René Derolez, "Runic Literacy among the Anglo-Saxons," in *Britain, 400–600: Language and History* (Anglistische Forschungen 205), ed. Alfred Bammesberger and Alfred Wollmann (1990); Frantzen, *Desire for Origins*, 130–67; Sarah Lynn Higley, *Between Languages: The Uncooperative Text in Early Welsh and Old English Nature Poetry* (University Park: Pennsylvania State University Press, 1993); Malcolm Godden and Michael Lapidge, *The Cambridge Companion to Old English Literature* (Cambridge: Cambridge University Press, 1991); Seth Lerer, *Literacy and Power in Anglo-Saxon Literature* (Lincoln: University of Nebraska Press, 1991); and Clare A. Lees and Gillian R. Overing, "Birthing Bishops and Fathering Poets: Bede, Hild, and the Relations of Cultural Production," *Exemplaria* 6 (1994): 35–66.

41. For references to the complex political project of reappropriating and refiguring Malinche (or Malintzin) among Chicana feminists, see Norma Alarcón, "Chicana's Feminist Literature: A Re-Vision through Malintzin; or, Malintzin: Putting Flesh Back on the Object," in *This Bridge Called My Back: Writing by Radical Women of Color*, ed. Cherríe Moraga and Gloria Anzaldúa (New York: Kitchen Table/Women of Color, 1981); Gloria Anzaldúa, "La conciencia de la mestiza: Towards a New Consciousness," in *Making Face, Making Soul*, ed. Gloria Anzaldúa (San Francisco: Aunt Lute Foundation, 1990); and Cherríe Moraga, "From a Long Line of Vendidas: Chicanas and Feminism," in *Feminist Studies/Critical Studies*, ed. Teresa de Lauretis (Bloomington: Indiana University Press, 1986). For a historical study of the figure of Malinche from sixteenth-century documents to contemporary Mexican feminism, see Sanra Messinger Cypess, *La Malinche in Mexican Literature: From History to Myth* (Austin: University of Texas Press, 1991). For another perspective, one that carefully avoids contemporary Chicana feminist appropriations of Malinche, see David E. Johnson, "Women, Translation, Nationalism: La Malinche and the Example of Juan García

Ponce," *Arizona Quarterly* 47, no. 3 (1991): 93–116 (I am grateful to Ted Cachey for sharing this reference).

42. See Frantzen, *Desire for Origins;* Lerer, *Literacy and Power;* and O'Keeffe, "The Developing Text of Caedmon's *Hymn.*"

43. See D. Emily Hicks, *Border Writing: The Multidimensional Text* (Minneapolis: University of Minnesota Press, 1991).

44. Said, "Representing the Colonized," 255.

45. Bhabha, "DissemiNation," 317.

46. Anzaldúa, "La conciencia de la mestiza," 379.

The Devil's Anal Eye: Inquisitorial Optics and Ethnographic Authority

I am grateful for the comments of pre- and early modern seminar participants at the University of California, Santa Cruz (Karen Bassi, Harry Berger, Valerie Forman, and Margo Hendricks), and of David Aers, Sujata Bhatt, Raoul Birnbaum, Steve Caton, Jim Clifford, Sarah Franklin, Carla Freccero, Katie King, Linda Lomperis, Lisa Rofel, and Cathy Soussloff on versions of this essay.

1. My readings in microhistory have concentrated on Carlo Ginzburg, "The Inquisitor as Anthropologist," in *Clues, Myths and the Historical Method* (Baltimore: Johns Hopkins University Press, 1989), 154–64 (on the dialogic nature of the archive, see p. 159; on the archive as "Eldorado," see p. 157); Emmanuel Le Roy Ladurie, *Montaillou: The Promised Land of Error,* trans. Barbara Bray (New York: Braziller, 1978), vii; Guido Ruggiero, *Binding Passions: Tales of Magic, Marriage, and Power at the End of the Renaissance* (New York: Oxford University Press, 1993), 19; and Georges Duby, "Affidavits and Confession," in *A History of Women in the West,* vol. 2, *The Silence of the Middle Ages,* ed. Georges Duby and Michelle Perrot (Cambridge, Mass.: Belknap, Harvard University Press, 1992), 483. I have chosen these texts for close reading on the basis of their strong methodological claims for the kind of "voice" that they can "hear" in *Inquisitorial* records. I am *not* here engaging the larger discursive field of microhistory beyond the Inquisition or "microhistories" that explicitly deal with inquisitions of Jews. The work, e.g., of R. Po-chia Hsia supports the argument about mourning that I develop here (see *The Myth of Ritual Murder: Jews and Magic in Reformation Germany* [New Haven, Conn.: Yale University Press, 1988], and *Trent 1475* [New Haven, Conn.: Yale University Press, 1992]). Carlo Ginzburg's "Microhistory: Two or Three Things That I Know about It" (*Critical Inquiry* 20 [Autumn 1993]: 10–35) underscored the importance

of foregrounding *mourning* with memory (Cleopatra's nose [p. 12], perhaps with the Jew's nose as meditated on in Sander Gilman, *The Jew's Body* [New York: Routledge, 1991]). Ginzburg begins an interesting discussion of memory in this essay but "retreats" to the safer grounds of "context" (p. 33) rather than engage in the painful problem of the borders of memory and mourning in history. Alternatively, see Dominick LaCapra's "Rhetoric and History," in *History and Criticism* (Ithaca, N.Y.: Cornell University Press, 1985), which underscored for me how "context" in history is invoked as a disavowal of mourning. Differences within the "microhistory" of Inquisitorial archives may, of course, also be found. For example, Mary O'Neil's work shares similarities of interest with Ruggiero's, but with a difference. O'Neil works from the ambiguity of magical operations for both the inquisitor and the love charmer and therefore distributes the problem of evidence and truth across discursive fields ("Magical Healing, Love Magic and the Inquisition in Late Sixteenth-Century Modena," in *Inquisition and Society in Early Modern Europe*, ed. Stephen Haliczer [Totowa, N.J.: Barnes & Noble, 1987]).

2. Ginzburg, "The Inquisitor as Anthropologist," 157.

3. In eliding ethnography/anthropology to mark the elision between fieldworker and writer/author, I follow Marilyn Strathern (*Partial Connections* [Savage, Md.: Rowman & Littlefield, 1991], 123). My critique of ethnography is also inspired by James Clifford, *The Predicament of Culture: Twentieth Century Ethnography, Literature and Art* (Cambridge, Mass.: Harvard University Press, 1988); Mary Louise Pratt, *Imperial Eyes: Travel Writing and Transculturation* (New York: Routledge, 1992); Roger Sanjek, ed., *Fieldnotes: The Makings of Anthropology* (Ithaca, N.Y.: Cornell University Press, 1990); Sara Suleri, *The Rhetoric of English India* (Chicago: University of Chicago Press, 1992); Michael Taussig, *Shamanism, Colonialism, and the Wild Man: A Study in Terror and Healing* (Chicago: University of Chicago Press, 1987); and Michel de Certeau, *The Writing of History* (New York: Columbia University Press, 1988), and *Mystic Fable* (Chicago: University of Chicago Press, 1992). For specific critiques of Ladurie's *Montaillou*, see James Clifford, "Naming Names," *Canto* 3 (1979): 142–53; Renato Rosaldo, "From the Door of His Tent: The Fieldworker and the Inquisitor," in *Writing Culture: The Poetics and Politics of Ethnography*, ed. James Clifford and George F. Marcus (Berkeley and Los Angeles: University of California Press, 1986), 77–97; and Claire Sponsler, "Medieval Ethnography: Fieldwork and the European Past," *Assays* 7 (1992): 1–30.

4. I am indebted to Sara Suleri and Michael Taussig for their discussions of colonial terror. Suleri eloquently notes that "to tell the history

of another is to be pressed against the limit's of one's own—thus culture learns that terror has a local habitation and a name" (*The Rhetoric of English India*, 2).

5. Ginzburg, "The Inquisitor as Anthropologist," 158.

6. Rosaldo, "From the Door of His Tent," 83, 93. See E. E. Evans-Pritchard, *The Nuer* (Oxford: Oxford University Press, 1940).

7. Sponsler, "Medieval Ethnography," 3.

8. This argument intersects with the discursive work on melancholia by Juliana Schiesari (*The Gendering of Melancholia: Feminism, Psychoanalysis, and the Symbolics of Loss in Renaissance Literature* [Ithaca, N.Y.: Cornell University Press, 1992]).

9. For insight into the shared borders of nineteenth-century histories of the Inquisition with British historical novels, see Michael Ragussis, "The Birth of a Nation in Victorian Culture: The Spanish Inquisition, the Converted Daughter, and the Secret Race," *Critical Inquiry* 20 (Spring 1994): 477–508. Susan Harding's "Representing Fundamentalism: The Problem of the Repugnant Other" (*Social Research* 58 [1991]: 373–94) has inspired me to try to think of the Inquisition outside the demonization-recuperation binary.

10. As an introduction to bibliography on the late medieval institutional history of the Inquisition and its archives, I have found useful Gustav Henningsen, John Tedeschi, and Charles Amiel, eds., *The Inquisition in Early Modern Europe: Studies on Sources and Methods* (Dekalb, Ill.: Northern Illinois University Press, 1986); and May Elizabeth Perry and Anne J. Cruz, eds., *Cultural Encounters: The Impact of the Inquisition in Spain and the New World* (Berkeley and Los Angeles: University of California Press, 1991). In concentrating on an Inquisitorial manual on witchcraft, I do not mean to imply that the prosecution of heretics and "crypto-Jews" is not crucial to fifteenth-century Inquisitorial activity. Rather, my point is that the witchcraft project of the Inquisition has specific ethnographic effects. The literature on witchcraft is vast. Works consulted are listed partially in n. 15. Marianne Hester also provides a succinct overview of English historiography of witchcraft in her *Lewd Women and Wicked Witches: A Study of the Dynamics of Male Domination* (New York: Routledge, 1992). Complementing her work are the comparative essays in *Early Modern European Witchcraft: Centres and Peripheries*, ed. Bengt Ankarloo and Gustav Henningsen (New York: Oxford University Press, 1990). Also relevant to the intersection of Inquisitorial practice and witchcraft are Edward Peters, *Torture* (New York: Blackwell, 1985); and Sabine MacCormack, "Demons, Imagination, and the Incas," *Representations* 33 (Winter 1991): 121–46.

11. See, e.g., Peter Hulme's *Colonial Encounters: Europe and the Native Caribbean, 1492–1797* (New York: Methuen, 1986), where he traces a tension between discourse of Oriental civilization traceable to Marco Polo and a discourse of savagery traceable to Herodotus in Columbus's journal. I am trying to map yet another engendered, sexualized discourse, a "European" ethnographic discourse of the Inquisition, a discourse of the cannibal within, to complicate this. For an interesting use of Hulme and a complication of cannibalism, see Carla Freccero, "Cannibalism, Homophobia, Women: Montaigne's 'Des cannibales' and 'De l'amitié,' " in *Women, "Race," and Writing in the Early Modern Period,* ed. Margo Hendricks and Patricia Parker (New York: Routledge, 1994).

12. For the use of the devil as a recording demon, a visual trope that emerges in the twelfth century during important transformations of the stakes of literacy, see Michael Camille, "The Devil's Writing: Diabolic Literacy in Medieval Art," in *World Art: Themes of Unity and Diversity,* ed. Irving Lavin (University Park: Pennsylvania State University Press, 1986). On demonic auditory technologies, in reference to witchcraft trials, Richard Godbeer calls for the full-scale study of narratology in *The Devil's Dominion: Magic and Religion in Early New England* (Cambridge: Cambridge University Press, 1992), 22, n. 33.

13. Gilles Deleuze, *Foucault* (Minneapolis: University of Minnesota Press, 1988), 13. The phrase reoccurs in Jonathan Crary, *Techniques of the Observer* (Cambridge, Mass.: MIT Press, 1990).

14. I have worked with the facsimile edited by Günter Jerouschek, *Malleus maleficarum 1487 von Heinrich Kramer* (*Institoris*) (New York: Georg Olms, 1992); the English translation by Montague Summers, *The Malleus maleficarum of Heinrich Kramer and James Sprenger* (1928; reprint, New York: Dover, 1971); Peter Segl, ed., *Der Hexenhammer: Enstehung und Umfeld des Malleus maleficarum von 1487* (Köln: Böhlau, 1988); and various works by Joseph Hansen, including "Der Malleus maleficarum, seine Drucksausgaben und die gefälschte Kölner Approbation vom J. 1487," *Westdeutsche Zeitschrift für Geschichte und Kunst* 17 (1898): 119–168, and *Quellen und Untersuchungen zur Geschichte des Hexenwahns und der Hexenverfolgung im Mittelalter* (Bonn: G. Georgi, 1901; reprint, Hildesheim: George Olms, 1963). Quotations given in the text in English are from Summers's translation, those in Latin from Jerouschek's facsimile. Page/folio numbers will be given in the text.

15. What follows is a brief selection of comments, largely contradictory, on the importance of the *Malleus maleficarum* culled from a selection of major histories of European witchcraft; much work remains to be done on the publication and translation histories of this text: Sydney Anglo, "Evident Authority and Authoritative Evidence: The *Malleus*

maleficarum," in *The Damned Art*, ed. Sydney Anglo (London: Routledge & Kegan Paul, 1977): "It now seems to be becoming fashionable to suggest that the *Malleus* has been accorded an exaggerated importance. This may well be true, for the influence of most books tends to be exaggerated by historians. On the other hand, it was reissued more frequently than any other major witch-hunting manual; it was long the most commonly cited; and it remained one of the works which the opponents of persecution sought especially to refute. But perhaps none of this matters" (p. 31). Julio Caro Baroja, *The World of Witches*, trans. O. N. V. Glendinning (Chicago: University of Chicago Press, 1964): "The views it advanced spread rapidly through Italy, Spain, France and countries in the north of Europe. Both Catholics and Protestants were influenced by it. And the more learned was the judge in charge of the trial, the more notice he took of it" (p. 250). Alan C. Kors and Edward Peters, eds., *Witchcraft in Europe, 1100–1700: A Documentary History* (Philadelphia: University of Pennsylvania Press, 1972): "First 'encyclopedia' of witchcraft beliefs, exhaustively analyzed the entire problem of witch beliefs and set out meticulously the ways by which witches could be found, convicted and executed" (p. 113). Norman Cohn, *Europe's Inner Demons* (London: Chatto, Heinemann, for Sussex University Press, 1975): "The importance of the most famous of the witch hunters' manuals, the *Malleus Maleficarum*, published in 1486, has been exaggerated" (p. 225). Stephen Greenblatt, "Shakespeare Bewitched," in *New Historical Literary Study* (Princeton, N.J.: Princeton University Press, 1993): "Faced with the necessity of producing the effect of the real of the materials of fantasy, the inquisitors turned to narrative. The *Malleus Maleficarum* rehearses dozens of tales crafted to redraw the boundary between the imaginary and the real, or rather to siphon off the darkest contests of the imagination and pour them, like a poison into the ear of the world" (p. 110). Richard Kieckhefer, *European Witch Trials: Their Foundations in Popular and Learned Culture, 1300–1500* (Berkeley: University of California Press, 1976): "Made available a fully developed manual for witch hunters" (p. 23). Ruth Martin, *Witchcraft and the Inquisition in Venice, 1550–1650* (New York: Blackwell, 1989): "There is no evidence that in their dealings with witchcraft Venetian Inquisitors made any use of the book. There was no demand for its reprinting and circulation amongst Inquisition tribunals within Italy and no mention or reflection of the Venetian witchcraft investigations during the period up to 1650" (p. 58). H. C. Erik Midelfort, *Witch Hunting in Southwestern Germany, 1562–1684* (Stanford, Calif.: Stanford University Press, 1972): "The *Malleus Maleficarum* failed to become generally accepted doctrine, and its influence and authority have been vastly exaggerated by most scholars" (p. 22). Jeffrey Burton Russell, *Witchcraft in the Middle Ages* (Ithaca, N.Y.: Cornell University Press, 1972): "Immediately achieved broad popularity among Inquisitors and throughout the church. . . . [I]t contributed little original to the witch phenomenon, but its careful organization and argumentation, combined with the papal approval that accompanied it, fixed the whole system of witch beliefs firmly in the mind of Inquisition and society in general" (pp. 230–31). William Monter, *Frontiers of Heresy: The Spanish Inquisition from the Basque Lands to Sicily* (New York: Cambridge University Press, 1990): "One tantalizing clue only deepens the mystery of the Suprema's encouragement of the Narvarrese witch-hunters in 1609–10. A brief letter in February 1608 ordered an overzealous comisario in Bilbao to release seventy-six copies of the newly-reprinted *Malleus Maleficarum,* the most famous handbook of witchhunting, which he had confiscated; they belonged to a Madrid bookseller named Francisco de Robles, who may well have sold a few copies to inquisitorial policy-makers that year. The Suprema had warned the Navarre Inquisitors about the *Malleus Maleficarum* seventy years previously: 'do not believe everything in it,' they had said, 'even if he [the authors] writes about it as something he himself has seen and investigated, for the cases are of such a nature that he may have been mistaken, as others have been'" (pp. 270–71). The German translation of the *Malleus maleficarum* may be found catalogued in Freud's London library (see Roger Dennis Simmons, "The Freud Library," *Journal of the American Psychoanalytic Association* 21 [1973]: 646–87).

16. The work of Jonathan Goldberg on the utter confusion of sodomy as a category and his exploration of "some of the terrains of confusion in the Renaissance" (p. 18) has informed my use of sodomy and my own exploration of the Inquisitorial fear of "the utter confusion of the world" (Jonathan Goldberg, *Sodometries: Renaissance Texts, Modern Sexualities* [Stanford, Calif.: Stanford University Press, 1992]).

17. For the English version of the passage under discussion, see Summers, trans., *Malleus maleficarum,* 75–76.

18. Michel de Certeau's chapter on ethnography in *The Writing of History* has guided my work here. The notion of the "picture of orality" comes from p. 209.

19. For discussion of the engendering and racializing of the space of cannibalism in late medieval/early modern Christendom, see my "Genders, Bodies, Borders: Technologies of the Visible," *Speculum* 68 (April 1993): 389–418, reprinted in *Studying Medieval Women,* ed. Nancy Partner (Cambridge, Mass.: Medieval Academy of America, 1993); and Carla Freccero, "Cannibalism, Homophobia, Women."

20. De Certeau, *Mystic Fable*, 66.

21. Goldberg, *Sodometries*, esp. 20.

22. See Joan Cadden, *Meanings of Sex Difference in the Middle Ages: Medicine, Science and Culture* (New York: Cambridge University Press, 1993); Danielle Jacquart and Claude Thomasset, *Sexuality and Medicine in the Middle Ages* (Princeton, N.J.: Princeton University Press, 1988); John Boswell, *Christianity, Social Tolerance, and Homosexuality* (Chicago: University of Chicago Press, 1980); and Kert Gerard and Gert Helima, eds., *The Pursuit of Sodomy: Male Homosexuality in Renaissance and Enlightenment Europe* (New York: Harrington Park, 1989).

23. For the overdetermination of blood as a border fluid, see Biddick, "Genders, Bodies, Borders." For interesting reflections on blood and symbolic relations, see Juliet Du Boulay, "The Blood: Symbolic Relationships between Descent, Marriage, Incest Prohibitions and Spiritual Kinship in Greece," *Man* 19 (1984): 533–56; and Françoise Héritier-Augé, "Semen and Blood: Some Ancient Theories concerning Their Genesis and Relationship," in *Fragments for a History of the Human Body*, vol. 3, ed. Michel Feher (New York: Zone, 1989). The conference "What's Blood Got to Do with It?: Kinship Reconsidered," organized by Sarah Franklin, was held at the University of California, Santa Cruz, in April 1994 to retheorize representations of kinship through the "blood tie."

24. Eve Kosofsky Sedgwick's "Privilege of Unknowing" (*Genders* 1 [1988]: 102–24) helps us understand the strategy of ignorance in the countereconomy imagined by the inquisitors.

25. Clifford, *Predicament of Culture*, 31.

26. Ibid., 40.

27. Dian Owen Hughes, "Distinguishing Signs: Ear-Rings, Jews and Franciscan Rhetoric in the Italian Renaissance City," *Past and Present* 112 (August 1986): 3–59.

28. See Louise O. Frandenburg, "Criticism, Anti-Semitism, and the Prioress's Tale," *Exemplaria* 1 (March 1989): 69–115.

29. I make these arguments in more detail in my "Genders, Bodies, Borders." The Inquisitorial anxiety regarding crypto-Jews must be read along the complicated fault lines of ethnographic co-construction. For work on the Inquisition and Jews, see the essays in *Cultural Encounters* and in *Inquisition and Society in Early Modern Europe*, esp. (in the latter) Stephen Haliczer's "The First Holocaust: The Inquisition and the Converted Jew of Spain and Portugal" and Nicolas Davidson's "The Inquisition and the Italian Jews."

30. Bruno Latour, *We Have Never Been Modern* (Cambridge, Mass.: Harvard University Press, 1993). For an important critique of La-

tour, see Donna Haraway, *Modest-Witness@Second-Millennium. Female Man©-Meets OncoMouse™* (New York: Routledge, 1997), 33–35.

31. Rosalind Krauss, *The Optical Unconscious* (Cambridge, Mass.: MIT Press, 1993), 157.

32. Joseph Leo Koerner, *The Moment of Self-Portraiture in German Renaissance Art* (Chicago: University of Chicago Press, 1993). This section of the essay is indebted to Koerner's work, which enabled me to make connections between demonology and technology. He discusses the *Vanitas* woodcut from *Der Ritter von Turm* on pp. 351–52. He includes a reproduction of the woodcut as fig. 166, p. 350. For further discussion, see Rudolf Kautzsch, *Die Holzschnitte zum Ritter von Turm,* Studien zur deutschen kunstgeschichte 44 (Strassburg: Heitz, 1903); and Frank Weitenkampf, "*Der Ritter von Turm* and the Dawn of the Renaissance in Book Illustration," *Bulletin of the New York Public Library* 35 (1931): 611–18. I consulted the copy of *Der Ritter von Turm* in the Newberry Library Collection, Chicago.

33. For comments on mirroring in fifteenth-century European painting, see Linda Seidel, "The Value of Verisimilitude in the Art of Jan van Eyck," in *Contexts: Style and Values in Medieval Art and Literature* (New Haven, Conn.: Yale University Press, 1991), 25–43.

34. Crary, *Techniques of the Observer,* 39.

35. I rely again on Koerner and his excellent study of Baldung in *Moment of Self-Portraiture.* I have also consulted *Hans Baldung Grien: Prints and Drawings,* ed. James Marrow and Alan Shestack (Chicago, 1981); G. F. Hartlaub, *Hans Baldung Grien: Hexenbilder* (Stuttgart, 1961); Sigrid Schade, *Schadenzauber und die Magie des Körpers* (Worms, 1983); Linda C. Hults, "Baldung and the Witches of Freiburg: The Evidence of Images," *Journal of Interdisciplinary History* 18, no. 2 (1987): 249–76, and "Baldung's *Bewitched Groom* Revisited: Artistic Temperament, Fantasy and the 'Dream of Reason,'" *Sixteenth-Century Journal* 15, no. 3 (1984): 259–80; Gustav Radbruch, "Hans Baldungs Hexenbilder," in *Elegantiae juris criminalis* (Basel, 1938); and Dale Hoak, "Art, Culture and Mentality in Renaissance Society: The Meaning of Hans Baldung Grien's *Bewitched Groom* (1544)," *Renaissance Quarterly* 38, no. 3 (1985): 488–510.

36. My discussion is based on Jonathan Goldberg's "Discovering America," in *Sodometries.* See also Michèle Duchet, *L'Amérique de Théodore de Bry: Une collection de voyages protestante de XVIe siècle* (Paris, 1987); and Bernadette Bucher, *Icon and Conquest* (Chicago: University of Chicago Press, 1981).

37. Peter's *Decade* (1555) is cited in Goldberg, *Sodometries,* 180.

38. This paper always runs the risk of repeating the position of Balboa, of "gesturing" toward the mimesis and alterity of Inquisitorial

exchanges in the New World, with its lability of devils, Jews, and witches, rather than articulating that gesture. I have tried to hold the tension of alterity as one interpretative problem in this section.

39. Suleri, *Rhetoric of English India*, 4.

40. Taussig, *Shamanism, Colonialism, and the Wild Man*, 196.

41. Ginzburg, "The Inquisitor as Anthropologist," 158.

42. Carlo Ginzburg, *Ecstasies: Deciphering the Witches' Sabbath* (New York: Pantheon, 1991), 150, n. 96.

43. The construction of European folklore awaits a critique as rigorous as the critique of nineteenth- and early twentieth-century ethnographies of the non-European primitive. For an important and suggestive way into this problem, see George W. Stocking, *Victorian Anthropology* (New York: Free Press, 1987), 53–56 and passim.

44. Ginzburg, *Ecstasies*, 242. For a provocative introduction to the mimetic problems that the construction of European folklore entails, mimetic problems that trouble microhistories, see Michael Taussig, *Mimesis and Alterity* (New York: Routledge, 1993), esp. the chapter "Search for the White Indian."

45. Ginzburg, *Ecstasies*, 214, 248, 249.

46. Ibid., 133.

47. Ibid., 307.

48. Margaret Murray, *The Witch Cult in Western Europe* (1921; reprint, Oxford: Clarendon, 1962).

49. Ginzburg, *Ecstasies*, 133.

50. Guido Ruggiero, too, uses the depositions of women before the Venetian Inquisition as a means to restore "the magic [that] is gone" in the contemporary world (*Binding Passions: Tales of Magic, Marriage, and Power at the End of the Renaissance* [New York: Oxford University Press, 1993], 224).

51. Cohn, *Europe's Inner Demons*, 262.

52. Ginzburg, *Ecstasies*, 242.

53. Ibid., 76.

54. *The Silence of the Middle Ages*, 4.

55. Ibid., 483.

56. For an analysis of this trial, see my "Paper Jews: Inscription/Ethnicity/Ethnography," *Art Bulletin* 78 (1996): 594–99.

Genders, Bodies, Borders: Technologies of the Visible

I am grateful to the History Department and the Medieval Institute of the University of Notre Dame for permission to teach a graduate seminar (autumn 1991) in preparation for writing this essay. The students of the seminar inspired me in their moments of resistance and insight: Stephen A. Allen, Jennifer Blatchford, Carolyn Edwards, Angela Gugliotta, Ann Hirschman, Elizabeth Jensen, Lezlie Knox, Tom Luongo, Dianne Phillips, Martin Tracy, Robert Vega, and Lisa Wolverton. The encouragement of Judith Bennett, Michael Camille, Marilyn Desmond, Robert Franklin, Madonna Hettinger, Sandra Joshel, Karma Lochrie, Peggy McCracken, Joan W. Scott, Susan St. Ville, Susan Simonaitis, John Van Engen, and the members of a writing group, Ted Cachey, Julia Douthwaite, and Barbara Green, was crucial. To Nancy Partner I owe a special debt of gratitude for her editorial advice and support.

1. This first citation gestures toward an abundant and discursive literature on modernity and its visualizations. My practice here and throughout is to cite those works that have been most important in guiding my thoughts for this essay. For a critique of history as a sign of the modern, see Nicholas B. Dirks, "History as a Sign of the Modern," *Public Culture* 2 (1990): 25–32. See also Jonathan Crary, *Techniques of the Observer: On Vision and Modernity in the Nineteenth Century* (Cambridge, Mass.: MIT Press, 1990); Barbara Duden, *The Woman beneath the Skin: A Doctor's Patients in Eighteenth-Century Germany* (Cambridge, Mass.: Harvard University Press, 1991); Bruno Latour, "Visualization and Cognition," in *Knowledge and Society* 6 (1986): 1–40; Michel Foucault, "The Political Technology of Individuals," in *Technologies of the Self: A Seminar with Michel Foucault*, ed. L. Martin, H. Gutman, and P. Hutton (Amherst: University of Massachusetts Press, 1988); Jane Gallop, *Thinking through the Body* (New York: Columbia University Press, 1988); and Barbara Maria Stafford, *Body Criticism: Imagining the Unseen in Enlightenment Art and Medicine* (Cambridge, Mass.: MIT Press, 1991).

2. See Michel de Certeau, "The New Science," in *Mystic Fable*, trans. Michael B. Smith (Chicago: University of Chicago Press, 1992).

3. Caroline Walker Bynum, *Holy Feast and Holy Fast: The Religious Significance of Food to Medieval Women*, The New Historicism: Studies in Cultural Poetics (Berkeley and Los Angeles: University of California Press, 1987) (page numbers for citations will be given in parentheses in the text). Readers should note that I occasionally use the word *gender* in the plural. This intended inconsistency invites us to think of gender as both a performed and a historically constrained construction exceeding the binary of sexual difference as it has been dominantly defined. If we allow for only two genders, we displace sexual difference into a discussion of gender. My reading concentrates on an engendering of historiography. A future reading is needed to untangle the sexualizing of

historiography. The two fields are not commensurate; the ways in which they intersect cannot be known in advance.

4. My ways of reading are influenced by Homi K. Bhabha, "Postcolonial Authority and Postmodern Guilt," in *Cultural Studies,* ed. Lawrence Grossberg, Cary Nelson, and Paula Treichler (New York: Routledge, 1992); Jonathan Dollimore, *Sexual Dissidence: Augustine to Wilde, Freud to Foucault* (New York: Oxford University Press, 1991); Donna Haraway, "Reading Buchi Emecheta: Contests for 'Women's Experience' in Women's Studies," in *Simians, Cyborgs, and Women: The Reinvention of Nature* (New York: Routledge, 1991); Bruno Latour, "The Politics of Explanation: An Alternative," in *Knowledge and Reflexivity: New Frontiers in the Sociology of Knowledge,* ed. Steve Woolgar (London: Sage, 1988); and Gayatri Chakravorty Spivak, "A Literary Representation of the Subaltern: A Woman's Text from the Third World," in *In Other Worlds: Essays in Cultural Politics* (New York: Metheun, 1987).

5. Gayatri Chakravorty Spivak, "French Feminism Revisited: Ethics and Politics," in *Feminists Theorize the Political,* ed. Judith Butler and Joan W. Scott (New York: Routledge, 1992), 58. Medieval historians have also urged feminist historians to beware of another metanarrative of European history: "progress" (see Susan Mosher Stuard, "The Chase after Theory: Considering Medieval Women," *Gender and History* 4, no. 2 [1992]: 135–46; and Judith M. Bennett, "Medieval Women, Modern Women: Across the Great Divide," in *Culture and History, 1350–1600: Essays on English Communities, Identities and Writing,* ed. David Aers [London: Harvester Wheatsheaf, 1992]). For a discussion of the difficulties of writing history without Europe as a referent, see Dipesh Chakrabarty, "Postcoloniality and the Artifice of History: Who Speaks for 'Indian' Pasts?" *Representations* 37 (Winter 1992): 1–26. For a series of suggestive contemporary studies that intertwine the imagination of Europe with norms of bodily and sexual behavior, see *Nationalisms and Sexualities,* ed. Andrew Parker, Mary Russo, Doris Sommer, and Patricia Yaeger (New York: Routledge, 1992). "Post-Oriental" theory and "postcolonial" theory are not monolithic and are also subject to critique; see Anne McClintock, *Imperial Leather: Race, Gender and Sexuality in the Colonial Context* (New York: Routledge, 1995).

6. Bynum relies on the following works in social psychology: Nancy Chodorow, *The Reproduction of Mothering: Psychoanalysis and the Sociology of Gender* (Berkeley and Los Angeles: University of California Press, 1978); and Carol Gilligan, *In a Different Voice: Psychological Theory and Women's Development* (Cambridge, Mass.: Harvard University Press, 1982).

7. Bynum notes Joan W. Scott's "Gender: A Useful Category of His-

torical Analysis" (*American Historical Review* 91, no. 5 [1986]: 1053–75) in n. 29 of chap. 10, p. 416. The debate over essentialism in critical feminist theory of the 1980s cannot be reduced to any simple description since readings of essentialism are historicized not only by gender but also by race, class, and the construction of homosexuality. Teresa de Lauretis wisely notes that the debate itself within feminism articulates "difference in the feminist conception of woman, women, world" ("The Essence of the Triangle, or Taking the Risk of Essentialism Seriously: Feminist Theory in Italy, the U.S., and Britain," *Differences* 1, no. 2 [1989]: 3). Essentialist and antiessentialist positions co-construct each other, as Dollimore shows in *Sexual Dissidence.* The African-American theorist bell hooks joins a critique of essentialism and race in *Yearning: Race, Gender and Cultural Politics* (Boston: South End, 1990). Donna Haraway usefully summarizes different historical positions in the essentialism debate in "'Gender' for a Marxist Dictionary: The Sexual Politics of a Word," in *Simians, Cyborgs, and Women.*

8. Bynum does mention the theoretical work of Luce Irigaray and Julia Kristeva sympathetically (pp. 416–17, nn. 35 and 41), after prefacing her remarks that "French feminist writing has been determinedly atheistical" (p. 416). For a study that brings Bynum and Kristeva together and extends them critically, see Karma Lochrie, *Margery Kempe and Translations of the Flesh* (Philadelphia: University of Pennsylvania Press, 1991). Important work criticizing the gendered production of knowledge was available when Bynum wrote *Holy Feast and Holy Fast.* She cites Scott's "Gender," in which Scott cautioned historians that the production of historical knowledge was itself gendered and called for an alliance between women's history and critical theory to begin to question how rhetorical practices in history used gender as a resource and produced gender as an effect: "It requires analysis not only of the relations between male and female experience in the past but also the connection between past history and current historical practice. . . . How does gender give meaning to the organization and perception of historical knowledge?" (p. 1055). Perhaps the most famous and widely known critique of the gendered production of knowledge dating to the period of the writing and publication of *Holy Feast and Holy Fast* is Evelyn Fox Keller, *Reflections on Gender and Science* (New Haven, Conn.: Yale University Press, 1985).

9. For different aspects of this debate, see esp. Joan W. Scott, "The Evidence of Experience," *Critical Inquiry* 17 (Summer 1991): 773–97. Dominick La Capra comments on the problem of "voices"—past and present—in *History and Criticism* (Ithaca, N.Y.: Cornell University Press, 1985); I have found these words of caution very helpful: "The

archive as fetish is a literal substitute for the 'reality' of the past which is 'always already' lost for the historian. When it is fetishized, the archive is more than the repository of traces of the past which may be used in its inferential reconstruction. It is a stand-in for the past that brings the mystified experience of the thing itself—an experience that is always open to question when one deals with writing and other inscriptions" (p. 92). Recent critical work on post-Orientalist history deeply troubles conventional uses of *experience* as a historical category (see Gyan Prakash, "Can the 'Subaltern' Ride? A Reply to O'Hanlon and Washbrook," *Comparative Studies in Society and History* 34, no. 1 [1992]: 168–84; Gayatri Chakravorty Spivak, "The Rani of Sirmur: An Essay in Reading the Archives," *History and Theory* 24, no. 3 [1985]: 247–72; and Michel de Certeau, *The Writing of History* [New York: Columbia University Press, 1988]).

10. During the mid-1980s, scholars of color and gay scholars called on academic feminism to grapple with its differences (racial, sexual, class). The citations can only gesture toward the literature. For historical crosshatching of the debates, see Jane Gallop, *Around 1981: Academic Feminist Literary Theory* (New York: Routledge, 1992). My citations are selective since this essay is not intended as a review of medieval women's history or of critical feminist theory. For an example of the growing critique of academic feminism for its racism, see *This Bridge Called My Back: Writings by Radical Women of Color,* ed. Cherríe Moraga and Gloria Anzaldùa (New York: Kitchen Table/Women of Color, 1983)—awarded the Before Columbus Foundation American Book Award in 1986. For an articulation of feminist theory in an internationalist frame, another pressing concern of the 1980s, see Gayatri Chakravorty Spivak, *In Other Worlds: Essays in Cultural Politics* (London: Methuen, 1987). For a recent criticism of a widely read essay in Spivak's *In Other Worlds,* see Silvia Tandeciarz, "Reading Gayatri Spivak's 'French Feminism in an International Frame': A Problem of Theory," *Genders* 10 (Spring 1991): 75–91. The critique of the presumption of heterosexuality organizing theories of sexual difference grew more vocal in the mid-1980s; see, e.g., Teresa de Lauretis, "Feminist Studies/Critical Studies: Issues, Terms and Contexts," in *Feminist Studies/Critical Studies,* ed. Teresa de Lauretis (Bloomington: Indiana University Press, 1986), and "The Female Body and Heterosexual Presumption," *Semiotica* 67, nos. 3/4 (1987): 257–59.

11. In spite of complex and subtle debates over medieval Christendom, scholars have not questioned how the construction of this category might be related to the construction of medieval genders. For a synthetic discussion of how medieval Europeans used the word *Christendom* (*Christianitas*), see John Van Engen, "The Christian Middle

Ages as an Historiographical Problem," *American Historical Review* 91, no. 3 (1986): 519–52. Van Engen notes that Raoul Manselli traced the origin of the concept to a "self-conscious, defensive reaction to Islam" (p. 539), but he drops the issue of the mutual construction of Islam, Judaism, and Christendom. The failure to look at these constructions *relationally* in an article self-conscious of complexity within Christendom shows the abiding cultural domination of a unitary notion of this category. We can look to theoretical tools developed by African-American feminist theorists, notably Hortense Spillers, to help us understand the historical ways in which cultural wholes are engendered through the exclusion and exteriorizing of the "Other(s)" that exist outside, but in relation to, a political and cultural interior. Through her study of the historical construction of gender in the juridical world of American slavery, Spillers has conceptualized the problem of discontinuous genders, i.e., genders exterior to, but in relation with, dominant juridical-kinship systems. Such systems typically conserve a notion of interiority, which is a notion of purity, by constructing a racial exterior. That exterior is also the cultural space where excluded cultural Others get located. Medievalists can usefully learn from this work and begin studying the problem of discontinuities of European genders produced juridically by medieval societies. (See Hortense J. Spillers, "Mama's Baby, Papa's Maybe: An American Grammar Book," *Diacritics* 17, no. 2 [1987]: 65–82.)

12. See Judith Butler, "Contingent Foundations: Feminism and the Question of the 'Postmodern,'" in *Feminists Theorize the Political.*

13. For a discussion of the problems of empathy and transference, see Dominick La Capra, "Is Everyone a *Mentalité* Case? Transference and the 'Culture' Concept," in *History and Criticism:* "Transference implies that the considerations at issue in the object of study are always repeated with variations—or find their displaced analogues—in one's account of it, and transference is as much denied by an assertion of the total difference of the past as by its total identification with one's own 'self' or 'culture'" (p. 72).

14. In *Holy Feast and Holy Fast* (p. 229), Bynum cites Victor Turner and her earlier article on his work, "Women's Stories, Women's Symbols: A Critique of Victor Turner's Theory of Liminality," in *Anthropology and the Study of Religion,* ed. Frank Reynolds and Robert Moore (Chicago: Center for the Scientific Study of Religion, 1984), reprinted in her *Fragmentation and Redemption: Essays on Gender and the Human Body in Medieval Religion* (New York: Zone, 1991). The work of Victor Turner has come in for some criticism in recent literature on ethnographic writing and dominant/dominating Western modes of repre-

sentation. For a mild version, see James Clifford, *The Predicament of Culture: Twentieth Century Ethnography, Literature and Art* (Cambridge, Mass.: Harvard University Press, 1990), 48–49, 52, 94. Michael Taussig is more critical of Turner as a proponent of a romantic notion of the symbol (see "Homesickness and Dada," in *Nervous System* [New York: Routledge, 1992], and *Shamanism, Colonialism, and the Wild Man: A Study in Terror and Healing* [Chicago: University of Chicago Press, 1987], 441–42).

15. See Clifford, *The Predicament of Culture,* 235. This historical concept of culture is, of course, under critique. Such criticism is the purpose of *The Predicament of Culture.* Also important is Edward W. Said, "Representing the Colonized: Anthropology's Interlocutors," *Critical Inquiry* 15 (Winter 1989): 205–25.

16. "There is thus an intentional or unintentional usage of Frazer's Law of Sympathy, a magical usage, not only in the actual rite itself, but in its representations, by the anthropologist-writer mimetically engaging the flow of events described with the flow of his theoretical argument, to the benefit and empowerment of the latter. Not the least impressive about this magical mimesis is that instead of obviously magicalizing the connectedness that holds the argument together, it naturalizes those connections" (Taussig, "Homesickness and Dada," 151). Taussig's critique is not a "modernist" one that denies an aspect of play or carnival in writing; rather, it insists that such play, carnival, rely on the marking of the gap.

17. Ibid., 151.

18. In an analysis of the rhetoric of a famous essay on symbols by Lévi-Strauss, in which he writes, among other things, that "the shaman provides the sick woman with a *language,* by means of which unexpressed and otherwise inexpressible psychic states can be immediately expressed" (ibid., 168), Taussig has demonstrated how the *anthropologist* provides the shaman with a language in order to give birth to structure that authorizes the anthropologist. (Taussig is analyzing Claude Lévi-Strauss, "The Effectiveness of Symbols," in *Structural Anthropology,* trans. Claire Jacobson and Brooke Grundfest Schoepf [New York: Basic, 1963], 198. This essay, dedicated to Raymond de Saussure, first appeared in *Revue de l'Histoire des Religions* [135 (1949): 5–27].) My analysis follows Taussig closely here. My criticisms of the cultural concept are situated in an extended literature of post-Orientalist critiques of culture that view culture as a historically essentialized notion and would encourage instead a refiguring of the concept: "Thus to see Others not as ontologically given but as historically constituted would be to erode the exclusivist biases we so often ascribe to cultures, our

own not the least. Cultures may then be represented as zones of control or abandonment, of recollection and forgetting, of force of dependence, of exclusiveness of sharing" (Said, "Representing the Colonized," 255). This criticism is also influenced by de Certeau, *The Writing of History;* Robert Young, *White Mythologies: Writing History and the West* (New York: Routledge, 1990); Homi Bhabha, ed., *Nation and Narration* (New York: Routledge, 1990); Dirks, "History as a Sign of the Modern," 25–32; and Timothy Mitchell, "Everyday Metaphors of Power," *Theory and Society* 19 (1990): 545–77, and *Colonising Egypt* (New York: Cambridge University Press, 1988).

19. I can cite no synthetic reference for the recent history of the critical studies of representations of fantasies of the maternal and theories of such fantasies. Judith Butler's *Gender Trouble: Feminism and the Subversion of Identity* (New York: Routledge, 1990) and Drucilla Cornell's *Beyond Accommodation: Ethical Feminism, Deconstruction, and the Law* (New York: Routledge, 1991) both provide useful critiques of some chief theorists of the maternal ranging from the social psychology school (Chodorow) to Lacanian-influenced theory (Kristeva). Kaja Silverman offers a study of how fantasies of the maternal are staged in films (see her *Acoustic Mirror: The Female Voice in Psychoanalysis and Cinema* [Bloomington: Indiana University Press, 1988]; as well as Mary Ann Doane, "Technophilia: Technology, Representation, and the Feminine," in *Body/Politics: Women and the Discourse of Science,* ed. Mary Jacobus, Evelyn Fox Keller, and Sally Shuttleworth [New York: Routledge, 1990], 163–76). The politics of rethinking the maternal is urgent since fantasies of the maternal produce specific historical bodies as sites of struggle (World Health Organization, *Maternal Mortality Rates: A Tabulation of Available Information* [Geneva, 1986]).

20. My thoughts here are inspired by Jane Gallop, who has emphasized the political importance of a postmodern engagement with "the anxiety produced by the absence of any certain access to the referent." My argument here is that Bynum forestalls that form of anxiety by using the maternal as a natural referent for the history of medieval women. This move creates anxieties of its own, but they are reductive rather than transformative anxieties (see Gallop, "The Body Politic," in *Thinking through the Body,* 96).

21. The earliest reviews of *Holy Feast and Holy Fast* were by John Frecerro in the *New York Times Book Review* (5 April 1987, 26), John Boswell in the *New Republic* (24 August 1987, 36–38), and Maurice Keen in the *New York Review of Books* (8 October 1987, 42–44). The following reviews appeared in major journals of church history and religious studies: Retha M. Warnicke, *Journal of the American Academy of Reli-*

gion 66, no. 3 (1988): 563–64; Glenn W. Olsen, *Church History* 57, no. 2 (1988): 225–27; John Howe, *Catholic History Review* 74, no. 3 (1988): 456–58; Bernard McGinn, *History of Religions* 28, no. 1 (1988): 90–92; George Holmes, *Journal of Ecclesiastical History* 40, no. 2 (1989): 274–75; and Amanda Porterfield, *Religion* 20 (April 1990): 187–88. Reviews in history journals considered for this essay include Lester K. Little, *Journal of Social History* 21 (Spring 1988): 597–99; Ann G. Carmichael, *Journal of Interdisciplinary History* 19 (Spring 1989): 635–44; Judith C. Brown, *American Historical Review* 94 (June 1989): 735–37; Rita Copeland, *Speculum* 64 (January 1989): 143–47; and Jack Goody, *English Historical Review* 105, no. 415 (April 1990): 429–31. Also considered is the review by Hester Goodenough Gelber, *Modern Language Quarterly* 48 (September 1987): 281–85. The reviews are short enough that quotations from them need not be documented by page number.

22. Bynum offers protocols of reading. Metaphors of food preparation suggest that her book is like food. She describes herself as holding a sieve and sifting "medieval experience," like flour, through a fine mesh (p. xv). Her book is also corporeal; it has a "heart" (p. 279). These reading protocols, suggestive of reading as eating, can also be traced to the structuralist frame of the book. We have seen how a structuralist notion of culture can result in a kind of "autocannibalism," the consumption of otherness. These images also raise interesting questions about distinguishing cannibalism from communion.

23. The notion of a divided empathy suggests that empathy traverses the path of transference.

24. My comments are restricted to rhetorical problems in *Holy Feast and Holy Fast;* I do not wish to imply here that the history of the construction of motherhood is not crucial. For an important historiographic step with a helpful bibliography, see Clarissa W. Atkinson, *The Oldest Vocation: Christian Motherhood in the Middle Ages* (Ithaca, N.Y.: Cornell University Press, 1991).

25. For a critique of the call for more context, see La Capra, "Rhetoric and History," in *History and Criticism,* 19. My thoughts about framing are inspired by Jacques Derrida's "The Parergon" (*October* 9 [Summer 1979]: 3–41; reprinted in his *The Truth in Painting* [Chicago: University of Chicago Press, 1987]). Derrida meditates on how a frame works as an "objectifying, representational essence, it is inside and outside, the criteria used in definition, the value attributed to the natural, and either secondarily or principally, the privileged position of the human body" (p. 22 of the *October* version).

26. Butler, *Gender Trouble,* 25. Feminists theorize performance as a

feminist practice and a way of questioning the "naturalized" links between anatomical sex, gender identity, and gender performance. This theorizing offers ways of historicizing the pain of gender performance, where doing "gender right" has been historically subject to political and social coercion. This theory appropriates in a utopian gesture a history of performance among gay and lesbian communities. It also questions gender as a representation (see Teresa de Lauretis, "Sexual Indifference and Lesbian Representation," in *Performing Feminisms: Feminist Critical Theory and Theatre,* ed. Sue-Ellen Case [Baltimore: Johns Hopkins University Press, 1990]). Judith Butler also theorizes gender as performance in *Gender Trouble* and in "Performative Acts and Gender Constitution: An Essay in Phenomenology and Feminist Theory," in *Performing Feminisms.* See also Cornell, *Beyond Accommodation.*

27. There is a discussion of iconographic evidence on p. 81 and mention of plates 1, 5, 7, 25, 26, and 30: "Iconographic evidence also suggests that medieval people of both sexes associated food and fasting with women." On pp. 268 and 270–72, there is a discussion of the lactating Virgin and reference to plates 13–16 and 20–30. It seems that plates 2–4, 6, 8–12, and 17–19 receive no mention. Michael Camille commented on the way the plates of *Holy Feast and Holy Fast* are used simply as illustrations to back up textual arguments rather than as semiotic objects in their own right that might not only reinforce but also contest and subvert textual arguments (see "Art History in the Past and Future of Medieval Studies," paper delivered at the conference The Past and Future of Medieval Studies, University of Notre Dame, 19–21 February 1992, reprinted in *The Past and Future of Medieval Studies,* ed. John Van Engen [Notre Dame, Ind.: University of Notre Dame Press, 1994]). In *The Gothic Idol: Ideology and Image-Making in Medieval Art* (New York: Cambridge University Press, 1989), Camille writes about medieval images, but the same could be said for their use as illustrations in current historical texts: "It [*The Gothic Idol*] also attempts to uncover realms of intervisual and not just intertextual meanings, where images do not just 'reflect' texts innocently but often subvert and alter their meanings" (p. xxvii).

28. "But historians have tended to correlate eucharistic concern with factors other than gender—for example, with religious order (particularly Cistercian or Dominican), with region (particularly the Low Countries or southern Germany), or with type of religious life (particularly monastic or anchoritic)" (p. 75). Issues of region and audience are complicated by different patronage and distribution patterns in different art markets in the later fifteenth century. To begin exploring

this problem, see Lynn F. Jacobs, "The Marketing and Standardization of South Netherlandish Carved Altarpieces: Limits on the Role of the Patron," *Art Bulletin* 71, no. 2 (1989): 208–29.

29. A historical understanding of medieval European gender requires a study of how gender came to mark as "naturalized" borders of interiority and exteriority of the body, the community, the institutions that institute kinship. The outlines of this complex history, which produced Jews, homosexuals, prostitutes, lepers, and heretics as an exterior to the "natural" European sex-gender system, are delineated in R. I. Moore, *The Formation of a Persecuting Society: Power and Deviance in Western Europe, 950–1250* (London: Blackwell, 1987). In using the word *homosexuals* here, I am not implying anachronistically a gay identity and lifestyle. For important discussion of how to talk about medieval gay people, see E. Ann Matter, "*MFN* Gay and Lesbian Issue," Simon Gaunt, "Gay Studies and Feminism: A Medievalist's Perspective," Carolyn Dinshaw, "The Heterosexual Subject of Chaucerian Narrative," Sylvia Huot, "Addressing the Issue of Lesbianism in a General Course on Women in the Middle Ages," Susan Schibanoff, "Chaucer's Lesbians: Drawing Blanks?" and Mary Anne Campbell, "Redefining Holy Maidenhood: Virginity and Lesbianism in Late Medieval England," *Medieval Feminist Newsletter* 13 (Spring 1992): 1–3, 3–8, 8–10, 10–11, 11–14, and 14–16. Historians tell us that such an identity began to form in the nineteenth century (see John Boswell, *Christianity, Social Tolerance, and Homosexuality: Gay People in Western Europe from the Beginning of the Christian Era in the Fourteenth Century* [Chicago: University of Chicago Press, 1980]). Eve Kosofsky Sedgwick offers a thoughtful and cogent analysis of the problem of speech acts in discussing histories of sexuality in *Epistemology of the Closet* (Berkeley and Los Angeles: University of California Press, 1990), 263. For a brilliant study of how medical and theological discourses on medieval sexuality are intertwined, see Danielle Jacquart and Claude Thomasset, *Sexuality and Medicine in the Middle Ages,* trans. Matthew Anderson (Princeton, N.J.: Princeton University Press, 1988).

30. For discussion of blood in medieval medical treatises, especially menstrual blood, see Jacquart and Thomasset, *Sexuality and Medicine.*

31. I am anticipating my argument here in two registers. Medieval Eucharistic devotion defined cultural boundaries that excluded Jews as Others in medieval society. Accusations of ritual cannibalism against Jews emerged with the formation of an institutionalized orthodox Eucharistic theology (Gavin I. Langmuir, *Toward a Definition of Antisemitism* [Berkeley and Los Angeles: University of California Press, 1990], 263–82), and that self-fashioning, the mental absorption of others as a

historical and contemporary rhetorical practice, deserves critical attention (Maggie Kilgour, *From Communion to Cannibalism: An Anatomy of Metaphors of Incorporation* [Princeton, N.J.: Princeton University Press, 1990]; see also *The Blood Libel Legend: A Casebook of Anti-Semitic Folklore,* ed. Alan Dundes [Madison: University of Wisconsin Press, 1991]; Gavin I. Langmuir, "From Anti-Judaism to Antisemitism," in *History, Religion, and Antisemitism* [Berkeley and Los Angeles: University of California Press, 1990], and *Toward a Definition of Antisemitism,* esp. chap. 11 on ritual cannibalism; Jeremy Cohen, *The Friars and the Jews: The Evolution of Medieval Anti-Judaism* [Ithaca, N.Y.: Cornell University Press, 1982]; Robert Chazan, *Daggers of Faith: Thirteenth-Century Christian Missionizing and Jewish Response* [Berkeley and Los Angeles: University of California Press, 1989]; Dian Owen Hughes, "Distinguishing Signs: Ear-Rings, Jews and Franciscan Rhetoric in the Italian Renaissance City," *Past and Present* 112 [August 1986]: 3–59; and Lionel Rothkrug, "Popular Religion and Holy Shrines: Their Influence on the Origins of the German Reformation and Their Role in German Cultural Development," in *Religion and the People (800–1700),* ed. James Obelkevich [Chapel Hill: University of North Carolina Press, 1979]). References to Eucharistic shrines built on the site of Jewish massacres appear in n. 23, p. 292, of *Holy Feast and Holy Fast;* see also Charles Zika, "Hosts, Processions and Pilgrimages: Controlling the Sacred in Fifteenth-Century Germany," *Past and Present* 118 [February 1988): 25–64; and R. Po-chia Hsia, *The Myth of Ritual Murder: Jews and Magic in Reformation Germany* (New Haven, Conn.: Yale University Press, 1988). For links between anti-Semitism and the propagation of broadsheets and woodcuts in fifteenth- and early sixteenth-century Europe, see David Kunzle, *History of the Comic Strip,* vol. 1, *The Early Comic Strip, Narrative Strips and Picture Series in the European Broadsheet from c. 1450–1825* (Berkeley: University of California Press, 1973), 11–28. Michael Camille discusses the Jew as image and asks about the medieval church, "Was it only by being on the image offensive that emphasis could be taken away from the questions 'what are *our* images for' and 'what relation does the image bear to its prototype?' and the finger pointed at the false images of the Other" (*The Gothic Idol,* 193). I am also indebted to Sander Gilman, *The Jew's Body* (New York: Routledge, 1991), and "The Jewish Body: A 'Footnote,'" *Bulletin of the History of Medicine* 64, no. 4 (1990): 588–602.

32. I borrow the term *the imaginary* from Lacanian psychoanalysis, where it has complex meanings. I use it in this essay in the following sense: "In relation to meaning, the Imaginary is that in which perceptual features like resemblance operate—that is to say, in areas where

there is a sort of coalescence of the signifier and the signified, as in traditional symbolism. For Lacan, the Imaginary relationship, of whatever kind, is also that of a lure, a trap. In this sense he is close to the normal usage of the word 'imaginary' to describe something we believe to be something else" (Jacques Lacan, *Speech and Language in Psychoanalysis,* trans. Anthony Wilden [Baltimore: Johns Hopkins University Press, 1968], 175).

33. Many readers of drafts of this essay expected it to turn into my own reading of Elizabeth of Hungary at this juncture. I have refused that move because this essay is not about better or different readings but about questions of engendering the visible and the invisible in our contemporary historiography. I wish to keep that problem open in the essay. For historical references for the Fulda persecution, see Gavin Langmuir's excellent "Ritual Cannibalism," in *Toward a Definition of Antisemitism.* The text of *Vox in Rama* appears in *Monumento germaniae historia,* ed. Carolus Rodenberg (Berlin: Weidman, 1883), 1:432–34. For Conrad's writings on Elizabeth of Hungary, see Albert Huyskens, *Quellenstudien zur Geschichte der hl. Elisabeth* (Marburg: N. G. Elwert'sche, 1908).

34. The motifs of this predella are virtually unique to Italian altarpieces of the period, but the story it illustrates circulated in popular plays and in northern Europe in broadsheets. Joos Van Ghent probably began the main panel of the altarpiece, *The Communion of the Apostles,* in 1473. The juxtaposition of a converted Jew (according to Marilyn Lavin's identification) in the Van Ghent panel with the predella suggests that the tragic scene of the predella is "correctible," but according to whose perspective? (see Marilyn Aronberg Lavin, "The Altar of Corpus Domini in Urbino: Paolo Uccello, Joos Van Ghent, Piero della Francesca," *Art Bulletin* 49 [March 1967]: 1–24; and John Pope-Hennessy, *Paolo Uccello* [New York: Phaidon, 1969], 156, pll. 87–100).

35. Franciscan preachers condemned Italian women for their appetite for finery, claiming that this avariciousness made them partners to the Jews (see Hughes, "Distinguishing Signs," 28). For a discussion of Franciscan involvement in the establishment of *mons pietatis* throughout Italy (there were over eighty *montes* in Italian cities at the end of the fifteenth century), see John T. Noonan, *The Scholastic Use of Usury* (Cambridge, Mass.: Harvard University Press, 1957), 295. Note that many of the northern Italian cities ordered that Jews wear distinguishing signs just a generation before the predella was executed: Padua in 1430, Perugia in 1432, and Florence and Siena in 1439 (Hughes, "Distinguishing Signs," 20).

36. We need comparative regional histories of the expulsion of Jews in

medieval Europe. Such histories would help pose comparative questions of how anti-Semitism and anxieties about pollution maintained themselves discursively both where Jews were present and where they were absent. Edward I ordered the first permanent expulsion of Jews from England in 1290; Phillip IV expelled Jews from France in 1306. Jews in southern Italian communities were subject to the Inquisition in the late thirteenth century, and many migrated to northern Italy or converted. In the 1420s and 1430s, many of the imperial cities of the Rhineland expelled their Jewish communities.

37. Hsia, *The Myth of Ritual Murder.*

38. See Kunzle, *The Early Comic Strip,* 11–28.

39. Hughes, "Distinguishing Signs," 28.

40. For the associations of Thomas Aquinas and the sterility of prostitutes, see Jacquart and Thomasset, *Sexuality and Medicine,* 156. For the well-established antipathy to homoeroticism, see Boswell, *Christianity, Social Tolerance and Homosexuality;* Michael J. Rocke, "Sodomites in Fifteenth-Century Tuscany: The Views of Bernardino of Siena," in *The Pursuit of Sodomy: Male Homosexuality in Renaissance and Enlightenment Europe,* ed. Kerit Gerard and Gert Helima (New York: Haworth, 1989); and John W. Baldwin, "Five Discourses on Desire: Sexuality and Gender in Northern France around 1200," *Speculum* 66, no. 4 (1991): 797–829.

41. It is the historically charged nature of these boundaries that undoubtedly accounts for the fact, according to Camille, that "the Host can be described as the single most important image to Christians from the middle of the thirteenth century onward, perhaps even overtaking veneration of the cross" (*Gothic Idol,* 215). Or, as Miri Rubin has brilliantly traced the many ways in which medieval Europeans used the Host to think with: "The eucharist was constructed to bear these meanings as a symbol which still retained an enormous space between signifier and signified to allow such a broad array of articulations. But it was becoming increasingly overdetermined" (*Corpus Christi: The Eucharist in Late Medieval Culture* [New York: Cambridge University Press, 1991], 344). I regret that Miri Rubin's "The Eucharist and the Construction of Medieval Identities" and Sarah Beckwith's "Ritual, Church and Theatre: Medieval Dramas of the Sacramental Body" (both in *Culture and History*), which have so much bearing on the argument of this essay, became available to me only as this essay was going to press.

42. Rubin, *Corpus Christi,* 70–71. Rubin quotes from *De sacramentis* by James of Vitry: "Because of possible danger the eucharist is not given to the laity under the species of wine" (p. 71).

43. Peter Stallybrass and Allon White make an important point about

exclusion and differentiation of the grotesque: "We have to avoid conflating the two different forms of the grotesque. If the two are confused [grotesque as excluded Other; hybrid grotesque as a boundary phenomenon of hybridization and inmixing], it becomes impossible to see that a fundamental mechanism of identity formation *produces* the second, hybrid grotesque at the level of the political unconscious *by the very struggle to exclude the first grotesque*" (*The Politics and Poetics of Transgression* [Ithaca, N.Y.: Cornell University Press, 1986], 193). Their theory can be related to the work of Homi Bhabha in the postcolonial theory of "doubling" (see "Interrogating Identity," in *The Real Me: Postmodernism and the Question of Identity* [ICA Documents 6], ed. Lisa Appignanesi [London: Institute for Contemporary Arts, 1987], and "Postcolonial Authority and Postmodern Guilt," in *Cultural Studies.* Dollimore's use of the notion of "proximate other" (*Sexual Dissidence,* 135), which I came across after completing the draft of this essay, could be fruitfully developed here.

44. Mikhail Bakhtin, *Rabelais and His World,* trans. Helene Iswolsky (Bloomington: Indiana University Press, 1984), 317. For references to the Corpus Christi procession, see ibid., 229–30. See also Rubin, *Corpus Christi,* 213–86. I am trying to negotiate and mark the tensions of constructing differences within and differences between in medieval European Eucharistic culture. Bynum cites Bakhtin in *Holy Feast and Holy Fast* for references to folk literature and the pleasures of eating, but she does not use his thoughts on the grotesque body in her analysis. For critical studies that question, among other things, Bakhtin's nostalgia and failure to address political questions of gendering the grotesque body, see Mary Russo, "Female Grotesques: Carnival and Theory," in *Feminist Studies/Critical Studies;* Stallybrass and White, *The Politics and Poetics of Transgression,* passim, esp. 1–26; and Dominick LaCapra, "Bakhtin, Marxism and the Carnivalesque," in *Rethinking Intellectual History: Texts, Contexts, Language* (Ithaca, N.Y.: Cornell University Press, 1983), 291–324.

45. Ella Shohat has called for study of the diverse modalities of hybridity—"forced assimilation, internalized self-rejection, political cooption, social conformism, cultural mimicry, and creative transcendence" ("Notes on the 'Post-Colonial,'" *Social Text* 31/32 [1992]: 110).

46. It is as if the Host functioned in the way in which the "phallus" does today in contemporary psychoanalytic debate. The Eucharist as the guarantee of the symbolic in medieval Europe helps us historicize the symbolic as a foundational category and understand power-charged aspects of its work without insisting that medieval Europeans describe

their symbolic in terms of the penis/phallus. Brian Stock makes the point that the Eucharist was good to think with: "The eucharistic debate in particular opened up two broad subjects to systematic study by medieval thinkers. One was the status of symbol and ritual in a theory of religion that was increasingly preoccupied with explanation in literate terms. The other was the beginning of reflection on observable nature, or, more precisely, on the relation of phenomenal appearances to an inner reality whose logical properties coincided with those of texts" (*Implications of Literacy: Written Language and Models of Interpretation in the Eleventh and Twelfth Centuries* [Princeton, N.J.: Princeton University Press, 1983], 241). Compare: "The eucharist emerged as a unifying symbol for a complex world. . . . [I]t possessed universal meaning" (Rubin, *Corpus Christi,* 348). The symbolic guaranteed by the phallus brings us into psychoanalytic discourse of the twentieth century; for an introduction, see *Feminine Sexuality: Jacques Lacan and the Ecole freudienne,* ed. Juliet Mitchell and Jacqueline Rose (New York: Norton, 1985). Feminist critiques of the Lacanian model abound; see most recently *Differences,* vol. 4, no. 1 (1992), an issue of essays dedicated to critical theory and the deconstruction of the phallus.

47. For a suggestive study of the host and Christian cannibalism, see Kilgour, *From Communion to Cannibalism,* passim, esp. 79–139. While I was making my final revisions, a copy of de Certeau's *Mystic Fable* became available to me. His is a much more detailed argument than Kilgour's.

48. My arguments in this section are based on Hans Belting, *The Image and Its Public in the Middle Ages: Form and Function in the Early Paintings of the Passion,* trans. Mark Bartusis and Raymond Meyer (New Rochelle, N.Y.: Aristide D. Caratzas, 1990), 82. Dianne Phillips pointed out the need for a study of the coexistence and co-construction of talking reliquaries and ostensories. It is too simplistic to say that one replaced the other.

49. Ibid., 212–14. Camille comments that the "very fabrication of a thing" (*Gothic Idol,* 9) became the cause of concern in thirteenth-century society. Belting also argues against any simple division between public cult and private devotion; he shows how each informed the other and how viewer and image were related mimetically. His work inspired me to question the gendering of mimesis and to wonder how mystics performed mimetically, whether their mimesis could be a kind of countermimesis that marked the gaps between object illusionism and the depicted subject's mimetic power (Belting, *The Image and Its Public,* 53). In a seminar conducted at the Medieval Institute at the University of

Notre Dame (23 March 1993), Brigitte Bedos-Rezak raised complementary questions about complex issues regarding visibility and authentication in the changing culture of charters in France, 1000–1200.

50. Belting, *The Image and Its Public,* 219.

51. This argument then questions the category *medieval female mystic.* My reading here complements that of Karma Lochrie: "We must begin looking at the body itself as an historical construction" (*Translations of the Flesh,* 15). Note also Lochrie's emphasis on the point that the two terms *body* and *sexuality* are not coterminous in the medieval mental maps of corporeality.

52. Stock, *Implications of Literacy,* 250, 249.

53. Could we think of this as a *historical* moment of the simulacrum, in spite of the problems posed by Jean Baudrillard's work? The feminine thus became a simulacrum, "never exchanging for what is real, but exchanging in itself" (Jean Baudrillard, *Simulations* [New York: Semiotext(e), 1983], 11). This discussion of the circulation of the sign of the feminine derives from a critique of Baudrillard's *Simulations* and represents an effort to question further his work by theorizing relations between what he calls *hyperreality* and what he ignores, embodiment.

54. Rubin, *Corpus Christi,* 169. For some selected references to important new work on gender and the problems of textual authority and authentication, see Lynn Staley Johnson, "The Trope of the Scribe and the Question of Literary Authority in the Works of Julian of Norwich and Margery of Kempe," *Speculum* 66, no. 4 (1991): 820–38; Sarah Beckwith, "Problems of Authority in Late Medieval English Mysticism: Language, Agency, and Authority in the *Book of Margery Kempe,*" *Exemplaria* 4, no. 1 (1992): 171–200; and Maureen Quilligan, "The Name of the Author: Self-Representation in Christine de Pizan's *Livre de la cité des dames,*" *Exemplaria* 4, no. 1 (1992): 201–28.

55. Camille, *Gothic Idol,* 224. Camille talks about a "crisis of overproduction" in reference to Marian images, and his subsequent comments are relevant here: "This would seem to be a response to what I have termed a 'crisis of overproduction,' a kind of relic inflation in which the proliferation of the image of the Virgin meant that she was to some extent fragmented and diminished."

56. My reflections on aura may seem anachronistic, but the medieval crisis of authentication provided interesting comparative terms for the problems of aura discussed by Walter Benjamin in "The Work of Art in the Age of Mechanical Reproduction," in *Illuminations,* ed. Hannah Arendt (New York: Schocken, 1968), 217–52. Jeffrey F. Hamburger works with similar ideas in his discussion of the mystic Heinrich Suso, "The Use of Images in the Pastoral Care of Nuns: The Case of Heinrich

Suso and the Dominicans," *Art Bulletin* 61 [March 1989]: 42); his model of gender comes closer to that of Bynum.

57. The feminine need not always be constructed negatively; for the positive (nevertheless gendered as feminine) valuation of the oral, see Sharon Farmer, "Persuasive Voices: Clerical Images of Medieval Wives," *Speculum* 61 (July 1986): 517–43.

58. For an interesting contemporary reading of female anorectics that raises issues about the politics of judgment of their practices, see Gillian Brown, "Anorexia, Humanism, and Feminism," *Yale Journal of Criticism* 5, no. 1 (1991): 189–215.

59. I deliberately risk anachronism here again to point to meditations on the body and tattoos by the contemporary performance artist and writer Kathy Acker (*Hannibal Lecter, My Father* [New York: Semiotext(e), 1991]).

60. Stock, *Implications of Literacy*, 252.

61. I found help in imagining this complicated textualizing process in Jacques Derrida, *On Grammatology* (Baltimore: Johns Hopkins University Press, 1976), esp. 27–73.

62. For discussion and illustrations, see Belting, *The Image and Its Public*, 53. The issues raised here can help historicize the practices of female mystics more fully and ask whether it is advisable to view these practices on a continuum from the twelfth to the seventeenth century. I would argue for ruptures in these practices and suggest that the brilliant work of Michel de Certeau on mystics, especially mystics of the seventeenth century, requires modification for the study of medieval mystics (see his "Mystic Speech," in *Heterologies: Discourse on the Other* [Minneapolis: University of Minnesota Press, 1986]). Sarah Beckwith makes the same point, that "to posit mysticism then as a natural source of resistance to orthodoxy is dangerously a-historical, both because the function of mysticism varies with the social and historical conditions in which it is produced and reproduced and because, over and above this, the very quality of mysticism which can empower its by-passing of official structure . . . removes both God and the human soul from history" ("A Very Material Mysticism: The Medieval Mysticism of Margery Kempe," in *Medieval Literature*, ed. David Aers [London: St. Martin's, 1986], 40).

63. Butler, *Gender Trouble*, 136. See also Cornell, *Beyond Accommodation.*

64. The kind of performance discussed here interrogates the basic epistemological assumption of Western representation, in urgent need of critical historicization, that a cultural text somehow has a separate nature distinct from a particular articulation or performance. For a

provocative discussion of abiding, seemingly naturalized dualism in current conceptions of power, see Mitchell, "Everyday Metaphors of Power." I am grateful to Lisa Rofel for drawing my attention to this reference.

65. Cornell, *Beyond Accommodation,* 78.

66. Benjamin, "The Work of Art," 222.

67. Drucilla Cornell's extended meditation on *dérèlection* inspires my comments (see *Beyond Accommodation*). For some further thoughts on the maternal function and its problems in contemporary technology, see my "Stranded Histories: Feminist Allegories of Artificial Life," this volume.

68. Scott, "The Category of Experience," 797.

69. For a postcolonial critique of the problem of dreaming the Middle Ages, a compelling image evoked by Umberto Eco in "Dreaming the Middle Ages" (in *Travels in Hyperreality,* trans. William Weaver [San Diego: Harcourt Brace Jovanovich, 1986]), my essay "Bede's Blush" above.

70. Toni Morrison, *Beloved* (New York: Penguin, 1987), 274.

Humanist History and the Haunting of Virtual Worlds: Problems of Memory and Rememoration

I thank Allucquere Rosanne Stone, chair of the Second International Conference on Cyberspace (Santa Cruz, 19–20 April 1991), for supporting inclusion of an early draft of this essay in that program. Colleagues in the Program for Science, Technology and Society and the Narrative Intelligence Group at the Media Lab at the Massachusetts Institute of Technology, who offered me their intellectual friendship during a sabbatical supported by a Lilly Endowment Open Faculty Fellowship (1990–91), listened critically to an early draft—my special thanks to Carol Strohecker, Mike Travers, and Marc Davis of the Media Lab. I also owe special thanks to Craig Adcock, Dana Benelli, Ted Cachey, Eva Cherniavsky, Istvan Csicsery-Ronay, Tom Foster, Robert Franklin, Barbara Green, Sandra Joshel, Bill Krier, Gloria-Jean Masciarotte, and Lisa Rofel for their encouragement and critical comments.

1. Michael Benedikt, introduction to *Cyberspace: First Steps* (Cambridge, Mass.: MIT Press, 1991), 23.

2. William Gibson cited this lyric, taken from the song "Sunday Morning," on *Velvet Underground and Nico* (MGM/Verve, 1967), by the Velvet Underground, as the epigraph he wanted for *Neuromancer* (Larry McCaffery, "An Interview with William Gibson," in *Storming the*

Reality Studio, ed. Larry McCaffery [Durham, N.C.: Duke University Press, 1991], 270). I am grateful to Tom Foster for drawing this interview to my attention.

3. William Gibson, *Neuromancer* (New York: Ace, 1984), *Count Zero* (New York: Ace, 1987), and *Mona Lisa Overdrive* (New York: Bantam, 1989). I read these books as trilogy and travel books. For "history lessons," see *Neuromancer,* 34–35, 51.

4. Gibson, *Neuromancer,* 51.

5. Benedikt, introduction to *Cyberspace,* 23. Michael Benedikt, School of Architecture, Don Fussell, Department of Computer Sciences, both of the University of Texas at Austin, William Gibson, and Charles Grantham, vice president of North Bay Consultancy, San Francisco, organized the first cyberspace conference. *Cyberspace* publishes the proceedings. Reference to cyberspace as a New World also appeared on p. iii of the collected abstracts, which were available for $15.00 from the School of Architecture, University of Texas at Austin, Austin, TX 78712.

6. Cited in John Perry Barlow, "Being in Nothingness," *Colonizing Cyberspace! The Race is On, Mondo 2000,* no. 2 (Summer 1990): 37.

7. Jonathan Dollimore offers an interesting discussion of camp in his *Sexual Dissidence: Augustine to Wilde, Freud to Foucault* (Oxford: Clarendon, 1991), 312.

8. Homi Bhabha, "Of Mimicry and Man: The Ambivalence of Colonial Discourse," in *Politics and Ideology,* ed. James Donald and Stuart Hall (Milton Keynes: Open University, 1986), 199. *Insula Hyspana* appears as one of the first titled woodcut illustrations of the New World. Tony Campbell discusses the maps and illustrations (with bibliography) that circulated in the printed Latin editions of Columbus's letter in *The Earliest Printed Maps: 1472–1500* (Berkeley and Los Angeles: University of California Press, 1987), 100–102.

9. Such rememoration can help short-circuit the profoundly damaging potential of virtual technologies, already encountered in the Persian Gulf War, the first cyberwar, a war of deterritorialization (Les Levidow and Kevin Robins, "Vision Wars," *Race and Class* 32 [1991]: 88–92). "Civilized modern societies are defined by processes of decoding and deterritorialization. But *what they deterritorialize with one hand, they reterritorialize with the other*" (Gilles Deleuze and Felix Guattari, *Anti-Oedipus: Capitalism and Schizophrenia* [Minneapolis: University of Minnesota Press, 1983], 257). I am relying on Toni Morrison for this use of the verb *to rememorate.* See her *Beloved* (New York: Penguin, 1987).

10. The anthropologist Michael Taussig has described the historical space of encounter as a "space of terror," a space of dismemberment, which, after five hundred years still proves resistant to "re-membering"

(*Shamanism, Colonialism, and the Wild Man: A Study in Terror and Healing* [Chicago: University of Chicago Press, 1987], and "Violence and Resistance in the Americas: The Legacy of Conquest," in *The Nervous System* [New York: Routledge, 1992]). Recent critical studies of European travel writing can help us read the trilogy for ways in which it goes about constructing virtual subjects of this New New World (see, e.g., Michel de Certeau, *The Writing of History,* trans. Tom Conley [New York: Columbia University Press, 1988]; Johannes Fabian, *Time and the Other: How Anthropology Makes Its Objects* [New York: Columbia University Press, 1983]; and Mary Louise Pratt, *Imperial Eyes: Travel Writing and Transculturation* [New York: Routledge, 1992]).

11. McCaffery, "An Interview with William Gibson," 270.

12. For an interesting discussion of the archival confinement of knowledge as an imperial fantasy, see Thomas Richards, "Archive and Utopia," *Representations* 37 (Winter 1992): 104–35. For the politics of erasure in the archive, see Gayatri Chakravorty Spivak, "The Rani of Sirmur: An Essay in Reading the Archives," *History and Theory* 24, no. 3 (1985): 247–72. Ironically, the separation between history and memory made by Gibson has an analogue in the dominant computer architecture of the first thirty years of computing. This so-called Von Neumann computer architecture, which separated memory from processing, yielded over the 1980s to parallel, distributed neural nets with recursive, associative memories (see Richard E. Smith, "A Historical Overview of Computer Architecture," *Annals of the History of Computing* 10, no. 4 [1989]: 277–303). Israel Rosenfield (*The Invention of Memory: A New View of the Brain* [New York: Basic, 1988]) makes important criticisms of early parallel distributed processors that still retain nineteenth-century notions of matching stimuli to fixed memory stores.

13. Case sees the "primitive ice" (p. 56) of the New York Public Library in *Neuromancer.*

14. Taussig, "Violence and Resistance in the Americas," 52. Taussig offers a way of thinking about voice outside the Western graphic epistemic without making it transcendent or essential. Linked to Taussig's project is Pratt's use of *autoethnography,* "instances in which colonized subjects undertake to represent themselves in ways that *engage with* the colonizer's own terms" (*Imperial Eyes,* 7). Within the limits of this discussion, suffice it to say that such recent films as *Dances with Wolves* and *Black Robe* and the documentary *The Civil War* by Ken Burns and Ric Burns can be cited as examples of popular historical representations of humanist history. For a critical review of the latter by a historian, see Ellen Carol Du Bois, *American Historical Review* 96, no. 4 (1991): 1140–42. For compelling essays warning historians of ventriloquism, see

Joan W. Scott, "The Evidence of Experience," *Critical Inquiry* 17 (Summer 1991): 773–97; and Peter de Bolla, "Disfiguring History," *Diacritics* 16 (Winter 1986): 49–58. For some thoughts on the complications of undoing humanist history, see Gyan Prakash, "Postcolonial Criticism and Indian Historiography," *Social Text* 31/32 (1992): 8–19; and David E. Johnson, "Voice, the New Historicism, and the Americas," *Arizona Quarterly* 48, no. 2 (1992): 81–116. I am grateful to my colleague Ted Cachey for this last reference.

15. Donna Haraway, "The Promises of Monsters: A Regenerative Politics for Inappropriate/d Others," in *Cultural Studies,* ed. Lawrence Grossberg, Cary Nelson, Paula Treichler (New York: Routledge, 1992), 327. See also her "Reading Buchi Emecheta: Contests for 'Women's Experience' in Women's Studies," in *Simians, Cyborgs, and Women: The Reinvention of Nature* (New York: Routledge, 1991).

16. Pratt, *Imperial Eyes,* 6.

17. The work of Donna Haraway has inspired my work on cyborg history (see Constance Penley and Andrew Ross, "Cyborgs at Large: Interview with Donna Haraway," and Donna Haraway, "The Actors Are Cyborg, Nature Is Coyote, and the Geography Is Elsewhere: Postscript to 'Cyborgs at Large,' " both in *Technoculture,* ed. Constance Penley and Andrew Ross [Minneapolis: University of Minnesota Press, 1991]).

18. The following criticisms of humanist history have influenced my thoughts in this essay: Dipesh Chakrabarty, "Postcoloniality and the Artifice of History: Who Speaks for 'Indian' Pasts," *Representations* 37 (Winter 1992): 1–26; de Certeau, *The Writing of History;* Nicholas B. Dirks, "History as a Sign of the Modern," *Public Culture* 2 (Spring 1990): 25–32; Fabian, *Time and the Other;* and Spivak, "The Rani of Sirmur."

19. Cited in Mary B. Campbell, *The Witness and the Other World: Exotic European Travel Writing, 400–1600* (Ithaca, N.Y.: Cornell University Press, 1988), 180.

20. Chandra Mukerji, "Visual Language in Science and the Exercise of Power: The Case of Cartography in Early Modern Europe," *Studies in Visual Communication* 10 (1984): 30–45; David Woodward, "Reality, Symbolism, Time and Space in Medieval World-Maps," *Annals of the Association of American Geographers* 75, no. 5 (1985): 510–21.

21. Michel de Certeau, "History: Science and Fiction," in *Heterologies: Discourse on the Other* (Minneapolis: University of Minnesota Press, 1986), 218, 205.

22. Taussig, *Shamanism, Colonialism, and the Wild Man,* 104–5.

23. For an evocation of nineteenth-century history as a kind of cryptology replete with mummies and vampires, see Laurence A. Rickels, *Aberrations of Mourning: Writing on German Crypts* (Detroit: Wayne

State University Press, 1988); and Nicolas Abraham and Maria Torok, *The Wolf Man's Magic Word* (Minneapolis: University of Minnesota Press, 1986).

24. Novels by such writers as Toni Morrison, Amitav Ghosh, Eduardo Galeano, and Leslie Marmon Silko write graffiti over the space of terror. Feminist autobiography as narrative/personal criticism can also disfigure the space of terror. The complexity and contradictions of feminist autobiography are produced in a note by Patricia Williams ("A Word on Categories," in *The Alchemy of Race and Rights* [Cambridge, Mass.: Harvard University Press, 1991]) where she describes the contest over categorizing her book for cataloging purposes. Williams wanted it referenced under the categories *autobiography, fiction, gender studies,* and *medieval medicine.* It is instead listed under *Afro-Americans–civil rights; United States–race relations; Williams, Patricia; law teachers–United States–biography; critical legal studies–United States,* and *feminist criticism–United States.* See also Jane Marcus, "The Asylums of Antaeus: Women, War and Madness: Is There a Feminist Fetishism?" in *The Difference Within: Feminism and Critical Theory,* ed. Elizabeth Meese and Alice Parker (Philadelphia: John Benjamins, 1989); and Nancy K. Miller, *Getting Personal: Feminist Occasions and Other Autobiographical Acts* (New York: Routledge, 1991).

25. Jean Baudrillard, *Simulations* (New York: Semiotext[e], 1983), 15.

26. Michel de Certeau, "Psychoanalysis and Its History," in *Heterologies,* 3.

27. Gibson, *Neuromancer,* 251.

28. Frances A. Yates, *The Art of Memory* (Chicago: University of Chicago Press, 1966), 209. See also Mary Carruthers, *The Book of Memory: A Study of Memory in Medieval Culture* (New York: Cambridge University Press, 1990).

29. During that time, the relations of knowledge to subjectivities were undergoing transformation. Rather than reflecting the world within memory and relying on internal images to construct subjectivities, the educated elite increasingly sought to construct the external world as an encyclopedia and to use memory as an aid to explore this externalized encyclopedia of nature (see Yates, *The Art of Memory,* 369).

30. For an overview of holographic and other competing models of memory in the neurosciences, see George Johnson, *In the Palaces of Memory: How We Build the Worlds inside Our Heads* (New York: Knopf, 1991).

31. Gibson, *Neuromancer,* 119.

32. According to Gibson, the film *Escape from New York* (John Carpenter, 1981) had a strong influence on *Neuromancer* (McCaffery, "An

Interview with William Gibson," 266). In the film, the character Snake Plissken has twenty-four hours to achieve a rescue mission before he suffers an irreversible effect of fatal toxins with which he has been inoculated. The film anxiously foregrounds the digital readout from a clock-like device that he wears on his wrist. This feature of the film's plot seems to have influenced Gibson's writing a digital display onto Molly's surgically inset silver lenses.

33. Gibson, *Neuromancer,* 201. There are several variants for the spelling of *voudou,* as if the word itself resisted easy appropriation. My use of the spelling *vodou* is based on the work of Karen McCarthy Brown in *Mama Lola: A Vodou Priestess in Brooklyn* (Berkeley and Los Angeles: University of California Press, 1991). The sunglasses with one lens missing worn by a female devotee of Pape Gede, the vodou trickster spirit of death and history, appears on p. 363 of *Mama Lola.*

34. The temporal prosthetic of Molly's glasses marks in an interesting way the crisis of history and its failure to think about noncommensurate transcultural temporalities: "The crisis in the conceptualization of 'narrative' appears as the other side of the crisis of the conceptualization of 'dimension' as geometrical narrative, the discourse of measurement of a reality visibly offered to all" (Paul Virilio, *Lost Dimension,* trans. Daniel Moshenberg, in *Semiotext[e]* [New York: Columbia University Press, 1991], 24). Virilio has interesting things to say about technocultural shifts in temporality and narrative. For a meditation on time, temporality, and the politics of space, see Paul Virilio and Sylvere Lotringer, *Pure War* (New York: Semiotext[e], 1983), 67–74: "Where there is no more field, our lives will be like a *terminal,* a machine with doors that open and close. A labyrinth for laboratory animals. If the parceling out of territory—of *territories of time*—is envisioned like that, according to a strict regulation and not a chrono-political understanding, there will be nothing left but absolute control, an immediacy which will be the worse kind of concentration" (p. 69).

35. Gibson, *Neuromancer,* 248, 269.

36. Gibson, *Count Zero,* 226.

37. The wedding of *Mona Lisa Overdrive* is hard to read. It involves corporeal death ("There's dying, then there's dying" [p. 301]) and afterlife in the cybermatrix: "Continuity [the AI entity] is there too, represented by a strolling scribble of silver tinsel" (p. 287). I first read the story as the marriage of Angie Mitchell to Continuity. In personal correspondence, Istvan Csicsery-Ronay Jr. wondered whether I was rewriting *Mona Lisa Overdrive* with this reading (for the stakes in rewriting science fiction, see Haraway, "The Promises of Monsters"). Our need for embodiment should not too easily tempt us to read the wed-

ding simply as Angie Mitchell and Bobby Newmark: "Is Bobby the solid rectangular mass of memory bolted above the stretcher?" (p. 286).

38. Here, the issues of postmodern political appropriation and the politics of pastiche and parody become vexed. Gibson mentions how he wrote the Haitian vodou into *Count Zero:* "A copy of *National Geographic* was lying around that had an article about Haitian voodoo in it" (McCaffery, "An Interview with William Gibson," 274). For a different politics of appropriation, see Brown, *Mama Lola.* Brown's encounter with Mama Lola rewrites the space of the encounter between self and Other and serves as an interesting counterpractice to Gibson's appropriation of the vodou pantheon from the *National Geographic.* Brown addresses the power issues of participant observation. She spent twelve years working with Mama Lola, who shares in the profits of Brown's book: "A true friendship is not over just because a writing project is done." This epigraph suggests an alternative process of postmodern appropriation in which "self" and "Other" coextend each other's worlds. See also Karen McCarthy Brown, "Writing about 'the Other,'" *Chronicle of Higher Education,* 15 April 1992, A56.

39. Taussig, *Shamanism, Colonialism, and the Wild Man,* 327.

40. Pauline Moffitt Watts, "Prophecy and Discovery: On the Spiritual Origins of Christopher Columbus's 'Enterprise of the Indies,'" *American Historical Review* 90 (1985): 92ff.

41. The relations of the Rastafarians and the Haitian spirits to "nature" in the trilogy deserve a separate essay.

42. Quoted in *A Joseph Cornell Album,* ed. Dore Ashton (New York: Viking, 1974), 45.

43. Gibson, *Count Zero,* 15.

44. See Brian Winston, "Reconsidering *The Triumph of the Will:* Was Hitler There?" *Sight and Sound* 30, no. 2 (1980–81): 102–7. I am grateful to Dana Benelli for this reference and for discussion. For a brilliant study of Walter Benjamin's appropriation of collage for history, see Susan Buck-Morss, *The Dialectics of Seeing: Walter Benjamin and the Arcades Project* (Cambridge, Mass.: MIT Press, 1989), esp. 60–71.

45. Walter Benjamin, "Theses on the Philosophy of History," in *Illuminations,* ed. Hannah Arendt (New York: Schocken, 1968), 255.

46. Israel Rosenfield, *The Strange, Familiar and Forgotten: An Anatomy of Consciousness* (New York: Knopf, 1962), 69.

47. Gibson, *Mona Lisa Overdrive,* 77.

48. See Zoe Sofia, "Exterminating Fetuses: Abortion, Disarmament, and the Sexo-Semiotics of Extraterrestrialism," *Diacritics* 14, no. 2 (1984): 57. See also my "Stranded Histories," *Research in Philosophy and Technology* 13 (1993): 167–84.

49. "I say remember the pain, because I believe true resistance begins with people confronting pain, whether it's theirs or someone else's, and wanting to do something to change it" (bell hooks, *Yearning: Race, Gender, and Cultural Politics* [Boston: South End, 1990], 215). Contacting the space of terror involves encounters with the fetishes that constitute the space of terror. "Get in touch with the fetish," urges Michael Taussig ("Maleficium: State Fetishism," in *The Nervous System,* 122). Taussig believes that the very intoxication of the fetish must be the starting point for its analysis and the force that can move it into transformative directions.

50. Gibson, *Mona Lisa Overdrive,* 308.

51. Haraway, "Promises of Monsters," 327.

52. Pratt, *Imperial Eyes,* 7.

53. Homi K. Bhabha, "Postcolonial Authority and Postmodern Guilt," in *Cultural Studies,* 59.

54. For a rigorous discussion of Freud's "A Child Is Being Beaten," see Parveen Adams, "Per Os(cillation)," *Camera Obscura* 17 (1988): 7–29.

55. François Du Creux S.J., *Historiae Canadensis* (Paris: Cramoisy, 1664), trans. Percy J. Robinson and James B. Conacher as *The History of Canada or New France* (Toronto: Champlain Society, 1951). This seventeenth-century text is a Latin compilation written in Bordeaux to appeal to cultivated literary tastes. Both the original Latin text and the modern translation feature a folded map of New France and thirteen plates. What I reproduce here as fig. 10 appeared as pl. 13 opposite p. 312 of the seventeenth-century edition. The modern edition reproduces all the plates and their original placing in the text.

56. Robert L. Reynolds, "The Ultimate Courage of Jean de Brébeuf," *American Heritage* 10, no. 6 (1959): 54–106.

57. The comic-book story of Isaac Jogues comes from the March 1945 issue of *Timeless Topix* (published in St. Paul, Minnesota). I am grateful to Carolyn T. Lee, curator of Rare Books and Special Collections at the Mullen Library, Catholic University of America, for her efforts in helping me try to locate the holy picture of my childhood and for sharing this reference with me.

58. Taussig, *Shamanism, Colonialism, and the Wild Man,* 105.

Stranded Histories: Allegories of Artificial Life

A Lilly Endowment Open Faculty Fellowship generously supported my sabbatical at the Massachusetts Institute of Technology (1990–91) and research for this essay. I am deeply grateful to the Lilly Endowment for the opportunities of that leave. Colleagues at MIT, both in the Program for Science, Technology and Society and in the Narrative Intelligence Reading Group at the Media Lab at MIT, offered me their intellectual generosity and friendship—I am indebted to Carol Strohecker, Mike Travers, Marc Davis, and Lily Kay. I also thank my colleagues in the Social Science History Association, especially Jon Liebowitz and Sonya Rose, who also gave this essay critical attention. The Gender Studies Faculty Forum at the University of Notre Dame provided me with helpful comments on a draft. I owe my special thanks to Sandra Joshel, Lisa Rofel, Joan Rothschild, and Joan Scott for their critical support and comments and to Anne Seelbach for the inspiration of her sculptured cyborgs.

1. Jonathon Crary, *Techniques of the Observer: On Vision and Modernity in the Nineteenth Century* (Cambridge, Mass.: MIT Press, 1990), 1; Vivian Sobchak, "A Theory of Everything: Meditations on Total Chaos," *Artforum* 19, no. 2 (1990): 153; Bill Nichols, "The Work of Culture in the Age of Cybernetic Systems," *Screen* 29, no. 1 (1988): 46. See also Richard Wright, "Computer Graphics as Allegorical Knowledge: Electronic Imagery in the Sciences," *Leonardo,* suppl. (1990), 65–74.

2. For an introduction to sociologies of representational practices in science, see *Representation in Scientific Practice,* ed. Michael Lynch and Steve Woolgar (Cambridge, Mass.: MIT Press, 1990). For an interesting, sympathetic criticism of the efforts of Bruno Latour, Lynch, and Woolgar, see Donna Haraway, "The Promises of Monsters: A Regenerative Politics for Inappropriate/d Others," in *Cultural Studies,* ed. Lawrence Grossberg, Cary Nelson, and Paula Treichler (New York: Routledge, 1992). For a meditation on dynamic subjects and objects in science, see Evelyn Fox Keller, "Dynamic Autonomy: Objects as Subjects," in *Reflections on Gender and Science* (New Haven, Conn.: Yale University Press, 1985).

3. The rhetorics of Renaissance art have been challenged in Svetlana Alpers, *The Art of Describing: Dutch Art in the Seventeenth Century* (Chicago: University of Chicago Press, 1983). For an interesting dialogue with her work, see Crary, *Techniques of the Observer,* 34–36. See also Michael Camille, "Walter Benjamin and Duerer's *Melancholia I:* The Dialectics of Allegory and the Limits of Iconology," *Ideas and Production* 5 (1985): 58–73. Benjamin used allegory in an oppositional way to its historicist use as a desire for origin (as described in Joel Fineman, "The Structure of Allegorical Desire," *October* 12 [1980]: 46–66).

4. Walter Benjamin, *The Origin of German Tragic Drama,* trans. John Osborne (London: Verso, 1977), 184. See also Susan Buck-Morss, *The*

Dialectics of Seeing: Walter Benjamin and the Arcades Project (Cambridge, Mass.: MIT Press, 1989), 184; Camille, "Walter Benjamin."

5. Buck-Morss, *The Dialectics of Seeing,* 184.

6. Benjamin, *The Origin of German Tragic Drama,* 183.

7. For a nonessential view of computers and the concept *computational object,* one "on the border between an abstract idea and a concrete physical object," see Sherry Turkle and Seymour Papert, "Epistemological Pluralism: Styles and Voices within Computer Culture," *Signs* 16, no. 1 (1990): 128–57.

8. Inspiration for recrafting these disembodied visualizations into specific, particular embodied images comes from Donna Haraway's "Situated Knowledges: The Science Question in Feminism and the Privilege of Partial Perspective" (*Feminist Studies* 14, no. 3 [1988]: 575–99) as well as from Benjamin and from the work of the artist Barbara Kruger (see Hal Foster, "Subversive Signs," in *Recodings* [Seattle: Bay, 1985]).

9. For a recent discussion of the problems and critical challenges of a nonfoundational history, see Joan Scott, "The Evidence of Experience," *Critical Inquiry* 17 (Summer 1991): 773–97; and Peter de Bolla, "Disfiguring History," *Diacritics* 16 (Winter 1986): 49–58.

10. A phrase of Richard Dawkins's, quoted in Chris Langton, "Toward Artificial Life," *Whole Earth Review* 58 (Spring 1988): 74–79.

11. Christopher Langton, preface to *Artificial Life,* vol. 6, ed. Christopher Langton (New York: Addison Wesley, 1989), xxii.

12. For a discussion of how cybernetic systems redefine relations to the real, see Nichols, "The Work of Culture"; Sobchak, "Total Chaos"; and Jonathan Crary, "Eclipse of the Spectacle," in *Art after Modernism: Rethinking Representations,* ed. Brian Wallis (New York: New Museum of Contemporary Art, 1984), 293–94.

13. Christopher Langton, "Toward Artificial Life," *Chronicle of Higher Education,* 4 December 1991, A30.

14. It is important to note the confusion between life and death articulated in some work by such postmodern theorists as Jean Baudrillard and Paul Virilio who claim that there is no life anymore on the planet, that there remains only the representation of life in its vital signs. In "Anorexic Ruins" (in *Looking Back at the End of the World* [New York: Columbia University Press, Semiotext(e), 1989]), Baudrillard writes, "As in the film *2001,* we are journeying into space, with the computer monitoring us. The information, communication, etc., keep the social body in a state of perfect survival ensuring that all vital functions continue: circulation, breathing, metabolism, heart tone, cell regeneration—just as the computer does it with the biophysiological

functions of the voyagers in *2001*. Quite simply, there is no life any longer. Nor is there in any of our societies. In a certain way there is no life anymore, but the information and the vital functions continue" (p. 39). See also Paul Virilio and Sylvere Lotringer, *Pure War* (New York: Columbia University, Semiotext[e], 1983): "No need to die, we're already the living dead" (p. 140).

15. For a compelling study of the fetal image, see Rosalind Pollack Petchesky, "Foetal Images: The Power of Visual Culture in the Politics of Reproduction," in *Reproductive Technologies: Gender, Motherhood and Medicine*, ed. Michelle Stanworth (Minneapolis: University of Minnesota Press, 1987).

16. Zoe Sofia, "Exterminating Fetuses: Abortion, Disarmament, and the Sexo-Semiotics of Extra-Terrestrialism," *Diacritics* 14, no. 2 (1984): 52; Donna Haraway, "A Cyborg Manifesto: Science, Technology, and Socialist-Feminism in the Late Twentieth Century," in *Simians, Cyborgs and Women: The Reinvention of Nature* (New York: Routledge, 1991), 149. See also Nichols, "The Work of Culture," 44, discussing engineered fetuses in the context of genetically based reproductive technologies as a "perfect cyborg."

17. Jacques Derrida, *The Post Card*, trans. Allan Bass (Chicago: University of Chicago Press, 1987).

18. Feminist theories of the maternal, maternity, and motherhood are working through power-charged debate over essentialism and antiessentialism. Such debates within feminism intersect with power-charged fantasies of the maternal and motherhood as the guarantee of "culture." For some constructive efforts to think through and beyond the opposition of essentialism and antiessentialism, see Teresa de Lauretis, "The Essence of the Triangle; or, Taking the Risk of Essentialism Seriously: Feminist Theory in Italy, the U.S., and Britain," *Differences* 1, no. 2 (1989): 3–38; Jane Gallop, "The Body Politic," in *Thinking through the Body* (New York: Columbia University Press, 1988); Lisa G. Bower, "'Mother-in-Law': Conceptions of Mother and the Maternal in Feminism and Legal Theory," *Differences* 3, no. 1 (1991): 20–38; and Drucilla Cornell, *Beyond Accommodation: Ethical Feminism, Deconstruction, and the Law* (New York: Routledge, 1991). See also reworkings of psychoanalytic theories of the maternal fantasy in Kaja Silverman, *The Acoustic Mirror: The Female Voice in Psychoanalysis and Cinema* (Bloomington: Indiana University Press, 1988), esp. 123–26; and Judith Butler, *Gender Trouble: Feminism and the Subversion of Identity* (New York: Routledge, 1990), esp. 79–92. These latter works reread the work of Julia Kristeva, including her famous essay "Stabat Mater" (in *The Female Body in*

Western Culture, ed. Susan Rubin Suleiman [Cambridge, Mass.: Harvard University Press, 1986]).

19. Mary Ann Doane, "Technophilia, Technology, Representation, and the Feminine," in *Body/Politics: Women and the Discourse of Science,* ed. Mary Jacobus, Evelyn Fox Keller, and Sally Shuttleworth (London: Routledge, 1990).

20. Marilyn Strathern, "Enterprising Kinship: Consumer Choice and the New Reproductive Technologies," *Cambridge Anthropology* 14, no. 1 (1990): 4.

21. For an incisive summary of the clash of biology and family ideology—"To what extent do such families [families generated by reproductive technologies] reproduce the grouping assumed in the ideal family type, that is, two parents plus children. . . . To what extent do these families reproduce the biological relationships assumed in the 'normal' family?" (p. 164)—see Erica Haimes, "Recreating the Family? Policy Considerations Relating to the 'New' Reproductive Technologies," in *The New Reproductive Technologies,* ed. Maureen McNeil, Ian Varcoe, and Steven Yearley (New York: St. Martin's, 1990). See also Valerie Hartouni, "Reproductive Discourse in the 1980s," in *Technoculture,* ed. Constance Penley and Andrew Ross (Minneapolis: University of Minnesota Press, 1991); and Jennifer Terry, "The Body Invaded: Medical Surveillance of Women as Reproducers," *Socialist Review* 89, no. 3 (1989): 13–44.

22. Hartouni, "Containing Women," 49.

23. Hortense J. Spillers, "Mama's Baby, Papa's Maybe: An American Grammar Book," *Diacritics* 17, no. 2 (1987): 74. I am indebted to a meditation on Spillers's article in Haraway's " 'Gender' for a Marxist Dictionary," in *Simians, Cyborgs and Women.*

24. Spillers, "Mama's Baby," 80.

25. For a meditation on sterilization, see Patricia J. Williams, *The Alchemy of Race and Rights* (Cambridge, Mass.: Harvard University Press, 1991), 216–36.

26. The gendered commodification of the biological materials of human reproduction has provoked anguishing debate and argument among feminists. The journal *Reproductive and Genetic Engineering: Journal of International Feminist Analysis* offers useful reports on current developments. Its editorial policy has tended to set up oppositions between so-called liberal and radical feminists on reproductive technologies. I would argue that these oppositions result from a failure to hold in tension the problems of "masculinist birthing" and the fantasy of a unified maternal.

27. Gayatri Chakravorty Spivak, "A Literary Representation of the Subaltern: A Woman's Text from the Third World," in *In Other Worlds: Essays in Cultural Politics* (New York: Routledge, 1988), 250.

28. Sofia, "Exterminating Fetuses."

29. Donna Haraway's "Monkeys, Aliens and Women: Love, Science and Politics at the Intersection of Feminist Theory and Colonial Discourse" (*Women's Studies International Forum* 12, no. 3 [1989]: 307–9) articulates the visions of Octavia Butler.

30. Samuel R. Delany, *Stars in My Pockets like Grains of Sand* (New York: Bantam, 1984), 86, 341.

31. Sofia, "Exterminating Fetuses," 51.

32. Erwin Schroedinger, *What Is Life? and Other Scientific Essays* (1944; reprint, New York: Doubleday), 61.

33. For discussion of the relation between war technologies and their contribution to changing logics of perception in the twentieth century, see Paul Virilio, *War and Cinema: The Logistics of Perception* (London: Verso, 1989). For the war work of Alan Turing, a "father" of the modern computer, in cryptanalysis, see Andrew Hodges, *Alan Turing: The Enigma* (New York: Simon & Schuster, 1983).

34. The document is translated and published in *Documents on the Holocaust,* ed. Yitzhak Arad, Yisreael Gutman, and Abraham Margaliot (New York: Ktav, 1982), 292.

35. Schroedinger, *What Is Life?* 88.

36. Ernst Simmel, *Kriegsneurosen und "Psychisches Trauma"* (1918), cited in Laurence A. Rickels, *Aberrations of Mourning: Writing on German Crypts* (Detroit: Wayne State University Press, 1988), 8. My thoughts on mourning are also inspired by Eric L. Santner, *Stranded Objects: Mourning, Memory and Film in Postwar Germany* (Ithaca, N.Y.: Cornell University Press, 1990).

37. Alan M. Turing, "The Chemical Basis of Morphogenesis," *Philosophical Transactions of the Royal Society* B237 (1952): 37–72. My reconstruction of Turing's work and his arrest, trial, and treatment is based on Hodges, *Alan Turing.* I am also indebted to David F. Channell's *The Vital Machine: A Study of Technology and Organic Life* (New York: Oxford University Press, 1991).

38. See Daniel Moynihan, *The Negro Family: The Case for Action* (Washington, D.C.: Office of Policy Planning, U.S. Department of Labor, March 1965). *The Moynihan Report and the Politics of Controversy* (ed. Lee Rainwater and William L. Yancey [Cambridge, Mass.: MIT Press, 1967]) also contains a full text of the March 1965 report on the Negro family. John von Neumann, *Theory of Self-Reproducing Automata,* ed. A. W. Burks (Urbana: University of Illinois Press, 1966). My

biographical comments on John von Neumann rely on Steve J. Heims's excellent *John von Neumann and Norbert Wiener: From Mathematics to the Technologies of Life and Death* (Cambridge, Mass.: MIT Press, 1980).

39. Von Neumann, *Self-Reproducing Automata,* 19.

40. "Government's Response to the Report (Nov. 16–18, 1965)," in *The Negro Family.*

41. *The Negro Family,* 29.

42. Langton, *Artificial Life,* 43.

43. Fineman, "The Structure of Allegorical Desire," 48.

44. Evelyn Fox Keller, "Reproduction and the Central Project of Evolutionary Theory," *Biology and Philosophy* 2, no. 4 (1987): 383.

45. Cited in Claude Lanzmann, "The Obscenity of Understanding: An Evening with Claude Lanzmann," *American Imago* 48, no. 4 (1991): 478.

Works Cited

Abraham, Nicolas, and Maria Torok. *The Wolf Man's Magic Word.* Minneapolis: University of Minnesota Press, 1986.

Acker, Kathy. *Hannibal Lecter, My Father.* New York: Semiotext(e), 1991.

Adams, Parveen. "Per Os(cillation)." *Camera Obscura* 17 (1988): 7–29.

Aers, David. "Justice and Wage-Labor after the Black Death." In *The Work of Work: Servitude, Slavery, and Labor in Medieval England,* ed. Allen J. Frantzen and Douglas Moffat. Glasgow: Cuithne, 1994.

Alarcón, Norma. "Chicana's Feminist Literature: A Re-Vision through Malintzin; or, Malintzin: Putting Flesh Back on the Object." In *This Bridge Called My Back: Writing by Radical Women of Color,* ed. Cherríe Moraga and Gloria Anzaldúa. New York: Kitchen Table/ Women of Color, 1981.

Aldrich, Megan. *Gothic Revival.* London: Phaedon, 1994.

Alonso, Anna Maria. "The Effects of Truth: Presentation of the Past and the Imagining of Community." *Journal of Historical Sociology* 1 (1988): 33–57.

Alpers, Svetlana. *The Art of Describing: Dutch Art in the Seventeenth Century.* Chicago: University of Chicago Press, 1983.

Anglo, Sydney. "Evident Authority and Authoritative Evidence: The *Malleus Maleficarum.*" In *The Damned Art,* ed. Sydney Anglo. London: Routledge & Kegan Paul, 1977.

Ankarloo, Bengt, and Gustav Henningsen, eds. *Early Modern European Witchcraft: Centres and Peripheries.* New York: Oxford University Press, 1990.

Anzaldúa, Gloria. "La conciencia de la mestiza: Towards a New Consciousness." In *Making Face, Making Soul,* ed. Gloria Anzaldúa. San Francisco: Aunt Lute Foundation, 1990.

Arad, Yitzhak, Yisreael Gutman, and Abraham Margaliot, eds. *Documents on the Holocaust.* New York: Ktav, 1982.

Arnold, Dana. "George Gilbert Scott and Bombay: India's Gothic Architecture." *Apollo* 123, no. 348 (1991): 87–90.

Ashton, Dore, ed. *A Joseph Cornell Album.* New York: Viking, 1974.

Atkinson, Clarissa W. *The Oldest Vocation: Christian Motherhood in the Middle Ages.* Ithaca, N.Y.: Cornell University Press, 1991.

Auguiste, Reece. "*Handsworth Songs:* Some Background Notes." *Framework* 35 (1988): 4–8.

Bakhtin, Mikhail. *Rabelais and His World.* Translated by Helene Iswolsky. Bloomington: Indiana University Press, 1984.

Baldwin, John W. "Five Discourses on Desire: Sexuality and Gender in Northern France around 1200." *Speculum* 66, no. 4 (1991): 797–829.

Balibar, Etienne. "Es Gibt Keinen Staat in Europa: Racism and Politics in Europe Today." *New Left Review* 186 (March/April 1991): 5–19.

Bann, Stephen. *The Clothing of Clio: A Study of the Representation of History in Nineteenth-Century Britain and France.* New York: Cambridge University Press, 1984.

Barlow, John Perry. "Being in Nothingness." *Mondo 2000,* no. 2 (1990): 37.

Baroja, Julio Caro. *The World of Witches.* Translated by O. N. V. Glendinning. Chicago: University of Chicago Press, 1964.

Baudrillard, Jean. *The Mirror of Production.* St. Louis: Telos, 1975.

——. *Simulations.* New York: Semiotext(e), 1983.

——. "Anorexic Ruins." In *Looking Back at the End of the World.* New York: Columbia University Press, 1989.

Beckwith, Sarah. "A Very Material Mysticism: The Medieval Mysticism of Margery Kempe." In *Medieval Literature,* ed. David Aers. London: St. Martin's, 1986.

——. "Problems of Authority in Late Medieval English Mysticism: Language, Agency, and Authority in the Book of Margery Kempe." *Exemplaria* 4, no. 1 (1992): 171–200.

——. "Ritual, Church and Theatre: Medieval Dramas of the Sacramental Body." In *Culture and History, 1350–1600: Essays on English Communities, Identities and Writing,* ed. David Aers. London: Harvester Wheatsheaf, 1992.

Bede. *A History of the English Church and People.* Translated by Leo Sherley-Price. Revised by R. E. Latham. Harmondsworth: Penguin, 1955.

Behlmer, Rudy, ed. *The Adventures of Robin Hood.* Madison: University of Wisconsin Press, 1979.

Belting, Hans. *The Image and Its Public in the Middle Ages: Form and Function in the Early Paintings of the Passion.* Translated by Mark Bartusis and Raymond Meyer. New Rochelle, N.Y.: Aristide D. Caratzas, 1990.

Benedikt, Michael. Introduction to *Cyberspace: First Steps.* Cambridge, Mass.: MIT Press, 1991.

Benjamin, Walter. *Illuminations.* Edited by Hannah Arendt. New York: Schocken, 1968. See esp. the chapters "Theses on the Philosophy of History," "The Work of Art in the Age of Mechanical Reproduction," and "On Some Motifs from Baudelaire."

——. *The Origin of German Tragic Drama.* Translated by John Osborne. London: Verso, 1977.

Bennett, Judith M. "Medieval Women, Modern Women: Across the Great Divide." In *Culture and History, 1350–1600: Essays on English Communities, Identities and Writing,* ed. David Aers. London: Harvester Wheatsheaf, 1992.

——. "Our Colleagues, Ourselves." In *The Past and Future of Medieval Studies,* ed. John Van Engen. Notre Dame, Ind.: University of Notre Dame Press, 1992.

Benson, Larry D., ed. *Riverside Chaucer.* 3d ed. New York: Houghton Mifflin, 1987.

Berry, Henry, ed. *Statutes and Ordinances and Acts of Parliament in Ireland.* Dublin: His Majesty's Stationery Office, 1907.

Bhabha, Homi. "Of Mimicry and Man: The Ambivalence of Colonial Discourse." In *Politics and Ideology,* ed. James Donald and Stuart Hall. Milton Keynes: Open University, 1986.

——. "Interrogating Identity." In *The Real Me: Postmodernism and the Question of Identity,* ed. Lisa Appignanesi. London: Institute for Contemporary Arts, 1987.

——. *Nation and Narration.* London: Routledge, 1990. See esp. the chapter "DissemiNation: Time, Narrative, and the Margins of the Modern Nation."

——. "Postcolonial Authority and Postmodern Guilt." In *Cultural Studies,* ed. Lawrence Grossberg, Cary Nelson, and Paula A. Treichler. New York: Routledge, 1992.

——. "How Newness Enters the World: Postmodern Space, Postcolonial Times and the Trials of Cultural Translation." In *The Location of Culture.* New York: Routledge, 1994.

Biddick, Kathleen. "Malthus in a Straitjacket? Analyzing Agrarian Change in Medieval England." *Journal of Interdisciplinary History* 20, no. 4 (1990): 623–35.

——. "Bede's Blush." In *The Past and Future of Medieval Studies,* ed. John Van Engen. Notre Dame, Ind.: University of Notre Dame Press, 1992.

——. "Decolonizing the British Past: Readings in Medieval Archaeology and History." *Journal of British Studies* 32 (1993): 1–23.

——. "Genders, Bodies, Borders: Technologies of the Visible." In *Studying Medieval Women,* ed. Nancy Partner. Cambridge, Mass.: Medieval Academy of America, 1993.

——. "Genders, Bodies, Borders: Technologies of the Visible." *Speculum* 68 (April 1993): 389–418.

——. Review of *The Navigator: A Medieval Odyssey,* by Vincent Ward. *American Historical Review* 97, no. 4 (1993): 1152–53.

——. "Stranded Histories: Feminist Allegories of Artificial Life." *Research in Philosophy and Technology* 13 (1993): 165–82.

——. "The Historiographic Unconscious and the Return of Robin Hood." In *The Salt of Common Life: Individuality and Choice in Medieval Town, Countryside, and Church,* ed. Edwin B. De Windt. Kalamazoo, Mich.: Medieval Institute Publications, 1996.

——. "Paper Jews: Inscription/Ethnicity/Ethnography." *Art Bulletin* 78 (1996): 594–99.

Birdwood, George M. *The Industrial Arts of India.* London: Chapman & Hall, 1880.

Bloch, R. Howard. "Naturalism, Nationalism, Medievalism." *Romanic Review* 76, no. 4 (1985): 341–60.

Bloch, R. Howard, and Stephen G. Nichols, eds. *Medievalism and the Modernist Temper.* Baltimore: Johns Hopkins University Press, 1996.

Boswell, John. *Christianity, Social Tolerance, and Homosexuality: Gay People in Western Europe from the Beginning of the Christian Era in the Fourteenth Century.* Chicago: University of Chicago Press, 1980.

——. Review of *Holy Feast and Holy Fast,* by Caroline Walker Bynum. *New Republic,* 24 August 1987, 36–38.

Bower, Lisa G. "'Mother-in-Law': Conceptions of Mother and the Maternal in Feminism and Legal Theory." *Differences* 3, no. 1 (1991): 20–38.

Boxam, Matthew Hobeche. "The Principles of Gothic Ecclesiastical Architecture." London: Tilt & Bogue Fleet, 1829.

Boyarin, Daniel. "'Épater l'embourgeoisement': Freud, Gender and the (De)Colonized Psyche." *Diacritics* 24 (1994): 17–41.

Boyd, William Douglas. "Books for the Young Businessmen: Mercantile Libraries in the United States, 1820–1865." Ph.D. diss., Indiana University, 1975.

Brentano, Robert. "The Sounds of Stubbs." *Journal of British Studies* 6 (1967): 1–14.

Brewster, David. *The Kaleidoscope: Its History, Theory and Construction.* London: John Murray, 1858.

Brown, Gillian. "Anorexia, Humanism, and Feminism." *Yale Journal of Criticism* 5, no. 1 (1991): 189–215.

Brown, Judith C. Review of *Holy Feast and Holy Fast,* by Caroline Walker Bynum. *American Historical Review* 94 (June 1989): 735–37.

Brown, Karen McCarthy. *Mama Lola: A Vodou Priestess in Brooklyn.* Berkeley and Los Angeles: University of California Press, 1991.

——. "Writing about 'the Other.'" *Chronicle of Higher Education,* 15 April 1992, A56.

Brown, Wendy. *States of Injury: Power and Freedom in Late Modernity.* Princeton, N.J.: Princeton University Press, 1995.

Brownlee, Marina S., Kevin Brownlee, and Stephen G. Nichols, eds. *The New Medievalism.* Baltimore: Johns Hopkins University Press, 1991.

Bucher, Bernadette. *Icon and Conquest.* Chicago: University of Chicago Press, 1981.

Buck-Morss, Susan. *The Dialectics of Seeing: Walter Benjamin and the Arcades Project.* Cambridge, Mass.: MIT Press, 1989.

Burke, Edmund. *A Philosophical Enquiry into the Origin of Our Ideas of the Sublime and Beautiful.* Edited by James Boulton. Notre Dame, Ind.: University of Notre Dame Press, 1968.

Burns, E. Jane, Sarah Kay, Roberta L. Krueger, and Helen Solterer. "Feminism and the Discipline of Old French Studies." In *Medievalism and the Modernist Temper,* ed. R. Howard Bloch and Stephen G. Nichols. Baltimore: Johns Hopkins University Press, 1996.

Burrow, J. W. "'The Village Community' and the Uses of History in Late Nineteenth-Century England." In *Historical Perspectives: Studies in English Thought and Society,* ed. Neil McKendrick. London: Europa, 1974.

Burt, Simon. Review of *The Last of England,* dir. Derek Jarman. *Times Literary Supplement,* 6 November 1987, 1225.

Butler, Judith. *Gender Trouble: Feminism and the Subversion of Identity.* New York: Routledge, 1990.

——. "Performative Acts and Gender Constitution: An Essay in Phenomenology and Feminist Theory." In *Performing Feminisms: Feminist Critical Theory and Theatre,* ed. Sue-Ellen Case. Baltimore: Johns Hopkins University Press, 1990.

——. "Imitation and Gender Insubordination." In *Inside/Out: Lesbian Theories, Gay Theories,* ed. Diana Fuss. New York: Routledge, 1991.

——. "Contingent Foundations: Feminism and the Question of the 'Postmodern.'" In *Feminists Theorize the Political,* ed. Judith Butler and Joan W. Scott. New York: Routledge, 1992.

——. *Bodies That Matter: On the Discursive Limits of "Sex."* New York: Routledge, 1993.

——. "Critically Queer." *Gay and Lesbian Quarterly* 1 (1993): 17–32.

Bynum, Carolyn Walker. "Women's Stories, Women's Symbols: A Critique of Victor Turner's Theory of Liminality." In *Anthropology and the Study of Religion*, ed. Frank Reynolds and Robert Moore. Chicago: Center for the Scientific Study of Religion, 1984.

——. *Holy Feast and Holy Fast: The Religious Significance of Food to Medieval Women*. The New Historicism: Studies in Cultural Poetics. Berkeley and Los Angeles: University of California Press, 1987.

——. "Women's Stories, Women's Symbols: A Critique of Victor Turner's Theory of Liminality." In *Fragmentation and Redemption: Essays on Gender and the Human Body in Medieval Religion*. New York: Zone, 1991.

——. "Why All the Fuss about the Body? A Medievalist's Perspective." *Critical Inquiry* 22 (1995): 1–34.

Cadden, Joan. *Meanings of Sex Difference in the Middle Ages: Medicine, Science and Culture*. New York: Cambridge University Press, 1993.

Callaghan, Dympna. "An Interview with Seamus Deane." *Social Text* 38 (1994): 38–50.

Camille, Michael. "Walter Benjamin and Duerer's *Melancholia I:* The Dialectics of Allegory and the Limits of Iconology." *Ideas and Production* 5 (1985): 58–73.

——. "The Devil's Writing: Diabolic Literacy in Medieval Art." In *World Art: Themes of Unity and Diversity*, ed. Irving Lavin. University Park: Pennsylvania State University Press, 1986.

——. *The Gothic Idol: Ideology and Image-Making in Medieval Art*. New York: Cambridge University Press, 1989.

——. "Philological Iconoclasm: Edition and Image in the *Vie de Saint Alexis*." In *Medievalism and the Modernist Temper*, ed. R. Howard Bloch and Stephen G. Nichols. Baltimore: Johns Hopkins University Press, 1996.

Campbell, Mary Anne. "Redefining Holy Maidenhood: Virginity and Lesbianism in Late Medieval England." *Medieval Feminist Newsletter* 13 (Spring 1992): 14–16.

Campbell, Mary B. *The Witness and the Other World: Exotic European Travel Writing, 400–1600*. Ithaca, N.Y.: Cornell University Press, 1988.

Campbell, Tony. *The Earliest Printed Maps, 1472–1500*. Berkeley and Los Angeles: University of California Press, 1987.

Cannon, Garland. *The Life and Mind of Oriental Jones: Sir William Jones, the Father of Modern Linguistics*. New York: Cambridge University Press, 1990.

Carmichael, Ann G. Review of *Holy Feast and Holy Fast*, by Caroline Walker Bynum. *Journal of Interdisciplinary History* 19 (Spring 1989): 635–44.

Carpenter, John, director. *Escape from New York*. Avco Embassy, 1981.

Caruth, Cathy. *Unclaimed Experience: Trauma, Narrative, and History.* Baltimore: Johns Hopkins University Press, 1996.

Carruthers, Mary. "The Wife of Bath and the Painting of Lions." *PMLA* 94 (1979): 209–22.

——. *The Book of Memory: A Study of Memory in Medieval Culture.* New York: Cambridge University Press, 1990.

Chakrabarty, Dipesh. "Postcoloniality and the Artifice of History: Who Speaks for 'Indian' Pasts?" *Representations* 37 (Winter 1992): 1–26.

Channell, David F. *The Vital Machine: A Study of Technology and Organic Life.* New York: Oxford University Press, 1991.

Chase, Cynthia. "Translating the Transference: Psychoanalysis and the Construction of History." In *Telling Facts: History and Narration in Psychoanalysis,* ed. Joseph H. Smith. Baltimore: Johns Hopkins University Press, 1992.

Chazan, Robert. *Daggers of Faith: Thirteenth-Century Christian Missionizing and Jewish Response.* Berkeley and Los Angeles: University of California Press, 1989.

Chodorow, Nancy. *The Reproduction of Mothering: Psychoanalysis and the Sociology of Gender.* Berkeley and Los Angeles: University of California Press, 1978.

Clifford, James. "Naming Names." *Canto* 3 (1979–81): 142–53.

——. "On *Orientalism.*" In *The Predicament of Culture: Twentieth-Century Ethnography, Literature, and Art.* Cambridge, Mass.: Harvard University Press, 1988.

——. *The Predicament of Culture: Twentieth-Century Ethnography, Literature, and Art.* Cambridge, Mass.: Harvard University Press, 1988.

Clouston, W. A. *The Additional Analogues.* EETS vol. 84. London: Early English Text Society, 1886.

Cohen, Jeremy. *The Friars and the Jews: The Evolution of Medieval Anti-Judaism.* Ithaca, N.Y.: Cornell University Press, 1982.

Cohn, Norman. *Europe's Inner Demons.* London: Chatto, Heinemann, for Sussex University Press, 1975.

Colgrave, Bertram, and R. A. B. Mynors, eds. *Bede's Ecclesiastical History of the English People.* Oxford: Clarendon, 1969.

Colls, Robert, and Phillip Dodd, eds. *Englishness: Culture and Politics, 1880–1920.* Beckenham: Croom Helm, 1986.

Copeland, Rita. Review of *Holy Feast and Holy Fast,* by Caroline Walker Bynum. *Speculum* 64 (January 1989): 143–47.

Cornell, Drucilla. *Beyond Accommodation: Ethical Feminism, Deconstruction, and the Law.* New York: Routledge, 1991.

Coss, P. R. "Aspects of Cultural Diffusion in Medieval England." *Past and Present* 108 (August 1985): 35–79.

Cotman, John Sell. *Specimens of Architectural Remains in Various Counties, but Principally in Norfolk.* London: Henry Bolin, 1838.

Crane, Susan. "The Writing Lesson of 1381." In *Chaucer's England: Literature in Historical Context,* ed. Barbara Hanawalt. Minneapolis: University of Minnesota Press, 1992.

Crary, Jonathan. "Eclipse of the Spectacle." In *Art after Modernism: Rethinking Representations,* ed. Brian Wallis. New York: New Museum of Contemporary Art, 1984.

——. *Techniques of the Observer: On Vision and Modernity in the Nineteenth Century.* Cambridge, Mass.: MIT Press, 1990.

Crépin, André. "Bede and the Vernacular." In *Famulus Christi: Essays in the Commemoration of the Thirteenth Centenary of the Birth of the Venerable Bede,* ed. Gerald Bonner. London: SPCK, 1976.

Crosby, Cristina. "Dealing with Differences." In *Feminists Theorize the Political,* ed. Judith Butler and Joan Scott. New York: Routledge, 1991.

——. *The Ends of History: Victorians and "the Woman Question."* New York: Routledge, 1991.

Cruz, Anne J., and May Elizabeth Perry, eds. *Cultural Encounters: The Impact of the Inquisition in Spain and the New World.* Berkeley and Los Angeles: University of California Press, 1991.

Curtiz, Michael, and William Keighley, directors. *The Adventures of Robin Hood.* Los Angeles: Warner Bros., 1938.

Cypess, Sanra Messinger. *La Malinche in Mexican Literature: From History to Myth.* Austin: University of Texas Press, 1991.

Davidson, Nicolas. "The Inquisition and the Italian Jews." In *Inquisition and Society in Early Modern Europe,* ed. Stephen Haliczer. Totowa, N.J.: Barnes & Noble, 1987.

Deane, Seamus, and Dympna Callaghan. "An Interview with Seamus Deane." *Social Text* 38 (1994): 38–50.

de Bolla, Peter. "Disfiguring History." *Diacritics* 16 (1986): 49–58.

de Certeau, Michel. *The Practice of Everyday Life.* Berkeley and Los Angeles: University of California Press, 1984.

——. *Heterologies: Discourse on the Other.* Minneapolis: University of Minnesota Press, 1986. See esp. the chapters "History: Science and Fiction" and "Psychoanalysis and Its History."

——. *The Writing of History.* Translated by Tom Conley. New York: Columbia University Press, 1988.

——. *Mystic Fable.* Translated by Michael B. Smith. Chicago: University of Chicago Press, 1992. See esp. the chapter "The New Science."

Delany, Samuel R. *Stars in My Pockets like Grains of Sand.* New York: Bantam, 1984.

de Lauretis, Teresa. "Feminist Studies/Critical Studies: Issues, Terms and Contexts." In *Feminist Studies/Critical Studies,* ed. Teresa de Lauretis. Bloomington: Indiana University Press, 1986.

——. "The Female Body and Heterosexual Presumption." *Semiotica* 67, nos. 3/4 (1987): 257–59.

——. "The Technology of Gender." In *Technologies of Gender: Essays on Theory, Film, and Fiction.* Bloomington: Indiana University Press, 1987.

——. "The Essence of the Triangle; or, Taking the Risk of Essentialism Seriously: Feminist Theory in Italy, the U.S., and Britain." *Differences* 1, no. 2 (1989): 3–38.

——. "Sexual Indifference and Lesbian Representation." In *Performing Feminisms: Feminist Critical Theory and Theatre,* ed. Sue-Ellen Case. Baltimore: Johns Hopkins University Press, 1990.

Deleuze, Gilles. *Foucault.* Minneapolis: University of Minnesota Press, 1988.

Deleuze, Gilles, and Felix Guattari. *Anti-Oedipus: Capitalism and Schizophrenia.* Minneapolis: University of Minnesota Press, 1983.

Derolez, René. "Runic Literacy among the Anglo-Saxons." In *Britain, 400–600: Language and History* (Anglistiche Forschungen 205), ed. Alfred Bammesberger and Alfred Wollman. Heidelberg: Carl Winter, 1990.

Derrida, Jacques. *On Grammatology.* Translated by Gayatri Chakravorty Spivak. Baltimore: Johns Hopkins University Press, 1976.

——. "The Parergon." *October* 9 (1979): 3–41.

——. *The Post Card.* Translated by Allan Bass. Chicago: University of Chicago Press, 1987.

——. *The Truth in Painting.* Chicago: University of Chicago Press, 1987.

——. "Signature Event Context." In *Limited INC,* ed. Gerald Graff. Evanston, Ill.: Northwestern University Press, 1988.

——. *Specters of Marx: The State of the Debt, the Work of Mourning and the New International.* Translated by Peggy Kamuf. New York: Routledge, 1994.

Dewey, Clive. "Images of the Village Community: A Study in Anglo-Indian Ideology." *Modern Asian Studies* 6 (1972): 291–328.

Dharmaraj, Glory. "Feminism, Medievalism, and the Other: Postcoloniality as Critique." Paper presented to the Medieval Institute, University of Notre Dame, 12 November 1991.

Dinshaw, Carolyn. "The Heterosexual Subject of Chaucerian Narrative." *Medieval Feminist Newsletter* 13 (Spring 1992): 8–10.

Dirks, Nicholas B. "History as a Sign of the Modern." *Public Culture* 2 (1990): 25–32.

Doane, Mary Ann. "Technophilia: Technology, Representation, and the Feminine." In *Body/Politics: Women and the Discourse of Science,* ed. Mary Jacobus, Evelyn Fox Keller, and Sally Shuttleworth. New York: Routledge, 1990.

Dobson, R. B., and John Taylor. *Rymes of Robyn Hood: An Introduction to the English Outlaw.* London: Heinemann, 1976.

Dollimore, Jonathan. *Sexual Dissidence: Augustine to Wilde, Freud to Foucault.* Oxford: Oxford University Press, 1991.

Douglas, David C., et al., eds. *English Historical Documents.* 12 vols. New York: Oxford University Press, 1955–77. See esp. vol. 4, covering 1327–1485.

DuBois, Ellen Carol. Review of *The Civil War,* dir. Ken Burns. *American Historical Review* 96, no. 4 (1991): 1140–42.

Du Boulay, Juliet. "The Blood: Symbolic Relationships between Descent, Marriage, Incest Prohibitions and Spiritual Kinship in Greece." *Man* 19 (1984): 533–56.

Duby, George. "The Emergence of the Individual." In *A History of Private Life,* vol. 2, *Revelations of the Medieval World.* Cambridge, Mass.: Harvard University Press, 1988.

——. "Affidavits and Confession." In *The Silence of the Middle Ages,* vol. 2 of *A History of Women in the West,* ed. Georges Duby and Michelle Perrot. Cambridge, Mass.: Belknap, Harvard University Press, 1992.

Duchet, Michele. *L'Amérique de Théodore de Bry: Une collection de voyages protestante de XVIe siècle.* Paris, 1987.

Du Creux, François, S.J. *Historiae Canadensis.* Paris: Cramoisy, 1664. Translated by Percy J. Robinson and James B. Conacher as *The History of Canada or New France.* Toronto: Champlain Society, 1951.

Duden, Barbara. *The Woman beneath the Skin: A Doctor's Patients in Eighteenth-Century Germany.* Cambridge, Mass.: Harvard University Press, 1991.

Dundes, Alan, ed. *The Blood Libel Legend: A Casebook of Anti-Semitic Folklore.* Madison: University of Wisconsin Press, 1991.

Eastlake, Charles L. *Hints on Household Taste.* 3d ed. London, 1868.

——. *A History of the Gothic Revival.* London: Longmans, 1872.

Eco, Umberto. "Dreaming the Middle Ages." In *Travels in Hyperreality.* New York: Harcourt Brace Jovanovich, 1986.

——. "The Return of the Middle Ages." In *Travels in Hyperreality.* New York: Harcourt Brace Jovanovich, 1986.

"EETS Report." London: Early English Text Society, 1869, 1877, 1868.

Ellmann, Maud. *The Hunger Artists: Starving, Writing, and Imprisonment.* Cambridge, Mass.: Harvard University Press, 1993.

English Historical Documents. Edited by David C. Douglas et al. 12 vols. New York: Oxford University Press, 1955–77.

Fabian, Johannes. *Time and the Other: How Anthropology Makes Its Object.* New York: Columbia University Press, 1983.

Farmer, Sharon. "Persuasive Voices: Clerical Images of Medieval Wives." *Speculum* 61 (July 1986): 517–43.

Felman, Shoshana. "Psychoanalysis and Education: Teaching Terminable and Interminable." In *Jacques Lacan and the Adventure of Insight: Psychoanalysis in Contemporary Culture.* Cambridge, Mass.: Harvard University Press, 1987.

Fineman, Joel. "The Structure of Allegorical Desire." *October* 12 (1980): 46–66.

Foster, Hal. "Subversive Signs." In *Recodings.* Seattle: Bay, 1985.

Foucault, Michel. *The Archaeology of Knowledge and the Discourse on Language.* Translated by A. M. Sheridan Smith. New York: Harper & Row, 1972.

——. *Discipline and Punish: The Birth of the Prison.* Translated by Alan Sheridan. New York: Pantheon, 1979.

——. *History of Sexuality.* Translated by Robert Hurley. 3 vols. New York: Vintage, 1978. See esp. vol. 1.

——. "The Political Technology of Individuals." In *Technologies of the Self: A Seminar with Michel Foucault,* ed. H. Gutman, P. Hutton, and L. Martin. Amherst: University of Massachusetts Press, 1988.

Frame, Robin. *The Political Development of the British Isles.* New York: Oxford University Press, 1990.

Frandenburg, Louise O. "Criticism, Anti-Semitism, and the Prioress's Tale." *Exemplaria* 1 (March 1989): 69–115.

——. "'Voice Memorial': Loss and Reparation in Chaucer's Poetry." *Exemplaria* 2 (1990): 169–202.

——. "'Be Not Far From Me': Psychoanalysis, Medieval Studies, and the Subject of Religion." *Exemplaria* 7 (1995): 41–54.

Frandenburg, Louise O., and Carla Frecerro. "The Pleasures of History." *Gay and Lesbian Quarterly* 1, no. 4 (1995): 371–84.

——, eds. *Premodern Sexualities in Europe* (special issue). *Gay and Lesbian Quarterly,* vol. 1, no. 4 (1995).

Frantzen, Allen J., and Charles L. Vengonie. "The Desire for Origins: An Archaeology of Anglo-Saxon Studies." *Style* 20, no. 2 (1986): 142–56.

——. *Desire for Origins: New Language, Old English, and Teaching the Tradition.* New Brunswick, N.J.: Rutgers University Press, 1990.

——. "Prologue: Documents and Monuments: Difference and Interdisciplinarity in the Study of Medieval Culture." In *Speaking Two Languages.* Albany: State University of New York Press, 1990.

Freccero, Carla. "Cannibalism, Homophobia, Women: Montaigne's 'Des cannibales' and 'De l'amitié.'" In *Women, "Race," and Writing in the Early Modern Period,* ed. Margo Hendricks and Patricia Parker. New York: Routledge, 1994.

Frecerro, John. Review of *Holy Feast and Holy Fast,* by Caroline Walker Bynum. *New York Times Book Review,* 5 April 1987, 26.

Freeman, Edward. *History of Architecture.* London: Joseph Masters, 1849.

Freud, Sigmund. "Mourning and Melancholia." In *A General Selection from the Works of Sigmund Freud,* ed. John Rickman. New York: Doubleday, 1957.

Furnivall, Frederick J., ed. *Wright's Chaste Wife.* EETS vol. 12. London: Early English Text Society, 1875.

Fusco, Coco. "A Black Avant-Garde? Notes on Black and Audio Film Collective and Sankofa." In *English Is Broken Here: Notes on Cultural Fusion in the Americas,* ed. Coco Fusco. New York: New Press, 1995.

Fuss, Diana, ed. *Inside/Out: Lesbian Theories, Gay Theories.* New York: Routledge, 1991.

Gallop, Jane. *Thinking through the Body.* New York: Columbia University Press, 1988. See esp. the chapter "The Body Politic."

———. *Around 1981: Academic Feminist Literary Theory.* New York: Routledge, 1992.

Gattrell, Peter. "Historians and Peasants: Studies of Medieval English Society in Russian Context." *Past and Present* 96 (1982): 22–50.

Gaunt, Simon. "Gay Studies and Feminism: A Medievalist's Perspective." *Medieval Feminist Newsletter* 13 (Spring 1992): 3–8.

Geertz, Clifford. "Deep Play: Notes on the Balinese Cockfight." In *The Interpretation of Culture: Selected Essays.* New York: Basic, 1973.

———. *Works and Lives: The Anthropologist as Author.* Stanford, Calif.: Stanford University Press, 1988.

Gelber, Hester Goodenough. Review of *Holy Feast and Holy Fast,* by Caroline Walker Bynum. *Modern Language Quarterly* 48 (September 1987): 281–85.

Geller, Jay. "'A Glance at the Nose': Freud's Inscription of Jewish Difference." *American Imago* 49 (1992): 445–66.

Gellrich, Jesse M. *Discourse and Dominion in the Fourteenth Century: Oral Contexts of Writing in Philosophy, Politics and Poetry.* Princeton, N.J.: Princeton University Press, 1995.

Genicot, Léopold. *Rural Communities in the Medieval West.* Baltimore: Johns Hopkins University Press, 1990.

Gerard, Kert, and Gert Helima, eds. *The Pursuit of Sodomy: Male Homosexuality in Renaissance and Enlightenment Europe.* New York: Harrington Park, 1989.

Gibson, William. *Neuromancer.* New York: Ace, 1984.

——. *Count Zero.* New York: Ace, 1987.

——. *Mona Lisa Overdrive.* New York: Bantam, 1989.

Gilligan, Carol. *In a Different Voice: Psychological Theory and Women's Development.* Cambridge, Mass.: Harvard University Press, 1982.

Gillingham, John. "The Beginnings of English Imperialism." *Journal of Historical Sociology* 5 (1992): 392–409.

Gilman, Sander. "The Jewish Body: A 'Footnote.'" *Bulletin of the History of Medicine* 64, no. 4 (1990): 588–602.

——. *The Jew's Body.* New York: Routledge, 1991.

——. *Freud, Race, and Gender.* Princeton, N.J.: Princeton University Press, 1993.

Gilroy, Paul. *"There Ain't No Black in the Union Jack": The Cultural Politics of Race and Nation.* London: Hutchinson, 1987.

Gilroy, Paul, and Jim Pines. "*Handsworth Songs:* Audiences/Aesthetic/Independence—Interview with the Black Audio Collective." *Framework* 35 (1988): 9–18.

Ginzburg, Carlo. "The Inquisitor as Anthropologist." In *Clues, Myths and the Historical Method.* Baltimore: Johns Hopkins University Press, 1989.

——. *Ecstasies: Deciphering the Witches' Sabbath.* New York: Pantheon, 1991.

——. "Microhistory: Two or Three Things That I Know about It." *Inquiry* 20 (Autumn 1993): 10–35.

Giroux, Henry A. "Resisting Difference: Cultural Studies and the Discourse of Critical Pedagogy." In *Cultural Studies,* ed. Lawrence Grossberg, Cary Nelson, and Paula A. Treichler. New York: Routledge, 1992.

Gleason, Philip. "American Catholics and the Mythic Middle Ages." In *Keeping the Faith: American Catholicism Past and Present.* Notre Dame, Ind.: University of Notre Dame Press, 1987.

Godbeer, Richard. *The Devil's Dominion: Magic and Religion in Early New England.* Cambridge: Cambridge University Press, 1992.

Godden, Malcolm, and Michael Lapidge, ed. *The Cambridge Companion to Old English Literature.* Cambridge: Cambridge University Press, 1991.

Goldberg, Jonathan. *Sodometries: Renaissance Texts, Modern Sexualities.* Stanford, Calif.: Stanford University Press, 1992.

Goody, Jack. Review of *Holy Feast and Holy Fast,* by Caroline Walker Bynum. *English Historical Review* 105, no. 415 (1990): 429–31.

Gordon, Rae Beth. *Ornament, Fantasy and Desire in Nineteenth-Century French Literature.* Princeton, N.J.: Princeton University Press, 1992.

Greenblatt, Stephen. Introduction to *Marvellous Possessions: The Wonder of the New World.* Chicago: University of Chicago Press, 1991.

——. "Shakespeare Bewitched." In *New Historical Literary Study.* Princeton, N.J.: Princeton University Press, 1993.

Pope Gregory. *Vox in Rama.* In *Monumenta germaniae historia,* ed. Carolus Rodenberg. Berlin: Weidman, 1883.

Grossberg, Lawrence, Cary Nelson, and Paula A. Treichler. "Cultural Studies: An Introduction." In *Cultural Studies,* ed. Lawrence Grossberg, Cary Nelson, and Paula Treichler. New York: Routledge, 1992.

Grundman, Roy. "History and the Gay Viewfinder: An Interview with Derek Jarman." *Cineaste* 18, no. 4 (1991): 24–27.

Haimes, Erica. "Recreating the Family? Policy Considerations Relating to the 'New' Reproductive Technologies." In *The New Reproductive Technologies,* ed. Maureen McNeil, Ian Varcoe, and Steven Yearley. New York: St. Martin's, 1990.

Halberstam, Judith. *Skin Shows.* Durham, N.C.: Duke University Press, 1995.

Halberstam, Judith, and Ira Livingston, eds. *Posthuman Bodies.* Bloomington: Indiana University Press, 1995.

Haliczer, Stephen. "The First Holocaust: The Inquisition and the Converted Jews of Spain and Portugal." In *Inquisition and Society in Early Modern Europe,* ed. Stephen Haliczer. Totowa, N.J.: Barnes & Noble, 1987.

Hall, Catherine. "The Economy of Intellectual Prestige: Thomas Carlyle, John Stuart Mill, and the Case of Governor Eyre." *Critical Inquiry* 12 (1989): 169–76.

Hall, Sir James. *Essay on the Origin, History and Principles of Gothic Architecture.* London, 1813.

Hamburger, Jeffrey. "The Use of Images in the Pastoral Care of Nuns: The Case of Heinrich Suso and the Dominicans." *Art Bulletin* 61 (1989): 20–46.

Hansen, Joseph. "Der Malleus maleficarum, seine Drucksausgaben und die gefälschte Kölner Approbation vom J. 1487." *Westdeutsche Zeitschrift für Geschichte und Kunst* 17 (1898): 119–68.

——. *Quellen und Untersuchungen zur Geschichte des Hexenwahns und der Hexenverfolgung im Mittelalter.* Bonn: G. Georgi, 1901; reprint Hildesheim: Georg Olms, 1963.

Haraway, Donna. "Situated Knowledges: The Science Question in Feminism and the Privilege of Partial Perspective." *Feminist Studies* 14, no. 3 (1988): 575–99.

——. "Monkeys, Aliens and Women: Love, Science and Politics at the Intersection of Feminist Theory and Colonial Discourse." *Women's Studies International Forum* 12, no. 3 (1989): 307–9.

——. "The Actors Are Cyborg, Nature Is Coyote, and the Geography Is Elsewhere: Postscript to 'Cyborgs at Large.'" In *Technoculture*, ed. Constance Penley and Andrew Ross. Minneapolis: University of Minnesota Press, 1991.

——. *Simians, Cyborgs and Women: The Reinvention of Nature.* New York: Routledge, 1991. See esp. the chapters "A Cyborg Manifesto: Science, Technology, and Socialist-Feminism in the Late Twentieth Century" and "Reading Buchi Emecheta: Contests for 'Women's Experience' in Women's Studies."

——. "'Gender' for a Marxist Dictionary." In *A Cyborg Manifesto: Science, Technology, and Socialist-Feminism in the Late Twentieth Century.* New York: Routledge, 1991.

——. "The Promises of Monsters: A Regenerative Politics for Inappropriate/d Others." In *Cultural Studies*, ed. Lawrence Grossberg, Cary Nelson, and Paula A. Treichler. New York: Routledge, 1992.

——. *Modest-Witness@Second-Millennium. Female Man©-Meets OncoMouse™*. New York: Routledge, 1997.

Harding, Susan. "Representing Fundamentalism: The Problem of the Repugnant Other." *Social Research* 58 (1991): 373–94.

Harrison, Robert Pogue. *Forests: The Shadow of Civilization.* Chicago: University of Chicago Press, 1992.

Hartlaub, G. F. *Hans Baldung Grien: Hexenbilder.* Stuttgart, 1961.

Hartman, Geoffrey H., ed. *Holocaust Remembrance: The Shapes of Memory.* Cambridge, Mass.: Blackwell, 1994.

Hartouni, Valerie. "Reproductive Discourse in the 1980s." In *Technoculture*, ed. Constance Penley and Andrew Ross. Minneapolis: University of Minnesota Press, 1991.

Harvey, Charles, and Jon Press. *William Morris: Design and Enterprise in Victorian Britain.* New York: St. Martin's, 1991.

Haverkampf, Anselm H. *Leaves of Mourning: Hölderlin's Late Work.* Albany: State University of New York Press, 1996.

Heims, Steve J. *John Von Neumann and Norbert Wiener: From Mathematics to the Technologies of Life and Death.* Cambridge, Mass.: MIT Press, 1980.

Henningsen, Gustav, John Tedeschi, and Charles Amiel, eds. *The In-*

quisition in Early Modern Europe: Studies on Sources and Methods. Dekalb: Northern Illinois University Press, 1986.

Héritier-Augé, Françoise. "Semen and Blood: Some Ancient Theories concerning Their Genesis and Relationship." In *Fragments for a History of the Human Body,* ed. Michel Feher. New York: Zone, 1989.

Hester, Marianne. *Lewd Women and Wicked Witches: A Study of the Dynamics of Male Domination.* New York: Routledge, 1992.

Hettinger, Madonna. "Defining the Servant: Legal and Extra-Legal Terms of Employment in Fifteenth Century England." In *The Work of Work: Servitude, Slavery, and Labor in Medieval England,* ed. Allen J. Frantzen and Douglas Moffat. Glasgow: Cuithne, 1994.

Hicks, D. Emily. *Border Writing: The Multidimensional Text.* Minneapolis: University of Minnesota Press, 1991.

Higley, Sarah Lynn. *Between Languages: The Uncooperative Text in Early Welsh and Old English Nature Poetry.* University Park: Pennsylvania State University Press, 1993.

Hilton, Rodney. *Peasants, Knights and Heretics.* New York: Cambridge University Press, 1976.

Hilton, R. H., and T. H. Aston, eds. *The English Rising of 1381.* Cambridge: Cambridge University Press, 1984.

Hoak, Dale. "Art, Culture and Mentality in Renaissance Society: The Meaning of Hans Baldung Grien's *Bewitched Groom* (1544)." *Renaissance Quarterly* 38, no. 3 (1985): 488–510.

Hobsbawn, Eric. *Primitive Rebels.* Manchester: Manchester University Press, 1959.

Hodges, Andrew. *Alan Turing: The Enigma.* New York: Simon & Schuster, 1983.

Holmes, George. Review of *Holy Feast and Holy Fast,* by Caroline Walker Bynum. *Journal of Ecclesiastical History* 40, no. 2 (1989): 274–75.

Holt, J. C. *Robin Hood.* New York: Thames & Hudson, 1982.

Holt, Thomas. *The Problem of Freedom: Race, Labor and Politics in Jamaica and Britain, 1832–1938.* Baltimore: Johns Hopkins University Press, 1992.

hooks, bell. *Yearning: Race, Gender and Cultural Politics.* Boston: South End, 1990.

Howe, John. Review of *Holy Feast and Holy Fast,* by Caroline Walker Bynum. *Catholic History Review* 74, no. 3 (1988): 456–58.

Hsia, R. Po-chia. *The Myth of Ritual Murder: Jews and Magic in Reformation Germany.* New Haven, Conn.: Yale University Press, 1988.

——. *Trent, 1475.* New Haven, Conn.: Yale University Press, 1992.

Hughes, Dian Owen. "Distinguishing Signs: Ear-Rings, Jews and

Franciscan Rhetoric in the Italian Renaissance City." *Past and Present* 112 (August 1986): 3–59.

Hulme, Peter. *Colonial Encounters: Europe and the Native Caribbean, 1492–1797.* New York: Methuen, 1986.

Hult, David F. "Gaston Paris and the Invention of Courtly Love." In *Medievalism and the Modernist Temper,* ed. R. Howard Bloch and Stephen G. Nichols. Baltimore: John Hopkins University Press, 1996.

Hults, Linda C. "Baldung's *Bewitched Groom* Revisited: Artistic Temperament, Fantasy and the 'Dream of Reason.'" *Sixteenth-Century Journal* 15, no. 3 (1984): 259–80.

——. "Baldung and the Witches of Freiburg: The Evidence of Images." *Journal of Interdisciplinary History* 18, no. 2 (1987): 249–76.

Hunt, William Holden, ed. *The Letters of William Stubbs, Bishop of Oxford, 1825–1901.* London: Constable, 1904.

Huot, Sylvia. "Addressing the Issue of Lesbianism in a General Course on Women in the Middle Ages." *Medieval Feminist Newsletter* 13 (Spring 1992): 10–11.

Huyskens, Albert. *Quellenstudien zur Geschichte der hl. Elisabeth.* Marburg: N. G. Elwert'sche, 1908.

Jacobs, Lynn F. "The Marketing and Standardization of South Netherlandish Carved Altarpieces: Limits on the Role of the Patron." *Art Bulletin* 71, no. 2 (1989): 208–29.

Jacquart, Danielle, and Claude Thomasset. *Sexuality and Medicine in the Middle Ages.* Translated by Matthew Anderson. Princeton, N.J.: Princeton University Press, 1988.

Jarman, Derek. *The Last of England.* Edited by David L. Hirst. London: Constable, 1987.

Jerouschek, Günter. *Malleus Maleficarum 1487 von Heinrich Kramer (Institoris).* New York: Georg Olms, 1992.

Jogues, Isaac. "Comic Book Story on Isaac Jogues." St. Paul, Minn.: Timeless Topix, 1945.

Johnson, David E. "Women, Translation, Nationalism: La Malinche and the Example of Juan García Ponce." *Arizona Quarterly* 47, no. 3 (1991): 93–116.

——. "Voice, the New Historicism, and the Americas." *Arizona Quarterly* 48, no. 2 (1992): 81–116.

Johnson, George. *In the Palaces of Memory: How We Build the Worlds inside Our Heads.* New York: Knopf, 1991.

Johnson, Lynn Staley. "The Trope of the Scribe and the Question of Literary Authority in the Works of Julian of Norwich and Margery of Kempe." *Speculum* 66, no. 4 (1991): 820–38.

Johnstone, Iain. Review of *The Last of England,* dir. Derek Jarman. *Sunday Times,* 25 October 1987, 65.

Jones, Owen. *The Grammar of Ornament.* London: Day & Son, 1856.

Justice, Steven. "Inquisition, Speech, and Writing: A Case from Late-Medieval Norwich." *Representations* 48 (1994): 1–29.

——. *Writing and Rebellion: England in 1381.* Berkeley and Los Angeles: University of California Press, 1994.

Kautzsch, Rudolf. *Die Holzschnitte zum Ritter von Turm.* Studien zur deutschen kunstgeschichte 44. Strassburg: Heitz, 1903.

Keen, Maurice. Review of *Holy Feast and Holy Fast,* by Caroline Walker Bynum. *New York Review of Books,* 8 October 1987, 42–44.

Kejariwal, O. P. *The Asiatic Society of Bengal and the Discovery of India's Past, 1784–1838.* Oxford: Oxford University Press, 1988.

Keller, Evelyn Fox. "Dynamic Autonomy: Objects as Subjects." In *Reflections on Gender and Science.* New Haven, Conn.: Yale University Press, 1985.

——. *Reflections on Gender and Science.* New Haven, Conn.: Yale University Press, 1985.

——. "Reproduction and the Central Project of Evolutionary Theory." *Biology and Philosophy* 2, no. 4 (1987): 383–96.

Kemp, Anthony. *The Estrangement of the Past: A Study in the Origins of Modern Historical Consciousness.* New York: Oxford University Press, 1991.

Kieckhefer, Richard. *European Witch Trials: Their Foundations in Popular and Learned Culture, 1300–1500.* Berkeley: University of California Press, 1976.

Kilgour, Maggie. *From Communion to Cannibalism: An Anatomy of Metaphors of Incorporation.* Princeton, N.J.: Princeton University Press, 1990.

Knight, Stephen. *Robin Hood: A Complete Study of the English Outlaw.* Cambridge, Mass.: Blackwell, 1994.

Koerner, Joseph Leo. *The Moment of Self-Portraiture in German Renaissance Art.* Chicago: University of Chicago Press, 1993.

Kors, Alan C., and Edward Peters, eds. *Witchcraft in Europe, 1100–1700: A Documentary History.* Philadelphia: University of Pennsylvania Press, 1972.

Krauss, Rosalind. *The Optical Unconscious.* Cambridge, Mass.: MIT Press, 1993.

Kristeva, Julia. "Stabat Mater." In *The Female Body in Western Culture,* ed. Susan Rubin Suleiman. Cambridge, Mass.: Harvard University Press, 1986.

Kruger, Barbara. Review of *Handsworth Songs*. *Artforum* 27 (September 1988): 143–44.

Kunzle, David. *History of the Comic Strip*. Vol. 1. *The Early Comic Strip, Narrative Strips and Picture Series in the European Broadsheet from c. 1450–1825*. Berkeley: University of California Press, 1973.

Lacan, Jacques. *Speech and Language in Psychoanalysis*. Translated by Anthony Wilden. Baltimore: Johns Hopkins University Press, 1968.

LaCapra, Dominick. "Bakhtin, Marxism and the Carnivalesque." In *Rethinking Intellectual History: Texts, Contexts, Language*. Ithaca, N.Y.: Cornell University Press, 1983.

——. *History and Criticism*. Ithaca, N.Y.: Cornell University Press, 1985. See esp. the chapters "Is Everyone a *Mentalité* Case?" and "Rhetoric and History."

——. "The Temporality of Rhetoric." In *Chronotypes: The Construction of Time*, ed. John Bender and David Wellbery. Stanford, Calif.: Stanford University Press, 1991.

Ladurie, Emmanuel Le Roy. *Montaillou: The Promised Land of Error*. Translated by Barbara Bray. New York: Braziller, 1978.

Langmuir, Gavin I. "From Anti Judaism to Antisemitism." In *History, Religion, and Antisemitism*. Berkeley and Los Angeles: University of California Press, 1990.

——. *Toward a Definition of Antisemitism*. Berkeley and Los Angeles: University of California Press, 1990. See esp. the chapter "Ritual Cannibalism."

Langton, Christopher. "Toward Artificial Life." *Whole Earth Review* 58 (Spring 1988): 74–79.

——. "Preface to Artificial Life." Paper presented at the Interdisciplinary Workshop, Santa Fe Institute in the Sciences of Complexity, Santa Fe, N.M., 1989.

——. "Toward Artificial Life." *Chronicle of Higher Education*, 4 December 1991, A30.

Lanzmann, Claude. "The Obscenity of Understanding: An Evening with Claude Lanzmann." *American Imago* 48, no. 4 (1991): 478.

Lapidge, Michael. "The School of Theodore and Hadrian." *Anglo-Saxon England* 15 (1986): 45–72.

Latour, Bruno. "Visualization and Cognition." *Knowledge and Society* 6 (1986): 1–40.

——. "The Politics of Explanation: An Alternative." In *Knowledge and Reflexivity: New Frontiers in the Sociology of Knowledge*, ed. Steve Woolgar. London: Sage, 1988.

——. *We Have Never Been Modern*. Cambridge, Mass.: Harvard University Press, 1993.

Lavin, Marilyn Aronberg. "The Altar of Corpus Domini in Urbino: Paolo Uccello, Joos Van Ghent, Piero della Francesca." *Art Bulletin* 49 (March 1967): 1–24.

Lerer, Seth. *Literacy and Power in Anglo-Saxon Literature.* Lincoln: University of Nebraska Press, 1991.

Levine, Phillipa. *The Amateur and the Professional: Antiquarians, Historians and Archaeologists in Victorian England, 1838–1886.* New York: Cambridge University Press, 1986.

Levidow, Les, and Kevin Robins. "Vision Wars." *Race and Class* 32 (1991): 88–92.

Lévi-Strauss, Claude. "The Effectiveness of Symbols." *Revue de l'histoire des religions* 135 (1949): 5–27.

——. *Structural Anthropology.* Translated by Claire Jacobson and Brooke Grundfest Schoepf. New York: Basic, 1963. See esp. the chapter "The Effectiveness of Symbols."

Libeskind, Daniel. "Between the Lines: The Jewish Museum, Berlin." *Research in Phenomenology* 22 (1992): 82–87.

Libeskind, Daniel, and Cecil Balmond. *Unfolding.* Rotterdam: NAI, 1997.

Little, Lester K. Review of *Holy Feast and Holy Fast,* by Caroline Walker Bynum. *Journal of Social History* 21 (Spring 1988): 597–99.

Lochrie, Karma. *Margery Kempe and Translations of the Flesh.* Philadelphia: University of Pennsylvania Press, 1991.

Lochrie, Karma, Clare A. Lees, and Gillian R. Overing. "Feminism within and without the Academy." *Medieval Feminist Newsletter* 22 (1996): 27–31.

Lormer, Douglas A. *Color, Class and the Victorians: English Attitudes to the Negro in the Mid-Nineteenth Century.* New York: Holmes & Meier, 1978.

Lotringer, Sylvere, and Paul Virilio. *Pure War.* New York: Columbia University/Semiotext(e), 1983.

Lubbock, Jules. *The Tyranny of Taste: The Politics of Architecture and Design in Britain, 1550–1960.* New Haven, Conn.: Yale University Press, 1995.

Lydon, James F. "Nation and Race in Medieval Ireland." In *Concepts of National Identity in the Middle Ages,* ed. Simon Forde, Lesley Johnson, and Alan V. Murray. Leeds Texts and Monographs. Leeds: University of Leeds, 1995.

Lynch, Michael, and Steve Woolgar. "Representation in Scientific Practice." Cambridge, Mass.: MIT Press, 1990.

MacCormack, Sabine. "Demons, Imagination, and the Incas." *Representations* 33 (Winter 1991): 121–46.

Macfarlane, Alan. *The Origins of English Individualism: The Family, Property, and Social Transition.* Oxford: Oxford University Press, 1978.

Maine, H. S. *Village Communities in the East and West.* London, 1871.

Maitland, F. W. *Domesday Book and Beyond.* Cambridge: Cambridge University Press, 1901.

Marcus, Jane. "The Asylums of Antaeus: Women, War and Madness: Is There a Feminist Fetishism?" In *The Difference Within: Feminism and Critical Theory,* ed. Elizabeth Meese and Alice Parker. Philadelphia: Benjamins, 1989.

Marrow, James, and Alan Shestack, ed. *Hans Baldung Grien: Prints and Drawings: Exhibition Catalogue.* Chicago, 1981.

Martin, Ruth. *Witchcraft and the Inquisition in Venice, 1550–1650.* New York: Blackwell, 1989.

Matter, E. Ann. "*MFN* Gay and Lesbian Issue." *Medieval Feminist Newsletter* 13 (Spring 1992): 1–3.

McCaffery, Larry. "An Interview with William Gibson." In *Storming the Reality Studio,* ed. Larry McCaffery. Durham, N.C.: Duke University Press, 1991.

McClintock, Anne. *Imperial Leather: Race, Gender and Sexuality in the Colonial Contest.* New York: Routledge, 1995.

McGatch, Milton. "The Medievalist and Cultural Literacy." *Speculum* 66, no. 3 (1991): 591–604.

McGinn, Bernard. Review of *Holy Feast and Holy Fast,* by Caroline Walker Bynum. *History of Religions* 28, no. 1 (1988): 90–92.

Menocal, María Rosa. *Shards of Love: Exile and the Origins of the Lyric.* Durham, N.C.: Duke University Press, 1994.

Metcalf, Thomas. *An Imperial Vision: Indian Architecture in Britain's Raj.* Berkeley and Los Angeles: University of California Press, 1989.

Midelfort, H. C. Erik. *Witch Hunting in Southwestern Germany, 1562–1684.* Stanford, Calif.: Stanford University Press, 1972.

Miele, Christopher E. "The Gothic Revival and Gothic Architecture: The Restoration of Medieval Churches in Victorian Britain." Ph.D. diss., 1991.

——. "The First Conservation Militants: William Morris and the Society for the Protection of Ancient Monuments." In *Preserving the Past: The Rise of the Heritage Industry,* ed. Michael Hunter. Stroud: Aldon Sutton, 1996.

Miller, Nancy K. *Getting Personal: Feminist Occasions and Other Autobiographical Acts.* New York: Routledge, 1991.

Mitchell, Juliet, and Jacqueline Rose, eds. *Feminine Sexuality: Jacques Lacan and the Ecole Freudienne.* New York: Norton, 1985.

Mitchell, Timothy. *Colonising Egypt.* Cambridge: Cambridge University Press, 1986.

——. "Everyday Metaphors of Power." *Theory and Society* 19 (1990): 545–77.

Mitter, Partha. *Much Maligned Monsters: History of European Reactions to Indian Art.* Oxford: Clarendon, 1977.

Mohanty, Chandra Talpade. "On Race and Voice: Challenges for Liberal Education in the 1990s." *Cultural Critique* 14 (Winter 1990): 179–208.

Monter, William. *Frontiers of Heresy: The Spanish Inquisition from the Basque Lands to Sicily.* New York: Cambridge University Press, 1990.

Moore, R. I. *The Formation of a Persecuting Society: Power and Deviance in Western Europe, 950–1250.* London: Blackwell, 1987.

Moraga, Cherríe. "From a Long Line of Vendidas: Chicanas and Feminism." In *Feminist Studies/Critical Studies,* ed. Teresa de Lauretis. Bloomington: Indiana University Press, 1986.

——. *The Last Generation.* Boston: South End, 1993.

Moraga, Cherríe, and Gloria Anzaldúa, eds. *This Bridge Called My Back: Writings by Radical Women of Color.* New York: Kitchen Table, 1983.

Morris, William. *To the Working-Men of England.* 1887.

——. "Some Hints on Pattern-Designing." 1890. In *News from Nowhere.* New York: Penguin, 1993.

——. *A Dream of John Ball and a King's Lesson.* London: Longman, Green, 1924.

——. *The Collected Letters of William Morris.* Edited by Norman Kelvin. 4 vols. Princeton, N.J.: Princeton University Press, 1987. See esp. vol. 2, covering 1881–84.

Morrison, Toni. *Beloved.* New York: Penguin, 1987.

——. "Unspeakable Things Unspoken: The Afro-American Presence in American Literature." *Michigan Quarterly Review* 28, no. 1 (1989): 11.

Mukerji, Chandra. "Visual Language in Science and the Exercise of Power: The Case of Cartography in Early Modern Europe." *Studies in Visual Communication* 10 (1984): 30–45.

Müller, F. Max. *My Autobiography: A Fragment.* London: Longmans, 1901.

Myers, A. R., ed. *English Historical Documents.* Edited by David C. Douglas. New York: Oxford University Press, 1966. See esp. vol. 4, covering 1327–1485.

Nichols, Bill. "The Work of Culture in the Age of Cybernetic Systems." *Screen* 29, no. 1 (1988): 46.

Noonan, John T. *The Scholastic Use of Usury.* Cambridge, Mass.: Harvard University Press, 1957.

O'Hanlon, Rosalind, and David Washbrook. "After Orientalism: Culture, Criticism, and Politics in the Third World." *Comparative Studies in Society and History* 34 (1992): 1–26.

O'Keeffe, Katherine O'Brien. "Orality and the Developing Text of Caedmon's *Hymn.*" *Speculum* 62, no. 1 (1987): 1–20.

Olender, Maurice. "The Danger of Ambiguity: Friedrich Max Müller." In *The Languages of Paradise: Race, Religion, and Philology in the Nineteenth Century.* Cambridge, Mass.: Harvard University Press, 1992.

Olsen, Glenn W. Review of *Holy Feast and Holy Fast,* by Caroline Walker Bynum. *Church History* 57, no. 2 (1988): 225–27.

O'Neil, Mary. "Magical Healing, Love Magic and the Inquisition in Late Sixteenth-Century Modena." In *Inquisition and Society in Early Modern Europe,* ed. Stephen Haliczer. Totowa, N.J.: Barnes & Noble, 1987.

Overing, Gillian R., and Clare A. Lees. "Birthing Bishops and Fathering Poets: Bede, Hild, and the Relations of Cultural Production." *Exemplaria* 6 (1994): 35–66.

Palmer, D. J. *The Rise of English Studies: An Account of the Study of the English Language and Literature from Its Origins to the Making of the Oxford School.* Oxford: Oxford University Press, 1965.

Parker, Andrew, Mary Russo, Doris Sommer, and Patricia Yaeger, eds. *Nationalisms and Sexualities.* New York: Routledge, 1992.

Patterson, Annabel M. *Pastoral and Ideology: Virgil to Valéry.* Berkeley and Los Angeles: University of California Press, 1987.

Patterson, Lee. *Negotiating the Past: The Historical Understanding of Medieval Literature.* Madison: University of Wisconsin Press, 1987.

———, ed. *Literary Practice and Social Change in Britain, 1380–1530.* Berkeley and Los Angeles: University of California Press, 1990.

———. " 'No Man His Reason Herde': Peasant Consciousness, Chaucer's Miller, and Structure of the Canterbury Tales." In *Literary Practice and Social Change in Britain, 1380–1530,* ed. Lee Patterson. Berkeley and Los Angeles: University of California Press, 1990.

———. "On the Margin: Postmodernism, Ironic History, and Medieval Studies." *Speculum* 65, no. 1 (1990): 87–108.

———. "The Return of Philology." In *The Past and Future of Medieval Studies,* ed. John Van Engen. Notre Dame: University of Notre Dame Press, 1994.

Penley, Constance, and Andrew Ross. "Cyborgs at Large: Interview with Donna Haraway." In *Technoculture,* ed. Constance Penley and Andrew Ross. Minneapolis: University of Minnesota Press, 1991.

Perry, Mary Elizabeth, and Anne J. Cruz, eds. *Cultural Encounters: The Impact of the Inquisition in Spain and the New World.* Berkeley and Los Angeles: University of California Press, 1991.

Petchesky, Rosalind Pollack. "Foetal Images: The Power of Visual Culture in the Politics of Reproduction." In *Reproductive Technologies: Gender, Motherhood and Medicine,* ed. Michelle Stanworth. Minneapolis: University of Minnesota Press, 1987.

Peters, Edward. *Torture.* New York: Blackwell, 1985.

Pope-Hennessy, John. "Paolo Uccello." New York: Phaidon, 1969.

Port, M. H., ed. *The Houses of Parliament.* New Haven, Conn.: Yale University Press, 1976.

Porterfield, Amanda. Review of *Holy Feast and Holy Fast,* by Caroline Walker Bynum. *Religion* 20 (April 1990): 187–88.

Prakash, Gyan. "Writing Post-Orientalist Histories of the Third World: Perspectives from Indian Historiography." *Comparative Studies in Society and History* 32, no. 2 (1990): 383–408.

——. "Can the 'Subaltern' Ride? A Reply to O'Hanlon and Washbrook." *Comparative Studies in Society and History* 34, no. 1 (1992): 168–84.

——. "Postcolonial Criticism and Indian Historiography." *Social Text* 31/32 (1992): 8–19.

Pratt, Mary Louise. *Imperial Eyes: Travel Writing and Transculturation.* New York: Routledge, 1992.

Quilligan, Maureen. "The Name of the Author: Self-Representation in Christine de Pizan's *Livre de la cité des dames.*" *Exemplaria* 4, no. 1 (1992): 201–28.

Radbruch, Gustav. "Hans Baldungs Hexenbilder." In *Elegantiae juris criminalis.* Basel, 1938.

Raffalovich, Mark André. *Uranisme et unisexualité.* Lyon: A. Stanck, 1896.

Ragussis, Michael. "The Birth of a Nation in Victorian Culture: The Spanish Inquisition, the Converted Daughter, and the Secret Race." *Critical Inquiry* 20 (Spring 1994): 477–508.

——. *Figures of Conversion: The "Jewish Question" and English National Identity.* Durham, N.C.: Duke University Press, 1995.

Rainwater, Lee, and William L. Yancey, eds. *The Moynihan Report and the Politics of Controversy.* Cambridge, Mass.: MIT Press, 1967.

Rancière, Jacques. *The Names of History: On the Poetics of Knowledge.* Minneapolis: University of Minnesota Press, 1994.

Reynolds, Robert L. "The Ultimate Courage of Jean de Brébeuf." *American Heritage* 10, no. 6 (1959): 54–106.

Richards, Thomas. "Archive and Utopia." *Representations* 37 (Winter 1992): 104–35.

Rickels, Laurence A. *Aberrations of Mourning: Writing on German Crypts*. Detroit: Wayne State University Press, 1988.

Rickman, Thomas. *Attempts to Discriminate the Styles of English Architecture from the Conquest to the Reformation*. London, 1819.

Robertson, Fiona. *Legitimate Histories: Scott, Gothic and the Authorities of Fiction*. Oxford: Clarendon, 1994.

Rocke, Michael J. "Sodomites in Fifteenth-Century Tuscany: The Views of Bernardino of Siena." In *The Pursuit of Sodomy: Male Homosexuality in Renaissance and Enlightenment Europe*, ed. Kert Gerard and Gert Helima. New York: Haworth, 1989.

Rogers, Thorold. *History of Agricultural Prices*. 6 vols. Oxford: Clarendon, 1866–1902. See esp. vols. 3–4.

Rosaldo, Renato. "From the Door of His Tent: The Fieldworker and the Inquisitor." In *Writing Culture: The Poetics and Politics of Ethnography*, ed. James Clifford and George F. Marcus. Berkeley and Los Angeles: University of California Press, 1986.

Rosenfield, Israel. *The Strange, the Familiar and the Forgotten: An Anatomy of Consciousness*. New York: Knopf, 1962.

——. *The Invention of Memory: A New View of the Brain*. New York: Basic, 1988.

Roth, Michael S. *The Ironist's Cage: Memory, Trauma, and the Construction of History*. New York: Columbia University Press, 1995.

Rothblatt, Sheldon. "How 'Professional' Are the Professionals? A Review Article." *Comparative Studies in Society and History* 37 (1995): 194–205.

Rothkrug, Lionel. "Popular Religion and Holy Shrines: Their Influence on the Origins of the German Reformation and Their Role in German Cultural Development." In *Religion and the People (800–1700)*, ed. James Obelkevich. Chapel Hill: University of North Carolina Press, 1979.

Rubin, Miri. *Corpus Christi: The Eucharist in Late Medieval Culture*. New York: Cambridge University Press, 1991.

——. "The Eucharist and the Construction of Medieval Identities." In *Culture and History, 1350–1600: Essays on English Communities, Identities and Writing*, ed. David Aers. London: Harvester Wheatsheaf, 1992.

Ruggiero, Guido. *Binding Passions: Tales of Magic, Marriage, and*

Power at the End of the Renaissance. New York: Oxford University Press, 1993.

Rushdie, Salman. Review of *Handsworth Songs,* dir. John Akomfrah. *Guardian,* 12 January 1987, 7.

——. *Satanic Verses.* New York: Viking, 1988.

Ruskin, John. *The Complete Works of John Ruskin.* Edited by E. T. Cook and Alexander Wedderburn. 39 vols. London: George Allen, 1903–12.

Russell, Jeffrey Burton. *Witchcraft in the Middle Ages.* Ithaca, N.Y.: Cornell University Press, 1972.

Russo, Mary. "Female Grotesques: Carnival and Theory." In *Feminist Studies/Critical Studies,* ed. Teresa de Lauretis. Bloomington: Indiana University Press, 1986.

Said, Edward W. "Representing the Colonized: Anthropology's Interlocutors." *Critical Inquiry* 15 (Winter 1989): 205–25.

Sanjek, Roger, ed. *Fieldnotes: The Makings of Anthropology.* Ithaca, N.Y.: Cornell University Press, 1990.

Santner, Eric L. *Stranded Objects: Mourning, Memory and Film in Postwar Germany.* New York: Cornell University Press, 1990.

——. *My Own Private Germany: Daniel Paul Schreber's Secret History of Modernity.* Princeton: Princeton University Press, 1996.

Scarry, Elaine. *The Body in Pain: The Making and Unmaking of the World.* Oxford: Oxford University Press, 1985.

Schade, Sigrid. *Schadenzauber und die Magie des Körpers.* Worms, 1983.

Schibanoff, Susan. "Chaucer's Lesbians: Drawing Blanks?" *Medieval Feminist Newsletter* 13 (Spring 1992): 11–14.

Schiesari, Juliana. *The Gendering of Melancholia: Feminism, Psychoanalysis, and the Symbolics of Loss in Renaissance Literature.* Ithaca, N.Y.: Cornell University Press, 1992.

Schroedinger, Erwin. *What Is Life? and Other Scientific Essays* (1944). Reprint, New York: Doubleday, 1956.

Scott, Joan Wallach. "Gender: A Useful Category of Historical Analysis." *American Historical Review* 91, no. 5 (1986): 1053–75.

——. "History in Crisis? The Others' Side of the Story." *American Historical Review* 94, no. 3 (1989): 680–92.

——. "The Evidence of Experience." *Critical Inquiry* 17 (Summer 1991): 773–97.

——. "After History?" *Common Knowledge* 5 (1996): 8–26.

Sedgwick, Eve Kosofsky. *Between Men: English Literature and Male Homosocial Desire.* New York: Columbia University Press, 1985.

——. *The Coherence of Gothic Conventions.* New York: Methuen, 1986.

——. "Privilege of Unknowing." *Genders* 1 (1988): 102–24.

——. *Epistemology of the Closet.* Berkeley and Los Angeles: University of California Press, 1990.

——. "Queer Performativity: Henry James's *The Art of the Novel.*" *Gay and Lesbian Quarterly* 1 (1993): 1–16.

Segl, Peter, ed. *Der Hexenhammer: Enstehung und Umfeld des Malleus maleficarum von 1487.* Köln: Böhlau, 1988.

Seidel, Linda. "The Value of Verisimilitude in the Art of Jan van Eyck." In *Contexts: Style and Values in Medieval Art and Literature.* New Haven, Conn.: Yale University Press, 1991.

Shohat, Ella. "Notes on the 'Post-Colonial.'" *Social Text* 31/32 (1992): 110.

Silverman, Kaja. *The Acoustic Mirror: The Female Voice in Psychoanalysis and Cinema.* Bloomington: Indiana University Press, 1988.

Simmons, Roger Dennis. "The Freud Library." *Journal of the American Psychoanalytic Association* 21 (1973): 646–87.

Smith, Anna Marie. *New Right Discourse on Race and Sexuality.* New York: Cambridge University Press, 1994.

Smith, Lindsay. *Victorian Photography, Painting and Poetry: The Enigma of Visibility in Ruskin, Morris and the Pre-Raphaelites.* Cambridge: Cambridge University Press, 1995.

Smith, Richard E. "A Historical Overview of Computer Architecture." *Annals of the History of Computing* 10, no. 4 (1989): 277–303.

Sobchak, Vivian. "A Theory of Everything: Meditations on Total Chaos." *Artforum* 19, no. 2 (1990): 153.

Sofer, Reba. *Discipline and Power: The University, History, and the Making of an English Elite, 1870–1930.* Stanford, Calif.: Stanford University Press, 1994.

Sofia, Zoe. "Exterminating Fetuses: Abortion, Disarmament, and the Sexo-Semiotics of Extra-Terrestrialism." *Diacritics* 14, no. 2 (1984): 47–59.

Son of Robin Hood. Directed by George Sherman. Argo Films, 1959.

Spiegel, Gabrielle M. "History, Historicism, and the Social Logic of the Text in the Middle Ages." *Speculum* 65 (1990): 59–86.

Spillers, Hortense J. "Mama's Baby, Papa's Maybe: An American Grammar Book." *Diacritics* 17, no. 2 (1987): 65–82.

Spivak, Gayatri Chakravorty. "The Rani of Sirmur: An Essay in Reading the Archives." *History and Theory* 24, no. 3 (1985): 247–72.

——. *In Other Worlds: Essays in Cultural Politics.* London: Methuen, 1987. See esp. the chapters "A Literary Representation of the Subaltern: A Woman's Text from the Third World" and "Subaltern Studies: Deconstructing Historiography."

——. "Can the Subaltern Speak?" In *Marxism and the Interpretation of Culture.* Urbana: University of Illinois Press, 1988.

——. "The New Historicism: Political Commitment and the Postmodern Criticism." In *The Postcolonial Critic: Interviews, Strategies, Dialogues,* ed. Sarah Harasym. New York: Routledge, 1990.

——. "French Feminism Revisited: Ethics and Politics." In *Feminists Theorize the Political,* ed. Judith Butler and Joan W. Scott. New York: Routledge, 1992.

Sponsler, Claire. "Medieval Ethnography: Fieldwork and the European Past." *Assays* 7 (1992): 1–30.

Stafford, Barbara Maria. "Body Criticism: Imagining the Unseen in Enlightenment Art and Medicine." Cambridge, Mass.: MIT Press, 1991.

Stallybrass, Peter. " 'Drunk with the Cup of Liberty': Robin Hood, the Carnivalesque, and the Rhetoric of Violence in Early Modern England." In *The Violence of Representation: Literature and the History of Violence,* ed. Nancy Armstrong and Leonard Tennenhouse. New York: Routledge, 1989.

Stallybrass, Peter, and Alon White. *The Politics and Poetics of Transgression.* Ithaca, N.Y.: Cornell University Press, 1986.

Stock, Brian. *Implications of Literacy: Written Language and Models of Interpretation in the Eleventh and Twelfth Centuries.* Princeton, N.J.: Princeton University Press, 1983.

——. *Listening for the Text: On the Uses of the Past.* Baltimore: Johns Hopkins University Press, 1990.

Stocking, George W. *Victorian Anthropology.* New York: Free Press, 1987.

Stone, Lawrence. "Interpersonal Violence in English Society." *Past and Present* 101 (1983): 22–33.

Storm, Melvin. "Alisoun's Ear." *Modern Language Quarterly* 42 (1981): 219–26.

Strachey, John, ed. *Rotuli parliamentorum.* 6 vols. London, 1767–77. See esp. vol. 3.

Strathern, Marilyn. *The Gender of the Gift: Problems with Women and Problems with Society in Melanesia.* Berkeley and Los Angeles: University of California Press, 1988.

——. "Enterprising Kinship: Consumer Choice and the New Reproductive Technologies." *Cambridge Anthropology* 14, no. 1 (1990): 4.

——. *After Nature: English Kinship in the Late Twentieth Century.* Cambridge: Cambridge University Press, 1991.

——. *Partial Connections.* Savage, Md.: Rowman & Littlefield, 1991.

Strohm, Paul. *Hochon's Arrow: The Social Imagination of Fourteenth-Century Texts.* Princeton, N.J.: Princeton University Press, 1992.

Stuard, Susan Mosher. "The Chase after Theory: Considering Medieval Women." *Gender and History* 4, no. 2 (1992): 135–46.

Stubbs, William. *Seventeen Lectures on the Study of Medieval and Modern History* (1886). Reprint, New York: Howard Fertig, 1967.

Suleri, Sara. *The Rhetoric of English India.* Chicago: University of Chicago Press, 1992.

Summers, Montague. *The Malleus Maleficarum of Heinrich Kramer and James Sprenger.* New York: Dover, 1971.

Tandeciarz, Silvia. "Reading Gayatri Spivak's 'French Feminism in an International Frame': A Problem of Theory." *Genders* 10 (1991): 75–91.

Taussig, Michael. *Shamanism, Colonialism and the Wild Man: A Study in Terror and Healing.* Chicago: University of Chicago Press, 1987.

——. *The Nervous System.* New York: Routledge, 1992. See esp. the chapters "Homesickness and Dada," "Maleficium: State Fetishism," and "Violence and Resistence in the Americas: The Legacy of Conquest."

——. *Mimesis and Alterity.* New York: Routledge, 1993.

Terry, Jennifer. "The Body Invaded: Medical Surveillance of Women as Reproducers." *Socialist Review* 89, no. 3 (1989): 13–44.

Thirsk, Joan. "The Family." *Past and Present* 27 (1964): 116–22.

Thompson, E. P. *William Morris: Romantic to Revolutionary.* 1st American ed. New York: Pantheon, 1977.

Trinh T. Minh-ha. *Woman, Native, Other: Writing Postcoloniality and Feminism.* Bloomington: Indiana University Press, 1989.

Turing, Alan M. "The Chemical Basis of Morphogenesis." *Philosophical Transactions of the Royal Society* B237 (1952): 37–72.

Turkle, Sherry, and Seymour Papert. "Epistemological Pluralism: Styles and Voices within Computer Culture." *Signs* 16, no. 1 (1990): 128–57.

Turville-Petre, Thorlac. *England the Nation: Language, Literature, and National Identity, 1290–1340.* Oxford: Clarendon, 1996.

Van Engen, John. "The Christian Middle Ages as an Historiographical Problem." *American Historical Review* 91, no. 3 (1986): 519–52.

——, ed. *The Past and Future of Medieval Studies.* Notre Dame, Ind.: University of Notre Dame Press, 1994.

Veeser, Harold, and Gayatri Spivak. "The New Historicism: Political Commitment and the Postmodern Criticism." In *The New Historicism,* ed. Harold Veeser. New York: Routledge, 1989.

Velvet Underground. "Sunday Morning." On *Velvet Underground and Nico.* New York: MGM/Verve, 1967.

Vinogradoff, Paul. *Villainage in England.* Oxford: Clarendon, 1892.

Virilio, Paul. *War and Cinema: The Logistics of Perception.* London: Verso, 1989.

——. *The Aesthetics of Disappearance.* New York: Semiotext(e), 1991.

——. *Lost Dimension.* Translated by Daniel Moshenberg. New York: Semiotext(e)/Columbia University Press, 1991.

Virilio, Paul, and Sylvere Lotringer. *Pure War.* New York: Columbia University /Semiotext(e), 1983.

Viswanathan, Gauri. *Masks of Conquest: Literary Study and British Rule in India.* New York: Columbia University Press, 1989.

——. "Raymond Williams and British Colonialism." *Yale Journal of Criticism* 4 (1991): 47–66.

von Neumann, John. *Theory of Self-Reproducing Automata.* Edited by A. W. Burks. Urbana: University of Illinois Press, 1966.

Wallace, David. *Chaucerian Polity: Absolutist Lineages and Associational Forms.* Stanford, Calif.: Stanford University Press, 1997.

Wallace, Elizabeth. *Goldwin Smith, Victorian Liberal.* Toronto: University of Toronto Press, 1957.

Warnicke, Retha M. Review of *Holy Feast and Holy Fast,* by Caroline Walker Bynum. *Journal of the American Academy of Religion* 66, no. 3 (1988): 563–64.

Watts, Pauline Moffitt. "Prophecy and Discovery: On the Spiritual Origins of Christopher Columbus's 'Enterprise of the Indies.'" *American Historical Review* 90 (1985): 73–102.

Webb, Benjamin. "On the Adaptation of Pointed Architecture in Tropical Climates." *Transactions of the Cambridge Camden Society* 1 (1849): 198–218.

Weitenkampf, Frank. "*Der Ritter von Turm* and the Dawn of the Renaissance in Book Illustration." *Bulletin of the New York Public Library* 35 (1931): 611–18.

White, James F. *The Cambridge Movement: "The Ecclesiologist" and the Gothic Revival.* Cambridge: Cambridge University Press, 1962.

Wigley, Mark. *The Architecture of Deconstruction: Derrida's Haunt.* Cambridge, Mass.: MIT Press, 1993.

Wilde, Oscar. "The English Renaissance in Art." In *The First Collected Edition of Works of Oscar Wilde,* ed. R. Ross. New York: Macmillan, 1908.

Williams, N. J. "Stubbs's Appointment as Regius Professor, 1866." *Bulletin of the Institute for Historical Research* 33 (1960): 121–25.

Williams, Patricia J. *The Alchemy of Race and Rights.* Cambridge, Mass.: Harvard University Press, 1991.

Willis, Sharon. "Disputed Territories: Masculinity and Social Space." *Camera Obscura* 19 (1989): 5–23.

Winston, Brian. "Reconsidering *The Triumph of the Will:* Was Hitler There?" *Sight and Sound* 30, no. 2 (1980–81): 102–7.

Wood, R. Derek. "The Diorama in Great Britain in the 1820s." *History of Photography* 17 (1993): 284–95.

Woodward, David. "Reality, Symbolism, Time and Space in Medieval World-Maps." *Annals of the Association of American Geographers* 75, no. 5 (1985): 510–21.

Workman, Leslie J., ed. *Studies in Medievalism.* Vol. 4 of *Medievalism in England.* Cambridge: Brewer, 1992.

Workman, Leslie J., and Kathleen Verduin, eds. *Studies in Medievalism.* Vol. 7 of *Medievalism in England II.* Cambridge: Brewer, 1995.

World Health Organization. *Maternal Mortality Rates: A Tabulation of Available Information.* Geneva, 1986.

Wrathmell, Stuart. "Peasant Houses, Farmsteads and Villages in Northeast England." In *Rural Settlements of Medieval England: Studies Dedicated to Maurice Beresford,* ed. Michael Aston, David Austen, and Christopher Dyer. Oxford: Blackwell, 1989.

Wright, Richard. "Computer Graphics as Allegorical Knowledge: Electronic Imagery in the Sciences." *Leonardo,* suppl. (1990): 65–74.

Yates, Frances A. *The Art of Memory.* Chicago: University of Chicago Press, 1966.

Young, Robert. *White Mythologies: Writing History and the West.* New York: Routledge, 1990.

Zika, Charles. "Hosts, Processions and Pilgrimages: Controlling the Sacred in Fifteenth-Century Germany." *Past and Present* 118 (February 1988): 25–64.

INDEX

Kathleen Biddick is Associate Professor of History and Director of the Gender Studies Program at the University of Notre Dame.

Library of Congress Cataloging-in-Publication Data

Biddick, Kathleen.
The shock of medievalism / by Kathleen Biddick.
p. cm.
Includes bibliographical references and index.
ISBN 0-8223-2182-3 (cloth : alk. paper). — ISBN 0-8223-2199-8 (pbk. : alk. paper)
1. Civilization, Medieval—Study and teaching. 2. Literature, Medieval—History and criticism. 3. Medievalism. I. Title.
CB353.B5 1998
909.07—dc21 97-32456